Dharam's Law of Inquiry Commissions in India

Dharam's Law of Inquiry Commissions in India

Volume–I

Dharam Paul Sharma

ATLANTIC
PUBLISHERS & DISTRIBUTORS (P) LTD

Published by
ATLANTIC
PUBLISHERS & DISTRIBUTORS (P) LTD
7/22, Ansari Road, Darya Ganj,
New Delhi-110002
Phones : +91-11-40775252, 23273880, 23275880, 23280451
Fax : +91-11-23285873
Web : www.atlanticbooks.com
E-mail : orders@atlanticbooks.com

Branch Office
5, Nallathambi Street, Wallajah Road,
Chennai-600002
Phones : +91-44-64611085, 32413319
E-mail : chennai@atlanticbooks.com

Printed in India at Nice Printing Press, A-33/3A, Site-IV, Industrial Area, Sahibabad, Ghaziabad, U.P.

To
My wife Santosh
who has been the
inspiring force behind
this endeavour

Acknowledgements

I owe a lot to many people but for whose involvement and cooperation this book would not have been completed. Apart from those whose contributions are specifically acknowledged hereinafter, there are many others whom it may not be possible to thank by names for one reason or the other. Nonetheless, I feel a sense of gratitude towards all of them and take this opportunity to formally acknowledge the same and convey my sincere thanks to all of them for having helped me in the completion of this book.

I owe special thank and gratitude to my beloved wife, Santosh Sharma, for shouldering the entire responsibility of the family, which would have otherwise been borne and shared by me during this period. I salute her for her all-round generous support and inspiration. I specially thank all elders and youngsters in the family, who have been deprived of my care and attention during the writing of this book. Thank you Maa, Babuji, Archana, Dinesh, Vimanyu, Rushil, Archita, Pawan and Vanshika, Saiyansh, Dr. Vivek and Dr. Poonam. I also wish to convey my sincere and heartiest thanks to all the members of my enlarged family who have been involved and contributed in one way or the other in the completion of this book.

I am grateful to Shri Sarvesh Chandra, former Chairman, Foreign Regulation Appellate Board and Foreign Management Appellate Tribunal and former Joint Secretary and Legal Adviser, Ministry of Law for sparing his precious time for making valuable suggestions which have made qualitative contribution to this book.

The task of completing this book has been made easier by unstinting cooperation of my supporting staff, viz. Ms. Anjana Battu, Iqbal Singh, S.C. Aggarwal, Harish Chandra, Diwakar, Tek Chand and Sher Singh. They have willingly borne the brunt and the rigors of tight working schedule and consequential inconvenience and discomfort. I am pleased to convey my sincere thanks to all of them.

Last but not least, I am beholden to Lord Almighty and Maa Bhawani for bestowing upon me their blessings and vesting in me the necessary inspiration, ability and competency for writing this book and crowning my humble endeavour with success.

Dharam Paul Sharma

Preface

The genesis of this book can be traced to my stint as Additional Secretary in the Ministry of Law, Government of India about six years back when I had an occasion to deal with certain issues concerning commissions of inquiry. I requisitioned necessary reference books from the library and was provided with an old edition of a book along with the volume of *AIR Manual* relating to the Commissions of Inquiry Act, 1952 but these did not help much in dealing with the matter at hand as the same had not received any judicial consideration. After some time, I was confronted with certain additional issues in the same matter. I knew that there was dearth of reference material on the subject. That prompted me to go into the history of the Commissions of Inquiry Act, 1952, the nature, scope and object of commissions of inquiry with a view to ensuring that any view expressed in the matter should at least be in conformity with the underlying rationale of the Act. In the meantime, another book appeared in the market. However, the same was found to be more of a compilation rather than being a treatise on the principles of law governing inquiry commissions. These instances sufficiently aroused my interest in the subject, which I found very fascinating and thought-provoking. The short framework of the Act and the paucity of standard text material on it provided added attraction to the subject. The paucity of material on the subject could be attributed to commercial expediency on the one hand and lack of development of much case law on the subject on the other. And, then, although the Act is more than fifty years old, yet the number of cases reported on the subject is around hundred and that too relating mostly to three or four sections of the Act. The result has been that in certain high profile cases, the points, which ought to have been raised by the counsels of high repute who appeared therein, were not raised, and consequently, the courts could not have occasions to deal with certain most fascinating aspects of such matters. Had it been done, the cases might have assumed different dimensions. One such aspect relates to the legality of reconstitution of a commission of inquiry. Although the apex court has held long back that the Act does not vest in the appropriate Government the power to reconstitute a commission, yet the fact remains that commissions are quite often reconstituted without its legality being questioned in courts. Surprisingly, the courts too fail to take notice of it, possibly on account of the necessary plea having not been raised by the parties (technical absence) in the cases. Obviously, such a scenario could be attributed to some extent to the lack of necessary reference material being readily available in the market. This gap is sought to be bridged by this book. I have gone through the reported cases and not only dealt with the pleas that were judicially upheld but also those that were judicially dismissed and referred to them at appropriate places in order to identify and highlight the principles governing the commissions of inquiry. Thus, efforts have been made to make the book exhaustive and self-contained on the subject.

Of late, commissions' litigation appears to be on the increase. Quite often, decisions to institute inquiry commissions are political ones and, at times, are resorted to gain political mileage. The courts too have recognized this aspect of the matter and have found nothing wrong or objectionable to it, subject of course, to the overall rider of mala fides vitiating all administrative actions. Many political heads have rolled in the past as a result of reports of such inquiry commissions. And, the inquiry commissions' reports are forgotten and not pursued after such casualties have been inflicted. However, this is in no way intended to belittle and denigrate the importance and utility of inquiry commissions that have certainly served the public cause and interest to a great extent in many respects. Thus, one may tend to conclude that the institution of inquiry commissions has been very much used and abused. Besides, there are certain peculiarities of the system of inquiry commissions that have further confounded the matter. To begin with, anything that can be humanly conceived is amenable to be the subject of inquiry. To add to it, the same incident or event can be the subject of inquiry by different commissions but with different objects and purposes or at different times. And, then, once the requirements of law for instituting an inquiry are satisfied, the motive behind such institution is not at all relevant as has been held by courts, barring the exception of mala fides. There is no absolute legislative mandate for completing an inquiry within a given time frame. Although the law requires the time to be specified within which a commission of inquiry should complete its functions and submit its report to the appropriate Government, yet there is no guarantee that the time so fixed once will not be extended further. The Liberhan Commission is a glaring example of this. The commission that was set up on December 16, 1992 as a sequel to demolition of Babri Masjid at Ayodhya, submitted its report to the Government on 30th June 2009 after about 17 years of its constitution that saw 399 sittings and 48 extensions involving an expenditure of rupees nine crore approximately. Nonetheless, the moot question is should there be any time limit for commissions of inquiry to complete their inquiries and submit reports lest these may be used to deflect the public attention from the matters of public importance that are subject of inquiries by sheer delay. And, there are cases where the reports of inquiry commissions are not acted upon for long and then suddenly taken up for action, at times, for extraneous considerations as well. There is nothing in the Act to regulate such unintended consequences. The question that arises in this context is should there be any time limit for taking action on the reports of inquiry commission or beyond which such reports should not be acted upon. From the case law on the subject, one can gather that any such limit or restriction is likely to be counter-productive. It is also open to the appropriate Government to change its opinion on the desirability of appointing a commission of inquiry from time to time as well as to take into consideration additional matters, besides report of the commission, while deciding upon the action to be taken in a case. Another interesting feature of the inquiry commissions system is that a commission of inquiry can be appointed to inquire into any definite matter of public importance. However, the existence of a definite matter of public importance does not render it obligatory on the appropriate Government to appoint a commission of inquiry. Even where such a commission has been appointed, its report is not binding on the Government and other agencies concerned. One may wonder, then why all this fuss! All these peculiarities bring to the fore the distinct character of the inquiry commissions' institution, having varieties of uses but nevertheless being essentially a tool of information gathering as well as a part of administrative decision-making process and above all, being a mechanism of restoring public confidence and trust in the established institutions and systems. It needs to be remembered that no system can yield its intended objects and results on its own. It all depends on the men who operate it. In the case of inquiry commissions, these men are the governmental agencies, who appoint such commissions, the commissioners themselves, the lawyers, the judges and the public concerned with the subject of inquiry and to some extent, the persons whose conduct might have been inquired into. Let us hope that all concerned will aim at raising the respect for the institution to a greater height. This book too is a step in that direction.

Efforts have been made to make this book exhaustive and self-contained on the subject of inquiry commissions. Accordingly, the subject of inquiry commissions has been examined not just with reference to the Act. Inquiries made in exercise of executive powers too have been suitably referred to. This would help the authorities concerned in deciding as to which type of inquiry may be resorted to in a given case. Besides, references have been made to inquiries that may be instituted under other statutes. Up-to-date case laws have been included after having gone through all the reported cases as far as possible. Certain intricate issues, which have so far not received judicial consideration such as interaction between commissions of concurrent jurisdiction and status of reconstituted commission, have also been examined and clarified. The book not only presents section-wise commentaries on the Act as it exists but also provides historical backdrop by tracing the amendments made in the Act since its enactment. The book contains the text of all the amendment Bills and the amendment Acts. The Act empowers the appropriate

Government to make rules to carry out the purposes of the Act. Accordingly, the Commissions of Inquiry (Central) Rules, 1972 have been made by the Central Government. Many State Governments follow these rules as well. However, there are certain States that have made their own rules under the Act. These rules are not readily available. Such rules too have been included in the book. To add to it, the report of the Select Committee and two reports of the Law Commission of India on the Act have also been included in the book. All these have added to the referential value of the book.

In order to impart practical utility to the book, text of certain notifications which have been subject matter of litigation, has been culled out from the reported cases by way of illustrations, and the relevant courts' ruling thereon are briefly stated to focus on such aspects as have been questioned for being objectionable. Similarly, extracts of the terms of references of various commissions from the reported cases are also included in the book to indicate the range of the subjects of inquiries. The book includes a special section containing head-notes of practically all the reported cases under the Act as ready references. Texts and extracts of certain allied laws have also been appended to make the book self-contained as well as for quick references. I believe that I have brought in this book all the relevant material that will be useful and necessary for its users. I am indeed indebted to the authors of all published materials that I have dwelt upon for the completion of this book. They have been duly acknowledged in the footnotes. Of course, errors if any, remain my responsibility. Also, I shall be glad to receive any suggestion for further improvement of the book in its later edition.

I hope and trust that this book will be of use and interest to all its readers and will serve the cause of inquiry commissions in India.

Dharam Paul Sharma
dr.dpsharma@nic.in

Contents

VOLUME 2

Table of Cases

Kaushalya Devi *v.* Bachittar Singh
AIR 1960 SC 1168; 274

Kehar Singh *v.* State AIR 1988 SC 1883;
1988 (3) SCC 609; 103, 244, 329, 332, 338

Khatri *v.* State of Bihar AIR 1981 SC 1068; 253

(The) King *v.* Minister of Health (1929)
1 KB 619; 166

(The) King *v.* Parmanand AIR 1949 Pat 222; 201

(Mrs.) Kiran Bedi *v.* Delhi Administration 1989 (2)
Delhi Lawyer 190; 62, 89, 94, 169, 344, 353

Kiran Bedi and Jinder Singh *v.* Committee of Inquiry
AIR 1988 SC 2252; 366

(Smt.) Kiran Bedi *v.* Committee of Inquiry
AIR 1989 SC 714; 254, 354, 357, 360, 369

Kochuni *v.* State of Madras AIR 1959 SC 725; 267

Krishna Ballabh Sahay *v.* Commission of Inquiry
AIR 1969 SC 258; 146, 166, 199

Lal Krishna Advani *v.* State of Bihar
AIR 1997 Patna 15; 144, 170, 356

Laker Airways Ltd. case (1976)3 WLR 537; 74

Laker Airways Ltd. case (1977) 2 WLR 234; 74

Laughton *v.* Bishop of Sodor (1872) LR 4
PC 495; 309, 311-12

Lincoln *v.* Deniels (1961) 3 All ER 740, 306

M. Karunnanidhi *v.* Union of India
AIR 1977 Mad 192; 125, 152, 181, 190, 207, 281

M.L. Jain *v.* Union of India AIR 1993 SC 1150; 240

M.P. Sharma *v.* Satish Chandra AIR 1954 SC 300; 332

M. Sathyanesan *v.* State of Kerala AIR 2003
Kerala 356; 144

Orient Paper Mills *v.* Union of India
AIR 1979 Cal 114; 66, 69, 98, 132, 134-35, 162, 164, 182, 267, 275-76, 300

P. Janardhana Reddy *v.* State of Andhra Pradesh
AIR 2001 SC 2631; 71

P.K. Kunju *v.* State of Kerala AIR 1970
Kerala 252; 109, 163, 182

P.P.M. Thangaiah Nadar Firm *v.* Govt. of
Tamil Nadu AIR 2007 (NOC) 954 (Mad); 116-17

P.R. Nayak *v.* Union of India ILR (1973)
I Delhi 747; 33, 62, 64, 123, 127, 179-80, 184, 193, 198-99, 222, 289, 349, 371, 402

P.V. Jagannath Rao *v.* State of Orissa (1968)
34 Cut LT 666; 66, 68-69, 114, 131-32, 137-38, 163, 202

P.V. Jagannath Rao *v.* State of Orissa
AIR 1969 SC 215; 98, 104, 110, 114, 136, 166, 199, 205, 306

Padfield *v.* Minister of Agriculture, Fisheries and
Food (1968) 1 All ER 694; 74-75, 85

Panday Surinder Nath Sinha *v.* Bageshwari Prasad
AIR 1961 Patna 164; 307

Parry-Jones *v.* Law Society (1968) 2 WLR 397; 370

Parshva Properties Ltd. *v.* CIT 104 ITR 631; 200

Peoples Union for Democratice Rights *v.*
Ministry of Home Affairs AIR 1985 Delhi 268; 88, 90, 94, 207, 210

(Re) Pergamon Press Ltd. 1970 ALL ER 535; 218

Perspective Publications (P) Ltd. *v.* State of
Maharashtra AIR 1971 SC 221; 401

Prafulla Chandra *v.* State of Orissa
AIR 1988 Orissa 18; 143, 386

Prafulla Kumar Mukherjee *v.* Bank of Commerce Ltd., Khulna AIR 1947 Privy Council 60; 49

Praga Tools Corporation *v.* Schri C.A. Imanual (1969) 3 SCR 773; 265-66

Pratap Singh *v.* State of Punjab AIR 1964 SC 72; 164

Puhlhofer *v.* Hillingdon London BC (1986) 1 All ER 467 (HL); 79

Puhupram *v.* State of Madhya Pradesh 1968 MPLJ 629; 105, 202, 299, 324-25, 338

Queen *v.* Collins 50 ALJR 471; 280

R. *v.* Comborne Justices (1954) 2 All ER 850; 213

R. *v.* Criminal Injuries Compensation Board Ex Parte Lain (1967) 2 QBD 864; 264

R. *v.* Electricity Commr. (1924) 1 KB 171; 263, 270, 294

R. *v.* Legislative Assembly of the Church Assembly (1928) 1 KB 411; 264

R. *v.* Lewisham Union (1897) 1 QB 498; 266

R. *v.* Metropolitan Police Commissioner (1968) 1 All ER 763; 115

R. Balakrishna Pillai *v.* State of Kerala AIR 1989 Kerala 99; 79

R. Rajagopal *v.* State of Tamil Nadu (1994) 6 SCC 632; 313, 319

(Dr.) Raghubir Saran *v.* State of Bihar AIR 1964 SC 1; 144

Rai Sahib Ram Jawaya Kapur *v.* State of Punjab AIR 1955 SC 549; 11

(Dr.) Rai Shivendra Bahadur *v.* The Governing Body of the Nalanda College (1962) Supp. 2 SCR 144; 267

THE COMMISSIONS OF INQUIRY ACT, 1952

ACT NO. 60 OF 1952[1]

An Act to provide for the appointment of Commissions of Inquiry and for vesting such Commissions with certain powers

(14th August 1952)

Be it enacted by Parliament as follows:

Assent and Commencement

The Commissions of Inquiry Act, 1952 received the assent of the President on 14th August 1952 and was, thereafter, brought into force on 1st October 1952 by Notification No. S.R.O. 1670, dated 30th September 1952, issued by the Central Government under Section 1(3) of the Act.[2]

Importance of Inquiry Commissions

The Commissions of Inquiry are an age-old institution. It even existed long before the passing of the present Commissions of Inquiry Act, 1952. Even today, inquiries can be legitimately instituted de hors the Act. Its genesis can be traced to the

---

1. This Act has been extended to:
   Goa, Daman and Diu (w.e.f. 1-2-1965) by Reg. 12 of 1962, S. 3 and Sch.
   Dadra and Nagar Haveli (w.e.f. 1-7-1965) by Reg. 6 of 1963, S. 2 and Sch. I.
   Pondicherry (w.e.f. 1-10-1963) by Reg. 7 of 1963, S. 3 and Sch. I.
   Kohima and Mokokchung in the State of Nagaland (w.e.f. 15-2-1972) by Notification No. 74(E) dated 14-2-1972.
   State of Jammu and Kashmir (w.e.f. 6-3-1972) by Notification No. 94(E) dated 4-3-1972.
   Sikkim (w.e.f. 12-12-1977) by S.O. 83(E) dated 12-12-1977.
2. Published in Gazette of India, Pt. II, S. 3, Ext., dated 30-9-1952, No. 135, p. 861.

practice of Parliamentary Committees to inquire into definite matters of public importance. In fact, the very purpose of instituting an inquiry into any matter of public importance is to restore the public confidence and faith in the public institutions and the system that might have been shaken by the matter/event under inquiry. To add to it, such inquiries, being of fact-finding nature, also help the authorities concerned to take appropriate measures to deal with a given situation and devise plans to prevent its recurrence. The utility and importance of the institution need no further emphasis.

The Commissions of Inquiry Act, 1952 is a small but important piece of legislation. Small as it contains only twelve sections. Important because of its wide sweep and all pervasive impact at times. There is no definite information as to the number of inquiry Commissions instituted so far in India, in pre- and post-independence era. The exact figures of Commissions of inquiry as on date are not available. However, as a matter of fact, the number of Commissions of Inquiry in the post-independence era has certainly been on the increase. There have been large numbers of Commissions for variety of reasons to inquire into wide spectrum of matters, which, inter alia, include accidents involving bus, rail, air-crashes, bridges and dams, mines' explosions and fire accidents, incidents of deaths and medical treatments of political personalities, contamination of river/water, food poisoning and liquor tragedy cases, police firing, excesses and inaction, custodial deaths, communal disturbances and riots, epidemics, favouritism, nepotism, corruption and abuse of authority by public officials and politicians, various scams and scandals, mismanagement of public and charitable institutions, land grabbing cases, sinking of Lord Buddha's statute in Hussain Sagar lake, and economics of newspaper industry, etc. It is not possible to catalogue such matters in entirety. However, the fact remains that the subject of inquiries can cover in its range all definite matters of public importance that are amenable to be conceived by human sense in the world. The appointments of Commissions under the Act have assumed new dimensions after its enactment. The proceedings under the Act are of paramount importance in a democratic country like ours, having a written constitution and governed by rule of law. Quite often, there have been public demands to have inquiries on issues of public importance with a view to know true facts and such inquiries have proved to be great satisfaction to the public at large and also helpful to the concerned agencies in taking necessary remedial and preventive measures.

Legislative Entries

The Commissions of Inquiry Act, 1952, falls under Entry 94, List I (Inquiries for the purposes of any of the matters in List I) and Entry 45, List III (Inquiries for the purposes of any of the matters in List II or List III) in the Seventh Schedule to the Constitution. The two entries between themselves cover inquiries into any aspect of the matters included in any of the three Legislative Lists and, thus, the scope of the matters which can be inquired into by the Commission appointed under the Act is wide and extensive.[3]

Statement of Objects and Reasons

Bill No. 39 of 1952 (Act No. 60 of 1952)

"Commissions and Committees of Inquiry are at present appointed by Government under executive order; there is no central law to regulate the powers of such bodies. Some of them have felt handicapped because of the absence of any statutory power to enforce the attendance of witnesses and the production of documents. In order to remove this difficulty, ad hoc legislation has been passed from time to time, such as, for example, the Sugar Crisis Inquiring Authority Act, 1950. It is felt that there should be a general law authorizing Government to appoint an inquiring authority on any matter of public importance, whenever considered necessary, or when a demand to that effect is made by the Legislature and that such law should enable the inquiring authority to exercise certain specific

---

3. Law Commission of India, Twenty-fourth Report (The Commissions of Inquiry Act, 1952), December 1962, Para 19, pp. 13-14; see also *Ram Krishna Dalmia* v. *Mr. Justice S.R. Tendolkar and Others*, AIR 1958 SC 538.

powers including the powers to summon witnesses, to take evidence on oath, and to compel persons to furnish information. The Bill is designed to achieve this object."[4]

Bill No. 131 of 1971 (Act No. 79 of 1971)

"Certain difficulties and deficiencies experienced in the working of the Commissions of Inquiry Act, 1952 were referred to the Law Commission for suggesting suitable amendments to the Act. Taking into account the importance of the Act and the need for a proper system of inquiries, the Law Commission undertook a comprehensive examination of the entire Act and made a number of recommendations in their Twenty-Fourth Report for the revision of the Act in several respects.

2. The main recommendations of the Law Commission have generally been accepted by Government after considering the views expressed on those recommendations by the State Governments, Union Territory Administrations and the Ministries of the Government of India. To give effect to the accepted recommendations of the Law Commission, the Commissions of Inquiry (Amendment) Bill, 1969 was introduced in the Lok Sabha on 21st November, 1969 and was later on referred to a Joint Committee of Parliament. The Joint Committee submitted their report to both the Houses of Parliament on 9th November, 1970. However, on the dissolution of the Fourth Lok Sabha, the Bill as reported by the Joint Committee lapsed. The present Bill seeks to give effect to the provisions of the Bill as reported by the Joint Committee with some minor modification which appears to Government to be necessary.

3. The notes on clauses explain the provisions of the Bill in detail."[5]

Bill No. 73 of 1986 (Act No. 36 of 1986)

"Sub-section (4) of Section 3 of the Commissions of Inquiry Act, 1952 provides that the appropriate Government shall cause

---

4. Gazette of India, Pt. II, S. 2, dated 7-6-1952, p. 206. For Report of the Select Committee, see Gazette of India, Pt. II, S. 2, dated 7-6-1952, p. 325.
5. Gazette of India, 18-11-1971, Pt. II, S. 2, Ext., p. 664.

to be laid before the House of the People or, as the case may be, the Legislative Assembly of the State, the report, if any, of any Commission on the inquiry made by it together with a memorandum of the action taken thereon, within a period of six months of the submission of the report by the Commission to the appropriate Government.

2. To provide for the situations where the fulfillment of the statutory obligation to lay the report of the Commission before the House of the People or the Legislative Assembly of a State involves practical difficulties or where a Commission of Inquiry is appointed to inquire into sensitive matters of public importance and the inquiry report may contain matters of sensitive nature on account of which it may not be desirable in the public interest to lay such report before the House of the People or the Legislative Assembly, the Commissions of Inquiry Act, 1952 was amended by the Commissions of Inquiry (Amendment) Ordinance, 1986 (6 of 1986) promulgated by the President on the 14th May, 1986. The Ordinance inserted two new sub-sections (5) and (6) in Section 3 of the Act. New sub-section (5) provides that the provisions of sub-section (4) of the said Section 3 shall not apply in cases where the appropriate Government, being satisfied that in the interests of the sovereignty and integrity of India, the security of the State, friendly relations with foreign States or in the public interest, it is not expedient to lay such report before the House of the People or the Legislative Assembly of the State, issues a notification to that effect in the Official Gazette. By virtue of the new sub-section (6), the appropriate Government is required to lay every notification issued under sub-section (5) before the House of the People or the Legislative Assembly and seeks approval thereon within the period mentioned therein.

3. The Bill seeks to replace the aforesaid Ordinance."[6]

Bill No. 102 of 1988 (Act No. 63 of 1988)

"Section 10A of the Commissions of Inquiry Act, 1952 provides for penalty for acts calculated to bring a Commission

---

6. Gazette of India, 18-07-1986, Pt. II, S. 2, Ext., p. 27, No. 27.

of Inquiry or any member thereof into disrepute and provides for the procedure for taking cognizance of such offence. Under the procedure specified in the section, the provisions of the Code of Criminal Procedure will apply and no prosecution can be launched except with the previous sanction of the Central Government or the State Government, as the case may be. It is proposed to amend this section to change this procedure to provide that an offence under this section is triable by the High Court by ordinary procedure prescribed under the Code of Criminal Procedure on a report of the Commission of Inquiry concerned without committal proceedings and that the personal attendance of the members of the Commission of Inquiry as complainants would not be necessary.

2. Opportunity is being availed of to give effect to the recommendations of the Committee on Subordinate Legislation of both the Houses of Parliament to the effect that the Commissions of Inquiry Act should be amended to make specific provision for appointment of assessors and for payment of traveling allowance and dearness allowance to assessors and witnesses. Such a provision at present exists in the Commissions of Inquiry (Central) Rules, 1972, made under the Act.

3. The Bill seeks to achieve the above objects."[7]

Bill No. 97 of 1989 (Act No. 19 of 1990)

"Sub-section (4) of Section 3 of the Commissions of Inquiry Act, 1952 casts an obligation on the appropriate Government to lay the report of the Commission of Inquiry appointed under sub-section (1) thereof before the House of the People or, as the case may be, the Legislative Assembly concerned, together with a memorandum of action taken thereon, within a period of six months of the submission of the report. However, in 1986, Section 3 had been amended so as to provide therein that under certain circumstances the report of the Commission of Inquiry may not be so laid.

2. A Commission of Inquiry is always set up for the purpose of making an inquiry into any definite matter of public

7. Gazette of India, 29-8-1988, Pt. II, S. 2, Ext., p. 4, No. 45.

importance. As such, the report submitted by such a Commission should not be withheld from the House of the People or the Legislative Assembly under any circumstances and the public should have access to information which is of vital importance and interest to them. It is felt that the amendments made in 1986 should be done away with.

3. The Bill seeks to achieve the above object."[8]

Inquiry—A Tool of Information Gathering

'Information' is not only an important tool of administration, it is also a source of administrative power. It can be obtained from different sources both formal and informal, in varied forms and degrees. It is noticed, more often than not, that human mind tries to hide or subvert the truth or to cover it up, as and when it suits him or may serve his purpose best. It has never been easy to find out the correct and true facts but the task is becoming more and more difficult with growing social complexities. Various ways and means have been explored and deployed for the purposes of finding out the true facts, at different levels for different purposes.[9] Inquiries are essentially means of information gathering. As such, these are an integral part of administration and are invariably made for various purposes, e.g. policy making, taking corrective and remedial measures, law enforcement and administration and even determination of rights and duties as well as adjudication of disputes and in connection with trial of offences. The most common and important aspect of these inquiries has been 'the facts-finding' as may be relevant to the matter under consideration in a given case. This helps in identifying the causes leading to a given situation as well as in deciding the future course of action to meet that situation. The quality of administrative decision, or for that matter, any decision largely depends on the quality of inputs that include correct and relevant facts having bearing on

8. Received the assent of the President on 28-8-1990 and published in the Gazette of India, Extra., Pt. II, S. 1, dated 29-8-1990, pp. 1-2.

9. *Sardar Malkeet Singh and Another* v. *State of U.P. and Others*, AIR 1993 Allahabad 343.

the matters in respect of which such a decision is required to be taken. Incorrect and irrelevant facts may vitiate the propriety and utility of any such decision. It may not always be feasible to have the relevant information from secondary sources or the concerned authorities directly. At times, there may be different versions on the relevant facts. In such a case, it may become necessary to have the relevant facts duly authenticated by an independent authority in an objective manner. Inquiries enable one to have first-hand information through the instrumentality of 'Commission' especially appointed for that purpose with a view to inform the mind of the authority concerned based on which it may take an objective view and decision in the matter without being fettered in any way by the information so obtained. Even where the facts are known, an inquiry commission can do well to place a stamp of judicial impartiality on these facts. This may help in garnering requisite support to, and acceptability of, any decision that may be taken on the basis of such authenticated facts.

The Commissions of Inquiry Act, 1952 is one of the legislations through which the effort is made to find out the true facts. It is a general law that empowers both the Central and State Governments to institute a Commission of Inquiry to enquire into any definite matter of public importance, falling in their respective competence and jurisdiction. The phrase 'definite matter of public importance' is wide and flexible enough to encompass in its ambit any and all conceivable matters in the discretion of the appropriate Government. Nonetheless, the purpose of all such inquiries is to ascertain the facts or the causes leading to an event or a situation and fixing responsibility therefor; determination of the existing malpractice or problem, if any, and the legislative, administrative or judicial action that needs to be taken in view of the outcome of such inquiries. But this Act and appointment of a Commission under it, does not ensure that the machinery is necessarily set in motion to achieve its object. There may still be many unforeseen hurdles, which often come in the way retarding the progress of enquiry,[10] such

10. *Sardar Malkeet Singh and Another* v. *State of U.P. and Others,* AIR 1993 Allahabad 343.

as challenging the appointment of a Commission on the ground of mala fide, political considerations, alien purposes, lack of competency and jurisdiction; or challenging the appointments of the Commissioners; or the lack of infrastructural support; or even the change of political regime and changed senario. Notwithstanding all this the institution of Commission of Inquiry, has been found to be necessary and quite useful, justifying its underlying object and purpose.

A former judge of the Supreme Court, referred in a manner characteristic of him, to the 'public inquiries jurisprudence' and the 'harvest of Commission litigation' developing in this country. The jurisprudence indeed seems to develop and the 'Commission litigation' appears to be on the increase.[11]

Other Statutory Inquiries

Besides, there are several statutes that enjoin upon the authorities concerned to institute inquiries in compliance with the statutory requirements in specified situation for prescribed purposes. Thus, inquiries may be instituted to enquire if a statutory body is complying, with the provisions of the Acts[12] or any violation of law being committed by some one[13] or where the affairs of a person/body are being conducted in a manner prejudicial to public interest[14] or to the detriment of any class of persons[15] or for a fraudulent or unlawful purpose[16] or in the happening of an event such as accidents.[17] The Code of Criminal Procedure, 1973 also provides for certain inquiries. Section 2(g) of the Code defines the term 'inquiry'. Accordingly, 'inquiry' means every inquiry, other than a trial, conducted under the Code by a Magistrate or a Court. The legality of such inquiries

---

11. *S.V. Purushothaman* v. *State of Kerala and Others*, AIR 1983 Kerala 118.
12. See for example, S. 54 of Dentists Act, 1954.
13. See for example, Factories Act, 1948; Income Tax Act, 1961.
14. See Industries (Development and Regulation) Act, 1951.
15. See Banking Companies Act, 1949.
16. See Companies Act, 1956.
17. See Railway Act, 1890; Motor Vehicles Act, 1939; Merchant Shipping Act, 1858 and Indian Aircraft Act, 1934.

and validity of their actions are governed by the statutory provisions under which they are held. It will, therefore, be necessary to ensure that there is no violation of any statutory provisions in cases of such inquiries.

Executive Inquiries

Apart from such inquiries as may be instituted in exercise of any statutory powers, administrative authorities in exercise of their executive powers may also institute inquiries. Power to institute such an inquiry is inherent in any administrative authority de hors any Act or statute. Such administrative inquiries have been in vogue from the time immemorial and are quite often instituted even after the passing of the Commissions of Inquiry Act, 1952.

It may not be possible to frame an exhaustive definition of what executive function means and implies. Ordinarily, the executive power connotes the residue of governmental functions that remain after legislative and judicial functions are taken away. The Indian Constitution has not indeed recognized the doctrine of separation of powers in its absolute rigidity but the functions of the different parts or branches of the Government have been sufficiently differentiated and consequently it can very well be said that our Constitution does not contemplate assumption, by one organ or part of the State, of functions that essentially belong to another. The executive indeed can exercise the powers of departmental or subordinate legislation when such powers are delegated to it by the legislature. It can also, when so empowered, exercise judicial functions in a limited way. The executive Government, however, can never go against the provisions of the Constitution or of any law. This is clear from the provisions of Article 154 of the Constitution but, it does not follow from this that in order to enable the executive to function there must be a law already in existence and that the powers of the executive are limited merely to the carrying out of these laws. The limits within which the executive Government can function under the Indian Constitution can be ascertained without much difficulty by reference to the form of the executive which our Constitution has set up. Our Constitution, though federal in its structure, is modelled on the British Parliamentary system where the executive is deemed to have the primary responsibility for the formulation of governmental policy and its transmission into law though the condition precedent to the exercise of this responsibility is in retaining the confidence of the legislative branch of the State. The executive function comprises both the determination of the policy as well as carrying it in to execution. This evidently includes the initiation of legislation, the maintenance of order, the promotion of social and economic welfare, the direction of foreign policy, in fact, the carrying on or supervision of the general administration of the State.[18]

While executive power of the Central Government under Article 73 of the Constitution would be available to the Central Government for any subject for which the Parliament can make legislation, i.e. any subject falling in List I (Union list) or in List III (Concurrent list), such executive power is always circumscribed by any existing legislation on the relevant subject. Since the Parliament has specifically mandated in the proviso to sub-section (1) of Section 3 that the Central Government shall not appoint another Commission to inquire into the same matter for so long as the State Commission is functioning, the Central Government could not have appointed a Commission to inquire into the cause of fire in some coaches of Sabarmati Express near Railway Station at Godhra which is admittedly in the State of Gujarat. What cannot be done directly by the Central Government under Section 3 of the Commission of Inquiry Act cannot be done indirectly by one of its department (Railway Administration) by invoking the executive power under Article 73 of the Constitution.[19]

Executive Inquiries vis-à-vis Statutory Inquiries

Inquiries may, thus, be held either in exercise of the executive powers on an informal and ad hoc basis or in exercise of powers

18. *Rai Sahib Ram Jawaya Kapur and Others* v. *The State of Punjab*, AIR 1955 SC 549, pp. 555-56.
19. *Union of India* v. *NilkanthTulsidas Bhatia* (2006) 2 GLR 952. It is understood that the Union of India, has preferred a Special Leave Petition against this judgment in the Supreme Court and the matter is yet to attain finality.

conferred under a statute. Both these kinds of inquiries have their own respective advantages and disadvantages. Barring cases where there may be statutory mandate to go for a statutory inquiry in terms of the requirements of the concerned statute, the authorities concerned may have to consider several factors before deciding upon the mode of inquiry, i.e. whether to go in for an executive inquiry or a statutory one. Executive inquiries are relatively having more flexibility than the statutory ones, which are circumscribed by the statutory provisions under which these are held. Then, statutory inquiries are quite often held in public which is not variably the case with the executive inquiries that can be held in administrative confidentiality and secrecy away from public and media scrutiny. Sources of information from which required information may have to be gathered may also have a bearing as to which of the two kinds of inquiries is to be resorted to. Thus, if the information sought can be obtained in the documents and records available with the authority concerned or to which it has easy access, executive inquiry would be more appropriate. However, where coercive measures may have to be applied in order to obtain the required information, statutory inquiry would be preferable. Furthermore, the evidentiary value of the statements obtained in the course of inquiries, and immunities in respect thereto, differ in the cases of executive inquiry on the one hand and statutory inquiry on the other. In the case of former, such a statement can be used against its maker, without affording him any immunity, it is not so in case of statutory inquiries wherein the maker of such a statement is invariably protected against any use of his statement in evidence in any proceedings, civil or criminal to which he may be a party. He may also have immunity in respect of any self-incriminating statement otherwise available to him under the law. Another relevant aspect is that of the right to hearing in case he is likely to be adversely affected by such an inquiry. Denial of such a right affording opportunity of being heard before being indicted or adversely affected may vitiate the inquiry's finding and report. It may not be so in case of executive inquiries. Another important aspect in this regard is that in executive inquiries, it may even be possible to recommend action against delinquent persons, in order to punish them for their lapses or by way of redressal or otherwise. It may not be so in case of statutory inquiries of fact-finding nature or other statutory inquiries which are governed by their statutory mandate. Above all, the purpose of instituting an inquiry may, at times, be decisive as to which type of inquiry needs to be instituted in a given case. Thus, in cases of Nation-wise or State-wise crises and/or emergencies, when restoration of public confidence and faith in established institution and public way of life is warranted, a statutory public judicial inquiry would be more appropriate than an executive one. It may, however, be mentioned that executive inquiries can be converted into statutory ones by extending the provisions of the Commissions of Inquiry Act, 1952.

Genesis of the Act

The appointment of Commissions under the present law owes its historical origin to the Anglo-Saxon jurisprudence, as it was in vogue in United Kingdom. It may be recalled that during seventeenth century and till almost the last phase of nineteenth century, events of great public importance and misconduct of Ministers or public servants used to be inquired by Parliamentary Select Committee appointed by the Parliament in England. One of the earliest of such committees was appointed by the Republic opposition against the Lord High Admiral, the Duke of York to investigate into the charges against the Navy and misappropriation and wastage of public funds. The war with Napoleaon and the Kremlin War also became the subject-matter of investigation by such a Committee in the nineteenth century. The Act was passed for the first time in 1921 in England which was called Tribunals of Inquiry (Evidence) Act, 1921 which was made for setting up of a Tribunal for inquiring into a definite matter of public importance as per the resolution of both Houses of Parliament. There, the power of contempt and enforcing the attendance of witnesses and calling a person to answer the questions was given and they were having the rights and privileges of a High Court. The working of these tribunals was then reviewed by Right Hon'ble Lord Justice Salmond as Chairman of the Royal Commission on Tribunals of Inquiry and the working of the Act was reviewed. The Act was retained though some safeguards were introduced.

In India, the Commissions of Inquiry Act came on the statute book for the first time in 1952. It was enacted after due consultation with State Governments to facilitate the setting up of Commissions with requisite powers to inquire into and report on any matter of public importance. Government realized, on the basis of its previous experience that the expedient of promoting special legislation for setting up a Commission of inquiry each time the need for it arose involved a tardy process which more often than not ended in the withdrawal of the proposals for inquiry. On the other hand, Government felt convinced of the utility of such inquiries as a means of arriving at a proper appraisal of matters of public importance and of infusing the confidence of the public in its administration and conduct. As the necessity for such inquiries was bound to be a recurring one, it was felt advantageous to have an enactment generalizing the powers which Commissions of inquiry may exercise and leaving it to the Government to constitute a Commission as and when necessary. Such in short is the genesis of the Commissions of Inquiry Act, 1952.[20]

The Commissions of Inquiry Bill, 1952, as was originally introduced in the Parliament, contained only eight clauses. The Bill was referred to the Select Committee. The Committee was consisted of thirty members and was headed by Dr. Kailash Nath Katju as Chairman. The report of the Committee was submitted to the House of People on 25 July 1952. The Bill as amended by the Select Committee contained twelve clauses as against eight clauses contained in the original Bill. The major amendments recommended by the Select Committee, inter alia, included that amendment of Clause 3 to provide that the time limit within which the Commission should complete its inquiry and submit its Report should be specified in the notification appointing the Commission. Then, under the existing proviso to Clause 3(1), it was not competent for any State Government,

20. Law Commission of India, Twenty-fourth Report—The Commissions of Inquiry Act, 1952, December 1962, Para 2, p. 1.

except with the approval of the Central Government, to appoint a State Commission to inquire into any matter which was being already inquired into by a Central Commisison for so long as that Central Commission was functioning and for two years thereafter. The Committee considered that the restriction imposed on a State Government to appoint a Commission for two years even after the Central Commission had ceased to function was unnecessary and should be omitted. They were further of the opinion that there should also be a prohibition on the Central Government to appoint a Central Commission when a State Commission was functioning unless the Central Government was of the opinion that the scope of the inquiry should be extended to two or more States. Accordingly, Clause 3 was amended to achieve these objects. Clause 4 was amended so as to empower the Commission to requisition copies of public records. As regards original Clauses 4(2) (3) and (4), now Section 5, the Committee was of the opinion that it was not necessary to vest in any of the Commissions appointed under Section 3 all the powers referred to in sub-clauses (2) to (4) of Clause 4. If, however, the appropriate Government was satisfied, having regard to the nature of the inquiry and other circumstances of the case, that such powers should be vested in any particular Commission, the appropriate Government might, by notification, vest such powers in that particular Commission. For this purpose, Clause 5(1) was inserted. Clause 5(3) was amended to provide that no officer below the rank of a Gazetted officer should be authorized by the Commission to have powers of search and seizure. The sole and the only minute of dissent by Shri K.S. Raghavachari was in respect of this clause, which Shri Raghavachari recommended to be omitted for the reason such a clause was necessary only to prevent evasion of taxation and the Bill under consideration was not expected to cover such cases. Sub-clauses (5) and (6) of Clause were inserted as new Clauses 8 to 10 and subsequent clauses were renumbered. The renumbered Clause 11 was slightly redrafted with a view to clarify that even under this clause, the appropriate Government should specify in the notification whether all or only some of the provisions of the Act should apply to a particular inquiring authority. The Bill as amended by the Select Committee was passed by the Parliament. It received the President's assent on 14-8-1952. It came into force on 1-10-1952.

The Act is based largely on the English Act. But it differs from the English Act in certain respects. The Indian Act empowers the Government to set up a Commission of Inquiry suo motu. There is no corresponding provision in the English Act. The English Act does not make the resolution of the Parliament or, as the case may be, Legislature of a State binding on the Government, although normally the Government would respect the wishes of the Parliament or the State Legislature; but in India the resolution of the Parliament or the State Legislature is binding on the Central Government or the State Government, as the case may be. The English Act provides that if any contempt of the Tribunal is committed, the Tribunal can refer the matter to the High Court which will punish or take steps for the punishment of the person guilty of contempt in like manner as if he had been guilty of contempt of the High Court. There is no such provision in the Indian Act. The English Act expressly provides that an inquiry shall generally be held in public. The Indian Act leaves it to the Commission to hold its sittings in public or in private. The Indian Act provides that where any authority, by whatever name called, other than a Commission appointed under the Act has been, or is set up, under any resolution or order of the Government for the purpose of making an inquiry into any matter of public importance, the Government may direct that all or any of the provisions of the Act shall be applicable to that authority. There is no corresponding provision in the English Act.[21]

The Law Commission of India, in its 24th report submitted in 1962, reviewed this Act. In the light of the defects and drawbacks of inquiries by Commissions as revealed in the working of the Act, the Law Commission considered two issues, namely (1) whether the Commissions of Inquiry Act, 1952 should at all be on the statute book? (2) if so, what safeguards

---

21. Law Commission of India, Twenthy-fourth Report, *ibid.*, Para 6, p. 4.

should be provided to mitigate the rigour of the Act? The first question was answered by the Law Commission in the affirmative. In support of this, the Law Commission referred to the reply of the Lord Chancellor, Viscount Kilmuir to the debate in the House of Lords in the Water case wherein he made a spirited and vigorous defence of the English Act in the following words:[22]

> Let me state quite shortly the arguments for some such procedure as the present. The sanction of the public inquiry is necessary on occasions for the purpose of maintaining a high standard of public administration and, indeed, of public life. The modern system has developed in consequences of the inadequacies of the machinery of inquiry by Select Committee on the one hand and the limitations of the ordinary process of law on the other.... The ordinary processes of law are geared to a charge or claim brought by one person against another. They do not fit when it is necessary to discover what has actually happened before the responsibility of or between individuals can arise, and, as has been discussed earlier in this debate, there are other fields, such as wreck inquiries, inquiries into accidents, courts of inquiry in the Services and the Committee of Privileges of the House of Commons, where the inquisitorial procedure is a necessary concomitant of their work. In all those cases the question of discovering what has actually happened is of prime importance.... After the true facts have been found and stated it may be necessary to stigmatise conduct which, although not a criminal offence or a civil wrong, falls short of the requisite standards of our public life. It may be necessary to kill harmful rumours which are found to be unjustified. It may be necessary—and this I am sure was very much in the minds of the Government who introduced this measure—to restore public confidence in public conduct and administration. These ends may well be of such importance to the life of the nation as to justify means which inflict hardship on individuals.

22. Parliamentary Debates, Lords, 1958-59, Vol. 216, "The Waters Tribunal", pp. 470-72.

The Law Commission found the arguments set out by the Lord Chancellor in defence of the English Act equally applicable to the Indian Act. In the view of the Law Commission, there seems to be sufficient justification for an Act like the Commissions of Inquiry Act, 1952. The Law Commission observed: "It is true that in some cases, the Government does not take any action on the report of a Commission of Inquiry. But that does not mean that the inquiry has not been useful. The Commission either exonerates the persons involved in the inquiry or holds them guilty. In either case the inquiry serves a useful purpose. In the first case, the inquiry sets at rest some ugly rumours which led to the appointment of the Commission. In the second case, the guilty persons are exposed to the public eye. The prosecution is not the only method of punishing persons who pollute the pure springs of public administration. Many persons would prefer to suffer a sentence in secret rather than face the public with their dark deeds. The glaring publicity which attaches to such inquiries is both its strength and its weakness. Such publicity exposes the wrong-doers to the public eye and there lies its strength. Sometimes, however, such publicity results in unmerited mud-slinging on some innocent persons who are denied the safeguards of the ordinary judicial procedure to vindicate themselves and there lies its weakness. But no human system of justice can be perfect. Cases of miscarriage of justice are not unknown in the ordinary courts of law."[23]

Having come to the conclusion that the Commissions of Inquiry Act, 1952 should be on the Statute Book, the Law Commission proceeded to deal with the necessary safeguards to mitigate the rigour of the Act. In this regard, the Law Commission felt that "in a matter like this, there should be a just balance between the interests of the general public and the rights of individuals, between the claims of the State and civil liberties. The fundamental rights enshrined in our Constitution will have little meaning if they can be trampled upon by a law which, though conforming to the letter of the Constitution, yet violates

23. Law Commission of India, Twenty-fourth Report (The Commissions of Inquiry Act, 1952), December 1962, pp. 6-7.

its spirit. In order that the special procedure envisaged in the Commissions of Inquiry Act, 1952 does not work any hardship on citizens, there should be some safeguards."[24]

Accordingly, the Law Commission considered certain general points in relation to the Act. These include, inter alia, power of Government to appoint Commissions suo motu, contempt of Commission, application of the Indian Evidence Act, procedure of Commission, costs, publication of reports, assistance to Commission for the purpose of investigation, etc. Amongst various infirmities pointed out by the Law Commission one of the important infirmities was that in the absence of specific clear cut provision for the purpose there is a danger of inquiries being instituted in relation to matters in which the remedies available under the ordinary law are adequate and effective and the powers conferred on the Commission are left to be rather draconian in practice. Consequently, amendments were made in 1971.

Nevertheless, the working of some of the commissions of inquiry led some of the critics to doubt the utility of this institution as a whole. Thus, it has been said that invariably our commissions of inquiry begin with a bang and end in a whimper. One has only to look into the history of past commissions to understand how they, as Shakespeare would say, are full of sound and fury, signifying nothing.[24a] The Liberhan Commission is one such commission, which recently submitted its report on 30th June 2009. Coming 17 years after it was set up, the report at best may be an interesting source of material. Its only claim to fame seems to be that it is the longest commission. "If anything, the Liberhan Commission should serve as a model for the future is as to how a commission of inquiry should not be."[24b] There lies the utility even in such a case.

---

24. Law Commission of India, Twenty-fourth Report (The Commissions of Inquiry Act, 1952), December 1962, p. 7.

24a. Coomi Kapoor, "A Commission is Forever", *The Indian Express*, July 10, 2009, p. 10.

24b. "Organiser View from the Right—Liberhan Commission", *The Indian Express*, July 9, 2009, p. 11.

In India various commissions have been set up to inquire into the charges against Ministers or other public matters. Khanna Commission and S.R. Das Commission were appointed to inquire into allegations against Shri Biju Patnaik and Shri Pratap Singh Kairon. Chandrachud Commission and Methew Commission also inquired into the death of some of the important personalities like Shri Deen Dayal Upadhyaya and Shri L.N. Mishra. In Rajasthan Justice Mr. B.P. Beri was required to investigate into Jaipur firing, which took place during the tenure of Dr. Sampurnanand as Governor in 1967 when a political tousle in Ministry-making was going on. The Nathdwara temples jewellery having been alleged to be removed, the allegation of the involvement of the then Chief Minister Shri Mohan Lal Sukhadia became the subject-matter of investigation by the then Chief Justice Sarjoo Prasad Commission. Several other commissions like Ganganagar district, Bhadra, Sangharia and Churu firing, Bose Hostel excesses, scooter stampede in Udaipur, Bharatpur firing in factory and even the death of the earlier Chief Minister Shri Barkatualla Khan and the allegations and inquiries of medical treatment in it became subject-matter of various inquiries under the Commission of Inquiry Act.

As is evident from the above legislative history, the Commissions of Inquiry Act, 1952 is now quite old and it came into force on October 1, 1952 and immediately on its coming into force the first Commission was appointed within two days. The majority of the Commissions have been appointed for inquiring into the police firings; but the most important Commissions relate to other matters of public importance which cover much wider range than the stray cases of police firings or executive or administrative excesses. The Press Commission was appointed to inquire into the state of press in India and the lines of its present and future development in 1952, Plantation Inquiry Commission was appointed in 1954 to inquire into the economic conditions and problems of the tea, coffee and rubber industries. Hindu Religious and Charitable Trusts came up for inquiry by Neeladri Rao Commission in 1954. Vivian Bose Commission, Chagla Commission and Tendulkar Commission were appointed in 1956 to inquire into the affairs of M/s. Allen

Berry and Co., Mundhra Group of Companies and Dalmia Jain Group of Companies respectively. Sarjoo Prasad Commission was appointed in 1958 to inquire into the funds and valuables of Shrinathji at Nathdwara temple in Rajasthan. In 1963, Das Commission was appointed to inquire into the allegations of corruption, etc. against Sardar Pratap Singh Kairon, Chief Minister of Punjab.

Aiyer Commission and Mudholkar Commission were appointed for making inquiry into the allegations of corruption against Shri K.B. Sahai and five other Bihar Ministers and Shri Mahamaya Prasad Sinha and thirteen other ex-Ministers of Bihar, respectively. In the years 1967, 1968 and 1969 the then Chief Justice of Supreme Court of India was appointed as one-man Commission to inquire into the facts and circumstances relating to the death of Shri Deen Dayal Upadhayaya, the then President of Bhartiya Jan Sangh. Sarkar Commission inquired into the affairs of large industrial houses. In 1971, Dr. H.K. Mahtab's, ex-Chief Minister, Orissa, conduct was inquired into by Sarjoo Prasad Commission. Justice Methew inquired into late Shri L.N. Mishra's death and the circumstances pertaining to the accident, which occurred at Samastipur on January 2, 1975. This included the inquiry into the bomb blast and the serious injuries caused to Shri Mishra and others, and nature and adequacy of the security measures, medical attention and other connected matters. Allegations of misuse of official position, bribery and corruption on the part of the former D.M.K. Chief Minister of Tamil Nadu Shri Karunanidhi and some of his Cabinet colleagues became the subject-matter of probe and inquiry by Sarkaria Commission in the year 1976.

The above are some of the major commissions referred to, as it is almost impossible to recapitulate and to make a catalogue of all the commissions appointed as the number of them, according to Mr. A.P. Chakravati, M.P., given on May 18, 1979 in the Parliament, is 1,76,000.[25]

The post-emergency commissions appointed by the Union of India and the States came to limelight by the first appointment

25. These are inclusive of committees and study teams also.

of Justice Shah as one-man Commission to inquire into the emergency excesses. The affairs of the Maruti Limited are the subject-matter of inquiry by Gupta Commission appointed in 1977. Reddy Commission inquired into the affairs relating to Bansi Lal and also the Nagarwala affairs. The conduct of Karnataka Chief Minister Shri Dev Raj Urs and some of his Cabinet colleagues became the subject-matter of inquiry before the Grover Commission appointed on May 23, 1977. Grover Commission was appointed by the Central Government. Karnatak Government appointed Iqbal Hussain Commission to inquire into certain allegations levelled against the Chief Minister Shri Dev Raj Urs and some of his Cabinet colleagues. On April 21, 1977, Karnatak Government appointed Mr. Justice Santosh as one-man Commission to inquire into the alleged excesses committed on Shri Lawrence Fernandes and Mrs. Snehlata Reddy. The Andhra Pradesh Government referred to the alleged atrocities and killings of Naxalities in Andhra Pradesh for inquiry and Mr. Justice A.N. Bhargava was appointed as one-man Commission on July 10, 1977. The Central Government appointed Alva Commission to inquire into the medical treatment given to Shri Jai Prakash Narain during his detention, after proclamation of emergency on June 26, 1975, while he was being treated in Chandigarh. The allegation was that the damage to the kidneys of Jai Prakash Narayan occurred because of wrong or neglectful treatment at Chandigarh, and as a result of that his kidneys had been damaged permanently and beyond the scope of repair, before his release in November 1975. Dr. Nagappa Alva was a former Health Minister of Karnataka.

The emergency excesses alleged to have taken place at Rewasa village in Haryana as a result of the earlier rivalries between Shri Surendra Singh, son of ex-Defence Minister (the then Chief Minister of Haryana) Shri Bansilal and a Rajput youth Shri Bhanwar Singh, who were contemporaries in the Vaish College, Bhiwani, were inquired into by Capoor Commission.

Justice P.D. Sharma Commission inquired into the police firings for family planning excess at Pipli and Nagina during the emergency. A public inquiry into the alleged disappearance of a boy, Vijavan Nair alias Manian during the emergency, came to light after the Kerala High Court's orders in Rajan's case was inquired into by Kochu Koshy Commission. Vishwanath Aiyar Commission appointed by Kerala Government on May 2, 1977 inquired into Rajan, the missing Engineering college student, who was alleged to have been murdered while in police custody. R. Sadasivam Commission was appointed on May 4, 1977 to inquire into the allegations of ill treatment and beating of detenues and political prisoners in the Central Prison, Madras after proclamation of President's Rule following the dismissal of D.M.K. Ministry. The alleged assault on Shri P.L. Kaushik, later a Union Minister and Mr. Sudhir Mukherjee, C.P.M. leader on election-eve in March 1977 was inquired into by B.C. Shrivastava Commission. Vimadalal Commission appointed on May 19, 1977 inquired into the allegations of misuse of official position against the Chief Minister of the State, Mr. Vengala Rao and some of his Cabinet colleagues. The family planning programme incidents between August 24 and 27, 1976 in Muzaffarnagar were inquired into by Ram Ashrey Mishra Commission. The Nagaland incidents of looting, rioting, and arson on May 28, 1977 were inquired into by Uma Shankar Shrivastava Commission. The police firing at Rajhara near Durg was inquired into by Razzaque Commission.

In addition to the above, many other commissions were appointed to inquire into the various emergency excesses which related to the unjustified detention, torture in jails, the police tortures and police atrocities, unlawful removal of buildings, family planning excesses, etc. during emergency. It is not possible to catalogue them all. The above survey would only show that the appointments of commissions under the Commission of Inquiry Act have assumed new dimensions after the Act was enacted.

The above brief survey of the various commissions appointed under the Commissions of Inquiry Act, 1952 either by the Union of India or by the State Government would show that the subjects, fields, matters and scope and arena of inquiry have been so diverse that they include from rail accidents, excess of food contamination, police firing, fire accidents, deaths in police lock-up, bus accidents, failure of dam to corruption of Ministers, frauds and scandles in companies, death of Shri L.N. Misra, Upadhayaya, economics of newspaper industries and excess of emergency from house demolition and forcible family planning to MISA arrests and detentions. Even in the matters of the commissions set up to conduct the probe and post-mortem in the various emergency excesses, vast and diverse fields have been covered commencing from misuse of authority, excesses and malpractices committed by a public servant and other individuals who may have directed, abetted or otherwise associated with the commission of such acts during emergency; subversion of lawful process, maltreatment, torture and other atrocities on the persons detained under MISA or DIR, unauthorized demolition of houses, huts, shops, buildings, or direct misuse of authority for receiving funds for publication of souvenir or other advertising material by public servant, political party or other persons, the reasons and circumstances leading to the proclamation of internal emergency on June 25, 1975, undue favour shown or other benefit given to one or more Maruti concerns; the circumstances relating to and manner of dispossession of the occupants of land given to Maruti limited; all matters pertaining to the initiation, processing and clearing to the Maruti small car project; any deviation from any rule or established procedure in relation to or connected with the chain of events by taking out a sum of Rs. 60 lakh from State Bank of India and the subsequent proceedings against Nagarwala and his death, etc. This only shows the scope of Section 3 of the Commissions of Inquiry Act has been treated and taken to be very wide and comprehensive. In fact, the only rider, limitation or fetters, which the Legislature has put on the powers of the Government under Section 3, is contained in the outer limit conveyed by the words, 'any definite matter of public importance'. If any inquiry is to be conducted in any matter, the only requirement is that it must be a definite matter not only of some importance, but it should be of public importance. The term 'matter' does not require any interpretation because it can include an atom to sky and can cover in its range all matters, which could be conceived by any human sense in the world. How deep is the sea level and how high is the sky and whether scientific research indicating the findings on the mars or moon is correct can all be matters as used in Section 3. Of course, the rider or the limitations to this is that they are all based on the interpretation of the meaning and words 'definite' and 'public importance'.[26]

Prior to the coming into force of the present Act, the Government appointed Commissions and Committees of Inquiry by executive orders. But because of certain handicaps felt in the conduct of such Commissions and Committees of Inquiry, this Act has been enacted. The statement of the objects and reasons of the Act state so. It further states that in the absence of any statutory power to enforce the attendance of witnesses and the production of documents, it was felt that there should be general law authorizing Government to appoint an inquiring authority on any matter of public importance, whenever considered necessary, or when a demand to that effect is made by the Legislature and that such law should enable the inquiring authority to exercise certain specific powers including the power to summon witnesses, to take evidence on oath and to compel persons to furnish information. The preamble to the Act also states that the Act is to provide for the appointment of Commissions of Inquiry and for vesting such commissions with certain powers. Section 2 of the Act defines, inter alia, the appropriate Government, which means the Central Government or the State Government, as the case may be. The legislative and executive sanction to appoint Commissions of Inquiry is to be found in Entry 94 of List I and Entry 45 of List III in the Seventh Schedule to the Constitution.[27]

The Commissions of Inquiry Act, 1952 was enacted after due consultation with State Governments to facilitate the setting up of commissions with requisite powers to inquire into and report on any matter of public importance. Government realised on the basis of its previous experience that the expedient of promoting special legislation for setting up a commission of

---

26. *Brijpal Dass* v. *Justice B.P. Beri and Another*, ILR (1981) 31 Raj., 361.

27. *Bhagwat Dayal Sharma* v. *Union of India and Others*, ILR (1974) I Delhi 847.

inquiry each time the need for it arose involved a tardy process, which more often than not ended in the withdrawal of the proposals for inquiry. On the other hand, Government felt convinced of the utility of such inquiries as a means of arriving at a proper appraisal of matters of public importance and of infusing the confidence of the public in its administration and conduct. As the necessity for such inquiries was bound to be a recurring one, it was felt advantageous to have an enactment generalizing the powers, which commissions of inquiry may exercise and leaving it to the Government to constitute a commission as and when necessary. Such, in short, is the genesis of the Commissions of Inquiry Act, 1952.[28] The Commissions of Inquiry Act, 1952 has been used for a variety of purposes.[29]

It may be investigative in nature. For example, a one-man judicial commission headed by Justice S.C. Mahapatra was appointed to inquire and report on the violence in Kandhmal in Orissa which claimed 43 lives besides damaging houses and churches in the wake of the killing of VHP leaders Swami Lakshman and Saraswati last year.[29a]

A Commission of inquiry may also be set up as a part of policy formulation process. Thus, a Commission headed by retired Gujarat High Court Judge, Justice B.J. Sethna has been appointed by the State Government notification dated June 6, 2009 to map and study migration and polarisation of religious communities in Gujarat since independence. The Commission will submit its report by January 31, 2011. The notification states that "there have been allegations made in the court as well as media that polarisation of population on the basis of religion is taking place in Gujarat. The government feels that such

---

28. Law Commission of India, Twenty-fourth Report on the Commissions of Inquiry Act, 1952, Government of India, Ministry of Law (1962), p. 1.

29. *Ibid.*, see Appendix III for a statement showing the commissions appointed under the Act.

29a. Reconversion of converts led to Kandhmal riots: Panel *Times of India*, July 4, 2009, p. 17. See also 'Need two more years to blame anyone' Kandhamal probe panel: *Indian Express*, July 4, 2009.

allegations and unscientific conclusions create heart burn and distance among citizens. The Commission will recommend steps to stop polarisation. As per the terms of reference of the Commission, it will map the total area in square metres covered by people following different religious in the State as on August 15, 1947. Then it will progressively show the changes taking place every 10 years. The Commission will also map area-wise proportion of people following different religions in new residential areas which have come into being only after August 15, 1947. Its primary objective will be to find out reasons of polarisation of population in terms of law and order and socio-economic development.[29b] Sometime back, there was a proposal to set up a one-man commission headed by former Lok Sabha Speaker, Somnath Chatterjee to study parliamentary privileges.[29c]

Another example of Commission being a tool of policy of formulation is the Kremlin Commission which has recently been established by Russia "to counter attempts to falsify history to the detriment of Russia's interest." Its task will be to trace and analyse historical untruths and draw up proposals on how to counter them. Apart from countering foreign falsehoods about Soviet history, the Kremlin Commission will be called upon to combat a decisive view of Russia's communist past among its own people.[29d]

The Commissions of Inquiry Act, 1952 is similar to and is modelled on the corresponding English statute, which provides the historical background for the Indian statute. The purpose of

---

29b. Gujarat panel to study communal divide, *Times of India*, July 4, 2009, p. 17. See also Justice Sethna at the center of a storm, again—The former High Court Judge who will chair Gujarat's inquiry Commission into 'polarisation of population' is no stranger to controversies, *The Indian Express*, July 9, 2009, p. 9. National Network.

29c. PM mulls new role for retired Somnath—May ask him to take charge of one-man commission to study parliamentary privileges, *Business Standard*, 29 June 2009.

29d. Vladimir Radyuhin, "Russia: Fighting Historical Lies", *The Hindu*, June 24, 2009, p. 12.

such an enactment is aptly summarized in the speech of Lord Salmon on 'Tribunals of Inquiry' as under:

> In all the countries, certainly in those which enjoy freedom of speech and a free Press, moments occur when allegations and rumours circulate causing a nation-wide crisis of confidence in the integrity of public life or about other matters of vital public importance. No doubt this rarely happens, but when it does it is essential that public confidence should be restored, for without it no democracy can long survive. This confidence can be effectively restored only by thoroughly investigating and probing the rumours and allegations so as to search out and establish the truth. The truth may show that the evil exists, thus enabling it to be rooted out, or that there is no foundation in the rumours and allegations by which the public has been disturbed. In either case, confidence is restored. How, in such circumstances, can the truth best be established?

It is for the purpose of ascertaining the truth in such circumstances that the Commissions of Inquiry Act, 1952 has been enacted. While construing the provisions of the enactment, it would be useful to bear in mind its object if occasion arises for illumination of any grey areas with reference to the object of the enactment as a permissible aid to construction.[30]

The proceedings under the Act are of paramount importance in a democratic country like ours, having a written Constitution and governed by rule of law. In our country on issues of public importance the demand of the public is to have a judicial enquiry to know the true facts and such enquiries have proved to be of great satisfaction to the public at large. Very many issues of public importance are now being set at rest by appointment of Commissions of Inquiry under the Act for, to use the words of Sir Cyril Salmon, public confidence without which no democracy can long survive, can be effectively restored only by thoroughly investigating and probing the rumours and allegations so as to search out and establish the truth. It is for

---

30. *State of Madhya Pradesh* v. *Ajay Singh and Others* (1993) 1 SCC 302, pp. 314-15.

this reason that more often than not, the demand of the public is to have a judicial enquiry by a Supreme Court Judge (sitting or retired) or by a High Court Judge (sitting or retired) because the public have faith in the fairness and impartiality of the Judges of the Supreme Court and the High Court. Therefore, it is of fundamental importance to ensure that the enquiry is fair and impartial and in appointing Commissions under the Act. The germane consideration should be that the public confidence is strengthened or restored, as the case may be, lest it should be shattered.[31]

Synopsis of the Act

The Act is a short one, consisting of 20 sections, numbering 1 to 12. Section 2 defines, inter alia, 'appropriate Government' to mean the Central Government in relation to any matter relatable to any of the entries in List I or List II or List III in the Seventh Schedule of the Constitution and the State Government in relation to any matter relatable to any of the entries in List II or List III in that Schedule. Under Section 3, a Commission of Inquiry for the purposes of making an inquiry into any definite matter of public importance may be appointed by the 'appropriate Government' of its own motion; but if a resolution in this behalf is passed by each House of Parliament or, as the case may be, the Legislature of the State, it is obligatory on the appropriate Government to appoint such a Commission. Where a Commission is appointed by the Central Government, a State Government cannot appoint another Commission to enquire into the same matter except with the approval of the Central Government and conversely, where a Commission is appointed by a State Government, the Central Government is barred from appointing another Commission to inquire into the same matter unless the Central Government is of the opinion that the scope of the inquiry should be extended to two or more States. A Commission of Inquiry may consist of one or more members. Section 4 confers on a Commission of Inquiry certain powers of a Civil Court (e.g. summoning and enforcing the attendance of

31. *K. Vijaya Bhaskar Reddy* v. *Government of Andhra Pradesh*, AIR 1996 A.P. 62, p. 70.

witnesses and examining them on oath, etc.). Section 5 empowers the 'appropriate Government' to confer some additional powers on a Commission of Inquiry relating to the production of information and seizure of books of account or documents. Sub-section (4) of Section 5 lays down that a Commission of Inquiry shall be deemed to be a Civil Court and when any offence as is described in Section 175, Section 178, Section 179, Section 180 or Section 228 of the Indian Penal Code is committed in the view or presence of the Commission, it may forward the case to the concerned competent court for trial. Sub-Section (5) of Section 5 enacts that any proceeding before a Commission shall be deemed to be a judicial proceeding for the purpose of Sections 193 and 228 of the Indian Penal Code. Section 5A empowers the Commission to utilise the services of certain officers and investigation agencies for conducting investigation pertaining to inquiry with the concurrence of the Central Government or the State Government, as the case may be. Under Section 5B, the Commission may, for the purpose of conducting any inquiry, appoint persons having special knowledge of any matter connected with the inquiry as assessors, to assist and advise the Commission in the inquiry. Section 6 confers upon persons giving evidence before the Commission protection from prosecution except for perjury. Section 6A, however, provides that nothing in the Act shall be deemed to compel any person giving evidence before the Commission to disclose any secrete process of manufacture except in cases where a Commission is expressly required to inquire into the process of manufacture of any goods. Section 7 empowers the 'appropriate Government' to dissolve a Commission when its continuance becomes unnecessary or, in case of a Commission appointed pursuant a resolution of the Parliament or the State Legislature, as the case may be, a resolution for the discontinuance is passed by each House of Parliament or, as the case may be, the Legislature of the State. Under Section 8 the Commission may regulate its own procedure subject to any rules made by the 'appropriate Government'. Section 8A provides that inquiry will not be interrupted by reason of vacancy or change in the constitution of the Commission. Section 8B provides for hearing to persons likely to be prejudicially affected by the inquiry. Section 8C deals with right of cross-examination and representation by legal practitioner. Section 9 contains the usual indemnity for action taken in good faith and Section 10 provides that members of a Commission and other officers appointed by it to exercise functions under the Act shall be deemed to be public servants within the meaning of the Indian Penal Code. Section 10A provides penalty for acts calculated to bring the Commission or any member thereof into disrepute. Under Section 11 the provisions of the Act may also be made applicable to a Commission of Inquiry set up by the appropriate Government in the exercise of its executive power. Section 12 authorises the appropriate Government to make rules to carry out the purposes of the Act.

The following propositions emerge from an analysis of the relevant statutory provisions:[32]

I. (i) If the appropriate Government is of the opinion that it is necessary so to do, it may appoint a Commission of Inquiry for the purpose of making an inquiry into any definite matter of public importance. [Section 3(1)]

(ii) If a resolution in this behalf is passed by each House of Parliament or, as the case may be, the

32. *Union of India* v. *Nilkanth Tulsidas Bhatia and 7 Ors* (2006) 2 GLR 952. These observations were made by a Division Bench of the High Court of Gujarat at Ahmedabad in its judgment dated 20-03-2006, in a Letter Patent Appeal, against an interim order of a Single Judge of that High Court in the case of *Nilkanth Tulsidas Bhatia* v. *Union of India and 7 Ors* dated 7-3-2006, which has not been reported. The Division Bench pointed out one more proposition as "V. Where a Commission of Inquiry is appointed under CoI Act to inquire into an accident, the Railway Administration or its officers cannot proceed with any pending inquiry, investigation or other proceeding in relation to that accident, meaning thereby after the appointment of a Commission of Inquiry under CoI Act, the Railway Administration or its officers cannot commence any inquiry or investigation." It is understood that the judgment of the Division Bench is under challenge in a Special Leave Petition filed by the Union of India, in the Ministry of Railway and final verdict in the matter is yet to come.

Legislature of the State, the appropriate Government shall appoint a Commission of Inquiry for the purpose of making an inquiry into any definite matter of public importance. [Section 3(1)]

II. The appropriate Government may apply the provisions of the CoI Act to any authority (by whatever named called) set up for the purpose of making any inquiry into any definite matter of public importance. [Section 11]

III. The proviso to sub-section (1) of Section 3 imposes the following prohibitions on exercise of powers under Section 3(1) or under Section 11:

(a) Where any such Commission has been appointed to inquire into any matter by the Central Government, no State Government shall, except with the approval of the Central Government, appoint another Commission to inquire into the same matter for so long as the Central Commission is functioning.

(b) Where any such Commission has been appointed to inquire into any matter by the State Government, the Central Government shall not appoint another Commission to inquire into the same matter for so long as the State Commission is functioning unless the Central Government is of the opinion that the scope of the inquiry should be extended to two or more States.

IV. The above prohibitions (a) and (b) forming part of the proviso to sub-section (1) of Section 3 are applicable, irrespective of the fact whether the Commission is appointed by the appropriate Government on the formation of its opinion or whether such Commission is appointed by the appropriate Government upon a resolution having been passed by the Parliament or the State Legislature, as the case may be.

It may, however, be noted that even after the enactment of this Act, a Commission or Committee of Inquiry can be constituted in exercise of executive power and de hors the Act. Section 11 of the Act which provides for application of the Act to other inquiring authorities, other than those set up under Section 3 of the Act, makes it clear that there can be inquiring authorities which are set up outside this Act. In *P.R. Nayak* v. *Union of India and Others*,[33] it was observed: "It cannot be disputed that a Commission of Inquiry can be constituted de hors the Act in which case it will be an authority appointed in exercise of the executive powers of the Government and if such an authority has been or is set up under a resolution or order of the appropriate Government for the purpose of making inquiry into any definite matter of public importance, then upon the issue of a notification under Section 11 of the Act this authority is deemed to be a Commission appointed under Section 3 for the purposes of the Act." It is, thus, clear that the Government, independent of the provisions of the Commissions of Inquiry Act, can constitute a Commission or a Committee. In other words, a Commission or Committee can be constituted by the Government de hors the provisions of the Commissions of Inquiry Act.[34]

Commissions under the Constitution and Other Statutes

The Constitution of India also contemplates the appointment of certain commissions for certain purposes. Some of these commissions and the related constitutional provisions are: Finance Commission under Articles 280, 243-I and 243-Y; Public Service Commissions for the Union and the States under Article 315; Election Commission under Article 324; National Commission for Scheduled Castes under Article 338; National Commission for Scheduled Tribes under Article 338-A; Commission to investigate the conditions of backward classes under Article 340; Commission on official language under Article 344.

33. ILR (1973) I Delhi 747.

34. *Brahma Nand Gupta* v. *Delhi Administration and Others*, 1989 (4) Delhi Lawyer (DB) 94.

Certain commissions have also been set up under various Acts of Parliament such as Monopolies and Restrictive Trade Practices Commission, Competition Commission, Human Right Commission, National and State Commissions for Consumer Dispute Redressal and Regulatory Commissions for telecom, electricity, insurance, etc.

Part III of the Code of Civil Procedure, 1908 deals with incidental proceedings. This Part contains four sections, viz. sections 75 to 78. This Part deals with 'Commissions'. Under Section 75, the Court may issue a Commission for the following purposes, namely: (a) to examine any person; (b) to make a local investigation; (c) to examine or adjust accounts; (d) to make a partition; (e) to conduct sale of property which is subject to speedy and natural decay and which is in the custody of the Court pending the determination of the suit; and (f) to perform any other ministerial act. Order XXVI of the Code contains detailed provisions for such Commissions. The Code further provides for issue of a Commission to another Court in Section 76 and also for Commission issued by foreign Courts in Section 78 of the Code.

Part B of Chapter XXIII of the Code of Criminal Procedure, 1973, consisting of Sections 284 to 289, deals with Commissions for the examination of witnesses.

In view of the aforesaid, a Commission may be set up under the Constitution, an Act of Parliament or State Legislature or in exercise of the executive power of the State. A Commission of Inquiry may thus be set up either in exercise of the executive power of the State or under the Commissions of Inquiry Act.

Commission—Meaning

In *DK Illustrated Oxford Dictionary*,[35] the words 'commission' and 'commissioner' have been assigned the following meanings, viz.

Commission *n.* **1a** the authority to perform a task or certain duties. **b** a person or group entrusted esp. by a government with such authority. **c** an instruction or duty given to such a group

35. 1998 Edition, pp. 169-70.

or person (*their commission was to simplify the procedure*). **2** an order for something, esp. a work of art, to be produced specially. **3** *Mil.* **a** a warrant conferring the rank of officer in any army, navy or air force. **b** the rank so conferred. **4a** the authority to act as agent for a company etc. in trade. **b** a percentage paid to the agent from the business obtained (*his salary is low, but he gets 20% commission*). **5** the act of committing (a crime, sin, etc.). **6** the office or department of a commissioner. *v.tr.* **1** authorize or empower by a commission. **2** a give (an artist etc.) a commission for a piece of work. **b** order (a work) to be written. **3** *Naul.* **a** give (an officer) the command of a ship. **b.** prepare (a ship) for active service. **4** bring (a machine, equipment, etc.) into operation. **in commission** (of a warship etc.) manned, armed, and ready for service. **out of commission** (esp. of a ship) not in service; not in working order. [related to commit]

Commissioner *n* **1.** a person appointed by a commission to perform a specific task. **2.** (esp. in titles) a person appointed as a member of a government commission (Civil Service Commissioner). **3.** a representative of the supreme authority in a district, department, etc.

In Bouvier's Law Dictionary and Concise Encyclopedia by John Bouvier[36] the word 'commission' has been assigned the following meaning, viz.

Commission (Lat. *Commissio*; from *committere,* to intrust to).

An undertaking without reward to do something for another, with respect to a thing bailed. Rutherforth, Inst. 105.

A body of persons authorized to act in a certain matter. 5 B. & C. 850.

The act of perpetrating an offence.

An instrument issued by a court of justice, or other competent tribunal, to authorize a person to take depositions, or do any other act by authority of such court or tribunal, is called a Commission.

---

36. Third Revision (being the Eighth Edition) by Francis Rawle, Vol. I, p. 547.

Letters-patent granted by the Government, under the public seal, to a person appointed to an office, giving him authority to perform the duties of his office. The commission is not the appointment, but only evidence of it, and, as soon as it is signed and sealed, vests the office in the appointee. *Marbury* v. *Madison*, 1 Cra. (U.S.) 137, 2 L.Ed.60; *State* v. *Billy*, 2 N. & McC. (S.C.) 357. See *Talbot* v. *Simpson*, 1 Pet C. C. 194, Fed. Cas. No. 13, 730; *U.S.* v. *Vinton*, 2 Sumn. 299, Fed. Cas. No. 16,624; *Scofield* v. *Lounsbury*, 8 Conn. 109. In this sense it is much used in Great Britain; the great seal is sometimes placed in commission by the crown in the hands of one or more persons; judges assigned to certain duties are appointed thereto by commission; the royal assent to bills in parliament is usually given by commissioners appointed for the purpose.

In Common Law. A sum allowed, usually a certain per cent, upon the value of the property involved, as compensation to a servant or agent for services performed. See COMMISSIONS.

In *Black's Law Dictionary*[37] by Bryan A. Garner, Editor-in-Chief, the words 'commission' and 'commissioner' have been defined as under:

Commission, n 1. A warrant or authority from the government or a court, that empowers the person named to execute official acts <the student received his commission to the U.S. Navy after graduation>. 2. the authority under which a person transacts business for another <the client gave her attorney express commission to sign the contract>. 3. A body of persons acting under lawful authority to perform certain public services <the Federal Communications Commission>.

Public Service Commission. A commission created by a legislature to regulate public utilities or public-service corporations.

4. The act of doing or perpetrating (as a crime) <the perpetrator fled to Mexico after commission of the assault>. 5. A fee paid to an agent or employee for a particular transaction, usu. as a percentage of the money received from the transaction <a real-estate agent's commission>.

37. Seventh Edition, pp. 264-65.

Commissioner. 1. a person who directs a commission; a member of a commission. 2. The administrative head of an organization, such as a professional sport.

In Wharton's Law Lexicon or Dictionary of Jurisprudence:[38] explaining the technical words and phrases employed by The Seberal Departments of English Law; including the various legal terms used in commercial business; together with an explanatory as well as literal translation of the Latin Maxims contained in the writings of the ancient and modern commentators by J. Shiress Will, Esq., the word 'commission' has been assigned the following meaning, viz.

Commission, the warrant or letters-patent which all persons exercising jurisdiction, either ordinary or extraordinary, have to authorize them to hear or determine any cause or action, or do other lawful things, as the commission of the judges, etc. There was formerly a High Commission Court founded on 1 Eliz. c. 1, but it was abolished in the reign of Charles II, though an impotent attempt was made to re-establish it during the succeeding reign.

In commerce, the order by which any one traffics or negotiates for another; also the percentage given to factors or agents for transacting the business of others.

In Stroud's Judicial Dictionary of words and phrases[39] by Daniel Greenberg and Alexandra Millbrook, the word 'commission' has been assigned the following meaning, viz.

Commission. "Commission" is taken for the warrant or letters patents which all men using jurisdication, either ordinarie or extraordinarie, have for their power to hear or determine any matter or action (Termes de la Ley). The word 'Commission' is one of equivocal meaning. It is used to denote a trust or authority exercised, or the instrument by which the authority is exercised, or the persons by whom the trust or authority is exercised (per *Abbott C.J.*, *R.* v. *Dudman*, 4 B. & C. 854).

---

38. The Sixth Edition, pp. 198-99.

39. Sixth Edition Volume 1 : A-F, p. 446.

Tribunals and Inquiries

The distinction between a 'tribunal' and an 'inquiry' has been discussed in Garner on Administrative Law[40] as follows:

> Neither expression is defined in any statute, but it is submitted that for an investigating agency to be properly described as a 'tribunal', it must be constituted under statutory authority, it must have a regular or permanent existence and also a defined jurisdiction within which it is required to exercise its powers to hear and determine dispute.... In ordinary language also a tribunal connotes something similar to or approaching a judicial body. An 'inquiry', on the other hand, is an investigating agency constituted specially (in this context under statutory authority, but not necessarily in pursuance of a statutory requirement) to inquire into a particular matter, and it may have few analogies with a court of law. In general, a tribunal will come to a conclusion and be responsible therefor, but an inquiry may or may not arrive at any conclusion, and will often be required only to make a report or recommendations to some other Government agency (for example, a Minister of the Crown) so as to enable that agency the better to come to a conclusion on the matter. In the case of a tribunal, an individual (often a 'person aggrieved') will normally have a statutory right to request his complaint to be heard and determined by the tribunal. In the case of an inquiry, the individual's statutory rights will most frequently be a right to appeal to a Minister, the statute then providing that the Minister shall convene an inquiry to hear the matter and report to him thereon so that he may make a decision.
>
> This distinction between tribunals and inquiries is rather descriptive than precise. The only precise classification seems to be one based on legal status....

Then dealing directly with tribunals of inquiry it has been observed[41] as follows:

---

40. Second Edition, p. 168.
41. *Ibid.*, p. 171.

> A tribunal of this kind is constituted in particular circumstances to inquire into a definite matter described in the Resolution as of 'urgent public importance'.... These tribunals give rise to special difficulties of their own. They have the powers of the High Court and usually consist of a small number of persons, presided over by a High Court Judge. Their procedure is investigatory and inquisitorial rather than in accordance with the more normal accusatory pattern of tribunals in this country, in which the issues before the tribunal are to some extent defined and any person concerned knows the case he has to meet.... Because of their quite exceptional nature, however, these Tribunals of Inquiry cannot be fitted logically into any scheme of classification of tribunals and inquiries.

A Tribunal of Inquiry is not a tribunal exercising judicial functions or deciding any disputes between two parties. Its procedure is investigatory and inquisitorial rather than judicial.[42]

It is interesting to note what Sir Cyril Salmon, Lord Justice of Appeal, said in a lecture on Tribunals of Inquiry:

> In all countries, certainly in those which enjoy freedom of speech and a free Press, moments occur when allegations and rumours circulate causing a nation-wide crisis of confidence in the integrity of public life or about other matters of vital public importance. No doubt this rarely happens, but when it does it is essential that public confidence should be restored, for without it no democracy can long survive. This confidence can be effectively restored only by thoroughly investigating and probing the rumours and allegations so as to search out and establish the truth. The truth may show that the evil exists, thus, enabling it to be rooted out, or that there is no foundation in the rumours and allegations by which the public has been disturbed. In either case, confidence is restored.

---

42. *The Statesman* v. *The Fact Finding Committee*, AIR 1975 Cal. 15, pp. 22-23. In this case, the writ petition was opposed, inter alia, on the ground that the Fact Finding Committee not being a Tribunal or a statutory body, was not amenable to writ jurisdiction. The Court did not uphold this objection in the facts of the case.

In the lecture mentioned above, it was pointed out that the Tribunals of Inquiry (Evidence) Act, 1921, was passed in England to displace the procedure by which Select Parliamentary Committees were used "to investigate alleged wrong doing in high places". About the Select Committee procedure he said:

> Such a method of investigation by a political tribunal was wholly unsatisfactory. Being a progressive people, it took us only more than about 300 years to do anything about it. In the United States of America, however, which is still more progressive than we are, they still use virtually the same method. Congressional Committees of Investigation, like our Parliamentary committees, consist of members representing the relative strength of the majority and minority parties. Clearly such bodies can never be free from party political influences. This is a very defect in any tribunal investigating allegations of public misconduct—particularly as the subject-matter of the inquiry often has highly charged political overtones.

He observed:

> The history of such investigations in England by Parliamentary committees is, to say the least, unfortunate. Let me give you but one example. Early in the present century there occurred what became known as the Marconi Scandal. In 1912 the Post Master General in a Liberal Government accepted a tender by the English Marcony Company for the construction of State-owned wireless telegraph stations throughout the Empire. There followed widespread rumours that the Government had corruptly favoured the Marconi Company and that certain prominent members of the Government had improperly profited by the transaction. The Select Parliamentary Committee appointed to investigate these rumours represented the respective strengths of the Liberal and Conservative Parties. The majority report of the Liberal members of the Committee exonerated the members of the Government concerned whereas a minority report by the Conservative members of the Committee found that these members of the Government had been guilty of gross impropriety. When the reports came

to be debated in the House of Commons, the House divided on strictly party lines and by a majority exonerated the Ministers from all blame. This is the last instance of a matter of this kind being investigated by a Select Committee of Parliament.

In other words:

It was because in England investigation by a political tribunal of matters causing grave public disquiet had been discredited that the Tribunals of Inquiry (Evidence) Act, 1921, was passed with a view to setting up some permanent investigations machinery to be available for use when required.

Furthermore, he pointed out that even in America ad hoc tribunals are not infrequently appointed to avoid a matter being referred to a Congressional Committee, as, for example, the Warren Commission to investigate the murder of President Kennedy.

It is, thus, clear that in democratic countries not only modern practice but statute can provide for inquiries of the kind which are meant to be conducted under our Act of 1952.[43]

Judicial Inquiry

Quite often, judges are appointed on the Commissions of Inquiry appointed under the Act. In common parlances, inquiries conducted by Courts or Judges are known as judicial inquiries. As such, appointments of such Commissions under the Act are colloquially called 'judicial inquiries'.[44] It may, however, be noted that non-judicial persons are also appointed on the Commissions of Inquiry under the Act and the Commissions appointed thereunder do not perform judicial functions.

Vires of the Act

The question whether the Act is ultra vires the Constitution, came up for consideration before the Supreme Court in the case of *Ram Krishna Dalmia* v. *Justice S.R. Tendolkar*.[45] The validity of the Act was called in that case in two ways. In the first place,

---

43. *State of Karnataka* v. *Union of India*, AIR 1978 SC 68, pp. 89-90.
44. *Janamohan Das* v. *State of Orissa*, AIR 1993 Orissa 157, p. 159.
45. AIR 1958 S.C., 538.

it was said that it was beyond the legislative competency of Parliament to enact a law conferring such a wide sweep of powers. Referring to the provisions of Article 246 read with Entry 94 in List I and Entry 45 in List III of the Seventh Schedule to the Constitution, it was urged that Parliament might make a law with respect to inquiries but could not under these entries make a law conferring any power to perform any function other than the power to hold an inquiry. It was pointed out that the law, which the appropriate Legislature was empowered to make under these entries must be with respect to inquiries for the purposes of any of the matters in the relevant lists and it was urged that the words "for the purpose of" made it abundantly clear that the law with respect to inquiries to be made under these two entries must be for the purpose of future legislation with respect to any of the legislative heads in the relevant lists. In other words, the argument was that under these two entries the appropriate Legislature might make a law authorizing the constitution of a Board or Commission of Inquiry to inquire into and ascertain facts so as to enable such Legislature to undertake legislation with respect to any of the legislative topics in the relevant lists to secure some public benefit or advantage or to prevent some evil or harm befalling the public and thereby to protect the public from the same. But if an inquiry became necessary for, say, administrative purposes, a law with respect to such an inquiry could not be made under these two entries. And far less could a law be made with respect to an inquiry into any wrongs alleged to have been committed by an individual person or company or a group of them for the purpose of punishing the suspected delinquent. It was urged that such an inquiry could neither be for any legislative nor for any administrative purpose, but was a clear usurpation of the functions of the judiciary. The Parliament could not, it was urged, undertake to inquire or investigate into alleged individual wrongs or private disputes nor could it bring the supposed culprit to book or gather materials for the purpose of initiating proceedings, civil or criminal, against him, because such inquiry or investigation was clearly not in aid of legislation. It was argued that if a criminal prosecution was to be launched, the preliminary investigation must be held under the Code of Criminal

Procedure and it should not be open to any Legislature to start investigation on its own and thereby to deprive the citizen of the normal protection afforded to him by the provisions of the Code of Criminal Procedure. The principal ground urged in support of the contention as to the invalidity of the Act was founded on Article 14 of the Constitution. Negating all these contentions, the Supreme Court upheld the constitutionality of the Act. The Court did not accept the view that the law with respect to inquiries to be made under the two entries must be for the purpose of future Legislation with respect to any of the legislative heads in the relevant lists as that would mean adding words to the two entries so as to read "inquiries...for the purpose of *future legislation with respect to* any of the matters in..." the List or Lists mentioned therein. It was further observed that Parliament, under Article 246 had no power to make a law with respect to any of the matters enumerated in List II. Therefore, when Parliament made a law under Article 246 read with entry 45 in List III with respect to an inquiry for the purposes of any of the matters in List II, such law could never be one for inquiry for the purpose of future legislation by Parliament with respect to any of those matters in List II. It was further held that the law with respect to inquiries for the purpose of any of the matters in the lists might also be for administrative purposes and the scope of the inquiry under such a law would cover all matters that might properly be regarded as ancillary to such inquiries. It was further observed that Parliament had made a law with respect to inquiry and had left to the appropriate Government to set up a Commission of Inquiry under certain circumstances referred to in Section 3 of the Act. The Central Government, in its turn, had, in exercise of the powers conferred on it by the Act, set up the Commission. It was, therefore, not correct to say that Parliament or the Government had undertaken to hold any inquiry. It was further observed that as the Commission could only make recommendations, which were not enforceable *proprio vigore*,[46] there could be no question of usurpation of judicial

46. *Advance Law Lexicon* by P. Ramanatha Aiyer, 3rd Edition, 2005, p. 3801: "*Proprio vigore*. Lat. by its own force; by its intrinsic meaning".

functions. It was further observed that Section 3 empowered the appropriate Government, in certain circumstances therein mentioned, to appoint a Commission of Inquiry into any definite matter of public importance and performing such functions within such time as might be specified in the notification. This delegation of authority, however, was not unguided or uncontrolled, for the discretion given to the appropriate Government to set up a Commission of Inquiry must conform to the conditions of the section, i.e. that there must exist a definite matter of public importance into which an inquiry was, in the opinion of the appropriate Government, necessary or was required by a resolution in that behalf passed by the House of the People or the Legislative Assembly of the State. It was accordingly held that it could not be said that an arbitrary and uncontrolled power had been delegated to the appropriate Government and that, therefore, the law itself was bad.

Short title, extent and commencement.

1. (1) This Act may be called the Commissions of Inquiry Act, 1952.

[47] **[(2) It extends to the whole of India:**

Provided that it shall apply to the State of Jammu and Kashmir only in so far as it relates to inquiries pertaining to matters relatable to any of the entries enumerated in List I or

---

47. Subs. by Act 79 of 1971, S. 2, for sub-section (2). The Act came into force in the State of Jammu and Kashmir on 6-3-1972 vide Notification No. 94(E) dated 4th March 1972 and in the districts of Kohima and Mokokchung in the State of Nagaland on 15-2-1972, vide Notification No. 74(E) dated 14th February, 1972, both issued under Section 15 of Act 79 of 1971, which reads as: "15. *Principal Act as amended to come into force in Jammu and Kashmir and in certain districts of Nagaland.*—The Principal Act, as amended by this Act, shall come into force in the State of Jammu and Kashmir and in the districts of Kohima and Mokokchung in the State of Nagaland on such date as the Central Government may, by notification in the Official Gazette, appoint." The Act has been extended to Sikkim subject to modifications with immediate effect vide S.O. 831(E) dt. 12-12-1977, Gazette of India, dated 12-12-1977, Part II, S. 3(ii) Ext., p. 2947.

List III in the Seventh Schedule to the Constitution as applicable to that State.]

(3) It shall come into force on such date[48] as the Central Government may, by notification in the Official Gazette, appoint.

Objects and Reasons

The Commissions of Inquiry Act, 1952 does not, at present, extend to the State of Jammu and Kashmir and to the districts of Kohima and Mokokchung in the State of Nagaland. The clauses seek to extend the Act to the State of Jammu and Kashmir and to the aforesaid districts. However, in relation to the State of Jammu and Kashmir, the Act will apply only in so far as it relates to inquiries pertaining to matters relatable to entries enumerated in List I and List III in the Seventh Schedule to the Constitution as applicable to that State.[49]

Definitions.

2. In this Act, unless the context otherwise requires,—

"appropriate Government" means—

(i) the Central Government, in relation to a Commission appointed by it to make an inquiry into any matter relatable to any of the entries enumerated in List I or List II or List III in the Seventh Schedule to the Constitution; and

(ii) the State Government, in relation to a Comission appointed by it to make an inquiry into any matter relatable to any of the entries enumerated in List II or List III in the Seventh Schedule:

---

48. 1st October 1952, vide Notification No. S.R.O. 1670, dated the 30th September 1952, Gazette of India, Extraordinary, Pt. II, S. 3, p. 861. This Act, as amended by Act 79 of 1971, came into force in the State of Jammu and Kashmir on 6-3-1972 and in the districts of Kohima and Mokokchung in the State of Nagaland on 15-2-1972, vide Notification Nos. 94(E), dated 4-3-1972 and 74(E), dated 14-2-1972 respectively, issued under S. 15 of Act 79 of 1971.

49. Notes on Clause: Clauses 2 and 3, the Commissions of Inquiry (Amendment) Bill, 1971, Gazette of India, 18-11-1971, Part II, Section 2, Extraordinary, p. 665.

[50][Provided that in relation to the State of Jammu and Kashmir, these clauses shall have effect subject to the modification that—

(a) in sub-clause (i) thereof, for the words and figures "List I or List II or List III in the Seventh Schedule to the Constitution", the words and figures "List I or List III in the Seventh Schedule to the Constitution as applicable to the State of Jammu and Kashmir" shall be substituted;

(b) in sub-clause (ii) thereof, for the words and figures "List II or List III in the Seventh Schedule to the Constitution", the words and figures "List III in the Constitution as applicable to the State of Jammu and Kashmir" shall be substituted;]

(c) "Commission" means a Commission of Inquiry appointed under section 3;

(d) "prescribed" means prescribed by rules made under this Act.

"Appropriate Government"—Meaning and Scope

The definition of appropriate Government in Section 2(a) shows that the Central Government is the appropriate Government for appointment of a Commission to make an enquiry into any matter relatable to any of the entries in List I or List II or List III in the Seventh Schedule. The State Governments are, however, empowered to appoint Commissions of Inquiry to make enquiry into any matter relatable to the entries in List II or List III in the Seventh Schedule.

While the Central Government has the power to appoint a Commission relatable to all the entries enumerated in List I, List II and List III of the Seventh Schedule, the State Governments have only power to constitute Commissions of Inquiry for the State under Section 3 in respect of matters relating to List II and List III. In case of overlapping, what is to happen that is dealt with in the proviso. But in respect of matters relatable to entries

---

50. Added by Act 79 of 1971, S. 3.

enumerated in List I, it is the Central Government and the Central Government alone which is entitled to constitute a body or appoint a Commission under the Act and in respect of that the Central Government, under the Act, has no authority or no power to delegate its functions or give any consent to any State. Indeed, giving approval or consent arises only in respect of entries enumerated in List II and List III where the Central Government has already appointed a Commission for the purpose of avoiding overlapping. Therefore, reading Section 2(a) along with Section 3 of the Act, it appears to be clear that the Central Government alone is competent to appoint Commission in respect of matters relatable to items mentioned in List I of the Seventh Schedule of the Constitution.[51]

It is well settled that the expression 'relatable' is of widest amplitude. In the case of *State of Karnataka* v. *Union of India*,[52] Mr. Justice Kailasham has treated the expression 'relatable' as synonymous to 'relating'. But whatever be the width of the amplitude of the expression used, this must be read in conjunction with other provisions of the Act. Section 2(a) read with Section 3 makes it clear that the framers of the Act had in contemplation different Governments, namely, Central Government, State Governments. In view of our federal structure, they demarcated the areas of the operation of the commission or authority contemplated by the Act. The matters relatable to List I are in the domain of the Union Government or the Central Government alone is competent to enquire into any offences or matters arising of the same. Now, the expression 'relatable' is one which indicates something which is in relation to or in relation of or which can be said to be relatable. This expression has been differently construed in different context in different cases. Anything which can be said to be related must be relatable to that matter and especially this expression 'relatable to' List I must be read in conjunction and in contradistinction to List II and List III. Therefore, if an Act is passed by virtue of power of

51. *Motahar Hossain* v. *Haratosh Chakrabarty* (1980) 84 C.W.N. 560, p. 573.

52. AIR 1978 SC 68.

List I, then implementation or carrying out and the effects of that Act are things or matters which will be relatable to matters of List I of the Seventh Schedule. That seems to be the clear meaning and the demarcation of the powers. If that is the position, then assuming for a moment that there have been excesses or abuses of powers in implementing the Act passed by virtue of powers conferred by List I then that would be a matter relatable or related to the matter enumerated in List I in the Seventh Schedule. If that is so, then the Central Government and the Central Government alone, has the authority. The Commissions of Inquiry Act, 1952 deals with the constitution of the Commission and in that matter neither the Central Government nor the Commission that it has appointed, can by any consent or any approval confer any authority to the State Government or a Commission to constitute such a body. For implementation of a Central Act if there is any excess or abuse of the power simplicter without reference to the user or application of the Central Act which endangers public order or any abuse or power which creates public disrespect in the administration whether the State Government may or may not be able to constitute a body, is an open question.[53]

The question whether a particular subject falls in one List or the other, has arisen on several occasions in the past, not only after coming into force of the Constitution, but even under Section 100 of the Government of India Act, 1935. In *Subramanyan Chettiar* v. *Muttuswami Goundan*,[54] Sir Maurice Gwyer CJ, said:[55]

> It must inevitably happen from time to time that legislation, though purporting to deal with a subject in one List, touches also on a subject in another List, and the different provisions of the enactment may be so closely inter-twined that blind adherence to a strictly verbal interpretation would result in

53. *Motahar Hossain* v. *Haratosh Chakrabarty*, 84 C.W.N. 560, pp. 576-77.
54. 1940 FCR 188: AIR 1940 FC 47: ILR (1941) Kar. FC 25: 192 IC 225(FC).
55. At p. 201.

a large number of statutes being declared invalid because the Legislature enacting them may appear to have legislated in a forbidden sphere. Hence, the rule which has been evolved by the Judicial Committee, whereby the impugned statute is examined to ascertain its pith and substance or its true nature and character for the purpose of determining whether it is legislation with respect to matters in this List or in that.

This was approved and followed by the Privy Council in the case of *Prafulla Kumar Mukherjee* v. *Bank of Commerce Ltd., Khulna*[56] when Lord Porter observed that the aforesaid passage of Gwyer CJ correctly described the grounds upon which the rule was founded. Their Lordships further observed that "It is not possible to make so clean a cut between the powers of the various Legislatures: they are bound to overlap from time to time.... Subjects must still overlap and where they do the question must be asked what in pith and substance is the effect of the enactment of which complaint is made and in what list is its true nature and character to be found. If these questions could not be asked, much beneficent legislation would be stifled at birth, and many of the subjects entrusted to Provincial Legislation could never effectively be dealt with.... (T)he extent of the invasion by the Provinces into subjects enumerated in the Federal List has to be considered. No doubt it is an important matter, not, as their Lordships think, because the validity of an Act can be determined by discriminating between degrees of invasion, but for the purpose of determining what is the pith and substance of the impugned Act. Its provisions may advance so far into Federal territory as to show that its true nature is not concerned with Provincial matters, but the question is not, has it trespassed more or less, but is the trespass, whatever it be, such as to show that the pith and substance of the impugned Act is not money-lending but promissory notes or banking? Once that question is determined the Act falls on one or the other side of the line and can be seen as valid or invalid according to its true content."

---

56 AIR 1947 PC 60.

The above dictum of Lord Porter speaking for the Privy Council has been repeatedly approved by the Hon'ble Supreme Court as laying down the correct rule to be applied in resolving conflicts which arise from overlapping powers in mutually exclusive lists in the Seventh Schedule to the Constitution.[57]

In *Union of India* v. *State of Manipur*,[58] the Government of Manipur by an order dated 12-3-1998 appointed a Commission of Inquiry to inquire into the incident that took place in the midnight on 13-2-1998. The terms of reference of the Inquiry Commission were as follows:

(a) the sequence of events leading to the disappearance of Shri Y. Sanamacha Singh;

(b) to find out whether the Army picked up Shri Y. Sanamacha Singh around the midnight of February 12, 1998 from his house and if affirmative, to find out the whereabouts of Shri Y. Sanamacha Singh since then;

(c) to find out the persons who are responsible for the disappearance of Shri Y. Sanamacha Singh; and

(d) to recommend the corrective remedies and measures needed to be taken to prevent recurrence to such incident in future.

The incident giving rise to the setting up of the Commission, as above, was that on 13-2-98 in the midnight an Army column rushed to Angtha village on receiving an information that some underground (sic) are operating in the said area. The Army column proceeded to the house of one Y. Binakumar Singh and apprehended four persons. Due to the interference and attack by the women folk 'Meira Paibi' of Angtha village, two persons, namely Shri Y. Binakumar Singh and Y. Sanamacha Singh managed to escape and the remaining two persons who were detained by the Army were handed over to Yairipok Police Station on 13-2-98 along with a written report. The officer-in-

---

57. *State of Bombay* v. *Narothamdas Jethabhai*, 1951 SCR 51; *State of Bombay* v. *F.N. Balsara* (1951) SCR 682: AIR 151 SC 318.

58. AIR 1999 Gauhati 15.

charge Yairipok P.S., on the basis of the said report, registered a case being FIR Case No. 15(2) 98 YPK P.S. u/s. 13 U.A. (P) Act, and 25(1-B) Arms Act. In the said report, the Army also requested the police to take appropriate action against the women folk of Angtha village.

The Union of India filed the writ petition challenging the competence of the State Government to set up the Commission of Inquiry on the ground, inter alia, that the inquiry in pursuance of its terms of reference, related to Entries 2 and 2A of List I of the Seventh Schedule to the Constitution of India as it involves investigation into the action of the Armed Forces of the Union for an act performed by them during the course of performing their duties in aid of civil power. This, however, did not find favour with the Court as can be seen from the following observations:

> In the instant case also it appears from the terms of reference that the Commission will inquire about the disappearance of Shri Y. Sanamacha Singh and whether he was arrested by the forces of the Union and if so how he has disappeared on that night in Angtha village. If possible, the Commission will also ascertain the facts about the whereabouts of Y. Sanamacha Singh. From the terms of reference, it does not appear that the Commission will make any inquiry about the powers and functions of the members of the force of the Union or it will inquire about the jurisdiction and privileges of such members. Consequently, I am of the view that the present, Sanamacha Inquiry Commission set up by the State of Manipur falls within the purview of public order as enumerated in Item 1 of List II of the Seventh Schedule to the Constitution of India. Since the disappearance of Y. Sanamacha Singh on the night of 12-2-98 has assumed character of great importance and it has created deterioration in the law and order of the State, I am of the view that no illegality or error has been committed by the State Government by setting up the Sanamacha Inquiry Commission. Further, I am of the view that there cannot be any bar for any inquiry by the Commission even in the face of the pendency of two habeas corpus petitions. It is true that question of prejudice

may be raised by a party, but there can be no legal prejudice in view of the provisions of Section 6 of the Commissions of Inquiry Act as the evidence before the Commission cannot be used in any civil or criminal proceedings for any purpose.[59]

In *Col. Jagmohan Singh and Others* v. *The State of Manipur*,[60] the State Government's competence in appointing a Commission to enquire into alleged killing of a cadre banned outfit PLA in custody of Assam Rifles Personnel, came up for consideration. The State Government sought to justify the same with reference to Entry 1 of List II relating to 'public order' in view of the series of bandhs and strikes consequent upon the alleged killing that paralysed the normal civil life in the State and created unprecedented law and order situation. Although the terms of reference de hors the recital part of the impugned notification at the first look suggested that the matter related to 'public order' as defined in Entry 1 of List II, but the notification indeed showed that the allegations that were subject of enquiry, related to the alleged excesses committed by the 17th Assam Rifles. Accordingly, it was held that the appropriate Government in the case was the Central Government to which the members of the Assam Rifles were accountable for such excesses.[61] As per Entry 1 of List II, the State Legislature is vested with the legislative powers relating to public order excluding the use of any naval, military or air force or any other armed force of the Union or any other force subject to the control or the Union or any contingent or unit thereof in aid of the civil power. The exclusion part shows that the use of the armed forces of the Union in aid of the civil power shall be subject to the control of the Union Government. Entry 2A of List I empowers the Parliament to make laws on deployment of the armed forces of the Union in any State in aid of civil power; powers, jurisdiction, privileges and liabilities of the members of such forces on deployment subject to control of the Union Government. The

---

59. AIR 1999 Gauhati 20.
60. AIR 2006 Gauhati 33.
61. *Naga People's Movement of Human Rights* v. *Union of India*, AIR 1998 SC 431, was relied upon.

two Entries in List I and List II read together make it abundantly clear that in relation to a Commission to make an enquiry into any matter relating to the armed forces on deployment in a State in aid of civil power; it is the Union Government which is the appropriate Government to make such appointment. This otherwise postulates that the State Government cannot be construed as the appropriate Government to appoint a Commission to make enquiry of the alleged excesses committed by the Assam Rifles personnel, or, for that matter, forces of the Union deployed in aid of civil power in any State. The powers for appointing a Commission has to be traced out from the legislative competence in terms of Section 2(a) of the Act read with Entry 2A of the Union List and Entry 1 of the State List. The Court distinguished the decision in *Border Security Force* v. *State of Meghalaya*[62] for the reason of having been delivered in a different context, as the BSF in that case was not acting in the aid of civil power when they opened the fire in the crowd.

In *Border Security Force* v. *State of Meghalaya*,[63] the State Government appointed a one man Inquiry Commission to report on the causes and nature of the disturbances; circumstances under which the fire was opened by the BSF and action taken thereafter. This was challenged by the BSF on the ground, inter alia, that it being an armed force of the Union and, as such, subject to the control of the Central Government. It was further contended that whenever their force is deployed, whether on invitation by civil authorities or otherwise, then the State Government has no authority to enquire into the acts of the personnel of such a force. The Court did not find this contention supported by any statutory provision or principle or the case law on the subject. It was held that the State Government desired to have a report as to the cause of 'disruption' to peace and tranquility, the subject of law and order is their allotted sphere in the list of powers of the Seventh Schedule of the Constitution and as such, it was held, the impugned notification did not suffer from any constitutional vice whatever.

62. AIR 1989 Gauhati 81.

63. AIR 1989 Gauhati 81; *Border Security Force* v. *State of Meghalaya*, AIR 1989 Gauhati 20.

In *Union of India* v. *Nilkanth Tulsidas Bhatia*,[64] the State Government appointed a Commission of Inquiry to inquire into what is popularly known as Godhara Kand in which certain coaches of Sabarmati Express engulfed in fire. Subsequently, the Central Government appointed a High Level Committee to inquire into same incident and suggest measures to prevent recurrence of such incidents in future and to ensure safety of railway passengers and property. The provisions of the Commissions of Inquiry Act, 1952 were extended to this Committee vide notification issued under Section 11 thereof. The validity of the appointment of the Committee was challenged in view of the functioning of the Commission appointed by the State Government. It was, inter alia, contended that the Committee was appointed by the Railway Administration to inquire into the events which involved damage to the railway property and also loss of life or injuries to railway passengers and, therefore, the railways being the subject at Entry 22 in List I, the Central Government alone had the authority to appoint a Commission to make an inquiry into the incidents. On the other hand, it was submitted on behalf of the State Government that essentially the inquiry by the State Commission related to the incident which involved commission of offences investigated by State police and to be tried by the Courts in the State of Gujarat, that it was law and order problem or public order problem and, therefore, the matter fell in List II. Applying the rule of pith and substance, a Division Bench of the Gujarat High Court held that the scope or subject of inquiry of the Commission appointed by the State Government was not in pith and substance with respect to a railway coach or railway passengers as such but was in relation to the incident which resulted into death of 58 persons and injuries to more than 40 persons in the context of the allegations made in criminal complaints filed on the same day that a mob had set some coaches of the Sabarmati Express on fire, which triggered off subsequent incidents of violence in the State, the adequacy of administrative measures to prevent and deal with the said disturbances and the role of the Chief

64. (2006) 2 GLR 952.

Minister, other Ministers, Police Officers and other individuals and organizations in Godhra incident and in the subsequent disturbances.[65]

Whereas both the Central Government and a State Government cannot simultaneously appoint their own respective commission to inquire into the same subject matter, yet more than one commission can be appointed by any one of them to inquire into the same matter one after another at different times. Thus, in 1999, the Manoj Mukherjee Commission was set up to find out whether Subhash Chandra Bose had indeed died in the air crash of 1945. The Mukherjee panel was the third commission to look into the very same matter for which earlier Pandit Jawaharlal Nehru had constituted the Shah Nawaj Commission and Indira Gandhi the Khosla Commission. Again, the 1983, Indira Gandhi appointed the Sarkaria Commission to examine Centre-State relations. Later on, the government appointed Justice M.M. Punchi to head a commission to look into Centre-State relations once more. The same subject incidentally was also covered partially by the high-powered Venkatachalliah Commission which reviewed the Constitution.[65a]

Union Territories

The definition of 'appropriate Government' does not contain any reference to Union Territories. The definition of 'State' in Section 3(58) of the General Clauses Act, 1897 includes Union Territory. The definition given in the General Clauses Act is subject to any context being repugnant. Accordingly, there is no fetter on the power of the President to make regulations for any Union Territory in accordance with the proviso to Article 240(1) of the Constitution of India so long there is no Legislature in a Union Territory. The inclusive definition of 'State' in Section

65. It is understood that the Union of India has preferred a Special Leave Petition before the Supreme Court against the judgment of the Divison Bench of the Gujarat High Court and the matter is, thus, yet to attain finality.

65a. Coomi Kapoor, "A Commission is Forever—Jain, Mukherjee, Sarkaria.... The Reports that went Nowhere", *The Indian Express*, July 10, 2009, p. 10.

3(58) being repugnant to the subject or context of Article 246 of the Constitution does not apply by virtue of Article 367.[66] Subject to any such context being repugnant, the definition of 'State' would have to be read as including Union Territory.

Appropriate Government and President's Rule

During the Presidential Rule, the employees of the State Government do not cease to be the employees of the State and become the Central Government employees. It is true that they act through the direction of the Governor given by the President on the advice of the Central Council of Ministers but even then they remain and continue to be the State Government employees and, in appropriate cases, their conduct has created such a situation where concerned matters of public order for the State, then, subsequently the appropriate Government can certainly appoint a Commission of Inquiry under the Commissions of Inquiry Act, 1952. Where there were killings of, and physical tortures or atrocitites committed on persons by public servants during any period, including the period of the Presidential Rule, the State Government can consider the matter whether it would be proper to form an opinion for constituting a Commission of Inquiry.[67]

In *T. Chitra* v. *The Chief Secretary to Government, Government of Tamil Nadu and Another*,[67a] the petitioner, inter alia, submitted that word 'State Government' in Section 2A defining the term 'appropriate Government' did not mean a single department of the Government, such as Public Department, which had issued the impugned notification, but collective wisdom of Council of Ministers should be reflected in the decision making process, both in respect of identifying the purpose for which Commission was to be appointed, approval of terms of reference, the identification of the name of the Judge to head the Commission, etc. were all to be brought as agenda

---

66. *T.M. Kanniyam* v. *Income Tax Officer, Pondicherry*, AIR 1968 SC 637.
67. *Sushil Chandra Chowdhury* v. *Secretary, Chakraborty Commission of Inquiry* (1980) 84 CWN 583, p. 599.

67a. (2008)1 MLJ 422 = MANU/TN/9409/2007.

for listing before the Council of Ministers in the Cabinet meeting. In the absence of the same, it was contended, the term 'appropriate Government', which alone could appoint a Commission in terms of Section 3 was not within the purview of the Act. Only a statement under Rule 110 of the Tamil Nadu Legislative Assembly Rules was made by the Portfolio Minister (Chief Minister) in the Tamil Nadu Legislative Assembly, which could not validate the order. These submissions did not find favour with a Division Bench of the Madras High Court in this case.

Construction of references to laws not in force in the State of Jammu and Kashmir.

[68][2A. Any reference in this Act to a law, which is not in force in the State of Jammu and Kashmir, shall, in relation to that State, be construed as a reference to the corresponding law, if any, in force in that State.]

Objects and Reasons

Certain law as referred to in the Commissions of Inquiry Act, 1952 are not in force in the State of Jammu and Kashmir. This clause provides that any reference to such law shall, in relation to the State of Jammu and Kashmir, be construed as a reference to the corresponding law, if any, in force in that State. This provision has become necessary consequent on the proposed extension of the Act to the State of Jammu and Kashmir.[69]

Appointment of Commission.

3.(1) The appropriate Government may, if it is of opinion that is necessary so to do, and shall, if a resolution in this behalf is passed by [each House of Parliament or, as the case may be, the Legislature of the State,][70] by notification in the Official Gazette, appoint a Commission of Inquiry for the purpose of making an inquiry into any definite matter of public importance and performing such functions and within such time as may be

---

68. Ins. by S. 4, the Commissions of Inquiry (Amendment) Act, 1971.
69. Notes on Clauses, Clause 4, the Commissions of Inquiry (Amendment) Bill, 1971.
70. Subs. by Act 19 of 1990, S. 2, for words "the House of the People or, as the case may be the Legislative Assembly of the State".

specified in the notification, and the Commission so appointed shall make the inquiry and perform the functions accordingly:

Provided that where any such Commission has been appointed to inquire into any matter—

(a) by the Central Government, no State Government shall, except with the approval of the Central Government, appoint another Commission to inquire into the same matter for so long as the Commission appointed by the Central Government is functioning;

(b) by a State Government, the Central Government shall not appoint another Commission to inquire into the same matter so long as the Commission appointed by the State Government is functioning, unless the Central Government is of opinion that the scope of the inquiry should be extended to two or more States.

(2) The Commission may consist of one or more members appointed by the appropriate Government, and where the Commission consists of more than one member, one of them may be appointed as the Chairman thereof.

[71][(3) The appropriate Government may, at any stage of an inquiry by the Commission fill any vacancy which may have arisen in the office of a member of the Commission (whether consisting of one or more than one member).

(4) The appropriate Government shall cause to be laid before [72][(each House of Parliament or, as the case may be, the Legislature of the State), the report, if any, of the Commission on the inquiry made by the Commission under sub-section (1) together with a memorandum of the action taken thereon, within a period of six months of the submission of the report by the Commission to the appropriate Government.] (5) and (6) [***][73]

71. Ins. by Act 9 of 1971, S. 5.

72. Subs. and omitted by Act 19 of 1990, S. 2.

73. Sub-sections (5) and (6) were inserted by Act 36 of 1986, S. 2 (w.e.f 14-5-1986). These were substituted and omitted by Act 19 of 1990, S. 2. These sub-sections read as:

Objects and Reasons

"Judging from the experience gained in the working of the Commissions of Inquiry Act, 1952, it is considered desirable to provide expressly for the filling up of vacancies in the membership of the Commission, whenever the Government thinks it necessary or expedient to do so. The new sub-section (3) to Section 3 of the Act seeks to give effect to this proposal (vide paragraph 26 of the Report).[74] During the course of the evidence given before the Joint Committee, it was brought to their notice that many a time Reports of Commissions of Inquiry on important issues of national interest could not see the light of the day even though considerable money from public funds had been spent thereon. The Joint Committee, therefore, considered it necessary that a specific provision should be made in the Act requiring the

---

(5) The provisions of sub-section (4) shall not apply if the appropriate Government is satisfied that in the interest of the sovereignty and integrity of India, the security of the State, friendly relations with foreign States or in the public interest, it is not expedient to lay before the House of the People or, as the case may be, the Legislative Assembly of the State, the report, or any part thereof, of the Commission on the inquiry made by the Commission under sub-section (1), and issues a notification to that effect in the Official Gazette.

Explanation.—For the purpose of sub-section (5), "report" includes an interim report and all proceedings of a Commission.

(6) Every notification issued under sub-section (5) shall be laid before the House of People or, as the case may be, the Legislative Assembly of the State, if it is sitting, or within seven days of its re-assembly, and the appropriate Government shall seek the approval of the House of the People or, as the case may be, the Legislative Assembly of the State, to the notification by a resolution moved within a period of fifteen days beginning with the day on which the notification is so laid before the House of the People or, as the case may be, the Legislative Assembly of the State and if the House of the People or, as the case may be, the Legislative Assembly of the State makes any modification in the notification or directs that the notification should cease to have effect, the notification shall thereafter have effect only in such modified form or be of no effect, as the case may be.

74. Twenty-fourth Report of the Law Commission of India on the Commissions of Inquiry Act, 1952.

appropriate Government to cause the Report of every Commission of Inquiry to be laid before the House of the People or the Legislative Assembly, as the case may be, together with the Memorandum in regard to the action taken thereon, within a period of six months from the date of submission of the Report. The new sub-section (4) of Section 3 of the Act seeks to give effect to this recommendation of the Joint Committee."[75]

"Sub-section (4) of Section 3 of the Commissions of Inquiry Act, 1952 provides that the appropriate Government shall cause to be laid before the House of People or, as the case may be, the Legislative Assembly of the State, the report, if any, of any Commission on the inquiry made by it together with a memorandum of the action taken thereon, within a period of six months of the submission of the report by the Commission to the appropriate Government.

2. To provide for the situations where the fulfilment of the statutory obligation to lay the report of the Commission before the House of the People or the Legislative Assembly of a State involves practical difficulties or where a Commission of Inquiry is appointed to inquire into sensitive matters of public importance and the inquiry report may contain matters of sensitive nature on account of which it may not be desirable in the public interest to lay such report before the House of the People or the Legislative Assembly, the Commissions of Inquiry Act, 1952 was amended by the Commissions of Inquiry (Amendment) Ordinance, 1986 (6 of 1986) promulgated by the President on the 14th May, 1986. The Ordinance inserted two new sub-sections (5) and (6) in Section 3 of the Act. New sub-section (5) provides that the provisions of sub-section (4) of the said Section 3 shall not apply in cases where the appropriate Government, being satisfied that in the interests of the sovereignty and integrity of India, the security of the State, friendly relations with foreign States or in the public interest, it is not expedient to lay such report before the House of the People or the Legislative Assembly of the State, issues a notification to that effect in the

75. Notes of Clauses, Clause 5, the Commissions of Inquiry (Amendment) Bill, 1971.

Official Gazette. By virtue of the new sub-section (6), the appropriate Government is required to lay every notification issued under sub-section (5) before the House of the People or the Legislative Assembly and seek approval thereon within the period mentioned therein.

3. The Bill seeks to replace the aforesaid Ordinance."[76]

"Sub-section (4) of Section 3 of the Commissions of Inquiry Act, 1952 casts an obligation on the appropriate Government to lay the report of the Commission of Inquiry appointed under sub-section (1) thereof before the House of the People or, as the case may be, the Legislative Assembly concerned, together with a memorandum of action taken thereon, within a period of six months of the submission of the report. However, in 1986, Section 3 had been amended so as to provide therein that under certain circumstances the report of the Commission of Inquiry may not be so laid.

2. A Commission of Inquiry is always set up for the purpose of making an inquiry into any definite matter of public importance. As such, the report submitted by such a Commission should not be withheld from the House of the People or the Legislative Assembly under any circumstances and the public should have access to information which is of vital importance and interest to them. It is felt that the amendments made in 1986 should be done away with.

3. The Bill seeks to achieve the above object."[77]

General

Fact-finding inquiries have been held in Britain first by Parliamentary Committees from 1660 onwards and then under the Tribunals of Inquiry (Evidence) Act, 1921 and lastly in India under the Commissions of Inquiry Act, 1952.[78] A Commission of Inquiry can be constituted de hors the Act in

76. Statement of Objects and Reasons, the Commissions of Inquiry (Amendment) Bill, 1986.

77. Statement of Objects and Reasons, the Commissions of Inquiry (Amendment) Bill, 1989.

78. *G.S. Harnal* v. *Union of India and Others*, ILR (1971) II Delhi 129, 142.

which case it will be an authority appointed in exercise of the executive powers of the Government. The Act, however, contains provision[79] for applying the provisions of this Act to any inquiring authority, by whatever name called, set up under any resolution or order of the appropriate Government. A Commission set up under Section 3 of the Act is not governed by such a provision as the provisions of the Act are otherwise applicable to it and there will be no need for issuing any notification extending the provisions of the Act to it. In respect of other inquiring authorities not so set up under the Section 3 of the Act, such authorities will be deemed to be Commissions appointed under Section 3 for the purposes of the Act if necessary notifications are issued so as to extend the provisions of the Act to such authorities.[80] Where the Commission is only a creature of executive discretion (and not of a statutory obligation), the notification setting up such a Commission being non-statutory, it cannot override Sections 3 and 8A of the Act.[81]

Requirements for Appointment of a Commission

As a matter of construction of sub-section (1) of Section 3 of the Act, the appropriate Government is under a statutory obligation to appoint a Commission of Inquiry in a case where a resolution in that behalf is passed by any House of Parliament or, as the case may be, the Legislature of a State and the appropriate Government has no option or discretion in the matter. In the absence of such a resolution, the power to

---

79. Section 11 of the Commissions of Inquiry Act, 1952.
80. *P.R. Nayak* v. *Union of India and Others*, ILR (1973) I Delhi 747, 757.
81. (Mrs.) *Kiran Bedi* v. *Delhi Administration*, 1989 (2) Delhi Lawyer 190. In this case, the Administration notified that a Committee consisting of two Judges whose names too were mentioned in the notification would examine the matter. A notification under Section 11 of the Act was issued, extending thereby the provisions of the Act to the Committee. Later on, one of the two Judges resigned and the remaining Judge continued with the inquiry. This was challenged on the ground, inter alia, that the duty of the Administration to appoint the second Judge was a statutory duty under Section 3(3) of the Act and Committee proceedings by a Single Judge were incompetent and void. The Court did not accept this.

appoint a Commission is optional and discretionary even if there is any definite matter of public importance. A Commission may be appointed by the appropriate Government if it is of the opinion that it is necessary so to do. This opinion is, by the words of the section, subjective. In other words, even if there is any definite matter of public importance, the appropriate Government may not appoint a Commission of Inquiry if it is of opinion that it is not necessary to do so.[82]

The appointment of a Commission of Inquiry under the Act is, thus, provided by Section 3 thereof. Sub-section (1) of this section requires (i) the formation of an opinion by the appropriate Government that it is necessary to appoint a Commission of Inquiry, (ii) for making an inquiry into any definite matter of public importance. Upon the formation of such opinion, the appropriate Government may appoint a Commission of Inquiry by notification in the Official Gazette to perform its functions within such time as may be specified in the notification. It is an enabling section except in cases where a resolution is passed by the Parliament or the Legislature of a State. If such a resolution has been passed, the appropriate Government has to appoint a Commission of Inquiry in the manner stated. Section 3 does not in terms require a notification in its technical sense. The only requirement of the section is that the opinion of the appropriate Government that it is necessary to appoint a Commission of Inquiry should be published in the Official Gazette. It is immaterial to the validity of the appointment of the Commission, subject to other conditions of Section 3 being satisfied whether the opinion of the appropriate Government has been expressed in the form of a resolution or of a notification or whether these are published in any particular part of the Official Gazette. Even where the appointment of the Commission was by an order and the provisions of the Central Secretariat Manual of Office Procedure were not complied with in respect of its publication in the Official Gazette, it would not matter whether this order is styled as a notification or as a resolution so long as it is notified

---

82. *Bhagwat Dayal Sharma* v. *Union of India and Others*, ILR (1974) I Delhi 847.

or published in the Official Gazette for the rules in the Manual are not statutory and are merely rules of office procedure. It is also not necessary to recite the formation of opinion in the resolution or notification itself as the formation of such opinion can be proved by evidence aliunde and even by affidavits filed in Court.[83]

On a careful analysis of the terms in sub-section (1) of Section 3, it, thus, appears that the question of appointment of a Commission would arise only if, in the opinion of the Government, it is found necessary to appoint one or when the Government is compelled to do so as a result of the resolution passed in that behalf, either by the Parliament or by the Legislature of the State concerned. The expression "if it is of opinion" used in the sub-section makes it abundantly clear that, unless compelled by the Parliament or by the Legislature of the State concerned, the Government has the discretion to appoint or not to appoint a Commission in terms of Section 3 of the Act, depending upon its opinion.[84]

It may be noted in this regard that Article 340 of the Constitution empowers the President of India to appoint a Commission to investigate the conditions of socially and educationally backward classes within the territory of India and the difficulties under which they labour and to make recommendations as to the steps that should be taken by the Union or any State to remove such difficulties to improve their conditions and as to the grants that should be made for the purpose by the Union or any State and the conditions subject to which such grants should be made. It is under this power that the Kalekar and the Mandal Commissions were appointed. But

---

83. *Swadeshi Cotton Mills Co. Ltd.* v. *State Industrial Tribunal, U.P. and Others*, AIR 1961 SC 1381; *The State of Jammu and Kashmir and Others* v. *Bakshi Gulam Mohammed and Another*, AIR 1967 SC 122; *Ganga Bishnu Swaika and Another* v. *Calcutta Pinjrapole Society and Others*, AIR 1968 SC 615; *Gullapalli Nageswara Rao and Others* v. *Andhra Pradesh State Road Transport Corporation and Another*, 1959 (Suppl.) SCR 319; *P.R. Nayak* v. *Union of India and Others*, ILR (1973) I Delhi 747.

84. *Rajendran* v. *Home Secretary*, AIR 1983 Kerala 59.

it does not follow from this Article that once the President appoints a Commission, the State is disabled from, or prohibited from appointing a Commission for one or more of the purposes mentioned in Article 340. It is also open to the State Government to appoint a Commission for such purposes under the Commissions of Inquiry Act, 1952. Even apart from the 1952 Act, the executive power of the State extends to appointing a body or a Committee to investigate a particular factual situation, including the ascertainment/identification of socially and educationally backward classes and to suggest measures for their amelioration.[85] The analogy of the proviso to sub-section (1) of Section 3 would not be applicable to the Commission appointed under Article 340 vis-à-vis the Commission appointed under Section 3 of the Commissions of Inquiry Act, 1952.

Resolution to Appoint Commission Lost in Parliament—Effect

The question is whether a Government, who is responsible to Parliament, can act contrary to the resolution of Parliament in exercising its discretionary power to appoint a Commission under Section 3 of the Act. Section 3 of the Act has got two parts. It confers power upon the Central Government to appoint a Commission if there exists definite matter of public importance and forms an opinion that it is necessary so to do. The appointment of such Commission is discretionary. But in case where there is a resolution either by the Parliament or the State Legislature, it is obligatory upon the appropriate Government to appoint a Commission of Inquiry. Two parts are mutually exclusive. The sources are different. Obligation on the Government to appoint a Commission arises only when there is a resolution by the Parliament. When a resolution to appoint a Commission is lost in Parliament, in that case there is no resolution and accordingly, it is not obligatory upon the Government to appoint a Commission. The discretionary power to appoint a Commission, however, is not fettered when the resolution to appoint a Commission is lost in Parliament. Where two sources of powers of appointing the Commission are distinct

85. *V. Narayana Rao* v. *State of A.P.*, AIR 1987 A.P. 53: 1987 Lab. I.C. 152.

and different, obviously, it cannot be exercised simultaneously. There is no bar to appoint a Commission by the Government in exercising its discretionary power even when a resulution to appoint a Commission is lost in Parliament inasmuch as it does not attract the other part of Section 3 of the Act.[86]

Appointment of Commission by State and Article 257

The question whether the appointment of a Commission by the State Government to inquire into identical matters, in respect of which once the Central Government refused to appoint a Commission, will be contrary to Article 257(1), came up for consideration in *P.V. Jagannath Rao* v. *State of Orissa*.[87] The Court held that "the appointment of the present Commission does not impede or prejudice the exercise of the executive power of the Union. Section 3 of the Act lays down the principles with reference to which the power would be exercised and where the State Government would not appoint a Commission where the Central Government had already exercised the power. If the State Government does not violate any of the prescriptions made in Section 3, Article 257(1) is no bar to the appointment by the State Government of such a Commission."[88]

Multiple Commissions for Same Matter

In *Nadendla Bhaskara Rao* v. *Government of Andhra Pradesh*,[89] the learned Advocate General contended on behalf of the State Government that Section 3(1) did not prohibit the constitution of more than one Inquiry Commission by the State Government. Referring to the language of sub-section (1) of Section 3, it was pointed out that there were only limitations on the constitution of an Inquiry Commission concurrently by the State Government and the Central Government. Negating this contention, the Court held: "By necessary implication Section 3 does not confer power on the State Government to appoint more than one Commission to inquire into the same charges or

---

86. *Orient Paper Mills* v. *Union of India*, AIR 1979 Cal. 114, p. 124.
87. (1968) 34 Cut LT 666.
88. *Ibid.*, 714.
89. AIR 1989 A.P. 186.

allegations." Whether two Commissions exercise concurrently power to inquire into the same matter or not, is a question of fact. If they do exercise such concurrent power, the one appointed later in point of time would be bad in law being contrary to the provisions of Section 3 of the Act. Section 3 does not contemplate a situation where there could be clash of two Commissions concurrently inquiring into the same matter and, as such, the State Government cannot exercise power to appoint two separate Commissions to inquire into the same allegations. The rule of harmonious construction cannot be invoked so as to construe that one Commission would be dealing with specific matter while the remaining matter in general would be dealt with by the other Commission so long as it is open to the one Commission to inquire into the matter that has been referred to the other Commission as well for inquiry. The Court further observed: "It is needless to emphasize that multiplicity of Commissions should be avoided. It is convenient from all points of view that a Commission of Inquiry, when it is appointed, is empowered to go into all allegations against an individual instead of breaking up the allegations into different classes and appointing different Commissions of Inquiry. Such a course, apart from the inconvenience and hardships to an accused individual, is also inconvenient to the Government and other individuals to cope up with the inquiry by different persons. No special reasons have been brought to the notice of this Court as to why the Government considered it expedient to appoint the Menon Commission in so far as the petitioner is concerned having appointed the Agarwal Commission with wide terms of reference. Having regard to all these facts and circumstance, the contention of the petitioner that the appointment of the Menon Commission, in the face of the Agarwal Commission already appointed is bad and violates the provisions contained in Article 14 of the Constitution and Section 3(1) of the Commissions of Inquiry Act has to be accepted."

Formation of Opinion by Appropriate Government—Justiciability

The discretion given to the Government to set up a Commission of Inquiry is guided by the policy laid down in the

Act and the executive action is to be taken only where there exists a definite matter of public importance into which an inquiry is necessary.[90] In *A.M. Rasheed* v. *State of Kerala*,[91] the Supreme Court said that in all statutes where such expression as "opinion", "reason to believe", "satisfied" are used, the Court would not readily defer to the conclusiveness of an executive authority's opinion as to the existence of a matter of law or fact upon which the validity of the exercise of power is predicated. Where a reasonable conduct is expected the criterion of reasonableness is not subjective but objective. Administrative decisions in exercise of power even if conferred in subjective terms must be made in good faith and on relevant considerations. The Courts would inquire whether a reasonable man could have come to that decision in question, without misdirecting himself on the law and facts. The Courts will find out whether the conditions precedents to the formation of the opinion have a factual basis.

Thus, the subjective satisfaction would not empower the appropriate Government to appoint a Commission in the absence of definite matter of public importance. The Court has got the power of judicial review within a very narrow compass as to whether there are materials to prove at least prima facie existence of definite matters of public importance. If a tentative conclusion can be arrived at on the allegations made, it is not open to the Court to go further and quash the Notification on the ground of insufficiency or impropriety of those materials. When the existence of definite matters of public importance is challenged, mere assertion on the part of the Government that those matters existed would not be enough. Some clue must be furnished which led to the conclusion as to their existence.[92] However, it is not the function of the Court to go into the merits of the allegations and to see whether they have been established. That

---

90. *State of Karnataka* v. *Union of India*, AIR 1978 SC 68, p. 172 (Per Kailasham, J).
91. AIR 1974 SC 2249.
92. *P.V. Jagannath Rao* v. *State of Orissa,* (1968) 34 Cut LT 666, 701: ILR (1966) Cut 482.

is the function of the Commission of Inquiry. The Court is only to see whether on the materials presented a prima facie case is made out for the subjective satisfaction of the State Government.[93]

Under Section 3 of the Act, the formation of opinion of the appropriate Government is subjective but such an opinion is required to be based on the circumstances/conditions as is provided for in that Section. The Section stipulates one condition or circumstance in this regard, namely, the subject-matter of inquiry must be definite matter of public importance. The exercise of power or formation of opinion under Section 3 of the Act is, therefore, limited or restricted only to definite matters of public importance. Factual existence of those materials is absolutely necessary. Those matters might be spelled out from the face of the order itself or by disclosing such matters in the affidavit of the Government when a challenge is thrown by the aggrieved party about the non-existence of definite matter of public importance. The case law on this subject laid down the following principles:— (a) the Courts are competent to decide whether the matters to be inquired into are definite matters of public importance, (b) the power conferred upon the appropriate Government is neither unfettered nor uncontrolled, and (c) the appropriate Government can appoint a Commission of Inquiry only when there exists a definite matter of public importance into which an inquiry is necessary.[94]

On a plain reading of the statutory provision it is clear that there is no prescribed form or particular manner for the appropriate Government to express its opinion that it is necessary to appoint a Commission of Inquiry. Such opinion may be expressed in any manner by which the public would get the information about such appointment. When the Chief Minister of the State expressed on the floor of the State Legislature that he has no objection for appointment of a Commission of Inquiry under the Act to inquire into the serious allegations

---

93. *P.V. Jagannath Rao* v. *State of Orissa* (1968) 34 Cut LT 666, 701: ILR (1966) Cut 703.

94. *Orient Paper Mills* v. *Union of India*, AIR 1979 Cal. 114, pp. 127-28.

regarding irregularities in payment of compensation for the acquired land, it is reasonable to presume that he has given necessary thought to the matter and on being satisfied that it is necessary so to do expressed his agreement for appointment of a Commission of Inquiry under the Act. The statement was made on behalf of the State Government. This was followed by the categorical statement of the Advocate General representing the State before the High Court that the requisite notification will be issued without delay and indeed such notification was issued. It is relevant to note that it was not the case of the writ petitioners that the subject-matter of inquiry was not a definite matter of public importance or that no inquiry into such matter was necessary. Indeed, there is little scope for doubt that the controversy is a matter of public importance and it is but appropriate that the State Government wanted a detailed enquiry in the matter for its information and guidance. The High Court, as noted, has simply held that since there is no specific order in the file, which would show that the State Government had formed such opinion as required under Section 3(1) of the Act, therefore, the notification appointing the Commission of Inquiry was not in accordance with law. On the facts and circumstances of the case, the Supreme Court expressed the view that the High Court took a hyper technical view of the matter in which the State Government, which is the repository of the authority, had made the appointment. A serious matter of public importance, which gave rise to criticism from different quarters against public functionaries and also private persons is a matter which calls for proper inquiry and if the State Government in its wisdom thought it proper to entrust the inquiry to a sitting or retired Judge of the High Court, no exception can be taken to such action. It is desirable that activities of public functionaries should be above board and if allegations and criticisms are received in that regard the matter should be promptly inquired into and appropriate follow-up action should be taken. The need is all the more important in matters relating to public money. The High Court, in the considered view of the Supreme Court, omitted to look to the main purpose of appointment of Commission of Inquiry under the Act and interfered with the notification issued by the State Government without firm basis in law and without justification on facts.[95]

In a society, aspiring to be governed by the rule of law, the scope and extent of judicial review in respect of an administrative action would depend not upon the question whether the power is statutory or constitutional but upon the terms of the grant of the power. If the power conferred is exercisable on fulfilment of certain conditions the exercise of powers subject to judicial review to the limited extent, that is to say, whether the powers have been exercised bona fide and the Court can enquire into whether there were relevant materials on which the power has been exercised. But the sufficiency of the materials found is not a matter for judicial review. It is, therefore, necessary to refer to the power granted. Power conferred under the Commissions of Inquiry Act is on the formation of opinion about the investigation of the matter of public importance. Therefore, the grounds or the materials necessary for the formation of the opinion must exist and when a challenge is thrown that there are no grounds at all for the formation of that opinion, then, by mere recital of that opinion in the notification or unless the notification so states as was in the case of *Ram Krishna Dalmia's* case,[96] it must be shown either by averments made on behalf of the State Government or otherwise that there are materials upon which the opinion is possible and not that the opinion necessarily follows. Accordingly, in *Sushil Chandra* v. *Secretary, Chakraborty Commission of Inquiry and Others*,[97] the impugned notification appointing the Chakraborti Commission of Inquiry was quashed as there were no materials disclosed upon which the State Government could have formed the necessary opinion and the proceedings were set aside. The Commission was also directed to make available to the State Government all that material that it had collected by its investigation whereupon the State Government, after due consideration of such materials, would

95. *P. Janardhana Reddy* v. *State of Andhra Pradesh and Others*, AIR 2001 SC 2631.

96. AIR 1958 SC 538.

97. 84 CWN 583.

take immediate steps for initiation of appropriate proceedings, civil or criminal against the delinquent persons. The State Government was also given liberty to form an opinion afresh for constituting a Commission of Inquiry.

The scope of judicial review in cases of exercise of discretionary statutory powers is well settled by a series of decisions of the Supreme Court, the House of Lords and other Courts. It will be expedient to mention only a few of them. Even at the outset, it should be stated, that a survey of decided cases shows that there is a great and eternal principle that there is nothing like "unfettered", or "absolute" discretion immune from judicial scrutiny or review, though Courts do not ordinarily go into the merits of the exercise of discretion. One of the earliest cases in which the Supreme Court had occasion to consider, about the meaning and content of the words occurring in a statute to the effect "in the opinion of the Government", is the case report in *Barium Chemicals Ltd.* v. *Company Law Board.*[98] The Court took the view that the formation of opinion is a subjective process and the scope of judicial review is strictly limited. The frontiers of judicial review were laid down in the different judgments delivered by the Court.[99]

In *I.T. Commissioner* v. *Mahindra and Mahindra Ltd.*,[100] the Supreme Court held[101] as follows:

> Indisputably, it is settled position that if the action or decision is perverse or is such that no reasonable body of persons, properly informed, could come to, or has been arrived at by the authority misdirecting itself by adopting a wrong approach, or has been influenced by irrelevant or extraneous matters the Court would be justified in interfering with the same. This Court in one of its later decisions[102] has

98. AIR 1967 SC 295.

99. *Ibid.*, see paragraph 10, p. 302, paragraph 39, p. 313 and paragraph 63, p. 324.

100. AIR 1984 SC 1182 : (1983) 3 SCR 773.

101. *Ibid.*, p. 1188, para 11.

102. *Smt. Shalini Soni* v. *Union of India,* (1981) 1 SCR 962 : AIR 1981 SC 431.

> observed thus: "It is an unwritten rule of the law, constitutional and administrative, that whenever a decision-making function is entrusted to the subjective satisfaction of a statutory functionary, there is an implicit obligation to apply his mind to pertinent and proximate matters only, eschewing the irrelevant and the remote."

In *State of U.P.* v. *Renusagar Power Co.*,[103] the Court observed[104] as follows:

> The exercise of power whether legislative or administrative will be set aside if there is manifest error in the exercise of such power or the exercise of the power is manifestly, arbitrary. Similarly, if the power has been exercised on a non-consideration or non-application of mind to relevant factors, the exercise of power will be regarded as manifestly erroneous. If a power (whether legislative or administrative) is exercised on the basis of facts, which do not exist, and which are patently erroneous, such exercise of power will stand vitiated.[105]

In *J.R. Raghupathy* v. *State of AP*[106], the Supreme Court held that the High Court in exercise of its jurisdiction under Article 226 of the Constitution of India cannot sit in appeal over Government's decision and proceed to evaluate merits and demerits of such decision with its own perspective. The Court also adverted to the statement of the law on the point as narrated in the book *Judicial Review of Administrative Action* by De Smith[107] 4th Edition, at pp. 285-87. The said passage is to the following effect:

> The authority in which a discretion is vested can be compelled to exercise that discretion, but not to exercise it in any particular manner. In general, a discretion must be exercised

---

103. AIR 1988 SC 1737.

104. *Ibid.*, pp. 1763-65.

105. *I.T. Commissioner* v. *Mahindra and Mahindra Ltd.* (1983) 3 SCR 773, pp. 786-87: AIR 1984 SC 1182, pp. 1188-89.

106. (1988) 4 SCC 364: AIR 1988 SC 1681.

107. Same passage was cited with approval in the case of *I.T. Commr.* v. *Mahindra and Mahindra Ltd.*, AIR 1984 SC 1182, p. 1189.

only by the authority to which it is committed. That authority must genuinely address itself to the matter before it: it must not act under the dictation of other body or disable itself from exercising a discretion in each individual case. In the purported exercise of its discretion it must not do what it has been forbidden to do, nor must it do what it has not been authorized to do. It must act in good faith, must have regard to all relevant considerations and must not be swayed by irrelevant considerations, must not seek to promote purposes alien to the letter or to the spirit of the legislation that gives it power to act, and must not act arbitrarily or capriciously. Nor where a judgment must be made that certain facts exist can a discretion be validly exercised on the basis of an erroneous assumption about those facts.

The Supreme Court in *Raghupathy's* case[108] also referred to the leading English decisions of the House of Lords and the Court of Appeal and textbooks of reputed authors. In particular, the decisions of the House of Lords in *Padfield* v. *Minister of Agriculture, Fisheries and Food,*[109] *Secretary of State* v. *Tameside*[110] and *Council of Civil Service Unions* v. *Minister for the Civil Service*[111] were cited with approval. The decision of the Court of Appeal in *Laker Airways Ltd.* case[112] wherein the passages from *Padfield* and *Tameside* cases were quoted and relied on was also referred to. The Supreme Court observed, "The general approach now is for the courts to require that the government must produce reasonable grounds for its action, even where the jurisdictional fact is subjectively framed."

In *Padfield* v. *Minister of Agriculture,*[113] the Court held that though the statute conferred unfettered discretion on a Minister, it will nevertheless be limited to the extent that it must not be

108. (1988) 4 SCC 364: AIR 1988 SC 1681.

109. (1968) 1 All ER 694.

110. (1976) 3 All ER 665.

111. (1964) 3 All ER 935.

112. (1977) 2 WLR 234, affirming 1976 (3) WLR 537.

113. (1968) 1 All ER 694.

so used whether by reason of misconstruction of the statute or other reason as to frustrate the object of the statute which conferred it and that the Minister was bound to exercise the discretion lawfully, i.e. not to misdirect himself in law, or to take into account irrelevant matters, nor to omit relevant matters from consideration.

In *Tameside* case[114] Lord Denning, MR stated the law, thus:

> To my mind, if a statute gives a Minister power to take drastic action if he is satisfied that a local authority have acted or are proposing to act improperly or unreasonably, then the Minister should obey all the elementary rules of fairness before he finds that the local authority are guilty or before he takes drastic action overruling them. He should give the party affected notice of the charge of impropriety or unreasonableness and a fair opportunity of dealing with it. I am glad to see that the Secretary of the State did so in this case. He had before him the written proposals of the new Council and he met their leaders. In addition, however, the Minister must direct himself properly in law. He must call his own attention to the matters he is bound to consider. He must exclude from his consideration matters, which are irrelevant to that which he has to consider. And the decision to which he comes must be one, which is reasonable in this sense that it is, or can be, supported with good reasons or any rate be a decision which a reasonable person might reasonably reach. Such is, I think, plain from *Padfield* v. *Minister of Agriculture, Fisheries and Food*[115] which is a landmark in our administrative law, and which we had in mind in *Secretary of State for Employment* v. *Associated Society of Locomotive Engineers and Firemen* (No. 2).[116] So much for the requirements if the Minister is to be 'satisfied'.... No one can properly be labeled as being

---

114. (1976) 3 All ER 665 (CA). The decision was affirmed by the House of Lords at (1976) 3 All ER 679.

115. (1968) 1 All ER 694: (1968) AC 997.

116. (1972) 2 All ER 949: (1972) 2 QB 455.

unreasonable unless he is not only wrong but unreasonably wrong, so wrong that no reasonable person could sensibly take that view.

In *Council of Civil Service Unions* v. *Minister for the Civil Service,*[117] Lord Diplock stated[118] the law, thus:

> Judicial review has I think developed to a stage today when, without reiterating any analysis of the steps by which the development has come about, one can conveniently classify under three heads the grounds on which administrative action is subject to control by judicial review. The first ground I would call 'illegality' the second 'irrationality' and the third 'procedural impropriety'....
>
> By 'illegality' as a ground for judicial review I mean that the decision-maker must understand correctly the law that regulates his decision-making power and must give effect to it. Whether he has or not is par excellence a justiciable question to be decided, in the event of dispute, by those persons, the judges, by whom the judicial power of the State is exercisable.
>
> By 'irrationality' I mean what can now be succinctly referred to as "Wednesbury unreasonableness".[119] It applies to a decision, which is so outrageous in its defiance of logic or of accepted moral standards that no sensible person who had applied his mind to the question to be decided could have arrived at it. Whether a decision falls, within this category is a question that judges by their training and experience should be well equipped to answer, or else there would be something badly wrong with our judicial system. To justify the court's exercise of this role, resort I think is today no longer needed to Viscount Radcliffe's ingenious explanation in Edwards[120] of irrationality as a ground for Court's reversal

---

117. (1984) 3 All ER 935.

118. *Ibid.*, pp. 950-51.

119. *Associated Provincial Picture Houses Ltd.* v. *Wednesbury Corpn.* (1947) 2 All ER 680 : (1948) 1 KB 223.

120. *Inspector of Taxes* v. *Bairstow* (1955) 3 All ER 48 : (1956) AC 14.

of a decision by ascribing it to an inferred though unidentifiable mistake of law by the decision-maker. "Irrationality" by now can stand on its own feet as an accepted ground on which a decision may be attacked by judicial review.

I have described the third head as 'procedural impropriety' rather than failure to observe basic rules of natural justice or failure to act with procedural fairness towards the person who will be affected by the decision. This is because susceptibility to judicial review under this head covers also failure by an administrative tribunal to observe procedural rules that are expressly laid down in the legislative instrument by which its jurisdiction is conferred, even where such failure does not involve any denial of natural justice.

Lord Roskill stated the law, thus:[121]

.... Executive action will be the subject of judicial review on three separate grounds. The first is where the authority concerned has been guilty of an error of law in its action, as for example purporting to exercise a power which in law it does not possess. The second is where it exercises a power in so unreasonable a manner that the exercise becomes open to review on what are called, in lawyers' shorthand, Wednesbury principles.[122] The third is where it has acted contrary to what are often called 'principles of natural justice'. As to this last, the use of this phrase is no doubt hallowed by time and much judicial repetition, but it is a phrase often widely misunderstood and, therefore, as often misused. That phrase perhaps might now be allowed to find a permanent resting place and be better replaced by speaking of a duty to act fairly. But that latter phrase must not in its turn be misunderstood or misused. It is not for the courts to determine whether a particular policy or particular decisions taken in fulfilment of that policy are fair. They are only concerned

121. *Council of Civil Service Unions* v. *Minister for the Civil Service*, (1984) 3 All ER 935, pp. 953-54.

122. *Associated Provincial Picture Houses Ltd.* v. *Wednesbury Corpn.* (1947) 2 All ER 680 : (1948) 1 KB 223.

> with the manner in which those decisions have been taken and the extent of the duty to act fairly will vary greatly from case to case as, indeed, the decided cases since 1950 consistently show. Many features will come into play including the nature of the decision and the relationship of those involved on either side before the decision was taken.
>
> My noble and learned friend Lord Diplock in his speech has devised a new nomenclature for each of these three grounds, calling them respectively 'illegality', 'irrationality' and 'procedural impropriety', words which, if I may respectfully say so, have the great advantage of making clear the differences between each ground.

The statement of the law contained in *Council of Civil Service Unions* v. *Minister for the Civil Service*[123] was reiterated by the House of Lords in *Wheeler* v. *Leicester City Council*.[124] Lord Roskill reiterated[125] the law thus:

> In his speech Lord Diplock[126] classified three already well established heads or sets of circumstances in which the Court will interfere. First, illegality, second irrationality, and third, procedural impropriety. If I may be forgiven for referring to my own speech in the case, a similar analysis appears therein.[127] Those three heads are not exhaustive and as Lord Diplock pointed out, further grounds may hereafter require to be added. Nor are they necessarily mutually exclusive.

In evaluating as to whether a decision is "reasonable", or in other words, the authority has acted "unreasonably", we should bear in mind the words of caution propounded by Lord Hailsham, L.C. *in Re, W* (an infant):[128] "Two reasonable (persons) can perfectly reasonably come to opposite conclusions

---

123. (1984) 3 All ER 935.
124. (1985) 2 All ER 1106.
125. *Ibid.*, p. 1111.
126. (1984) 3 All ER 935, 950 : (1984) 3 WLR 1174, p. 1196.
127. (1984) 3 All ER 935, 954 : (1984) 3 WLR 1174, p. 1200.
128. (1971) 2 All ER 49, p. 56.

on the same set of facts, without forfeiting their title to be regarded as reasonable." And, it is perhaps due to this note of caution, Lord Scarman said, in *Nottinghamshire County Council* v. *Secretary of State,*[129] that for the Courts to intervene on the ground of "unreasonableness", prima facie case should show that the official concerned has behaved "absurdly" or "must have taken leave of his senses".

Lord Brightman said in *Puhlhofer* v. *Hillingdon London BC*[130] as follows:

> The ground on which the Courts will review the exercise of an administrative discretion is abuse of power, e.g. bad faith, a mistake in construing the limits of the power, a procedural irregularity or unreasonableness in the Wednesbury sense[131], i.e. unreasonableness verging on an absurdity: see the speech of Lord Scarman in *Nottinghamshire CC* v. *Secretary of State for the Environment*,[132] where the existence or non-existence of a fact is left to the judgment and discretion of a public body and that fact involves a broad spectrum ranging from the obvious to the debatable to the just conceivable, it is duty of the Court to leave the decision of that fact to the public body to whom Parliament has entrusted the decision making power save in a case where it is obvious that the public body, consciously or unconsciously, are acting perversely.[133]

Whether Court has Jurisdiction to Direct Appointment of Commission?

Under Section 3 of the Act, the right to appoint a Commission of Inquiry vests in the appropriate Government. There are two situations in which a Commission may be appointed. The first is when the Government is of the opinion that it is necessary so

---

129. (1986) 1 All ER 199 (HL).

130. (1986) 1 All ER 467, p. 474 (HL).

131. *Associated Provincial Picture Houses Ltd.* v. *Wednesbury Corpn.* (1947) 2 All ER 680 : (1948) 1 KB 223.

132. (1986) 1 All ER 199, 202: (1986) 2 WLR 1, p. 5.

133. cf. *R. Balakrishna Pillai* v. *State of Kerala*, AIR 1989 Kerala 99.

to do and the second is when the Parliament or a State Legislature passes a resolution in that behalf, as the case may be. In the first case the appointment of a Commission is discretionary and in the second case it is obligatory. Once a resolution is adopted in terms of Section 3, the Government has no option but to appoint a Commission of Inquiry. In other cases, the Government is not bound to appoint a Commission of Inquiry. In other words, in the first situation, it is entirely discretionary with the Government to appoint a Commission or not to appoint a Commission. The Court cannot control the exercise of discretion by the executive. The opinion of the Government referred to in Section 3 of the Act is subjective and the petitioner cannot ask for a mandamus to compel the Government to appoint a Commission of Inquiry.[134] The Court does not have jurisdiction to direct the Government to appoint a Commission of Inquiry. It is entirely a matter to be decided by the appropriate Government.[135]

On a careful analysis of the terms in Section 3(1), it appears that the question of appointment of a Commission would arise only if in the opinion of the Government it is found necessary to appoint one or when the Government is compelled to do so as a result of the resolution passed in that behalf, either by the Parliament or by the State Legislature concerned. The expression "if it is of opinion" used in the sub-section (1) makes it abundantly clear that, unless compelled by the Parliament or the State Legislature concerned, the Government has the discretion to appoint or not to appoint a Commission in terms of Section 3 of the Act, depending upon its opinion.[136]

Section 3(1) of the Act permits the appropriate Government to appoint a Commission of Inquiry for the purpose of making inquiry into any definite matter of public importance. The notification by which the Commission is so appointed is to specify the time within which the Commission shall make the inquiry and perform the function. It is settled law that Section

---

134. *Maharshi Avadhesh* v. *State of U.P.*, AIR 1991 Allahabad 52.

135. *B. Jegnathan* v. *State of Tamil Nadu*, AIR 1990 Madras 69.

136. *Rajendran* v. *Home Secretary*, AIR 1983 Kerala 59.

3(1) of the Act confers discretion on the Government to appoint a Commission or not. The discretionary power that is conferred on the Government is not coupled with any duty. The said Section merely gives a power to the Government to appoint a Commission and does not, at the same time, confer any benefit on any person or group of persons, a corresponding right to call upon the Government to have an inquiry conducted. The Government is getting the power to inform its mind or to find out if certain facts exist. It is for the Government to consider whether to appoint a Commission for making an inquiry. In other words, no corresponding right is conferred on any person to compel the Government to appoint a Commission. When such is the right given to the Government, which is purely discretionary, the Courts have taken the view that Government cannot be compelled to appoint a Commission under the Act.[137]

Under Section 3(1) of the Act, it is discretionary with the appropriate Government to set up a Commission and it is only mandatory to set up a Commission if the resolution is passed by the Parliament or as the case may be by the Legislature of the State concerned. Where there is discretionary jurisdiction, no mandamus can be issued to the State Government to set up a Commission of Inquiry, for the purpose to make inquiry into the matter of public importance by notification in the Official Gazette. Therefore, the prayer, which has been made that this Court should set up a Commission of Inquiry under the provision of the Act, cannot be allowed. But it can hardly be disputed that the Court has power to appoint Commissioner/Commissioners and investigators to make inquiries, collect data, submit its report to the Court suggesting remedial measures, if any. In that case the report as aforesaid should be made available to both the parties who may be asked to give their objections, if any to the report and to file affidavits, and then the Court may give such directions as it deems proper in public interest to the State Government.[138]

---

137. *Jan Sangharsh Manch* v. *State of Gujarat and Another*, AIR 1998 Gujarat 133.

138. *Sidda Raj Dhadda* v. *State of Rajasthan*, AIR 1990 Rajasthan 34.

According to sub-section (1) of Section 3, it is incumbent upon the appropriate Government to appoint a Commission of Inquiry in a case where a resolution in that behalf is passed by the Parliament or, as the case may be, the Legislature of the State. In other words, there is a statutory obligation on the appropriate Government to appoint a Commission of Inquiry in case a resolution in that behalf is passed by the the State Legislature. In such circumstances, the appropriate Government has no option or discretion in the matter. However, in the absence of a resolution, the power to appoint a Commission is discretionary and optional even in a case of "any definite matter of public importance". In that case, a Commission can only be appointed by the appropriate Government, if in its opinion, it is necessary to do so. From the words, "if it is of opinion", it is abundantly clear that the opinion of the State Government in such a situation is subjective. There may be definite matter of public importance, but the appropriate Government may not feel inclined to appoint a Commission of Inquiry if it is of opinion that is not necessary so to do.[139]

An inquiry under the Act is not at all a judicial inquiry. The object of appointing a Commission of Inquiry is to enable the Government to make up its mind as to what legislative or administrative measures should be adopted to eradicate the evil found or to implement the beneficial objects it has in view. In other words, the Commission of Inquiry is only a fact-finding body for the benefit of the Government when there is a definite matter of public importance. A Commission of Inquiry may be appointed if it is necessary in the opinion of the appropriate Government to do so. Under Section 3, the appropriate Government is not under a legal or statutory obligation to appoint a Commission of Inquiry even on a definite matter of public importance except in a case of resolution by Parliament or the Legislature of the State in that behalf. It, therefore, necessarily follows that the petitioner has no legal or statutory right to compel the State Government to appoint a Commission of Inquiry even when there is a definite matter of public

---

139. *Vijay Mehta* v. *State of Rajasthan*, AIR 1980 Rajasthan 207.

importance. In *Kanhiayalal* v. *The University of Rajasthan*,[140] a Division Bench of the Rajasthan High Court held that in order to maintain a writ for grant of mandamus, the petitioner must show that there exists a right in him to compel the opposite party to act in a particular manner and in the absence of any such right, the petition for the grant of mandamus cannot be allowed. In *Calcutta Gas Company* v. *State of West Bengal*,[141] it was laid down that the existence of the right is the foundation of the exercise of jurisdiction of the High Court under Article 226 and the legal right that can be enforced under Article 226 like Article 32 must ordinarily be the right of petitioner himself who complains of infraction of such right and approaches the Court for relief. It was further held that the right that can be enforced under Article 226 should ordinarily be the personal or individual right of the petitioner himself though in the cases of some of the writs like *habeas corpus* and *quo warranto*, this rule may have to be relaxed or modified. It is not necessary to multiply the authorities in this regard, for there is catena of cases of the Supreme Court on the point. It is well settled that four pre-requisite conditions for issuance of a writ of mandamus are as follows:

1. Whether the petitioner has a clear and specific right to relief demanded by him?
2. Whether there is a duty imposed by law on the respondent?
3. Whether such duty is of an imperative ministerial character involving no judgment or discretion on the part of respondent? And
4. Whether petitioner has any remedy other than by way of mandamus for the enforcement of right, which has been denied to him?

In *Mani Subrat Jain* v. *State of Haryana*,[142] it was observed as under:

> It is elementary though it is to be restated that no one can ask for a mandamus without a legal right. There must be a

140. 1965 Raj LW 53: AIR 1965 Rajasthan 84.
141. AIR 1962 SC 1044.
142. AIR 1977 SC 276.

judicially enforceable right as well as a legally protected right before one suffering a legal grievance can ask for a mandamus. A person can be said to be aggrieved only when a person is denied a legal right by some one who has a legal duty to do something or to abstain from doing something.

It follows, therefore, that existence of a right is *sine qua non* for the issuance of a writ of mandamus. However, the right need not be in respect of a proprietary interest. In *Union of India* v. *Nilkanth Tulsidas Bhatia*,[143] the question of *locus standi* of the respondent (the original petitioner and a victim of Godhra incident) in challenging the Committee appointed by the Railway Administration to inquire into the said incident, being contrary to the provisions of the Commission of Inquiry Act, came up for consideration. It will be expedient to refer to the following observations made by a Division Bench of the Gujarat High Court, viz.

"We find considerable substance in the submission made by the learned counsel for the original petitioner that just as the accused has the right to fair trial, every witness and every victim of a crime also has the right to demand a fair trial. There is no dispute about the fact that the original petitioner was one of the passengers traveling in S-6 coach of the Sabarmati Express. In fact, the original petitioner had filed case No. OA 030027 against the Railway Administration for compensation alleging that when the train reached the Godhra Railway Station, the said coach was set on fire leading to deaths of, injuries to many passengers. The petitioner was taken to Civil Hospital at Godhra and then to Civil Hospital at Ahmedabad and discharged on 18-3-2002. As indicated earlier, the Tribunal held that the incident of the coach being set on fire under a violent attack was an admitted fact and that railway authorities had also made *ex gratia* payment of Rs. 500 to the petitioner and, the Tribunal thereafter passed the order directing the Railway Administration to pay the petitioner a sum of Rs. 20,000 by way of compensation. If such a victim of the incident comes before the Court and insists that the Committee appointed by the Railway

143. (2006) 2 GLR 952.

Administration two years after the date of incident is not only illegally appointed, but has also submitted an interim report which takes an absolutely contradictory view vis-à-vis the stand of the Railway Administration for the last two years and that the Committee should be restrained from proceeding further and that the authorities be restrained from giving publicity to the final report of the Committee, it cannot be said the petitioner has no personal interest in the matter. As held by the Apex Court in *Venkateswara Rao* v. *Govt. of Andhra Pradesh*,[144] ordinarily the petitioner who seeks to file an application under Article 226 of the Constitution should be one who has a personal or individual right in the subject matter of the petition, but a personal right need not be in respect of a proprietary interest. In exceptional cases as the expression ordinarily indicates, a person who has been prejudicially affected by an act or omission of an authority can file a writ even though he has no proprietary or fiduciary interest in the subject matter thereof. When the petitioner has been prejudiced by an administrative order or action, the petition under Article 226 of the Constitution at his instance is certainly maintainable".[145]

It may be expedient to refer here, the case *Padfield* v. *Minister of Agriculture, Fisheries and Food*,[146] on which considerable reliance is generally placed in such cases by the petitioners. It may, however, be stated that this case does not support the contention for issue of mandamus for appointment of a Commission of Inquiry. In this case, the complainants, who were members of the South-East Regional Committee of the Milk Marketing Board, filed a complaint to the Minister of Agriculture, Fisheries and Food under Section 19 of the Agriculture Marketing Act asking that their complaint be referred to the Committee of Investigation established under that Act.

---

144. AIR 1966 SC 828.

145. It is understood that the judgment of the Division Bench of the Gujarat High Court in this case has been challenged by the Union of India in a Special Leave Petition filed in the Supreme Court. The matter is, thus, yet to attain finality.

146. 1968 AC 997.

The Minister, however, declined to refer the matter to the Committee for he did not consider the question suitable for investigation. In support of this, he gave reasons. The House of Lords found that the Minister had proceeded upon a misconstruction of the statute and remitted the case with a direction to consider the complaint of the appellants according to law. In that case, the complainants were interested in the price structure of milk. Section 19(3)(b) of that Act contemplated the making of a complaint to the Minister by the Consumers Committee. It is correct that this judgment was referred in *M/s. Hochtief Gammon* v. *State of Orissa*,[147] wherein it was observed as under:

> The principles deducible from the decisions of this Court and the above decision of the House of Lords which, though not binding on us, appeals to us on principle may be set out as follows:
>
> The Executive have to reach their decisions by taking into account relevant considerations. They should not refuse to consider relevant matter nor should take into account wholly irrelevant or extraneous consideration. They should not misdirect themselves on a point of law. Only such a decision will be lawful. The courts have power to see that the Executive acts lawfully. It is no answer to the exercise of that power to say that the Executive acted bona fide nor that they have bestowed painstaking consideration. They cannot avoid scrutiny by courts by failing to give reasons. If they give reasons and they are not good reasons, the court can direct them to reconsider the matter in the light of relevant matters, though the propriety, adequacy or satisfactory character of those reasons may not be open to judicial scrutiny. Even if the Executive considers it inexpedient to exercise their powers they should state their reasons and there must be material to show that they have considered all the relevant facts.

A somewhat similar question arose before a Division Bench of the Delhi High Court in *Bhagwat Dayal Sharma* v. *Union of*

147. AIR 1975 SC 2226, paras 12 and 13.

India,[148] under Section 3 of the Act. The High Court took the view that the petitioner in that case who stated himself to be a citizen, a taxpayer, a member of the Rajya Sabha and a former Chief Minister of the State of Haryana had no right under the Act for the appointment of the Commission. It was observed:

> All that the petitioner has stated is that he is a citizen, a taxpayer, a member of the Rajya Sabha and a former Chief Minister of the State of Haryana. In essence, his status is no better than of a member of the public. Council for the petitioner has used, during arguments, high sounding words and phrases relating to democracy, integrity, corruption, nepotism, terrorism, enrichment at the cost of the public and the spirit of the construction to urge that every citizen has a right to see that those in power are not corrupt. These expressions may be used on and from other platforms but they are not relevant in a Court of law which is concerned with rights and obligations arising out of the Constitution and the laws. The petitioner has clearly no right under the statute, namely, the said Act[149] and therefore, no *locus standi* to move this petition for a writ of mandamus.

It is, therefore, not open to anyone to argue that the Government has been asked to exercise discretion under Section 3 of the Act by the appointment of the Commission of Inquiry as there is a matter of public importance which it failed to do. It cannot be said that a demand has been made but the discretion has not been exercised and that when a discretion is required to be exercised and it is not exercised as required by law, the Court has power to compel the authority or, for that matter, the State Government, to exercise it under Section 3 of the Act. The law on the subject is very clear. If the petitioner has no right to get the Commission appointed, then the demand for the appointment of Commission by the political parties or by the Ms.L.A. will not confer any right. There is no statutory duty on the appropriate Government to be discharged towards the petitioner. In these circumstances, the contention of the learned counsel that

148. ILR (1974) 1 Delhi 847.

149. The Commissions of Inquiry Act, 1952.

discretion vested in the appropriate Government under Section 3 of the Act has not been exercised and, therefore, the petitioner has a right to maintain the writ petition, is devoid of force.[150]

In *Peoples Union for Democratic Rights and Another* v. *Ministry of Home Affairs*,[151] Yogeshwar Dayal, J., speaking for the Division Bench, observed as under:

> Where the discretion is with the appropriate Government to appoint a Commission of Inquiry, it is not under a legal or statutory obligation to appoint a Commission of Inquiry even on definite matter of public importance except in the case mentioned in the section. It will be noticed that the distinction between the meanings of the word 'may' and 'shall' is in accord of the purposes of the Commission so appointed. The Commission is merely to investigate, record its findings and make its recommendations which are not enforceable proprio vigore. The inquiry or report cannot be looked upon as judicial inquiry in the sense of its being an exercise of judicial function properly so called.[152]

Accordingly, it was held that the petitioners had no legal or statutory right to compel the Government to appoint Commission of Inquiry even when there was a definite matter of public importance. The Court referred to and relied on the case of *Bhagwat Dayal Sharma* v. *Union of India*,[153] which squarely covered this question. The Court quoted with authority the following observations of Chief Justice S.N. Andley and S.N. Shankar, J., viz.:

> The appropriate Government is under a statutory obligation to appoint a Commission of Inquiry in a case where a resolution in that behalf is passed by the House of the People or, as the case may be, by the Legislative Assembly of the State and the appropriate Government has, in such a case, no option or discretion in the matter. In the absence of

150. *Vijay Mehta* v. *State of Rajasthan*, AIR 1980 Rajasthan 207.

151. AIR 1985 Delhi 268.

152. *Ram Krishna Dalmia* v. *S.R. Tendolkar*, 1959 SCR 279: AIR 1958 SC 538.

153. ILR (1974) I Delhi 847.

such a resolution, the power to appoint a Commission may be appointed by the appropriate Government if it is of the opinion that it is necessary so to do. This opinion is, by the words, even if there is any definite matter of public importance, the appropriate Government may not appoint a Commission of Inquiry if it is of opinion that it is not necessary so to do; that an enquiry under the Commissions of Inquiry Act is not a judicial inquiry and the object of constituting a Commission of Inquiry under the Act is to enable the Government to make up its mind as to what legislative or administrative measures should be adopted to eradicate the evil found or implement the beneficial objects it has in view. It is merely a fact finding body for the benefit of the Government and that is why even where there may be a definite matter of public importance, a Commission of Inquiry is appointed under the said Act only if it is necessary, in the opinion of the appropriate Government to do so. Except in the case of a resolution of Parliament or the Legislature of a State in that behalf, there is no statutory or other obligation upon the appropriate Government to appoint a Commission of Inquiry and, therefore, on the words of Section 3 of the Act, there cannot be a legal or statutory obligation upon the appropriate Government to appoint a Commission of Inquiry even if there is a definite matter of public importance. This conclusion by itself would displace the contention on behalf of the petitioner that he has a legal or statutory right to compel the appointment of a Commission of Inquiry whenever there is a definite matter of public importance, therefore, that the petitioner, a member of the public, has clearly no right under the statute, namely, the Commissions of Inquiry Act and, therefore, no *locus standi* to move a petition for a writ of mandamus for directing the Central Government to appoint a Commission of Inquiry.

In *Kiran Bedi* v. *Delhi Administration*,[154] the Court observed, "The word 'may' cannot be read as 'shall' for the reason that

154. 1989 (2) Delhi Lawyer 190.

there is no obligation on the Government to appoint a Commission of Inquiry at all. The opinion of the Government to appoint a Commission of Inquiry is subjective opinion. It does not create a legal obligation for the Government or a legal right in a citizen. Therefore no mandamus can be issued for directing the Government to appoint a Commission."

S.K. Mal Lodha, J. of Rajasthan High Court took the same view in the case reported as *Vijay Mehta* v. *State of Rajasthan*,[155] and also by Bhaskaran and Balakrishna Menon, JJ. of Kerala High Court in the case reported as *Rajendran* v. *Home Secretary*.[156]

Furthermore, it is a common practice in writ petition cases that the petitioners should first made a demand on the appropriate Government for necessary relief. In the context of the Commissions of Inquiry Act, 1952, where the petitioners never demanded from the appropriate Government the appointment of an Inquiry Commission, it has been observed that the petition in such a case is liable to be dismissed on this short point as they could have no right to claim a writ of mandamus without making such a demand. Notwithstanding that, the petitioners have otherwise no *locus standi* whatsoever for demanding the appointment of a Commission of Inquiry under the Commissions of Inquiry Act, 1952.[157]

In *Dhronamraju Satyanarayana* v. *N.T. Rama Rao*,[158] it was held that the Court would not be justified in issuing a writ of mandamus directing the Central Government to appoint a judicial Commission under the Commissions of Inquiry Act, 1952 for enquiring into the misdeeds of "corruption and abuse of authority by the first respondent", in view of the clear provision of Section 3 which gives a discretion to the appropriate Government to appoint or not to appoint a Commission even

155. AIR 1980 Rajasthan 207.

156. AIR 1983 Kerala 59.

157. *Peoples Union for Democratic Rights* v. *Ministry of Home Affairs*, AIR 1985 Delhi 268.

158. AIR 1988 Andhra Pradesh 144 (FB).

when it is found that there was a definite matter of public interest to be gone into by a Commission. It was, however, further held that "it is the right and the duty of this Court to see that ends of justice should not be allowed to be frustrated, but this Court should exercise its discretion in moulding the relief in such manner as would meet the situation, particularly in view of the fact that the comprehensive provisions of Article 226 of the Constitution empower the High Court to issue orders "for any other purpose", apart from writs for the enforcement of any of the rights conferred by Part III. Accordingly, the Court recorded its prima facie findings with respect to the allegations discussed in the order and directed the petitioner to implead within four weeks of the date of the Court's order all the persons who were likely to be affected by the final orders to be passed in the proceedings.

However, a different view was taken by the Orissa High Court in *Janamohan Das* v. *State of Orissa*[159] when it was observed: "Section 3 of the Act has conferred the power to order for judicial inquiry when the need to inquire into any matter of public importance is felt. So, the question would be, if there be a definite matter of public importance, can judicial inquiry be refused? According to us, the discretion conferred by Section 3 of the Act cannot be said to 'unfettered' inasmuch as the Parliament did think that if a definite matter of public importance would be there, a judicial inquiry should be ordered, if a need for the same exists according to the appropriate Government. There is no dispute so far. We would further say that if any reasonable man reasonably instructed in law would have come to the conclusion that the need for judicial inquiry exists, the denial of the same by the Government could, in the facts of a case, be regarded by the Court as meant to serve an alien purpose." In this case, a liquor tragedy took place on 7 May 1992 in which 124 persons died according to official statement. On the very next day, the State Government directed the Revenue Divisional Commissioner, Central Division, Cuttack to hold an administrative inquiry. The Commissioner submitted his report

159. AIR 1993 Orissa 157.

on 12-7-1992. The case of the State was that in view of the report of the Commissioner, the recommendations contained in which had been accepted by the Government, no need for a judicial inquiry existed, as whatever the State Government thought necessary to be informed about the tragedy had been done by the Commissioner, and no new facts of public importance had come to light warranting judicial inquiry. The case of the petitioner, on the other hand, was that the terms of reference of the inquiry entrusted to the Revenue Divisional Commissioner would show that a vital matter of public importance was left out. That matter was involvement of "certain Ministers and persons with powers", as stated in paragraph 21(b) of O.J.C. No. 3676 of 1992. The legal submission was that it was to protect the aforesaid persons that a judicial inquiry regarding the above matter was not being held, by which the Government was protecting its own Ministers and hereby achieving a purpose totally 'alien' to the Act. To put it different, the refusal to hold judicial inquiry to know about the above was fraud on power, a species of mala fide. Accordingly, the Court examined whether a case of mala fide had been made out and whether non-exercise of power, if mala fide, would render it bad so much so that a Court could issue a writ of mandamus to exercise that power and held that the refusal of judicial inquiry in the case was to serve an 'alien purpose' (which party in power would normally like to get matters involving its members inquired into by a judicial body?). The Court, thus, held that "The law, therefore, permits us to order for a judicial inquiry, which we hereby do." On 4-12-1992, the State filed the applications praying for recalling the directions as aforesaid on the sole ground that this Court had no jurisdiction to do so. The Court, holding, inter alia, that direction to institute judicial inquiry could also be given under Article 226 of the Constitution, dismissed the applications.[160] In this regard, the Court observed: "Nonetheless, it may be stated here that ouster of this Court's power of issuing mandamus for the purpose at hand cannot at all be read in the language of Section 3 of the Act. The two

160. *State of Orissa* v. *Janamohan Das*, AIR 1993 Orissa 180.

powers visualized by Section 3(1) of the Act are not dependent on each other but are independent—the one does not control the other—this Court's direction had related to the discretionary power conferred on the State Government, which is akin to the discretionary power conferred by any other statute, relating to the exercise of which writ of mandamus can undoubtedly be issued on a case for the same having been made out. No ground exists for treating the power conferred by the first part of Section 3 on the Government, which is discretionary in nature, in any way different from discretionary powers conferred by so many statutes on Government."

It may, thus, be seen from the aforesaid cases the preponderence of the judicial opinion has been that no mandamus can be issued directing the appropriate Government to appoint a Commission of Inquiry under the Act even there exists a definite matter of public importance that can be gone into in such an inquiry. The power to appoint a Commission of Inquiry has been statutorily vested in the appropriate Government. The Act does not make it obligatory for the appropriate Government to appoint a Commission of Inquiry in all cases where there exists a definite matter of public importance. Instead, it has been left to the discretion of the appropriate Government to appoint or not to appoint a Commission of Inquiry. The reason for this is quite obvious. The appropriate Government for the information of its own mind appoints a Commission of Inquiry in order that it should act on the basis of the correct facts and in a fair and objective manner. In other words, a Commission of Inquiry is a fact-finding body meant only to instruct the mind of the Government. Where the appropriate Government does not feel the necessity of being so informed and is otherwise in a position to act on its own in the matter, the Act does not enjoin upon the Government to appoint a Commission of Inquiry even in such a case. The Act does not require the Government to necessarily go for a Commission of Inquiry wherever and whenever a definite matter of public importance exists. It is entirely upto the Government to decide as to whether it feels the necessity of an inquiry by a Commission into any definite matter of public importance before acting in respect thereto. The Act does not confer any right on any one to demand the appointment of a Commission of Inquiry as a matter of right. Nor does it impose any corresponding duty on the Government to appoint one except where a resolution is passed by the Parliament or, as the case may be, the State Legislature for the appointment of such a Commission.

Thus, we have seen that High Courts of Allahabad,[161] Andhra Pradesh,[162] Delhi,[163] Gujarat,[164] Kerala,[165] Madras,[166] and Rajasthan[167] have held that the Court does not have jurisdiction to direct the Government to appoint a Commission of Inquiry for it is a matter to be decided by the appropriate Government itself. However, Andhra Pradesh and Rajasthan High Courts have qualified this proposition. After holding that Section 3 gives a discretion to the Government to appoint or not to appoint a Commission even when it was found that there was a definite matter to be gone into by a Commision, the Andhra Pradesh High Court[168] went on to observe that the Court would not allow the ends of justice to be frustrated and in appropriate cases, the Court would exercise its discretion in moulding the relief in such a manner as would meet the situation. In this

161. *Maharshi Avadhesh* v. *State of U.P.*, AIR 1991 Allahabad 52.

162. *Dhronamraju Satyanarayana* v. *N.T. Rama Rao*, AIR 1988 Andhra Pradesh 144 (FB).

163. *Bhagwat Dayal Sharma* v. *Union of India*, ILR (1974) I Delhi 847; *Peoples Union for Democratic Rights* v. *Ministry of Home Affairs*, AIR 1985 Delhi 268: *Kiran Bedi* v. *Delhi Administration*, 1989 (2) Delhi Lawyer 190.

164. *Jan Sangharsh Manch* v. *State of Gujarat*, AIR 1998 Gujarat 133.

165. *Rajendran* v. *Home Secretary*, AIR 1983 Kerala 59.

166. *B. Jegnathan* v. *State of Tamil Nadu*, AIR 1990 Mad 69.

167. *Vijay Mehta* v. *State of Rajasthan*, AIR 1980 Rajasthan 207; *Sidda Raj Dhadda* v. *State of Rajasthan*, AIR 1990 Rajasthan 34.

168. *Dhronamraju Satyanarayana* v. *N.T. Rama Rao*, AIR 1988 Andhra Pradesh 144 (FB). After recording its prima facie findings on the allegations, the Court directed the petitioner to implead all the persons who might be affected by the final orders passed in the case. However, it could not be gathered as to what final order was passed and how the Court ultimately moulded the final relief.

regard, the Court referred to the powers conferred under Article 226 to issue orders 'for any other purpose' apart from writs for the enforcement of fundamental or other legal rights. While declining the prayer that the Court should set up a Commission of Inquiry under the Act, the Rajasthan High Court[169] observed that it has power to appoint commissioner(s) and investigator(s) to make inquiries, collect data and submit report(s) to the Court suggesting remedial measures whereupon the Court might issue such directions to the Government as it deemed proper in public interest. However, the fact remains that both the High Courts affirmed that the appropriate Government couldn't be directed by the Court to appoint a Commission of Inquiry under the Act.

The only High Court that has taken a different view is the Orissa High Court[170] and issued order for judicial inquiry under the Act. On appeal,[171] the High Court declined to recall its order, holding that Section 3 did not oust the power under Article 226 to issue mandamus and the discretionary power conferred under Section 3 was in no way different from any other discretionary powers conferred under other statutes. The Orissa High Court's decision may be open to question as laying down correct law on the subject. The reasons for this are not far to seek. First, the power to appoint a Commission of Inquiry vests in the appropriate Government and the same cannot be exercised by the Court itself. Secondly, where the discretionary power under Section 3 is vitiated on any count, the Court can at best direct the Government to reconsider the matter in the light of the observations, if any, made by the Court. However, it will not be open to the Court to direct the Government to exercise its power in any particular matter or, for that matter, directing the Government to appoint a Commission of Inquiry notwithstanding whether the Government is of the opinion to appoint such a Commission or not. And, lastly, the Act does not

---

169. *Sidda Raj Dahadda* v. *State of Rajasthan*, AIR 1990 Rajasthan 34. However, no such directions that might have been given could be ascertained.

170. *Janamohan Das* v. *State of Orissa*, AIR 1993 Orissa 157.

171. *State of Orissa* v. *Janamohan Das*, AIR 1993 Orissa 180.

contemplate appointment of a Commission of Inquiry in all cases where exists a definite matter of public importance. The scheme of the Act is of enabling character and empowers the Government to appoint a Commission of Inquiry to inquire into any definite matter of public importance if that Government so desires. If the Government does not feel the necessity for such a Commisson, there is nothing in the Act that makes it obligatory for the Government to go in for such a Commission of Inquiry even in such a case.

To sum up, no direction can be given by the Court to the Government, whether Central or State, to appoint a Commission of Inquiry under the Act. In appropriate cases, the Court can at best direct the Governement to reconsider its decision in the matter, having regard to the observations that may have been made by the Court while disposing of the matter.

However, the cases of a judicial direction for appointment of a Commission of Inquiry as aforesaid should be distinguished from cases where the appropriate Government has decided to appoint a Commission of Inquiry to inquire into any definite matter of public importance but whose terms of reference or findings contained in its report, as the case may be, are found to be bad in law. The case of *Nair Service Society* v. *State of Kerala*[171a] should be noted in this regard wherein the Supreme Court not only set aside the report of the Narendran Commission but also directed the State to appoint a fresh Commission to go into all the aspects of the matter and submit its report thereon. In this case, interpretation of the Supreme Court's judgment as regard identification of 'creamy layer' amongst the Backward classes and their exclusion from the purview of reservation, vis-a-vis, the report of Justice K.K. Narendran Commission and acceptance thereof by the State of Kerala in issuing the impugned notification dated 2-5-2000 came up for consideration before the Supreme Court in the writ petition filed by Nair Service Society. The petitioner, inter alia, contended that in accepting the said report, the State violated the underlying principles

171a. (2007) 4 SCC 193.

contained in the judgments of *Indira Sawhney I*[171b] and *II*[171c] as also in *Ashoka Kumar Thakur*[171d] case. The respondent State, on the other hand, questioned the *locus standi* of the petitioner society on the ground that it represented forward classes and was not concerned with the correctness or otherwise of the Report of Narendran Commission. The Supreme Court held that it was not possible to dismiss the writ petition summarily on the ground of lack of *locus standi* on the part of the petitioner, especially when the question of such grave importance had been brought to the notice of the Supreme Court, having regard to the principle underlying the purport and object for which the "creamy layer" was sought to be excluded. In such a case, the Supreme Court could not shut its eyes and refuse to determine the question. The Supreme Court observed: "In terms of Article 141 of the Constitution of India, the declaration of law made by this Court is binding on all courts; a *fortiori* such directions would also be binding on all authorities. Article 142 empowers this Court to pass such order as is necessary to do complete justice to any cause or matter pending before it and Article 144 enjoins all authorities, civil and criminal, to act in aid of the Supreme Court." The Supreme Court further observed that, "in view of the decision of this Court in *Ram Krishna Dalmia* v. *Justice S.R. Tendulkar*[171e] it is no longer *res integra* that the terms of reference while appointing a commission may be subject to judicial review." The Supreme Court noted how Narendran Commission sat in appeal over the Joseph Committee Report despite the fact that the same had been accepted in toto by the Supreme Court. While placing on record its displeasure as to the manner in which Joseph Committee Report received severe criticism by the Narendran Commission, most of which were, in the opinion of the Supreme Court, wholly unwarranted, the Supreme Court observed that the tests adopted by Joseph Committee could not have been given a complete go-by the

---

171b. *Indira Sawhney* v. *Union of India* (1992) Supp. 3 SCC 217.

171c. *Indira Sawhney* v. *Union of India* (2000) 1 SCC 168.

171d. *Ashoka Kumar Thakur* v. *State of Bihar* (1995) 5 SCC 403.

171e. AIR 1958 SC 538.

Narendran Commission. The Apex Court further opined that the findings of a Commission in respect of a matter of such grave significance and importance should have been based on scientific data as also evidence of experts. There was no reason as to why a successor committee, without any just and cogent reasons, ignored the recommendations of the former committee. Accordingly, while setting aside the report of the Narendran Commission, the Supreme Court directed the State to appoint a fresh commission which should go into all the aspects of the matter and submit its report. Thus, it may be seen where the terms of reference of a commission or, as the case may be, the findings contained in the report of that Commission are violative of well established principles of law, the same would not receive the approval of the Court. The Court of competent jurisdiction will be well within its powers to issue appropriate directions in such a case. Furthermore, where the court itself appoints a commission as has been done by the Supreme Court in the case of *NOIDA Entrepreneurs Association* v. *NOIDA* and others;[171f] such a commission will not be treated as the one under the Act but it will be more in the nature of any fact finding body appointed de hors the Act.

Change of Opinion of Appropriate Government

The appropriate Government can change its subjective opinion to appoint a Commission of Inquiry because it was not necessary to do so at a particular point of time even when definite matters of public importance were in existence. But by changing its opinion, the Government cannot change an indefinite matter or matter of no importance into a 'definite' matter of public importance where in fact such a matter did not exist. If the opinion was changed in subsequent acquisition of such materials, which could be regarded as definite matters of public importance, then those new facts must be disclosed.[172] The appropriate Government is not barred by the principle of estoppel or *res judicata*. It is open to the Government to re-examine the

171f. 2005 (1) SCALE 621.

172. *P.V. Jagannath Rao* v. *State of Orissa*, AIR 1969 SC 215; *Orient Paper Mills* v. *Union of India*, AIR 1979 Calcutta 114.

matter from time to time and arrive at different conclusions if materials are found.[173]

There is, thus, no bar in Section 3(1) of the Act for changing opinion. But in any case the conditions precedent for appointing a Commission in terms of that Section must be satisfied.

Constitutionality of the Section

The constitutionality of Section 3(1) of the Act came up for consideration before Gauhati High Court in the case of *Manabendra Sarkar* v. *State of Assam and Others*.[174] Assailing the vires of the Section, the counsel of the petitioner, inter alia, contended that Section 3(1) of the Act was discriminatory and, as such, should be struck down as violative of Article 14 of the Constitution. It was submitted by the learned counsel for the petitioner that "if a resolution is passed by the House of People or by the State Legislative Assembly, the matters are discussed on the floor of the House by the representatives of the people and the State Government is obliged to appoint a Commission in pursuance of the resolution passed by the Legislature after appropriate discussion; but, on the other hand, Section 3(1) confers an arbitrary and uncanalised power on the State Government to appoint or not to appoint a Commission 'if it is of opinion that it is necessary so to do'". The power conferred on the State Government without any guidance whatsoever, is violative of Article 14 of the Constitution. These contentions, however, did not find favour with the Court for the following reasons, namely: "We do not see any objection to the Government having the discretion to appoint a Commission after taking into consideration circumstances as to its necessity for inquiring into definite matters of public importance. While a resolution of the House is binding on the Government, when Government's view will also be known and the elected members of the Legislature will have opportunity to take part in the discussion for a claim to a Commission of Inquiry with regard to definite matters of

---

173. *Dr. Harekrushna Mahtab* v. *The Chief Minister of Orissa*, AIR 1971 Orissa 175.

174. AIR 1974 Gauhati 46.

public importance, a further consideration by the Government after a resolution has been passed by the Legislature is absolutely unnecessary. The pattern of the Parliamentary Government, which is envisaged under the Constitution where no resolution could be passed by the Assembly against the wishes of the Government enjoying the confidence of the majority of the members of the Legislature, there is no purpose or relevance to having a further consideration by the Government of matters with regard to the necessity for appointing a Commission of Inquiry under the Act. While this is the legal position under Section 3(1) with regard to the exercise of powers by the Government in pursuance of the resolution of the Legislature, the same would not be the position obviously when the Government has to exercise its own discretion in appointing a Commission of Inquiry under the first part of Section 3(1). Merely because in one case the Government is obliged to appoint a Commission and in the other case the Government has the discretion to appoint or not to appoint a Commission, it does not make the section invalid under Article 14 of the Constitution. This is particularly so because there is sufficient guidance in Section 3(1) itself to enable Government in exercising power to appoint a Commission on its own initiative. The fact that only definite matters of public importance can be assigned for the purpose of inquiry under Section 3(1) clearly gives sufficient guidance in the matter. Whether the matters, which are referred to, are definite matters of public importance may in appropriate cases, be subject to judicial scrutiny. But that does not make Section 3(1) void under Article 14 of the Constitution. The opinion that the appropriate Government has to form is, no doubt, a subjective opinion on materials available to Government and that opinion is not subject to judicial scrutiny. But the necessity to appoint a Commission must be clear from the notification, as is clear from the words used in Section 3(1), viz. 'if it is of opinion that it is necessary so to do', and further the matters which are assigned to the Commission of Inquiry must be matters of definite public importance. We are, therefore, unable to accede to the submission that because there are two modes of appointing a Commission, namely, one when the

Government is of opinion that it is necessary to appoint the same, and secondly when there is a resolution of the Legislature to that effect, Section 3(1) of the Act is violative of Article 14 of the Constitution.[175]

Commission of Inquiry—Its Nature

An inquiry under the Act is not a judicial inquiry and the object of constituting a Commission of Inquiry under the Act is to enable the Government to make up its mind as to what legislative or administrative measures should be adopted to eradicate the evil found or to implement the beneficial objects it has in view. It is merely a fact-finding body for the benefit of the Government and that is why even where there may be a definite matter of public importance, a Commission of Inquiry is appointed under the Act only if it is necessary in the opinion of the appropriate Government to do so. Except in the case of a resolution by Parliament or the Legislature of a State in that behalf, there is no statutory or other obligation upon the appropriate Government to appoint a Commission of Inquiry and therefore, on the words of Section 3 of the Act there cannot be a legal or statutory obligation upon the appropriate Government to appoint a Commission of Inquiry even if there is a definite matter of public importance. No one has, thus, a legal or statutory right to compel the appointment of a Commission of Inquiry whenever there is a definite matter of public importance.[176]

A Commission of Inquiry is obviously appointed by the appropriate Government "for the information of its own mind", in order that it should not act, in exercise of its executive power, "otherwise than in accordance with the dictates of justice and equity". It is, therefore, a fact-finding body meant only to instruct the mind of the Government without producing any document of a judicial nature.[177] The only power that a Commission of Inquiry has is to inquire and make a report and

175. AIR 1974 Gauhati 46, p. 48.

176. *Bhagwat Dayal Sharma* v. *Union of India*, ILR (1974) I Delhi 847.

177. *M.V. Rajwade* v *Dr. S.M. Hassan*, AIR 1954 Nagpur 71, p. 76.

embody therein its recommendations. The Commission has no power of adjudication in the sense of passing an order, which can be enforced *proprio vigore*. A clear distinction must be drawn between a decision, which, by itself, has no force and penal effect, and a decision which becomes enforceable immediately or which may become enforceable by some action being taken. Therefore, as the Commission is merely to investigate and record its findings and recommendations without having any power to enforce them, the inquiry or report cannot be looked upon as a judicial inquiry in the sense of its being an exercise of judicial function properly so called.[178]

In view of the fact that the appointment of a Commission is made primarily for the purpose of information of the Government and the Commission does not adjudicate on any of the matter, the report as may be submitted by the Commission of Inquiry will not amount to giving any declaration in respect of the right and title of the parties.[178a]

Where a Commission of Inquiry was appointed under the Act of 1952 to enquire into a claim, it was held that the Commission of Inquiry had no judicial powers and it was appointed only to inquire, investigate, record its findings and make its recommendations. Its recommendations might be taken into consideration by the Government in arriving at decision but said decision of Government (a party to MOU containing arbitration clause), was not binding on the applicant, seeking appointment of an arbitrator, under the said MOU and the applicant was entitled to seek resolution of dispute regarding their claim of non-payment of their dues.[178b]

The Commission is a fact-finding body meant only 'to instruct the mind of the Government without producing any documents of a judicial nature'. It is neither a Civil Court nor

178. *Ram Krishna Dalmia* v. *Justice S.R. Tendolkar*, AIR 1958 SC 538, p. 546.

178a. *T. Chitra* v. *The Chief Secretary to Government, Government of Tamil Nadu and Another* (2008) 1 MLJ 422 : MANU/TN/9409/2007.

178b. *M/s B.H.C. Agro Pvt. Ltd.* v. *Director of Horticulture, Govt. of A.P. & Another*, AIR 2008 (NOC) 23 (A.P.).

its proceedings are judicial nor do the provisions of the Code of Civil Procedure or of the Evidence Act apply to its proceedings. The Commission is neither a quasi-judicial Tribunal nor does it exercise powers of such a Tribunal nor are its proceedings quasi-judicial.[179] If it is a fact-finding body it is difficult to envisage that the Legislature intended giving it the character of a judicial body or Tribunal exercising judicial functions.[180] In this case, the petitioner sought the removal of the Solicitor and the Secretary attached to the Commission on the grounds of being biased and interested. However, as the proceedings before the Commission are not of judicial or quasi-judicial in nature, the Court held, even if there is any bias or interest so far as the Solicitor and the Secretary attached to the Commission are concerned, they are not disqualified from being associated with the Commission.[181]

The Commission constituted under Section 3 of the Act is not a Court except for a limited purpose. The procedure of the Commission is inquisitorial rather than accusatorial.[182] In such an inquiry, there is no accuser, no accused and no specific charges for trial. Nor is the Government required to pronounce one way or other on the findings of the Commission. The Commission is appointed by the Government for getting information for its own mind so that it may not act in its sovereign character otherwise than in accordance with law and the dictates of justice and enquiry.[183] The Commission is, thus, only a fact-finding body meant only to instruct the mind of the Government without producing any document of a judicial nature.[184]

---

179. *M/s. Allen Berry and Co. Private Ltd. and Another* v. *Vivian Bose and Others*, AIR 1960 Punjab 86, p. 94.
180. *Ibid.*, p. 91
181. *Ibid.*, p. 95.
182. *Kehar Singh* v. *State*, (1988) 3 SCC 609, para 237.
183. In re., *Maharaja Madhav Singh*, ILR 32 Calcutta 1 (PC).
184. *M.V. Rajwade* v. *S.M. Hassan*, AIR 1954 Nagpur 71; *Mohammed Haneefa* v. *State of Kerala*, 1988 (2) KLT 919.

The inquiry cannot be looked upon as a judicial inquiry and the order ultimately passed cannot be enforced *proprio vigore*. The inquiry and the investigation by the Commission do not amount to usurpation of the functions of the Courts of law. The scope of the trial by the Courts of law and the Commission of Inquiry is altogether different. In any case, it cannot be said that the Commission of Inquiry would be liable for contempt of Court if it proceeds to enquire into matters referred to it by the Government Notification. In appointing a Commission of Inquiry under Section 3 of the Act the Government is exercising a statutory power and in making the inquiry contemplated by the notification, the Commission is performing its statutory duty. It is, therefore, not possible to accept the argument that the setting up of the Commission of Inquiry by the State Government or the continuance of the inquiry by the Commission so constituted would be tantamount to contempt of Court. To constitute contempt of Court, there must be involved some "act done or writing published calculated to bring a Court or a judge of the Court into contempt or to lower his authority" or something "calculated to obstruct or interfere with the due course of justice or the lawful process of the Courts".[185] Where the Government and the Commission have done nothing to obstruct or interfere with the lawful powers of the Court by acting bona fide and discharging statutory functions under the Commissions of Inquiry Act, there is no justification for holding that the issue of the notification under Section 3 of the Act or the conduct of the inquiry amount to contempt of Court.[186]

It is not necessary to stress that the inquiry, which the Commission is going to hold, is not an inquiry by a civil or a criminal Court and the proceedings thereof are not judicial proceedings of a Court of law.[187] The decisions on the subject

---

185. *Reg* v. *Gray* (1900) 2 Q B 31; *Arthur Reginald Perera* v. *The King*, 1951 AC 482.

186. *P.V. Jagannath Rao* v. *State of Orissa*, AIR 1969 SC 215, pp. 226-27.

187. *Chimansingh* v. *State*, AIR 1951 Madhya Pradesh 44; *M.V. Rajwade* v. *Dr S.M. Hassan*, AIR 1954 Nagpur 71: ILR 1954 Nagpur 1: 1954 NLJ 245 and *Ram Krishna Dalmia* v. *Justice S.R. Tendolkar*, AIR 1958 SC 538, p. 514.

point out what is "Court" and what are judicial proceedings of a Court of law. Judged by the tests laid down, in those decisions, there can be no doubt that the inquiry, which the Commission is going to hold, is not a judicial proceeding of a Court of law. The Commission has not been asked to give a decision as to the respective rights and liabilities of any person or to punish any wrong. In an inquiry of this nature, there is no issue between parties for the Commission to decide and no defendant or an accused person to be tried. There is no 'lis'. As Lord Shawross has said in the case of the analogous Tribunal in England, "the procedure of the Tribunal is inquisitional rather than accusatorial".[188] The Commission has been appointed to find the facts relating to the matters it has to enquire into. In ascertaining those facts, and having ascertained them in making a report on the basis of those facts, the Commission is no doubt obliged to proceed judicially and not arbitrarily and to bring to bear judicial mind, i.e. a mind to determine what is fair and just in accordance with law in respect of the matters under consideration. It is in this sense of a standard of conduct and freedom from bias or interest that the inquiry is judicial. The inquiry is not judicial in the sense of an inquiry done by a person in the exercise of his duties as a Judge of a Court.[189]

However, the proceedings before a Commission of Inquiry have been held to be quasi-judicial by a Division Bench of Delhi High Court.[190]

But a different view has been expressed by Andhra Pradesh High Court in *Mohd. Ibrahim Khan* v. *Susheel Kumar*.[191] In this case, the Court observed that "the Commission is purely a fact finding body and it performs no judicial or quasi-judicial

---

188. *Cases and Materials on Administrative Law in India* (Vol. 1), published by the Indian Law Institute, New Delhi.

189. *Puhupram* v. *State of Madhya Pradesh*, 1968 MPLJ 629, pp. 632-33.

190. *P.R. Nayak* v. *Union of India*, ILR (1973) I Delhi 747 at 774. An earlier decision of a Division Bench (Tatachari and Aggarwal, JJ) of Delhi High Court in Civil Writ No. 522 of 1972 decided on 10th October, 1972 was relied on.

191. AIR 1983 Andhra Pradesh 69.

functions. There is no lis to be decided. The decision does not prejudicially affect rights. Therefore, the use of the accolade judicial or quasi-judicial to such inquiries is inappropriate". The Court further observed: "It is true that the only power of the Commission is to enquire and make a report and embody therein its recommendations. The Commission has no power of adjudication of any questions of title or dispute and pass a decree which can be enforced *proprio vigore*. There is no charge as such against any person; nor is there any accused or accusor. There is neither a plaintiff nor a defendant. There are no pleadings raising issues to be tried. No one is punished. No serious disability or disqualification is incurred by the findings. The enquiry made by the Commission differs from a criminal trial. The Commission is only a machinery set up to enquire into a definite matter of public importance and to make a report so as to enable the Government to take such action as the Government may deem fit. Therefore, there is no definite judgment in the enquiry, nor is there any usurpation of judicial functions."

The Court further observed: "The question whether a person prejudicially affected gets a right to cross-examine the witnesses who have not been summoned and who have given affidavit in evidence, did not arise. Quasi-judicial decision equally pre-supposes as a true judicial decision the existence of a dispute between two or more parties. It involves: (i) presentation of their cases by the parties; (ii) the ascertainment of any disputed facts by the evidence adduced by the parties; (iii) submission of arguments; and (iv) a declaration of the liabilities of the parties. In an inquiry before the Commission, there is neither a dispute nor a decision, which prejudicially affects any right. There is an investigation and a mere report of the facts ascertained. There is no decision. Therefore, use of the accolade judicial or quasi-judicial to inquiries before a Commission of Inquiry appointed under the Commissions of Inquiry Act is inappropriate. The Commission is not an adjudicating body, but an assisting body that assesses the facts and assists the Government in the arrival at an appropriate decision."

Reference in this regard may be made to the case of *Arun Shridhar Bondale* v. *Government of A.P.*,[192] wherein a retired

192. 1992 (1) Andh LT 654.

learned Judge of Andhra Pradesh High Court was appointed as One Man Commission to find out the circumstances leading to the accident resulting in sinking of the Buddha statue and other equipments and also loss of life in Hussain Sagar Lake on March 10, 1990. In the course of the enquiry, the petitioner filed an application to cross-examine the Engineer-in-Chief. While rejecting that application, the Commission made some observations orally. Alleging mala fide and bias against the Commission on the ground that the Commission commented in open Court hall of the Commission about the competency of the counsel for the petitioner and threatened that he would impose costs of Rupees ten thousand if the counsel insisted on recalling the witness for cross-examination, the petitioner filed the writ petition in the High Court. The Division Bench, which dealt with the case, inter alia, observed that the doctrine of bias applied only to judicial and quasi-judicial bodies and as the Commission of Inquiry did not answer the description of either, the doctrine had no application.

Yet another different view was taken by the Andhra Pradesh High Court in *K. Vijaya Bhaskar Reddy* v. *Government of Andhra Pradesh*[193] wherein it was observed that "having regard to the nature of rights—conduct and reputation of a person—which are likely to be prejudicially affected by the enquiry and the safeguards provided to such persons by the Parliament under Sections 8B and 8C to protect those rights by affording an opportunity of hearing and conferring right to cross-examine the witness, we are of the view that while conducting enquiry on those aspects the Commission of Inquiry will be discharging a quasi-judicial function."

In *Sheikh Ghulam Rasul* v. *State of Jammu and Kashmir*,[194] the petitioner prayed for a writ of certiorari quashing the order of the Commission and further restraining the Commission from proceeding against the petitioner under Section 3(d) of the J&K Government Servants' Prevention of Corruption

193. AIR 1996 Andhra Pradesh 62.

194. AIR 1965 J&K 78.

(Commission) Act, 1962 on the ground, inter alia, that it violated Article 20(1) of the Constitution of India for the amendment in the said Act in 1964 put in other penalties which were not existing in the previous Act and that amendment was not retrospective. Negating the said contention, the Court observed, "Article 20 in its first part talks of convictions and offences. The Commission has no power of convicting a person. It is an advisory or a recommendatory body which after inquiring into certain matters can at the most make a recommendation to the Sadar-I-Riyasat for the prosecution of a certain person.... Article 20(1) dealt with what is known in legal language as the doctrine of ex post facto law. What this Article prohibits is the conviction of a person except for the violation of a law which was in force when the alleged act was committed. It does not at all affect the procedure of determining an offence which may be different after Constitution came into existence from what it was before the Constitution. As already stated, the Commission has no power to convict anybody; at best under Section 17(3) it can recommend that a person may be prosecuted for an offence in a court of law. Therefore, Art 20(1) has no application to the findings of the Commission."

In *Dhirendra Brahmachari* v. *Union of India*,[195] the petitioner invoked the provision of the Constitution by declining to take oath and give testimony when called upon to do so before a Commission appointed under the Commissions of Inquiry Act, 1952. The Commission being of the view that the said action of the petitioner constituted an offence under Sections 178 and 179 of the Penal Code directed the lodging of a complaint against the petitioner. The petitioner claimed that the lodging of the complaint was illegal and without jurisdiction inasmuch as the alleged refusal of the petitioner was in furtherance of the right guaranteed under Article 20(3) of the Constitution and so could not constitute an offence. Having regard to the nature of proceedings of the Commission of Inquiry, especially that there is no accused; the Court dismissed the claim for the applicability of Article 20(3) of the Constitution to the proceedings before

195. AIR 1979 NOC 91 (Delhi).

the Commission. Accordingly, it is well settled that in proceedings of Commissions under the Act there is no accuser, and no specific charges for trial before the Commission. The Commission under the Act is merely a fact-finding body meant to instruct the mind of the appropriate Government. The report and proceedings of the Commission are not documents of a judicial nature. A Commission should not deal with a matter if a civil or criminal Court is already seized of it. But this rule would not be attracted where there is only a possibility of prosecution. Merely because there was a possibility of the petitioner being prosecuted for an alleged offence in connection with unlawful import of an aircraft or alleged avoidance of payment of customs duty, it could not be said that in the larger context of subversion of established procedure the Commission was not empowered to go into the matter referred to it by the notification appointing it.

The Court further observed that two conditions must be satisfied before invoking aid of Clause (3) of Article 20 of the Constitution. First, the proceedings must be in the nature of criminal proceedings before a Court of law or a judicial Tribunal. Second, the person invoking Article 20(3) must be an accused. The observations in the proceedings of the Commission either by the Commission or by a counsel cannot be regarded as formal accusation or an accusation so as to attract Article 20(3). Evidence may have been placed before the Commission of what may constitute offence but the scope of the inquiry was not akin to criminal trial or even police investigation under Section 161 of the Cr.P.C. The issuance of notice or summons or the phraseology thereof would not make the petitioner an "accused" or the proceedings in regard to him a "prosecution". Clearly, therefore, the petitioner could not invoke Article 20(3).

Commission of Inquiry—Purpose and Scope

The purpose and the object of ordering an enquiry under the Commissions of Inquiry Act, 1952 is to preserve the purity and integrity of public administration. Section 3 of the Act effectuates this purpose.[196] This section empowers the appropriate

---

196. *P.K. Kunju* v. *State of Kerala*, AIR 1970 Kerala 252.

Government, in certain circumstances therein mentioned, to appoint a Commission of Inquiry for the purpose of making an inquiry into any definite matter of public importance and performing such functions within such time as may be specified in the notification. The section indicates that the appropriate Government can appoint a Commission of Inquiry only for the purpose of making an inquiry into any definite matter of public importance and into no other matter. In other words, the subject matter of inquiry can only be a definite matter of public importance. The appropriate Government, it follows, is not authorized by this section to appoint a Commission for the purpose of holding an inquiry into any other matter. Accordingly, on a proper construction of this section, the functions the performance of which is contemplated must be such as are ancillary to and in aid of the inquiry itself and cannot be read as a function independent of or unconnected with such inquiry.[197]

The question whether the Notification must state the purpose for which enquiry is to be made in order to be valid, was raised before the Supreme Court in *P.V. Jagannath Rao* v *State of Orissa*[198] but was not answered as no such omission was found in fact. In this case, an argument was put forth on behalf of the appellants that the appointment of the Commission was not valid, as the notification did not state the purpose for which the enquiry was to be made. To put it differently, the argument of the appellants was that the Notification was not related to any future Government action or legislative policy and hence the notification was bad. The contention in fact was that an enquiry for mere collection of facts unrelated to any future course of Government action did not fall within the purview of Section 3 of the Act and it was not a valid exercise of statutory power to appoint such a Commission. This contention did not find favour with the Court as it found that the purpose of the enquiry was stated in the Preamble to the Notification, which stated that "the matters aforesaid regarding the aforesaid persons should be enquired into through a Commission of Inquiry so

197. *Ram Krishna Dalmia* v. *Justice S.R. Tendolkar*, AIR 1956 SC 538, p. 549.
198. AIR 1969 SC 215.

that facts may be found which alone will facilitate rectification and prevention of recurrence of such lapses and securing the ends of justice and establishing a moral public order in future." In other words, the object of the enquiry to be made by the Commission appointed under Section 3 of the Act was to take appropriate legislative or administrative measures to maintain the purity and integrity of political administration in the State. It was accordingly held that the appointment of the Commission of Inquiry in the present case was in valid exercise of the statutory power by the State Government under Section 3 of the Act.

In *Dr. Harekrushna Mahtab* v. *The Chief Minister of Orissa and Others*,[199] it was, inter alia, contended that once the State Government had arrived at a conclusion that there was no prima facie case for appointing a Commission of Inquiry, it had no further jurisdiction to re-examine that conclusion and appoint any person to hold further inquiry, whether preliminary or otherwise. In this case, on 27-6-1967, a memorial was submitted to the President by certain Ms.LA. and Ms.P. alleging corruption and impropriety against certain former Chief Ministers, Deputy Chief Ministers and Ministers including the petitioner and praying for the appointment of a Commission of Inquiry. This memorial was sent by the then Home Minister to the then Chief Minister of the State for such action as the latter deemed proper. The Chief Minister wrote back to the then Home Minister saying that on examination of the records available with the State Government, no prima facie case was made out against anyone. He, however, said that if the Home Minister of India desired, he might get the matter examined by a sitting Judge of a High Court or the Supreme Court of India, the Home Minister replied that it would not be possible to ask any sitting Judge to do the job and the matter might be examined by the Chief Minister through a retired High Court or Supreme Court Judge. Sri Mudholkar (Opposite Party No. 3), a retired Judge of the Supreme Court, agreed to examine the matter. Accordingly, he was appointed on 3-5-1968 to conduct the inquiry as per the notification dated 3-5-1968, which, inter alia, provided that

199. AIR 1971 Orissa 175.

"On preliminary verification you are requested to report as to whether any prima facie case against any such person as aforesaid exists, and in case any prima facie case is found with respect to any of the allegations, you are also requested to report as to whether in public interest as at present a Commission of Inquiry should be established in order to have a full and complete enquiry in the said matters." Shri Mudholkar submitted his report on 29-9-1968, whose recommendations are sought to be quashed by the issue of a writ of certiorari on number of grounds, including the lack of State Government's jurisdiction to re-examine and change its opinion on the appointment of a Commission of Inquiry. The Court found no substance in this contention and observed: "The State Government is not barred by principles of estoppel or *res judicata*. The satisfaction reached by the State Government that there was no prima facie case for appointment of a Commission of Inquiry was entirely subjective and was a purely administrative decision. It is open to the State Government to re-examine the same conclusion from time to time and arrive at a different conclusion if materials are found. When there was a memorial to the President that there was a prima facie case for appointment of a Commission of Inquiry, the State Government acted very fairly in getting the matter examined by a High Judicial authority to determine whether a case for a further probe can be made out."

The question to be considered in each case would be whether the purpose of the inquiry is to take appropriate legislative and administrative measures to maintain purity and integrity of political administration and if the Commission is set up by a desire to set up and maintain high standards of moral conduct in the political administration, and not the "character assassination" of the leaders of the ex-ruling party, the appointment of a Commission is not ultra vires or mala fides.[200]

Suitability of Inquiry

Commissions of Inquiry are more suited for inquiring into such matters of public importance where the purpose is to find

200. *Brijpal Dass* v. *Justice Shri B.P. Beri*, 1981 ILR 31 Rajasthan 361, p. 380.

out the truth so as to learn lessons for the future and devise policies or frame legislation to avoid recurrence of lapses. Such Commissions do not suitably serve the object of punishing the guilty. In the facts and circumstances of the case of *Sanjiv Kumar* v. *State of Haryana*,[201] and looking at the nature of the allegations[202] made and the mighty people were alleged to be involved, the Apex Court opined that the better of option of the two was to entrust the matter to investigation by the Central Bureau of Investigation (CBI). While doing so, the Hon'ble Supreme Court, inter alia, observed: "We have given our thoughtful consideration to the respondents' proposal for entrusting the whole matter to a Commission of Inquiry, assisted by a special investigating task force. The flaw with Commissions of Inquiry, as revealed by experience, is that they do not have enough teeth and for their functioning they have to depend on the State's assistance. Commissions of Inquiry remain pending for unreasonable length of time. The reports submitted do not bind the State and in spite of transparency and public hearings which the Commissions often hold, at times with fanfare, the reports hardly serve any purpose. By the time the reports are submitted the public memory has already fainted and people are not any more bothered about the results. It is in the discretion of the State to take or not to take any action on the report submitted by the Commission of Inquiry and the experience is that the follow-up action depends more on political considerations rather than for public good."

An inquiry by the Public Accounts Committee in its very nature cannot be as thorough as an inquiry by Commission. Similarly, the inquiry by the Cabinet Sub-Committee is doubtless

201. (2005) 5 SCC 517.

202. The allegations referred to the rampant corruption in the corridors of politics and bureaucracy whereby unemployed persons belonging to the lower strata of society were granted jobs by adopting questionable means and with hidden consideration and underhand dealings instead of merits and equal opportunity to all, in respect of which directions for investigation were sought and also protection for the petitioner and his family members.

of a limited nature.[203] The appropriate authority has, therefore, to take its decision based on the object and the nature of inquiry and other relevant considerations and decide upon the kind of inquiry, and the authority by whom, to be made in any given matter.

Effect of Commission's Findings—Not Binding on Government

The Supreme Court had, on two occasions, pointed out that a Commission of Inquiry appointed under the Commissions of Inquiry Act was for fact-finding purposes and that the reports of the Commission had no force *proprio vigore*.[204] In *Manohar Lal* v. *Union of India*,[205] the petitioner, inter alia, prayed for issue of a suitable writ, or order, or direction be issued to implement the State Commission (called Punjab Boundary Commission) Report *in toto* and that certain areas mentioned in the petition be declared as included in the territories of the Haryana State in terms of the said report. Thus, Chandigarh Capital Project as also Lalroo, Derabassi, Pathankot and areas of Fazilka and Malaut were sought to be declared as included in the territories of the Haryana State. In view of the Supreme Court's judgments in *State of Jammu and Kashmir* v. *Bakshi Gulam Mohammad*[206] and *P.V. Jagannath Rao* v. *State of Orissa*,[207] and especially having regard to the fact that the Commission's report could have no force *proprio vigore*, to use the expression adopted by the Supreme Court in both these judgments, no merit was found in the petition and the same was dismissed accordingly. The Court observed that the Commission was asked to recommend adjustment of the existing boundary of the Hindi and Punjabi regions of the present State to secure linguistic homogeneity; and to indicate boundaries of the hill areas was of the present State which was contiguous to Himachal

---

203. *P.V. Jagannath Rao* v. *State of Orissa* (1968) 34 Cut LT 666, p. 721.

204. *State of Jammu and Kashmir* v. *Bakshi Gulam Mohammad*, AIR 1967 SC 122; *P.V. Jagannath Rao* v. *State of Orissa*, AIR 1969 SC 215.

205. AIR 1970 Delhi 178.

206. AIR 1967 SC 122.

207. AIR 1969 SC 215.

Pradesh and had cultural and linguistic affinities. It is, thus, clear that the Commission was only asked to make recommendations, which were made by the Commission. The Commission report, therefore, could have no force *proprio vigore*, to use the expression adopted by the Supreme Court in both the above said decisions.[208] Thus, the report of a Commission of Inquiry appointed under the Act is not binding on the Government appointing it and it is open to that Government not to take any action on, or pursuant to, such a report.

It is, thus, seen that the report and findings of the Commission of Inquiry are meant for information of the Government. Acceptance of the report of the Commission by the Government would only suggest that being bound by the Rule of law and having duty to act fairly, it has endorsed to act upon it. The duty of the police-investigating agency of the State—is to act in accordance with the law of the land. This is best described by the learned law Lord—Lord Denning—in *R. v. Metropolitan Police Commissioner*,[209] observed as follows:

> I hold it to be the duty of the Commissioner of Police, as it is of every chief constable, to enforce the law of the land. He must take steps so to post his men that crimes may be detected; and that honest citizens may go about their affairs in peace. He must decide whether or not suspected persons are to be prosecuted; and, it need be, bring the prosecution or see that it is brought; but in all these things he is not the servant of anyone, save of the law itself.

Acting, thus, the investigating agency may with advantage make use of the report of the Commission in its onerous task of investigation bearing in mind that it does not preclude the investigating agency from forming a different opinion under Section 169/170 of Cr.P.C. if the evidence obtained by it supports such a conclusion. The Courts, civil or criminal, are not bound by the report or findings of the Commission of Inquiry, as they have to arrive at their own decision on the evidence placed

208. AIR 1969 SC 181.

209. (1968) 1 All ER 763, p. 769.

before them in accordance with law.[210] The findings of the Commission of Inquiry are not binding on the Court when the Court has arrived to its own conclusions on the independent assessment of the persuasive evidence.[211]

The Full Bench of the High Court at Madras too held[212] very recently that the report of Commission is not binding on State nor its findings are binding on those against whom any recommendation is made. Conclusions of Commission of Inquiry are also not admissible in Court of law, in criminal case or even in civil case. Such conclusions are merely advisory in nature. However, such report to extent it is accepted by State, the State would be bound by its findings.

Reference in this regard may be made to a passage contained in the foreword by Mr. Justice Krishna Iyer, to the *Commissions of Inquiry Act, 1952* by K.A. Ramasubramaniam whereby the learned Judge observed:[213]

> We, in this country, currently live in an era of commissions and have accumulated sufficient experience of the utility and futility, the processual failing and political fall-outs and a host of other facets of these quasi-judicial though purely recommendatory operations. The time is ripe for a social functional audit of the Act in depth with the critical yet constructive purpose of modifying its structure and restyling its engineering so that the statute may be able to fill the bill.
>
> Again the learned Judge said:[214]
>
> These commissions, more or less function as a court of law, statements of person are recorded either by an affidavit or viva voce and, in any case, under oath. There is a public hearing, appearing on behalf of all those concerned, including

210. *T.T. Antony* v. *State of Kerala and Others*, AIR 2001 SC 2637.
211. *Sham Kant* v. *State of Maharashtra*, AIR 1992 Cri. LJ 3243, p. 3250: AIR 1992 SC 1879.
212. *P.P.M. Thangaiah Nadar Firm and Others* v. *Govt. of Tamil Nadu and Others*, AIR 2007 (NOC) 954 (Mad) (FB).
213. *Ibid.*, p. vi.
214. *Ibid.*, p. viii.

> witnesses. Affected parties whose reputation is likely to be prejudicially affected are given an opportunity to be heard, to cross examine the witnesses appearing against them and to adduce evidence in their defence, by and large, the Rules of the Evidence Act are followed. It is clothed with the essential powers of a court of law and is always presided over by a high judicial dignitary.

But again, the learned Judge said:[215]

> Yet, the pronouncements of this Commission are not binding on any one. It is most essential, these should be written into the Act, and perhaps, even in the Representation of People's Act that a person whose conduct has been adversely reported upon by a Commission of Inquiry should suffer some legal disqualification. He should be debarred from holding any elective office or contesting any election for a period and, if he is a civil servant, it should automatically spell his removal from public service. Otherwise these commissions become an expensive luxury ending in futility. If the object is to ultimately cleanse public life and cleanse the Augean Stables, they should be invested with some sanctions.

Mr. Krishna Iyer, therefore, deeply regrets that the reports of the commissions are not binding on any one.

With due respect to the learned Judge, it may be stated that his view may sound good as a matter of policy with some justification, having regard to the time, resources and money that go into such inquiries but it may not be so pragmatically. And, if so insisted upon, one may find, in the ultimate analysis, the remedy worst than the disease itself. One must bear in mind that inquiry commissions are essentially tools of information gathering that help the administrative authorities in taking sound objective decisions. These are part of proper decision-making process. In no way, these need to impinge upon the decision making process itself, especially having regard to the fact that such inquiries are not adjudicatory in nature and there being no lis involved at all. It may be stated that there is nothing

215. *P.P.M. Thangaiah Nadar Firm and Others* v. *Govt. of Tamil Nadu and Others*, AIR 2007 (NOC) 954 (Mad) (FB) ix.

wrong with the system of inquiry commissions. It has outlived for so long and obviously, must be for valid reasons and useful purposes. The fact that it might have been put to abuse in certain cases is not to denigrate and denounce the system as a whole. Such cases are only an aberration and not the rule for otherwise the system could not have survived for so long. In the ultimate analysis, the use, or, as the case may be, the abuse of the system of inquiry commissions lies in the bona fides or otherwise of those entrusted with the duties and responsibilities of the administration of the august institution of inquiry commissions. It may be useful to refer in this regard to the following observations made by the Supreme Court in *I.R. Coelho* v. *State of Tamil Nadu*:[216]

> Further, mere possibility of abuse is not a relevant test to determine the validity of a provision. The people, through the Constitution, have vested the power to make laws in their representatives through Parliament in the same manner in which they have entrusted the responsibility to adjudge, interpret and construe law and the Constitution including its limitation in the judiciary. We, therefore, cannot make any assumption about the alleged abuse of the power.[217]

Prohibiting Government from Accepting Report

As a writ cannot be issued directing the Government to accept and implement a Commission's Report *in toto*, in the same vein, a writ cannot be issued prohibiting the Government from accepting such a report. It is certainly for the Government

---

216. AIR 2007 SC 861, p. 879.

217. In this case, the Court was confronted with a very important yet not very easy task of determining the nature and character of protection provided by Article 31B of the Constitution of India, 1950 to the laws added to the Ninth Schedule by amendments made after 24-4-1973. It was, inter alia, contended that the power to pack up laws in the Ninth Schedule in absence of any idicia in Article 31B had been abused and that abuse was likely to continue. It was submitted that the Ninth Schedule which commenced with only 13 enactments had now a list of 284 enactments. While observing that the validity of Article 31B was not in question before the Court, their lordships made the above observations.

to consider the report and take a decision thereon. As observed by Justice Das:

> While the Commission must necessarily accept the responsibility for the correctness and (of?) its findings on the evidence laid before it and for the probity of its report, it must stoutly and emphatically disclaim all responsibility for the consequences that may ensure in the wake of this enquiry. The Commission has been charged only with the duty of finding the true facts as they emerge from the evidence admitted and assessed according to well established principles of law, and to make its report to the Central Government setting forth its findings and conclusions. Our Constitution has, on the other hand, trusted the Legislature and the Government with all matters of policy and reasons of State in relation to the governance of the country. The Commission has no doubt that those authorities will be readily willing to derive assistance from this Report in informing their minds about true state of affairs as they appear from the evidence laid before the Commission. But what action they will take, in the discharge of their own responsibilities, is no concern of the Commission.

Accordingly, it has been held that the Court cannot issue a writ of prohibition restraining the Government from accepting any finding recorded by the 3rd respondent-Commission in this case in the light of the legal position relating to the role of the Commission, and the duty and authority of the Government in such matters.[218]

However, in an unreported judgment of a Single Judge of the High Court of Gujarat at Ahemdabad delivered on 07-03-2006 in *Nilkanth Tulsidas Bhatia* v. *Union of India* (Special Civil Application No. 16500 of 2005 with Civil Application No. 12629 of 2005 in Special Civil Application No. 16500 of 2005 with Civil Application No. 12631 of 2005 in Special Civil Application No. 16500 of 2005), it was directed, by way of

---

218. *S.V. Purushothaman* v. *State of Kerala and Others*, AIR 1983 Kerala 118, pp. 123-24.

interim relief, that "during the pendency and till final disposal of the present Special Civil Application, the report submitted by High Level Committtee headed by Mr. Justice U.C. Benerjee, former Judge of the Supreme Court to the Central Government shall not be further acted upon and relied upon by any of the respondents, their agents and servants and anybody in any manner whatsoever. The aforesaid interim relief is granted considering the fact that in the present Special Civil Application the constitution of the Committee itself is under challenge and if ultimately at the time of final hearing this Court finds that the Committee could not have been constituted and is without jurisdiction and/or de hors the law, then all the further proceedings and even the report can be declared nullity and can be set aside, more particularly, when the Committee itself was constituted after a period of two years and seven months and therefore, if the matter is fixed for final hearing within four weeks and the interim relief is granted, no further prejudice will be caused to the respondents. Therefore, to see that the present Special Civil Application does not render infructuous the aforesaid limited interim relief is granted."

On an appeal, the aforesaid judgment of the learned Single Judge, restraining, by way of interim relief, the implementation of the Committee's report, was upheld by a Division Bench of the High Court of Gujarat in *Union of India* v. *Nilkanth Tulsidas Bhatia*.[219] While doing so, the Division Bench observed: In view of the above discussion, we are of the view that the original petitioner has made out a strong prima facie case that the appointment of the Committee by the Central Government under notification dated 4-9-2004 is absolutely illegal and contrary to the express mandatory provisions of Clause (b) in the proviso to sub-section (1) of Section 3 of the Commissions of Inquiry Act and also contrary to the express mandatory provisions of Section 119 of the Railways Act."[220]

---

219. (2006) 2 GLR 952.

220. It is understood that the Union of India, in the Ministry of Railways, has preferred a Special Leave Petition against this judgment in the Supreme Court and the matter is, thus, yet to attain finality.

Reference in this regard may also be made to the case of *Col. Jagmohan Singh* v. *State of Manipur*[221] wherein the appointment of the Commission by the State Government was held to be beyond its competence and accordingly it was held that the Commission could not be treated as one for the purposes of the Act. The Court further directed the State Government to forward the report of its Commission to the Central Government for consideration and necessary action at its end.

Should Notification Indicate the Purpose for which Commission is Constituted?

Section 3(1) does not expressly provide for mentioning the purpose in terms in the notification, although it may always be proper to indicate the same in the preamble. The absence of a recital of the necessity for the inquiry indicating the purpose and object thereof will not *per se* invalidate the notification if the same can be spelt out from the subject-matter of inquiry.[222]

Also, a notification under Section 3, not mentioning the names of persons to be proceeded against in enquiry but mentioning categories of such persons, is not vitiated. Where the notification specifically mentioned that the inquiry shall be in regard to conduct of political authorities, i.e. any member of the Council of Ministers of the State of Tripura Legislative Assembly or any other person holding any public office by reason of his political affiliation or association; public servant as defined in the Indian Penal Code; and friends and relations of such political person in whom such political authorities or public servants or other persons in whom such political authorities or public servants were interested, the notification could be viewed as clearly mentioning the categories of persons to be proceeded against even though the particulars of such persons were not mentioned. Further, if the notification contains the specific charges to be inquired into, it is not liable to be quashed for indefiniteness.[223]

---

221. AIR 2006 Gauhati 33.

222. *Manabendra Sarkar* v. *State of Assam and Others*, AIR 1974 Gauhati 46, pp. 49-50.

223. *Sukhamay Sen Gupta* v. *State of Tripura*, AIR 1979 Gauhati 63.

Definite Matter of Public Importance

The dictionary meaning of the word "*definite*" is: determinate, distinct, precise and not vague.[224] Therefore, it is to be seen whether the terms of reference of the Commission are distinct, precise and not vague.[225] The question whether the subject of inquiry is a "definite" matter of public importance in a given case is to be determined with reference to the Terms of the Reference with which the inquiry is instituted. It may be that the subject of inquiry *ex facie* includes within it various factors and may be understood in different ways by different persons. The correct approach in such a case is to examine and ascertain the subject in the context of the points/terms of reference. The notification, resolution or, as the case may be, order by which a Commission of Inquiry is set up, must be read as a whole and not piecemeal. If the terms of reference as contained in the document setting up the Commission of Inquiry clearly indicates what the Commission has to do and there is no room for any ambiguity as to the matters that are required to be considered or inquired into by the Commission so as to say that the Commission does not have to grope in the dark to find out the matters which it would consider for the purpose of the inquiry, then, the terms of reference cannot be said to be vague and indefinite. Applying these principles, the Calcutta High Court[226] upheld the setting up of a Committee, to which the provisions of the Act were subsequently extended in terms of Section 11 thereof, for the purpose of inquiring into the "economics of newspaper industry", being a definite matter of public importance. It has further been held by the Court in this case that if once the matter to be inquired is found to be a definite matter of public importance, the Court cannot enter into a further inquiry as to the propriety or otherwise of the questions framed by the Committee for the purpose of inquiry into the matter directed to be inquired into. In this case, a contention

---

224. *The Concise Oxford Dictionary*, 4th Edition.

225. *Brijpal Dass* v. *Justice Shri B.P. Beri* (1981) ILR 31 Rah 361, p. 378.

226. *The Statesman* v. *The Fact Finding Committee*, AIR 1975 Calcutta 15.

was raised by the petitioners in support of their plea of the subject of inquiry being vague and indefinite, that, in the questionnaire, there was no query as to the rehabilitation and modernization of printing machinery and equipment in the country. This contention, however, did not find favour with the Court, as the questionnaire was prepared by the Committee and not by the Government. The Court observed in this regard that "it is for the Committee to decide what evidence it will take and what information it requires for the purpose of its inquiry. The Court cannot take any notice of any omission on the part of the Committee to include in the questionnaire any particular question. The only question which is relevant is whether the matter which has been referred to the Committee is a definite matter".[227]

No argument can be made to say that the terms of reference are vague and/or indefinite merely because some references were made by the Commission to the Government to elucidate or even add to the terms of reference. Where there was an application of mind by the Government in the formulation of the original terms of reference and it was only because of some elucidation required by the Commission that the terms of reference were added to and not because the Government thought that the original terms of reference were vague and/or indefinite, the legality of the establishment of the Commission is not open to objection on the ground of its terms of reference being vague or indefinite.[228]

In *Motahar Hossain* v. *Haratosh Chakrabarty*,[229] the terms of reference of the impugned Commission were assailed on the ground, among others, being vague. It was alleged that the expressions like "well established conventions", "excess of power", "maltreatment", or "atrocious act", are expressions of vague import and could not be judged by any yardstick. The Court did not accept this contention and observed, "the expression used must be judged in the context in which it has

---

227. *The Statesman* v. *The Fact Finding Committee*, AIR 1975 Calcutta 14, p. 26.

228. *P.R. Nayak* v. *Union of India*, ILR (1973) I Delhi 747.

229. 84 CWN 560.

been used. It is true that the expression "convention" in one context may mean one thing and in other context it may mean other. But in the context in which the notification has been issued in my opinion, the expressions like "well established convention" or "excess of power" or "maltreatment" or "atrocious acts" are the expressions, which could be understood and which could not be said to be vague or uncertain. Though these expressions are capable of conveying different meanings but actually in public matters these are capable of conveying certain well established meanings and judged in that light, in my opinion, the present notification cannot be condemned as vague."

In *Sri Narayanadoss Mahant and Another* v. *Sri T. Neeladri Rao and Another*,[230] it was held that widespread mismanagement of public endowments dedicated to religious and charitable purposes and the eradication of that evil was a definite matter of public importance. It was further held that it was not necessary that the institutions whose affairs should be named in the notification before an inquiry could be ordered into a definite matter of public importance. The Court further observed: "The section speaks only of a definite matter and not of particulars or instances of such matter. The duty of ascertaining the institutions, in which there is mismanagement, is cast on the Special Officer and it is for him to inquire into the affairs of such institutions and make recommendations to the Government. The Special Officer is constituted as a fact-finding body for the purpose of finding out which of the institutions are being mismanaged, in what way and to what extent. He would proceed to hold an inquiry only if he is prima facie satisfied that a particular institution is a public temple or mutt or the like and that its properties are being mismanaged and diverted to private purposes."[231] A definite matter of public importance is a question which may arise even on allegations made.[232]

230. AIR 1959 Andhra Pradesh 148.

231. *Ibid.*, p. 151.

232. *State of Jammu and Kashmir* v. *Bakshi Gulam Mohammad*, AIR 1967 SC 122.

It is not necessary that the persons against whom the enquiry is sought to be proceeded should have been mentioned. There is no warrant for this. Under Section 3 of the Act, the inquiry may relate to anything covered under the Act and it may not relate to any person, as for instance, bomb explosion in a public place. At the stage, when the enquiry is ordered, the name and other particulars need not be mentioned. It is an enquiry into a matter of public importance relating to the allegations made by particular persons. As to who are the persons to be proceeded against will be decided at a later stage and if any person is aggrieved, he will have ample opportunity to defend himself before the Commission. The absence of mention of the names or the particulars of persons against whom the enquiry is to be proceeded in the memo will not vitiate the notification made under Section 3 of the Act.[233]

Nevertheless, Section 3(1) of the Act envisages "an inquiry into any definite matter of public importance" and this expression does not include in its ambit a roving inquiry into the conduct of persons unknown as yet, regarding incidents uncertain as yet, the only definite provision being certain ascertained periods. Only because certain allegations had been made against six named persons, it could not be held that the State Government was of the opinion that it was necessary to make an inquiry into all illegal gains, all corruptions, all favouritisms, all abuses of power, all other malpractices of all persons holding official positions in the whole of the State during certain periods. If it be held that the Commission had to inquire and report about all illegal gains, all corruptions and favouritisms indulged, in all abuses of power and all other malpractices taken recourse to by all persons holding official positions during certain periods mentioned in the notification, then it might be difficult to hold that such a direction could be supported by the provision of Section 3(1) of the Act.[234]

In *Brijpal Dass* v. *Justice Shri B.P. Beri*,[235] the petitioner challenged the notification appointing the Commission of Inquiry

---

233. *M. Karunanidhi* v. *Union of India*, AIR 1977 Madras 192, p. 196.

234. *Md. Anis Khan* v. *T.L.V. Aiyar*, AIR 1970 Patna 334.

235. 1981 ILR 31 Raj. 361.

on the ground, inter alia, that the scope of inquiry is too vague, wide, sweeping, covering a period of about 29 years and includes the power to inquire into the matters of slightest irregularities in the allotment of land or its conversion or gift; to the allegations of favouritism or nepotism or corruption or misuse of authority. Neither any particular incident has been named, nor any person has been named and by this process the Government has permitted the Commission to make a roving and fishing inquiry. It was also urged that the date of commencement of the period was also vague, because the formation of Rajasthan could not relate to a particular date as it was done in various phases and stages. Negating these contentions, the Court observed: "an area does not cease to be a definite merely because it is large. A circle remains a circle even if its radius is long because the circumference is ascertainable and definite. Since the matter of irregularities, illegalities, political favouritism or otherwise, all mentioned in the Notification, relate to a definite period commencing from the formation of Rajasthan, the matters have become definite. It may be that the period of 29 years or so, and all matters of land allotment or transfers or otherwise, as mentioned in the notification issued by the Government of Rajasthan can mean in inquiry into lacs and lacs of cases; but on account of that it cannot be said that the matters are uncertain or indefinite. The matters which can be covered by this Notification are certainly within a very wide range, but not vague. They are certainly spread over a very long period, but they are not spread for any indefinite period, they certainly cover the whole of Rajasthan wherein lacs and lacs of cases of irregularities and illegalities might have occurred deliberately or innocently, with personal and political influence, or even absence of proper knowledge of law, rules or facts in some cases nonetheless the area of Rajasthan is definite and the allotment and transfer or other matters referred to in the Notification are also on record of the Government. I, therefore, do not find anything unconstitutional or illegal in it, even though I am of the view that such wide terms of reference should be avoided for ruling out the possibility of misuse or abuse, avoidable harassment which may happen once a while in such broad and wide reference.... It is true that the allegations are neither contained in the memorandum or annexures to this Notification, nor any reference has been made. Any specific matter from any record or notified, would have been better for bringing preciseness in addition to definiteness; but on that account the Notification cannot be quashed. Since I am of the view that the matters are definite both from the point of view of time, as for the reasons given in the impugned order, and so from the point of view of the areas which restricted to Rajasthan, and further from the point of view of specific points mentioned in the Notification enumerated above, and therefore, they fall within the purview of Section 3 of the Act."

Where the matters that are the subject-matter of reference involve large amount of public funds and contemplate lack of probity on the part of officers/officials of the Government and Government undertakings, it would be a definite matter of importance for which a Commission of Inquiry can be validly constituted.[236] Land grabbing by a particular individual has been held to be a matter of public importance for the appointment of a Commission of Inquiry in *Mohd. Ibrahim Khan* v. *Susheel Kumar*.[237] Justice Murtaza Hussain Commission was constituted by Uttar Pradesh State Government on 9-12-1997 to inquire into the allegation related to irregularities in allotment and conversion of land in New Okhla Industrial Development Authority (in short, NOIDA).[238] A Commission was set up on 14-7-2005 to inquire into, and submit its report, on the alleged anomalies in the computerized draw of lots for the allotment of 1250 plots in various sectors of NOIDA on 2-7-2005.[239]

It is of public importance that public men failing in their duty should be called upon to face the consequences. It is certainly a matter of importance to the public that lapses on the part of the Ministers should be exposed. The cleanliness of

---

236. *P.R. Nayak* v. *Union of India*, ILR (1973) I Delhi 747.

237. AIR 1983 Andhra Pradesh 69.

238. *NOIDA Entrepreneurs' Association* v. *NOIDA and Others*, 2007 (2) SCALE 131.

239. Reported in *Hindustan Times*, 28-2-2007, p. 5, titles "Probe into Noida Plot Scam Going Nowhere".

public life in which the public should be vitally interested, must be a matter of public importance. The people are entitled to know whether they have entrusted their affairs to an unworthy man. Accordingly, in *State of Jammu and Kashmir and Others* v. *Bakshi Gulam Mohammad and Another*,[240] the Supreme Court upheld the setting up of Commission of Inquiry to inquire into the acquisition of assets and pecuniary resources of the Prime Minister of the State of Jammu and Kashmir and his family members and relatives by abusing the official positions held by him. The Supreme Court negated the contention that the notification by which the Commission of Inquiry was set up, was not justified by the J&K Commissions of Inquiry Act, 1962 because under the Jammu and Kashmir Constitution, a Minister was responsible for his acts only to the Legislature and no action could be taken against him except for criminal and tortuous acts in the ordinary courts of law, unless the Legislature by a resolution demanded it. The Court further held that matters which were otherwise of public importance, would not ceased to be for the reason that on the date of the issue of the notification, the person whose acts were to be inquired into, did not hold any office in the Government. Nor it was necessary that there must be some evidence of public agitation in respect of the acts complained of. Absence of such agitations would not show that the matters were not of public importance. Their lordships observed[241] that "What is to be inquired into in any case are necessarily past acts and it is because they have already affected the public well-being or their effect might do so, that they became matters of public importance. It is irrelevant whether the person who committed those acts is still in power to be able to repeat them. The inquiry need not necessarily be into his capacity to do again what he has already done and it may well be into what he has done. The fact that Bakshi Ghulam Mohammad is no longer in office does not affect the question whether his acts, already done, constitute matters of public importance. If once it is admitted, as it was done before us, that

240. AIR 1967 SC 122.

241. AIR 1967 SC 122, p. 127.

if he had been in office his acts would have been matters of public importance that would be acknowledging that his acts were of this character. His resignation from office cannot change that character. A Minister, of course, holds a public office. His acts are necessarily public acts if they arise out of his office. If they are grave enough, they would be matters of public importance. When it is alleged that a Minister has acquired vast wealth for himself his relations and friends, as is done here, by abuse of his official position, there can be no question that the matter is of public importance." Their lordships further observed:[242] "We are, however, unable to agree that a matter cannot be of public importance unless there was some public agitation over it. Public may not be aware of the gravity of the situation. They may not know the facts. Some members of the public may be aware of individual cases but the entire public may not know all of them. There may have been influences working to prevent public agitation. Again, whether a matter is of public importance or not has to be decided essentially from its intrinsic nature. If a matter is intrinsically of public importance, it does not case to be so because the public did not agitate over it. Take this case. Suppose the Government sets up a Commission to inquire into the mineral wealth in our country. The public are not likely to agitate over this matter for they would not know about the mineral wealth at all. Can it be said that the inquiry does not relate to a matter of public importance because they did not agitate over it? The answer must plainly be in the negative. This would be so whether there were in fact minerals or not. Considering the allegations contained in the Notification by themselves, we think for the reasons earlier mentioned, that they constitute matters of public importance even if there was no public agitation over them."

The Court further observed that the fact that the notification only mentioned that the matters were of public importance but did not say that they were definite matters of public importance, does not make any difference. A Court can decide whether the matters to be inquired into are definite matters of public

242. AIR 1967 SC 122, p. 128.

importance. "Definite" in this connection means something which is not vague.

It was also contended that the inquiry was into allegations of misconduct and an inquiry into allegations was not contemplated by the Act. The Court did not accept this contention and observed:

> Allegations may very well raise questions of great public importance.... It cannot also be said that allegations can never be definite. They can be as definite as any existing concrete matter. It must depend on what the allegation is.

There may be cases where certain expressions used in the terms of reference describing the subject of inquiry may be truly vague yet such expressions may have acquired certain connotations for which reason the notification appointing the Commission may not be open to objection on the ground of being vague. Reference in this regard may be made to the case of *Sushil Chandra Chowdhury* v. *Secretary, Chakraborty Commission and Others*[243] wherein the Court observed: "It is true that the terms of reference, so far as murder or killings for political motive are concerned, are vague expressions. In criminal law, as far as I know, murder or killing for political motive as such is not treated differently.... Killing for political motive cannot be called a class by itself. But unfortunately in India, perhaps due to past history of national liberation movement during the National Freedom struggle sometimes, we have given certain amount of legitimacy to killing or committing other crimes for political motive. Whether continuation of this attitude after national independence is good or bad, is a different matter and is a matter of policy, but it has to be recognized as a fact that killings of men for political motives have been treated in pubic mind often separately and differently from other killings though it is often difficult to separate that kind of killings, I would have hesitated, had it been necessary for me, to strike down this aspect of notification only on the ground of vagueness. The expression 'enjoying the patronage of the Ruling party' is again an expression of vague import because the expression

243. 84 CWN 583.

'patronage' may mean various things and will give a wide meaning but even in this country this political 'patronage of the Ruling party' or 'persons in power' are expressions which have achieved certain connotation. For that reason, I would have again hesitated, had it been necessary for me to strike down this notification as being a vague and there being no application of mind."

Relying upon the decision of the Supreme Court in *Bakshi Gulam Mohammad Case*,[244] the Orissa High Court[245] observed as follows:

> Thus, in order to be definite, all that is necessary is that the matters must not be vague. If general allegations are not vague, they are definite matters. Doubtless where a particular instance is given, the matter becomes definite. Absence of particulars or instances would nonetheless make matters definite. That would depend upon the nature of the general allegations depending on the facts and circumstances of each case.

Meaning of Public Importance

What is a matter of "public importance" has been considered by the Royal Commission on Tribunals of Inquiry, 1966 under the Chairmanship of the Rt. Hon'ble Lord Justice Salmon. In its report, Royal Commission felt that matters, which cannot be dealt with by ordinary, civil and criminal processes and/or rare occasions when a nationwide crisis of confidence occurs, the appointment of a Commission of Inquiry is justified. In the said report, it was observed as follows:[246]

> Normally persons cannot be brought before a Tribunal and questioned save in civil or criminal proceedings. Such proceedings are hedged around by long-standing and effective safeguards to protect the individual. The inquisitorial procedure is alien to the concept of justice generally accepted

---

244. *Supra*, AIR 1967 SC 122.
245. *P.V. Jagannath Rao* v. *State of Orissa* (1968) 34 Cut LT 666, p. 695.
246. Para 28 of the Report of Royal Commission on Tribunals of Inquiry, 1966.

in the United Kingdom. There are, however, exceptional cases in which such procedures must be used to preserve the purity and integrity of our public life without which a successful democracy is impossible. It is essential that on the very rare occasions when crisis of public confidence occur, the evil if it exists, shall be exposed so that it may be rooted out; or if it does not exist, the public shall be satisfied that in reality there is no substance in the prevalent rumours and suspicions by which they have been disturbed. We are satisfied that this would be difficult if not impossible without public investigation by an inquisitorial Tribunal possessing the powers conferred by the Act of 1921. Such a Tribunal is appointed by Parliament to inquire and report. The task of inquiring cannot be delegated by the Tribunal for it is the Tribunal which is appointed to inquire as well as to report. The public reposes its confidence not in some other body or person but in the Tribunal to make investigations and to produce the witnesses in order to arrive at the truth. It is only thus that public confidence can be fully restored.[247]

Public men failing in their duty should be called upon to face the consequences and that it was certainly a matter of public importance that lapses on the part of the Ministers should be exposed. The cleanliness in public life in which the public are vitally interested, is a matter of public importance.[248] Corruption, nepotism and misappropriation of public funds during a particular period are clearly definite matters of public importance.[249]

It may be pertinent to refer to the following observations made by the Rajasthan High Court in the case of *Brijpal Dass* v. *Justice Shri B.P. Beri*,[250] viz.

---

247. *Orient Paper Mills* v. *Union of India*, AIR 1979 Calcutta 114, pp. 131-32.
248. *State of Jammu and Kashmir* v. *Bakshi Gulam Mohammad*, AIR 1967 SC 122.
249. *P.V. Jagannat Rao* v. *State of Orissa* (1968) 34 Cut L T 666, p. 697.
250. 1981 ILR 31 Raj 361, p. 383.

Now coming to the question of public importance, the grabbing of land by person in authority, or by indulging in favouritism against law is certainly a matter of public importance inasmuch as it regards and is a negation of equitable distribution of wealth as enshrined in the directive principles of the Constitution. A tiller of the soil is entitled to be considered for the purpose of allotment of land when he is landless. The favouritism, nepotism, misuse and abuse of authority either by the Government officers or by those who held reigns of the Government, certainly is a matter in which the public at large is vitally interested. It is also important and of great importance for public that such persons who misused the public office are named by a competent authority like the Commission functioning under the statute. The impugned notification contains in its terms of reference a requirement from the Commission to suggest ways and means and even to the extent of suggesting the laws to be legislated for the purpose of taking action against such land grabbers to redeem the land from them. These are all matters relating to citizens at large who are interested and conscious community of people is always interested to see that the law is enforced and implemented, the law breakers are brought to book and howsoever highly placed a person may be, he is not allowed to take the benefit of any illegal act done to the detriment of the society. This, in substance, makes a matter of great public importance.

Ancillary or Incidental Functions of a Commission

Once there is a definite matter of public importance and the conditions precedent for appointment of the Commission are satisfied, then the Government may require the Commission to perform such ancillary or incidental functions as may be specified in the notification. The functions specified in the notification of the Commission can be those which are in aid of or for the purpose of conducting the inquiry into the definite matter of public importance. Where a Commission has been appointed to inquire into the definite matter of public importance, in that case, the question of its performing such functions as specified in the notification only arises.[251] The scope of inquiry is wide enough to cover anything reasonably related to the matter under inquiry.[252]

Additions of References to Commission

In *State of Madhya Pradesh* v. *Arjun Singh*,[253] during the pendency of the enquiry, the State Government by a fresh notification enlarged the terms of the original reference. The second reference was quashed by the High Court holding that it suffered from non-application of mind and invalid exercise of powers under Section 3 of the Act. The High Court, inter alia, took the view that there was no relevant material before the appropriate Government for enlarging the scope of existing enquiry. On appeal, the Supreme Court found as a matter of fact that the additions were substantively covered under the original reference and as such there could be no bar to the Commission to enquire into such matter under the original reference itself. However, as regards part of one of the additions, the Supreme Court held that the same was rightly quashed by the High Court, as there was no relevant material before the State Government for enlarging the scope of existing enquiry under the original reference. But the Supreme Court clarified that their judgment did not preclude the State Government from appointing any Commission of enquiry according to law after applying its mind to any fresh or further material placed before it. Such formation of opinion would depend on the subjective satisfaction of the appropriate Government but should be based on an objective or real material and not merely on some vague allegations or hearsay evidence or to make fishing enquiry.

Previous Investigation, or Its Absence, No Bar to Inquiry

There is no bar to appoint a Commission of Inquiry by the Government and refer those particular matters to the Commission of Inquiry even if those matters were previously investigated with and inquired into by different agencies of the Government

251. *Orient Paper Mills* v. *Union of India*, AIR 1979 Calcutta 114 , p. 126.
252. *State of Karnataka* v. *Union of India*, AIR 1978 SC 68: 1977 (4) SCC 608.
253. AIR 1993 SC 1239.

provided those matters are definite matters of public importance.[254]

In *Balakrishna Pillai* v. *State of Kerala*,[255] the State Government appointed, in exercise of its executive powers, two Commissions, consisting of retired High Court Judges, to inquire into certain allegations against the petitioners. The Commissions reported that none of the allegations were proved or established. The reports were, however, *ex parte* as the complainants did not appear before the Commissions. In the meantime, the Government in the State changed and the new Government did not accept the reports of the Commissions and appointed a new Commission, this time, under Section 3 of the Commissions of Inquiry Act, which was challenged by the petitioner. Holding that the appointment of the Commission under the Act was competent and valid, the Court observed as follows:

> The purpose of an enquiry under Section 3 of the Commissions of Inquiry Act is only to enable the Government 'to gather facts or information'. The information can be obtained or gathered in any manner. The proceeding before a Commission is not judicial or quasi-judicial. It is only a fact-finding authority. The enquiry is done or made to reach an ultimate administrative decision.
>
> It cannot be denied that the appointment of a Commission under Section 3 of the Commissions of Inquiry Act is generally impelled by a desire to set up and maintain high standard of moral conduct in public life and administration. This is a welcome step to maintain high standards in public life. It is definitely a matter which will result in cleanliness of public life in which the public are vitally interested. In this context, it would be useful to quote the observations of the Royal Commission on Tribunals of Inquiry, 1966 to the following effect:
>
> The evil, if it exists, shall be exposed so that it may be rooted out and if it does not exist, the public shall be satisfied that

254. *Orient Paper Mills* v. *Union of India*, AIR 1979 Calcutta 114, p. 127.

255. AIR 1989 Kerala 99: 1988 (2) KLT 1038.

in reality there is no substance in the prevalent rumours and suspicions by which they have been disturbed. We are satisfied that this would be difficult, if not impossible, without public investigation by an inquisitorial tribunal possessing the powers conferred by the Act of 1921.

It may also be stated that the appointment of a Commission, under Section 3 of the Commissions of Inquiry Act, for the purpose of enquiring into lapses on the part of Ministers, acquisition of vast wealth by Ministers or near relations by abuse of official positions, acts of malfeasance, misfeasance and misappropriation on the part of Ministers etc., have been held to be competent and valid by the decisions of the Supreme Court.[256] It has also been held that the existence of political rivalry by itself is insufficient to hold that the appointment of a Commission of Inquiry is illegal.[257] Once it is held that the purpose of Section 3 of the Act is to obtain information or collect facts or details to reach an ultimate administrative decision, normally, it cannot be stated that the said power is in any way curtailed, either qualitatively or quantitatively.

The earlier two Commissioners were appointed under executive orders. The scope, extent and power of the Commissioner appointed under the executive order is far different from the Commissioner appointed under the Commissions of Inquiry Act. On facts, the earlier enquiries were found to be unsatisfactory as these did not carry credibility on account of serious infirmities and there was serious criticism and persistent public demand for further and deeper probe, the Government, with the approval of the Cabinet, decided to have an enquiry under Section 3 of the Commissions of Inquiry Act. There is nothing to bar in the Act such an enquiry. There was nothing on the basis of which it could be said that the Government did not apply its mind, or acted without due care and caution or mala fide or failed to take into account relevant facts or took

256. *State of Jammu and Kashmir* v. *Bakshi Gulam Mohammed*, AIR 1967 SC 122.

257. *P.V. Jagannath Rao* v. *State of Orissa*, AIR 1969 SC 215.

into consideration irrelevant facts or acted unreasonably or arbitrarily in appointing the Commission under the Act.

In *V. Narayana Rao* v. *State of AP*,[258] the State Government accepted the recommendations of the earlier Commissions and issued orders in 1979 extending reservations up to 1991 whereupon the matter was to be reviewed further. Before the expiry of that period in 1991, the Government appointed the impugned Commission for this purpose. It was held that the Commission was not invalid and the plea that the review should have taken place only after 1991 was not tenable. The appointment of the Commission was also held not open to objection on the ground that there was no reference to a survey already made in 1986 on the socio-economic conditions of the backward classes in the State or the material collected in this survey while appointing the impugned Commission.

On the other hand, it was urged in *P.V. Jagannath Rao* v. *State of Orissa*,[259] that "the fact that on similar facts, no inquiry commission was appointed against different Ministers from 1947 to 1961 is evidence of the fact that irrelevant considerations weighed with the State Government in appointing the Commission". While negating this contention, the Court observed: "The long and short of the matter is whether failure to make inquiry against the ministers functioning from 1947 to 1961 is a consideration relevant or germane to the decision of the State Government to appoint a Commission to make the present inquiry. In our view, it is not. This argument suffers from the basic fallacy that whenever Government wants to appoint a Commission to have an inquiry into any definite matters of public importance under section 3 of the Act, it would be incumbent upon it to make also inquiry into all analoguous and similar matters, Government might choose to have inquiry in respect of some and not in respect of others. That would depend upon the gravity of the particular matters under consideration.... The contesting opposite parties in their

258. AIR 1987 A.P. 53: 1987 Lab. I.C. 152.

259. (1968) 34 Cut LT 666, p. 715.

counter state that the allegations made against some of the ministers functioning from 1947 to 1961 would be submitted for examination by a Retired Judge for determination if there is a prima facie case for acting under section 3 of the Act. If the necessary conditions are fulfilled another Commission would be appointed to go into those allegations. The memorial has been submitted to the President of India by Sri Sadasiba and others. Under section 3 of the Act, it is open to the Central Government to appoint a Commission to go into those allegations, if it is so satisfied. For all these reasons, the failure on the part of the State Government not to appoint a Commission to make inquiry into the allegations made against some ministers from 1947 to 1961 is not a consideration germane to the present inquiry."[260]

Status of a Commission—Not Appointed by Appropriate Government

The report of a Commission, which has not been appointed by the appropriate Government, cannot be treated as a report within the meaning of Section 3 of the Act. The report may, however, be treated as a report by a fact-finding Committee/ Body appointed by the Government that appointed it. Where interim directions were issued by the High Court under Article 226 permitting the Commission to proceed with the inquiry, such directions attributed some amount of legality to the report inasmuch as the report could be assumed to have been prepared under the direction of the Court. The State Government was, therefore, directed to hand over the report to the Union Government, being the appropriate Government, which would examine the report and pass orders/take appropriate action against the personnel, if any, indicted in the report.[261]

Report of Commission in Excess of Its Jurisdiction

If a Commission of Inquiry gives report, containing recommendations that travel beyond its terms of reference, what would be its status in law? In *Brahma Nand Gupta* v. *Delhi*

260. (1968) 34 Cut LT 666, pp. 715-20.

261. *Col. Jagmohan Singh* v. *State of Manipur*, AIR 2006 Gauhati 33.

Administration,[262] it was, inter alia, contended that the Justice Misra Commission could only give a report with regard to the definite matters of public importance which had been referred to it and the recommendations of the said Commission for a Committee, like the present one, being set up, inter alia, for monitoring the progress of the criminal cases was without jurisdiction and ultra vires. The Court did not find any merit in this contention and observed: "It is now well settled that the report of a Commission set up under the Commissions of Inquiry Act is recommendatory in nature, and it has no power to enforce its recommendations.[263] This being so, it is open to the Government to accept all or any of the recommendations given by the Commission. Assuming that the Commission has traveled beyond the scope of the reference made to it, it is, in our opinion, for the Government to decide and consider whether to accept or act on such a recommendation or not. The Government may choose to ignore any advice or recommendation, which is given but which is not sought for. But if an unsought for advice is tendered and the Government chooses to accept the same, then we fail to see as to how the acceptance of such an advice can be impugned. In exercise of its executive powers, the government is free to seek advice from any quarters. The advice so given helps the Government in coming to an administrative decision. De hors any statute a suggestion can be mooted to the Government to act, administratively, in a particular manner and we fail to see any legal impediment in the Government accepting such an advice. If, therefore, the Commission exceeded the terms of its reference and gave some recommendation or advice, which was not covered by the provisions of the Commissions of Inquiry Act, the Government, in our opinion, was not constrained by the provisions of any law in accepting such a recommendation."

It is true that the Commission's report by itself has no effect. But when it is found that the Commission has exceeded its jurisdiction in reporting upon an issue which was not referred to it and when it is further found that the Commission's finding

262. 1989 (4) Delhi Lawyer 94.

263. *Ram Krishna Dalmia* v. *Justice S.R. Tendolkar*, AIR 1958 SC 538.

is causing prejudice to the petitioner, there is no principle or authority that the report to that extent cannot be quashed. Such a finding is without jurisdiction and that much part of the report as contains such a finding must be quashed.[264]

It will also be useful to refer to the following observations made by the Kerala High Court in *Mohammed Haneefa* v. *State of Kerala*,[265] viz.

> The law relating to Commission of Inquiry as so understood shows that the function of the Commission is only to enquire and report. He does not decide. Government is also not bound by what the Commission says. They are not also confined to the report. It is for the Government to consider and take such action as they deem fit. The question of considering the validity or otherwise of the Commission's finding does not, therefore, really arise because Government is acting on its own on the evidence and materials available with it. The fact that the information has been furnished to Government by the report of the Commission (even assuming it was beyond the scope of the reference) does not mean that the Government is acting illegally or without jurisdiction. If the information or material is relevant, Government could take such action as is warranted against the petitioner if he is delinquent in any manner. They need not, in such circumstances, seek the support of the report of the Commission to sustain their action. The fact that the information available with Government is incorporated in the report of the Commission of Inquiry (even if it be in excess of the terms of reference) does not vitiate the action of the Government.... The question is whether Government has got the power to initiate action against the petitioner, if they have sufficient materials with them. Petitioner has no case that Government has no such power. His only grievance is that the materials relied on are not legal for the finding was rendered by a Commission beyond the scope of the reference. As stated earlier, the question for consideration is

264. *Dr. Ku. Sneh Rani Jain* v. *The State of M.P.*, 1978 Lab. IC NOC 43.
265. 1988 (2) KLT 919.

whether Government does have the jurisdiction. The source of the materials on which they are acting is immaterial so long as they are relevant. Even if the materials are gathered on the basis of a report made outside the scope of the reference, that cannot vitiate the Government's action if otherwise it is within jurisdiction.

In *V. Narayana Rao* v. *State of AP*,[266] the Government accepted recommendations of M.R. Commission appointed to make recommendations as to whether the backward classes enumerated earlier had progressed socially and culturally as to warrant deletion of some of them and reservation to be made in their favour in educational institutions. The same was challenged, inter alia, for the reason of being beyond the purview of the Commission. Negating this contention, the Court observed: "On this aspect, it is well to remember that appointment of Commission is not obligatory before making a special provision, or before providing for reservations under Articles 15(4) and 16(4). Even apart from the provisions of the Commissions of Inquiry Act, the executive power of the State extends to appointing a person or a Committee by whatever name it may be called to investigate the social and educational backwardness of any classes or groups in the State, and to act upon the report submitted by such person or committee. Indeed, it may even be open to the Government to make its own investigation and take appropriate measures. It, therefore, cannot be said just because the M.R. Commission made certain recommendations beyond its purview the acceptance of the said recommendations by the Government is *per se* illegal or incompetent...but, so far as the first contention of the learned Counsel for the petitioners is concerned, it is not possible to agree, that the Government acted illegally in accepting,[267] or acting upon the said recommendations

266. AIR 1987 Andhra Pradesh 53.

267. The Court, however, qualified these observations when it observed that "It is another matter to say that the recommendations of the Commission are not based upon relevant material, or to say that the government blindly accepted the said erroneous recommendations without any further investigation." Page 70, para 32 of the judgment.

because those recommendations were outside the purview of the Commission."

Failure to Report on Matters Referred for Inquiry

On the other hand, there may be cases where it could be alleged that the Commission did not properly or fully go into the questions specifically referred to it. It is essentially a matter of fact. It is for the Government to accept or not to accept the report of the Commission or to direct further inquiries in such matters. Where the Commission constituted for recommending backward classes for reservation, recommended inclusion into backward classes certain professional groups among Hindus such as barbers, washermen, fishermen, etc. without including corresponding groups among Muslims, the proceedings of the Commission were not held to have been vitiated on this ground in view of the fact that there was no link between caste and profession among Muslims as had been the case with Hindus wherein these homogeneous groups constituted a caste respectively. Similarly, the contention that there were certain groups that were socially and educationally backward such as rickshaw-pullers who were not confined to any one community and failure to include such groups in the list of backward classes recommended by the Commission and consequently, vitiating its proceedings, was not sustained for the reason that no such group was brought to the notice of the Commission nor any representation was made by any of these groups to the Commission. Although the Commission could have made its own inquiries in this regard, the Court held that it was not the province of the Commission as the Commission was constituted to review list of backward classes with a view to find out whether they had progressed socially and educationally so as to call for their deletion and also to find out whether any of the minority communities or groups deserved to be included in the list of backward classes.[268]

Commission's Report and Writ Jurisdiction

A Commission of Inquiry appointed under the provisions of the Act is simply a fact-finding body; therefore, its report is not

268. *V. Narayan Rao* v. *State of AP*, AIR 1987 Andhra Pradesh 53 (FB): 1987 Lab. IC 152.

binding on the Government. As such, any attempt to find out the correctness or otherwise of such a report may be beyond the scope of Articles 226 and 227 of the Constitution of India. The Court in exercise of its writ jurisdiction under Article 226 of the Constitution of India would not make a review of the evidence before the Inquiring Authority to substitute its own conclusion. However, there may be cases where the petitioners suffered an injury by virtue of the findings and recommendations of the Commission though the report of the Commission by itself has no force of any penal effect. Although the proceedings under Article 226 of the Constitution are not in the nature of appellate or revisional proceedings, yet a question of fact, which is unsupported by any evidence whatsoever, can be questioned in a proceeding under Article 226 of the Constitution. If a finding of fact is based on no evidence that would be regarded as an error of law, which can be corrected by a writ issued under Article 226 of the Constitution. It would not be a case of adequacy or sufficiency of evidence and an inference of fact can be drawn therefrom but it would be case of a finding of fact based on no evidence giving no scope for a possibility of different conclusion other than arrived at by the Inquiring Authority. Thus, adverse remarks made against senior police officers in the report of the Inquiring Authority based on presumptions and not on evidence have been held to be unjustified and liable to be quashed.[269]

Even though the Court is not concerned with the correctness of findings or otherwise of the reports, yet the question arises for consideration, in the facts of the case, whether in absence of a notice under Section 8B of the Act such findings which cast stigma against the conduct and prejudicial to the reputation of the petitioner can sustain. There cannot be any doubt that any judgment of a Court or report of a tribunal empowered by law to adjudicate and decide matters affecting rights of parties, cannot be assailed unless law permits it to be questioned or interfered with. But expunction of irrelevant and uncalled for remarks will not amount to alteration or amendment of report

---

269. *Prafulla Chandra* v. *State of Orissa and Others*, AIR 1988 Orissa 18.

or judgment. No doubt such exercise of power may affect a judgment or order to some extent but having regard to paramount importance of securing the ends of justice, the High Court will have no option but to exercise such power.[270]

Reference in this regard can be suitably made to a relevant passage from the judgment of the Apex Court in the case of *Dr. Raghubir Saran* v. *State of Bihar*[271] as follows:

> As already stated, expunction of irrelevant remarks does not amount to the alteration or amendment of a judgment or an order of a subordinate Court. No doubt, the exercise of such power will have the effect of taking out of the judgment or order something which was there before and thus in a limited way to interfere with the content of the document embodying the judgment or order. But bearing in mind the paramount importance of securing the ends of justice the High Court must be deemed to have such power.

In *M. Sathyanesan* v. *State of Kerala*,[272] the petitioner, a former District Committee Secretary of the Communist Party of India (Marxist), filed petition under Article 226 with the prayer that the report dated 28-9-2002 submitted by the Hon'ble Mr. Justice V.P. Mohankumar Commission of Inquiry be quashed as the Deputy Superintendent of Police on whose statement a notice had been given to the petitioner, had admitted during his cross-examination that there was no material indicating that the petitioner had received any money illegally and, therefore, the finding recorded by the Commission against the petitioner could not be sustained. This, however, did not find favour with the High Court which was of the view that the fact that the Deputy Superintendent of Police resiled from his statement did not mean that the Commission could not have taken into consideration the totality of the evidence that was available on the record. The Court further said that equally, it could not imply that because of the mere fact that the Deputy

---

270. *Lal Krishna Advani* v. *State of Bihar*, AIR 1997 Patna 15.

271. AIR 1964 SC 1, p. 10.

272. AIR 2003 Kerala 356.

Superintendent of Police had chosen to support the petitioner, the Commission could not have drawn an adverse inference even against the Officer. It was accordingly held by the High Court that the finding of the Commission, in the circumstances of the case, could not be said to be without any basis.

In *Mahila Atyachaar Virodhi Jan Andolan, Jaipur* v. *State of Rajsathan and Others*,[273] the petitioner who was a participant before the Justice Kokje Commission of Enquiry (Bhinmal incident) filed the writ petition aggrieved by the decision taken by the Commission not to examine certain witnesses on the ground of expediency. The Court found this decision of the Commission not based on sound ground and reasoning. Once the witnesses in question were found to be relevant and important and could surely throw sufficient light on the subject of inquiry and these witnesses had also expressed in writing their willingness to depose before the Commission but were not available to do so at a particular time for the reason of being away from the place of the venue of the Commission's hearings, it would not be proper on the part of the Commission in these circumstances owing to the expenditure involved in examining these witnesses by visiting the place where they were available at a given time. Saving of costs and time in not examining the material witnesses might not be a good reason for doing so. The Court observed in this regard: "It should be remembered that when the State Government sets up a Commission to enquire into an incident, it is its responsibility to provide required expenses for the Commission especially when the State Government itself considers the witnesses to be important and relevant. It cannot object to the expenditure involved in examining these by the Commission even by going to Tamil Nadu to the place where they are. The anxiety of the Commission to save time will also be taken care of by the Commission itself by going to the place where the witnesses are and the Commission will not have to wait till the year 2002 for availability of the witnesses in Rajsathan." Accordingly, the petition was disposed of by directing the

---

273. AIR 2002 Rajasthan 48.

Commission to reconsider the matter of examining these witnesses in the light of the observations made by the Court in its order.

In *D. Kandaswamy* v. *R. Kumaraswamy Naicker*,[274] a writ petition was filed against the appointment of the Commission of Inquiry to inquire into the clashes between various castes in certain places in Madurai district in September 1989. The petitioner alleged, inter alia, that the very appointment was not in consonance of the provisions laid down under Section 3 of the Commissions of Inquiry Act. It was further stated that it was not for a definite matter of public importance but only for information to find out the faults specifically with the people belonging to Scheduled Castes. It was further alleged that the appointment of the said Inquiry Commission was arbitrary and discriminatory, that the term of appointment of the said Inquiry Commission was to single out the Scheduled Castes community and to blame them for the alleged riots. It was further alleged that when the very term of appointment of the said Inquiry Commission assigned the alleged communal riots basically with the Adi Dravidas, it did not warrant for a distinct Inquiry. After having examined the notification and more particularly the terms of reference, the Court found the appointment of the Commission of inquiry perfectly valid as the inquiry was to find out the cause and circumstances leading to riots and other disturbances of law and order in various places. Though the preamble was shown as appointment of Commission to inquire into clashes between Adi Dravidas and other castes, but the terms of reference did not make any reference to Adi Dravidas at all. The Court further held that the Commission was only a fact-finding body and it was open to the petitioner to take part in the Commission's proceedings and file his objections on merits. Accordingly, the petition was dismissed.

Validity of Commission Appointed by Governor after Expiry of His Term

In *Krishna Ballabh Sahay* v. *Commission of Inquiry*,[275] the Governor of Bihar issued notification on 1-10-1967 under

274. (1990) I *MLJR* 163.

275. AIR 1969 SC 258.

Section 3 of the Commissions of Inquiry Act by which inquiry was ordered against the appellant and two others. This was challenged on the ground that the Governor's term having come to an end under the Constitution, he was functus officio and could not order the enquiry contemplated by the Government then in power. The Governor, in whose regime the notification was issued, was sworn in as Governor of Bihar on 6-5-1962. Under Article 156(3) he could hold office for a term of five years from the date on which he entered upon the office, that is to say, till 5-6-1967. The contention of the appellant, therefore, was that the Governor's continuance in office was illegal. The respondents relied upon the proviso to Article 156(3), viz. "Provided that Governor shall, notwithstanding the expiration of his term, continue to hold office until his successor enters upon office," and pointed out that there could not be an interregnum in view of this provision. In reply, the appellants' counsel referred to Article 160, viz. "Discharge of the functions of the Governor in certain contingencies: The President may make such provision as he thinks fit for the discharge of the functions of the Governor of a State in any contingency not provided for in this Chapter." His contention was that under the third clause of Article 156 the Governor's term was a closed term and if the term came to an end without the successor being named, the provisions of Article 160 must be used. The proviso, according to him, covered only the time lag before the successor entered office and not a case where no successor was appointed before the term of the holder was over. To hold otherwise, he submitted, might enable the appointing authority to set at naught the provisions of the main clause through the proviso. By way of analogy he referred to Articles 56 and 62(1) in respect of the President and the Vice President that enjoined that the election to fill the vacancies had to be completed in each case before the term ceased. The Court did not accept these contentions and observed: "There is no provision such as Article 62(1) or 68(1) in the scheme of the Governor's appointment. On the other hand, the proviso to Article 156(3) contemplates that the Governor is to continue to hold office 'notwithstanding the expiration of his term'. The effect of these words is to exclude all questions of the legality of the holding of office by a Governor after the expiry of his term. There must always be a Governor under Article 153 and the interregnum is avoided by the proviso.... Therefore, it is legitimate to hold that a person once appointed a Governor continues to hold that office till his successor enters upon his office. This successor may be appointed under Article 155 or an order may be made under Article 160. Whatever the position the former Governor continues to hold office till the new Governor enters his office. For these reasons we hold that Mr. M.A. Ayyangar acted validly as Governor on 1-10-1967."[276]

Validity of Commission Appointed by Governor During President's Rule

In *Gokulananda Roy* v. *Tarapada Mukharjee and Others*,[277] it was, inter alia, contended that after the Proclamation under Article 356 of the Constitution it was for the President alone to be satisfied about the necessity of an inquiry under the Commissions of Inquiry Act. It was argued that the President having assumed to himself all the functions of the Government of the State, and all powers vested in the Governor of the State, it was for him alone to be satisfied that an inquiry under the Act was called for, and also about the necessity of such inquiry. In other words, it was contended that it was for the President alone, to the exclusion of any other authority, to be satisfied about the necessity of an inquiry into a matter of public importance and on being so satisfied the President alone could issue the notification under Section 3 of the Commissions of Inquiry Act, 1952 and the Governor had no authority or jurisdiction to issue such a notification. It was argued that as this was not done and the notification was issued by the Governor on his own satisfaction about the necessity of the inquiry, the

---

276. The Court further observed that there might be cases in which neglect to appoint a Governor soon might lead to an inference and it might require further examination as to the remedy in such cases. However, this question was left unanswered as no facts bearing upon the failure to designate a successor were pleaded in this case.

277. AIR 1973 Calcutta 233: 76 CWN 411.

notification was invalid and for that reason the inquiry should not be held by the first respondent. It was further argued that even if it was held that the Governor was properly authorized to make the order appointing a Commission of Inquiry, he had no jurisdiction or authority to decide for himself about the necessity of such an inquiry. In other words, it was submitted, that it was one thing to make an order appointing a Commission of Inquiry, and quite another thing to form an opinion that such an inquiry was called for. It was for the President alone, it was argued, to form an opinion that an inquiry was necessary. It was submitted that what was delegated by the Presidential notification were the powers of the President, but not the duties or the statutory obligation, of forming an opinion that an inquiry was called for. These arguments did not find favour with the Court, which observed: "It seems to me that there is an inherent fallacy in this argument. This argument requires that the statutory obligation of forming an opinion about the necessity of an inquiry should be exercised by the President, and the order appointing the Commission of Inquiry may be made by the Governor by virtue of delegation of powers to him. If in this case, the opinion as to the necessity of the inquiry was formed by the President, and on such formation of opinion by the President, the Governor issued the notification appointing the Commission of Inquiry, the order would have been open to challenge on the ground that the opinion was formed by a person who did not make the order, appointing the Inquiry Commission, and that the order appointing the Inquiry Commission was made by a person who did not form the opinion. If such an order was made, it could not be sustained, because the opinion required to be formed about the necessity of the inquiry was not the opinion of the person, who made the order appointing the Commission of Inquiry." The Court further observed that "The question is, in a case, such as this, where the powers and duties and statutory obligations, are so inter-woven, inter-connected and inter-dependent on each other, can it be said that the delegation of the powers would not necessarily involve a delegation of the duty and the statutory obligation? In other words, in a case of delegation of power, where power and duty are inter-woven, inter-connected, and inter-dependent, can it be said that the power and the duty can be so separated and distinguished, that the delegation of the power only can be made, leaving the duty or statutory obligation with the principal? The answer to both these questions, in our opinion, must be in the negative. The delegation of the power in a case, such as this, operates as an implied delegation of the duties and the statutory obligations as well. It cannot, in our view, be held that while the power to appoint a Commission of Inquiry stood delegated to the Governor, the duty and the statutory obligation to form an opinion about the necessity of such an inquiry remained vested in the President. To hold otherwise, would be creating a situation where the exercise of the power itself would be invalid. Because, in that case the President will have to form the opinion about the necessity of the inquiry, and having formed such an opinion, he will have to leave it to the Governor to make the order appointing the Commission of Inquiry, though the Governor has formed no opinion about the necessity of such an inquiry." It was further observed by the Court, "Under Article 154(1) of the Constitution, the executive power of[278] the State is vested in the Governor and is to be exercised by him directly or through the Officers subordinate to him. The President delegated to the Governor not only the powers of the Governor, but also the functions of the State Government. Quite apart from the position that delegation of powers carries with such delegation the duties and statutory obligations connected with the power, delegation of the functions of the State Government to the Governor, would include within its ambit the power to form an opinion about the necessity of an inquiry under the Commissions of Inquiry Act."

In this case, it was further argued that if the Presidential notification was construed to effectuate a delegation of powers by the President to the Governor, then it should be held that the said notification was ultra vires the powers of the President, as the effect of the delegation would be that the President completely abdicated and surrendered the powers and responsibilities, which

278. Case law on delegation of powers and duties was discussed.

he had assumed by the Proclamation under Article 356. In other words, it was argued that by the Proclamation the President had assumed to himself the powers of the State Government and the State Governor, and it was for him alone to discharge the duties and obligations of the State Government and the Governor, and he could not divest himself of the powers which he had lawfully assumed, to the State Governor. Negating this argument, the Court said "It cannot be overlooked, and it should not be overlooked, that Article 356 itself enables the President when a Proclamation is made under that Article, to make incidental and consequential provisions. These incidental and consequential provisions are such as may appear to the President to be necessary for giving effect to the objects of the Proclamation. The terms of Clause (c) of Article 356(1) make it abundantly clear that, what incidental and consequential provisions are to be made is a matter entirely for the subjective satisfaction of the President. The validity or legality of the incidental and consequential provisions contemplated by Article 356(1)(c) is not justiciable.... Apart from the question of validity of an absolute delegation of power by the President to the Governor, resulting in a complete divestiture of the powers and functions which the President had assumed by reason of the Proclamation, it is to be noticed that the notification explicitly provides that the powers and functions delegated to the Governor, are to be exercised by the latter, subject to the superintendence, direction and control of the President of India. This provision in the notification leaves no room for doubt, that the President of India retains full control and superintendence over the Governor who exercises the powers delegated to him by the notification. The second answer to the contention that there was complete abdication of powers and duties by the President to the Governor is to be found in the last few words of the notification itself, namely, 'be exercisable also by the Governor of the said State'. The word 'also' appearing in the notification should not be lost sight of, in dealing with this question. It is quite clear that there is, by no means, a complete abdication or surrender of the powers, duties and functions which the President assumed by the Proclamation in favour of the Governor, as the President retains in his own hands, the authority and the jurisdiction to act, by virtue of the assumption of power under the Proclamation."

During the President's rule, the employees of the State Government do not cease to be the employees of the State and become the Central Government employees. It is true that they acted through the direction of the Governor given by the President on the advice of the Central Council of Ministers but even then they remained and continued to be the State Government employees and if, in appropriate cases, their conduct had created such a situation which concerned matters of public order for the State, subsequently the appropriate Government could certainly appoint a Commission of Inquiry to investigate under the Commissions of Inquiry Act, 1952.[279]

Appointment of Commission by Union Against State Ministers

The validity of a Commission of Inquiry appointed by the Union Government to inquire into the conduct of certain State Ministers was examined and upheld in the case of *M. Karunanidhi* v. *Union of India*.[280] The President's Rule was imposed in the State of Tamil Nadu by issue of the Proclamation under Article 356 on 31-1-1976. The Proclamation was based on the Governor's report made on 29-1-1976 in which the Governor had recommended the appointment of a Commission of Inquiry against the D.M.K. Government. Accordingly, on 3-2-1976, the Central Government notified the appointment of a Commission of Inquiry under Section 3 of the Commissions of Inquiry Act, 1952 to inquire into the allegations made by four persons who were named in the notification. The first and the foremost ground taken by the petitioner in challenging the appointment of the Commission of Inquiry was that "the federal nature of the Constitution does not empower the Central Government to lay down standards of good Government for the State Governments and to initiate an inquiry under the Commissions of Inquiry Act for what, in the opinion of the

---

279. *Sushil Chandra Chawdhury* v. *Secretary, Charaborty Commission of Inquiry and Others*, 1980, 84 CWN, p. 583.

280. AIR 1977 Madras 192.

Central Government might constitute maladministration." This contention did not find favour with the Court which upheld the Central Government's notification as intra vires its powers under Section 3 of the Commissions of Inquiry Act even though the inquiry was directed against State Ministers. In the Court's view, the words "federation", "autonomy" and "federating States" have varying meanings and what a particular word means will depend upon the context. To apply the meaning of the word "federation" or "autonomy" used in the context of the American Constitution to Indian Constitution would be totally misleading. The feature of the Indian Constitution is the establishment of a Government for governing the entire country. In doing so, the Constitution prescribes the powers of the Central Government and the powers of the State Governments and the relations between the two. According to the Constitution, as construed by the Supreme Court, there could be no difficulty in concluding that the State as such has no inherent power or autonomous power which cannot be encroached upon by the Centre. The very fact that the President has powers to take over the administration of the States would demolish the theory of any independent or autonomous existence of a State. These undeniable facts can give no room for the contention of the learned counsel for the petitioner that the Central Government is not empowered to order an enquiry against State Ministers, subordinating the State Ministers to the control of the Union Government.

The Supreme Court has gone a step further in *State of Karnataka* v. *Union of India*[281] and held that the power conferred by Parliament on the Central Government to appoint a Commission of Inquiry under Section 3(1) of the Act for the purpose of finding facts in regard to the allegations of corruption, favouritism and nepotism against a sitting Chief Minister or Ministers cannot be held to constitute interference with the executive functions of the State Government.[282] The facts giving rise to this case may be briefly stated in order to have better

281. AIR 1978 SC 68.

282. Para 183, p. 138 vide Chandrachud J. and Per majority, Kailasam J. contra.

understanding and appreciation of the issues involved therein. "Consequent upon the result of the elections held to the Karnataka Legislative Assembly in 1972, the Congress formed the Government with Shri D. Devraj Urs as the Chief Minister of the State. That party was then in power at the Centre too, but it lost its long held majority in the 1977 Lok Sabha elections after which the Janata Party formed the Government at the Centre. However in those elections to the Lok Sabha, 26 out of 28 allotted to the State of Karnataka were won by the Congress. Certain opposition members of the Karnataka Legislative Assembly submitted to the Union Home Minister a memorandum containing allegations of corruption, favouritism and nepotism against the Chief Minister, Shri Devraj Urs. In response to a request of the Union Home Minister, the Chief Minister offered his comments on the allegations but, while repelling the accusations as frivolous and politically motivated, the Chief Minister raised a point which forms the nucleus of the arguments advanced in the suit. He contended that the federal structure enshrined in the Constitution is the corner-stone of national integrity; that the Constitution is the source of the power of the Centre and the States; that the exercise of all powers, whether by the Central Government or by the State Governments, must conform to the scheme of distribution of powers devised under the federal scheme of our Constitution; that the erring Ministers of the State Government are accountable to the State Legislature only; and that, the Central Government has no authority or control over the Government of a State in respect of matters which are within the State's exclusive domain, save in exceptional times when an emergency is in operation. The Chief Minister asserted that an enquiry into the charges levelled against him could only be held by or at the instance of the State Government. By a notification dated 18-5-1977 issued under Section 3(1) the Commissions of Inquiry Act, 1952 the Government of Karnataka appointed a Commission of Inquiry consisting of Shri Mir Iqbal Hussain, a retired Judge of the Karnataka High Court, for the purpose of conducting an inquiry into the allegations specified in the notification. Within a few days thereafter, on May, 23, the Government of India issued a notification under the same

Act, appointing a Commission of Inquiry consisting of Shri A.N. Grover, a retired Judge of the Supreme Court, for inquiring into the charges made against the Chief Minister, as described in the notification. The validity of this notification is challenged by the State of Karnataka by the present suit under Article 131 of the Constitution."[283] In accordance with the view of the majority, the suit was dismissed with costs. The three issues framed in the suit were answered as follows, namely, (1) the suit was maintainable; (2) the Central Government's notification was valid; and (3) Section 3 of the Act was valid.

Test to Determine if the Subject Matter of Two Enquiries is the Same

Reading Section 3(1) along with the proviso, it is apparent that the intention of the Act is to enable the appropriate Government, i.e. the Central or the State Government to appoint a Commission of Inquiry into any definite matter of public importance. The Central Government can appoint a Commission to make an inquiry into any matter relatable to any of the Entries enumerated in List I, List II or List III of the Seventh Schedule of the Constitution while the State Government can appoint a Commission to inquire into any matter relatable to any of the entries enumerated in List II and List III of the Constitution. As both the Central Government and the State Government have power to appoint a Commission of Inquiry relatable to Entries in List II and List III there might arise occasions when there may be overlapping. In order to avoid such a contingency provisos (a) and (b) to Section 3(1) enact that when the Central Government has appointed a Commission of Inquiry the State Government shall not appoint another Commission to inquire into the same matter without the approval of the Central Government as long as the Commission appointed by the Central Government is functioning and the Central Government shall not appoint another Commission to inquire into the same matter as long as the Commission appointed by the State Government is functioning. These provisions are for the purpose of avoiding any conflict by the two Governments

283. Paras 153-55, p. 129.

appointing two separate Commissions to inquire into the same matter. In a speech made by the Minister for Law, Shri C.C. Biswas while introducing the Bill on 6-8-1952 in the Rajya Sabha, he explained the provisions of Section its underlying purposes as follows:

> Then there is also the question whether and how far there may be overlapping inquiries by the Centre appointing a Commission on its own and State also a Commission of its own to deal with the same matter. That is dealt with here in the proviso. The danger of overlapping is avoided by providing that if there is a Commission appointed by the Central Government already functioning then it will not be open to a State Government, except with the approval of the Centre, to appoint another Commission to inquire into the same matter. Similarly, if there is already a Commission appointed by a State Government functioning with respect to a matter which is within the jurisdiction of the State it will not be open to the Central Government to override the State Commission except in certain circumstances which are indicated, that is, unless the Central Government is of the opinion that the scope of inquiry should be extended to two or more States. Then of course this will be done, obviously not without reference to the State. So as you will see, Sir, provision is made in this clause for avoiding conflict between the Centre and the State.[284]

It may, thus, be seen that there cannot be two Commissions of Inquiry, one appointed by the Central Government and another by the State Government, functioning simultaneously with regard to the same subject-matter. The scheme of Section 3 is to avoid any conflict between the Central Government and a State Government in this regard. The question whether two enquiries are with regard to the same subject-matter or not, is essentially a question of fact. Nonetheless, different opinions were expressed on this aspect in the case of *State of Karnataka*

---

284. *State of Karnataka* v. *Union of India*, AIR 1978 SC 68, para 274, pp. 175-76.

v. *Union of India*,[285] indicating different angles from which the matter could possibly be seen and examined.

As per the majority opinion, the question as to whether two enquiries, one instituted by the Centre and another by a State, are with regard to the same "subject-matter" will have to be examined not only with reference to the precise terms of their enquiries but also with reference to the objectives with which these are so instituted. As per the majority opinion in the case of *State of Karnataka* v. *Union of India*,[286] "the interests of the State and of the Union are not antithetical when there are charges of corruption and misuse of power against those in authority anywhere. To serve the common interest of the whole people, on whose behalf our Constitution speaks, the States and the Union cannot stand apart. They must stand together united in purpose and action. It is as important that unjustified and malicious attacks and charges against individuals in high places should be unmasked and the reality behind them exposed for what it is worth, as it is that justified complaints must find adequate means of redress so that the interests of the dumb millions of our countrymen are duly safeguarded against unscrupulousness wherever found. If, as we find in this case, the State notification is meant only to superficially scratch the surface of the allegations made whereas the Central Government notification is meant to probe into the crux or the heart of what may or may not have gone wrong with the body politic in the State of Karnataka, we could not be too technical or astute in finding reasons to hold that the subject-matter of the two enquiries is substantially the same. Obviously, this could not really be so.... As we hold that the two notifications authorize inquiries into matters which are substantially different in nature and object, the enquiry by the Grover Commission cannot be said to be barred by reason of the State Government notification under proviso (b) to Section 3(1) of the Act, even if, in order to deal with the substantially different subject-matter, in view of the divergence in objects, certain areas of fact or rules governing

---

285. *State of Karnataka* v. *Union of India*, AIR 1978 SC 68, para 274, pp. 175-76.

286. *Ibid.*

transactions may be common. If the objectives are different the examination of common areas of fact and law for different purposes will still be permissible."[287]

Furthermore, as per the majority opinion,[288] there is no justification for reading down the provision of Section 3(1) so as to limit the power of the Central Government to appointing Commissions of Inquiry for inquiring into the conduct of persons in relation to matters concerning the affairs of the Union only. Section 3(1) empowers the Central Government to appoint a Commission for making an inquiry into any definite matter of public importance. It is inarguable that the conduct of Ministers of State Government in the purported discharge of their official functions is not a definite matter of public importance within the meaning of Section 3(1). There is no substance in the contention that the Central Government does not even possess the power to collect facts in regard to allegations of corruption made by a section of the State Legislature against sitting Ministers of the State Government. That power must undoubtedly be exercised sparingly and with restraint because under the guise of directing an inquiry under Section 3(1), the Central Government cannot interfere with day-to-day working of the State Government. One cannot also contradict that what appears to be a proper use of power may sometimes contain a veiled abuse of power, howsoever, infinitesimally. But statutory construction cannot proceed on distrust and suspicion of those who are charged with the duty of administering laws. Section 3(1) must, therefore, receive its proper construction with the reservation that mala fides vitiate all acts.

On the other hand, the minority opinion[289] is based more on the purpose underlying the provisions in Section 3 and accordingly, the need for a wide interpretation to achieve that purpose. Thus, it is said, "as the purpose of the two provisos to Section 3(1) is to avoid conflict, the words 'the same matter' in the proviso should be given wide interpretation and only matters

---

287. AIR 1978 SC 68, paras 16-23, pp. 85-88.

288. *Ibid.*, para 170, p. 134.

289. AIR 1978 SC 68, per Kailasam J., para 274, pp. 177-78.

that are not referable to the subject-matter of inquiry by the Commission appointed by the State can be taken over by the Center. We were not called upon to go into the two notifications and determine which item in the notification of the Central Government is not covered by the State Government notification. In giving a wider meaning to the words 'the same matter' with a view to avoid conflict, the contention of the Central Government that the inquiry into the conduct of the Chief Minister about the same incident will make it a different matter cannot be accepted."

In *Union of India* v. *Nilkanth Tulsidas Bhatia*,[290] the validity of the High Level Committee appointed by the Central Goverent, to which the provisions of the Act were subsequently extended under Section 11 thereof, was under challenge on the ground, inter alia, that its terms of reference was in conflict with the terms of reference of the Commission appointed by the State Government to inquire into the same incident. It was contended on behalf of the appellant, the Railway Administration, that there was no such conflict as the terms of reference of State Commission presupposed that the coach was set on fire, but the appellant appointed the impugned Committee to find out the precise cause of fire becaust it was after all the railway property which had suffered damage and the railway passengers had died or sustained injuries and, therefore, the Railway Administration was concerned with the safety of the passengers as well as the protection of its properties so that suitable measures for preventing recurrence of such incident can be taken. Strong reliance was placed on the decision of the Apex Court in *State of Karnataka* v. *Union of India*[291] in support of the contention that there might be some events and common areas of inquiry, but different authorities might make the inquiry for different purposes and from different angles and perspectives. In other words, the contention has been that even after appointment of Commission by the State Government under Section 3 of Commissions of Inquiry Act, the Central Government may appoint another

290. (2006) 2 GLR 952 (DB).

291. AIR 1978 SC 68.

Commission in order to deal with substantially different subject-matter relating to the same transactions; in view of the divergence in objects, certain areas of facts or rules governing transactions may be common and if the objects are different the examination of common areas of facts and law for different purposes will still be permissible. This contention, however, did not find favour with the High Court. The Court observed: "It is thus clear that while the State Commission has been looking into the incident that resulted into death of 58 lives and injury to more than 40 persons traveling in the Sabarmati Express on 27-2-2002 and also the subsequent incidents of violence in the State in the aftermath of the Godhra incident, and also the role of the Chief Minister and other Ministers in the incidents at Godhra as other incidents in the State (and there is not even a whisper that the Godhra incident is not being properly inquired into by the State Commission), the Committee appointed by the Railway Administration was also appointed to look into the same incident at Godhra which took place on 27-2-2002 and the other allied questions regarding the acts of negligence, defaults and wrongs on the part of the employees of the Railway Administration were allied or consequential issues added on the premise that the passengers in the train were mainly responsible for the eventual tragedy or on the premise that the fire was the result of an accident simpliciter. If at all the Railway Administration was keen to have an early inquiry made into any wrongful acts, negligence or defaults on the part of the officials and workmen of the Railway Administration and its security staff and into the preparedness of the rescue and relief operation and recommending measures for improving the quality of response in such situation, the Central Government could as well have called upon the State Government to request Justice Nanavati Commission to submit an interim report with regard to the facts, circumstances and course of the events of the incidents that resulted into fire in some coaches of the Sabarmati Express train on 27-2-2002 near Godhra Railway Station before concluding the inquiry into the subsequent incidents in the State of Gujarat." Accordingly, the Court expressed the view that "the original petitioner has made out a strong prima facie case that the appointment of the

Committee by the Central Government under notification dated 4-9-2004 is absolutely illegal and contrary to the express mandatory provisions of clause (b) in the proviso to sub-section (1) of Section 3 of the Commissions of Inquiry Act".

It is understood that this decision has been challenged by the Union of India in a Special Leave Petition before the Supreme Court. The matter is, thus, yet to attain finality. It is relevant to note that the judgment of the High Court has been on the application for the grant of interim relief and the main petition is yet to be disposed of on merits. It appears to be open to question if substantive relief in the petition can be granted by way of interim relief. Furthemore, it is not material as to what the Central Government could have done. What is material is whether it was within the competence and jurisdiction of the Central Government to appoint a Committee/Commission of its own to inquire into the same incident that was also being inquired into by the State Commission but with a different purpose. Nor it seems to be relevant that the Railway Administration has taken a different stand in respect of the incident in question. It is open to the Central Government to change its earlier stand upon receipt of additional inputs. The earlier stand will not be a fetter on the power of the Central Government to appoint a Committee/Commission if it is otherwise competent to do so. And, above all, the material distinction in the fact situtation of the *Karnataka* case does not appear to be germane to the issue that needs to be dealt with in accordance with the law on the subject. It will of interest to watch as to how the matter will be dealt with before the Apex Court.

Nonetheless, the fact that Nanavati Commission, set up by Gujarat Government, concluded that the train was set on fire because of a conspiracy as against the diametrically opposite conclusion of the Banerjee Commission that the fire in the train was accidental, only reinforces the suspicion that those who institute commissions select judges they believe will reflect their point of view. This also, therefore, reinforces the need for reviewing the majority view in the Karnataka case[291a] as to the

291a. *State of Karnataka* v. *Union of India*, AIR 1978 SC 68.

correct scope and ambit of Section 3 concerning the field of inquiry of commissions set up thereunder having regard to the ground realities that have emerged since the judgment in the Karnataka case.[291b]

Parliamentary Proceedings' Relevance

A question may arise how far and to what extent the Minister's speech in Parliament is relevant for determination of definite matter of public importance. The Minister's speech is neither conclusive nor binding on the Courts for determination whether the matters referred to by the Minister before Parliament are definite matters of pubic importance or not. But those speeches are relevant for the purpose of knowing the mind of the Government and its own opinion on the matters discussed about.[292]

Whether the Government can Exercise the Power for a Purpose Alien to the Statute

Misuse of power may arise either from breach of law conferring it or from the abuse of power in bad faith. There may be mala fides in three different ways, namely,

(1) The existence of a bias in the mind of the authority whose satisfaction is necessary. In other words, a biased mind cannot have a proper judgment.

(2) When the mind of the authority is not at all applied to the matters for consideration.

(3) When the mind is applied without bias, but is influenced by extraneous considerations, collateral purpose and ulterior object.

In a system where governance by political parties is prescribed by the Constitution, any inquiry initiated by any successor Government of a different political complexion is bound to be attacked as being influenced by oblique motives. The true tests

---

291b. Coomi Kapoor, "A Commission is Forever—Jain, Mukherjee, Sarkaria.... The Reports that went Nowhere," *The Indian Express*, July 10, 2009, p. 10.

292. *Orient Paper Mills* v. *Union of India*, AIR 1979 Calcutta 114, p. 131.

in such cases are whether there were any definite matters of public importance and whether the Government in power had a prima facie subjective satisfaction. If the essential conditions prescribed under Section 3 of the Act are fulfilled, then the appointment of the Commission cannot be attacked on the ground that prior to the election there was demand for such a Commission and that the successor Government formed by a different political party initiated the proceeding. It would be relevant to refer to the decision of the House of Lords in *Franklin and Others* v. *Minister of Town and Country Planning*[293] wherein their Lordships held that—

> The Minister of Town and Country Planning has no judicial or quasi-judicial duty imposed on him, so that considerations of bias in the execution of such a duty are irrelevant, the sole question being whether or not he genuinely considered the report and the objections.

Applying the same test, the appropriate Government has no judicial or quasi-judicial duty to reach the subjective satisfaction. If there is material on the basis of which the Government reached the satisfaction that there were definite matters of public importance, then the question of bias is irrelevant as the conclusion was genuinely reached on the materials before them.[294]

In *Ram Krishna Dalmia* v. *Justice S.R. Tendolkar*,[295] the Supreme Court observed that where power is misused but there is good faith the act is only ultra vires. But where the misuse of power is in bad faith there is added to the ultra vires character of act, another vitiating circumstance...misuse may arise from a breach of law or from an abuse of power in bad faith. In *P.K. Kunju* v. *State of Kerala*,[296] relying on the above observations of the Supreme Court, it was held that the use of power for achieving alien purpose for example wrecking Minister's

293. 1948 Appeal Case 87.

294. *P.V. Jagannath Rao* v. *State of Orissa* (1968) 34 Cut LT 666, pp. 721-22.

295. AIR 1958 SC 258.

296. AIR 1970 Kerala 252.

vengeance or of an officer's would be mala fide and a colourable exercise of that power. The Court observed in this case, "the exercise of a statutory power for an unauthorized purpose, or even professedly for an authorized purpose, but in fact for a different one with an ulterior object, would vitiate the exercise of power".[297]

In *Earl Fitz-William's Wentworth Estates Co. Ltd.* v. *Minister of Town and Country Planning*,[298] Lord Denning observed:

> So also the validity of Government action often depends on the purpose with which it is done. There, too, the same principle applies. If Parliament grants a power to a Government Department to be used for an authorized purpose, then the power is only validly exercised when it is used by the department genuinely for that purpose as its dominant purpose. If that purpose is not the main purpose, but is subordinate to some other purpose which is not authorized by law, then the Department exceeds its powers and the action is invalid. The Department cannot escape from this result by saying that its motive is immaterial. Just as its real purpose is crucial, so also is its true motive, because they are one and the same thing.[299]

The Supreme Court reiterated the same principle in *Pratap Singh* v. *State of Punjab*[300] when their Lordship observed:

> Sometimes, Courts are confronted with cases where the purposes sought to be achieved are mixed, some relevant and some alien to the purpose. The courts have, on occasions, resolved the difficulty by finding out the dominant purpose which impelled the action and where the power itself is conditioned by a purpose, have proceeded to invalidate the exercise of the power when any irrelevant purpose is proved to have entered the mind of the authority.

---

297. Page 257; See also *Orient Paper Mills* v. *Union of India*, AIR 1979 Calcutta 114.

298. (1951) 2 KB 284.

299. *Crofter Hand Woven Harris Tweed* Co. v. *Veitch* (1942) 1 All ER 142.

300. AIR 1964 SC 72.

The Court further observed that the two grounds of ultra vires and mala fide are most often inextricably mixed. Treating it as a question of ultra vires, the question is what is the nature of the power which has been granted to achieve a definite object in which case, it would be conditioned by the purpose for which it is vested. Taking the present case of the power vested in Government to pass the impugned orders, it could not be doubted that it is vested in Government for accomplishing a defined public purpose, viz. to ensure probity and purity in the public service by enabling disciplinary penal action against the members of the service suspected to be guilty of misconduct. The nature of the power, thus, discloses its purpose. In that context the use of that power for achieving an alien purpose wreaking the minister's vengeance on the officer would be mala fide and a colourable exercise of that power, and would therefore be struck down by the Courts.

Again in *Ram Manohar Lohia* v. *State of Bihar*,[301] it was observed:

> Although this Court has already stated that allegations of bad faith can be considered, it may be added that where statutory powers are converted to take drastic action against the life and liberty of a citizen, those who exercise it may not depart from the purpose. Vast powers in the public interest are granted but under strict conditions. If a person, under colour of exercising the statutory power, acts from some improper or ulterior motive, he acts in bad faith. The action of the authority is capable of being viewed in two ways. Where power is misused but there is good faith the act is only ultra vires but where the misuse of power is in bad faith there is added to the ultra vires character of act, another vitiating circumstance. Courts have always acted to restrain a misuse of statutory power and the more readily when improper motives underlie it. The misuse may arise from a breach of the Law conferring the power or from an abuse of the power in bad faith.

---

301. AIR 1966 SC 740.

It is well settled that if a statutory authority exercises its power for a purpose not authorized by the law the action of the statutory authority is ultra vires and without jurisdiction. In other words, it is a mala fide exercise of power in the eye of law, i.e. an exercise of power by a statutory authority for a purpose other than that which the Legislature intended.[302] But the question arises as to what is the legal position if an administrative authority acts both for an authorized purpose and for an unauthorized purpose. In such a case where there is a mixture of authorized and unauthorized purpose, what should be the test to be applied to determine the legal validity of the administrative act? The proper test to be applied in such a case is as to what is the dominant purpose for which the administrative power is exercised. To put it differently, if the administrative authority pursues two or more purposes of which one is authorized and the other is unauthorized, the legality of the administrative act should be determined by reference to the dominant purpose.[303] Applying this principle in *P.V. Jagannatha Rao* v. *State of Orissa*,[304] the Supreme Court upheld the validity of the notification setting up the Commission of Inquiry as the dominant purpose of setting up the Commission of Inquiry was to promote measures for maintaining purity and integrity of the administration in the political life of the State and not the character assassination of political rivals. The Court further observed that the existence of political rivalry is in itself not sufficient to hold that the appointment of the Commission of Inquiry is illegal.

In *Krishna Ballabh Sahay and Others* v. *Commission of Inquiry and Others*,[305] the setting up of a Commission of Inquiry was challenged on the ground, inter alia, "that the appointment

302. *The King* v. *Minister of Health* (1929) 1 KB 619.

303. *P.V. Jagannath Rao and Others* v. *State of Orissa and Others*, AIR 1969 SC 215; *Rex* v. *Brighton Corporation*; ex parte Shoosmith, (1907) 96 LT 762; and *Earl Fitz William's Wentworth Estate Co. Ltd.* v. *Minister of Town and Country Planning* (1951) 2 KB 284.

304. AIR 1969 SC 215.

305. AIR 1969 SC 258.

of the Commission is a campaign of vilification for political gain by a party in opposition and is based on personal animus against those who kept the members of that party out of office. The argument thus attributes malice and mala fides to the Governor's notification and abuse of the powers under the Commissions of Inquiry Act for an illegitimate purpose. Side by side there is the argument that a succeeding Ministry cannot inquire into the conduct of public and governmental affairs of the Ministry that goes out". Repelling these contentions, the Court observed: "It hardly needs any authority to state that the inquiry will be ordered not by the Minister against himself but be some one else. When a Ministry goes out of office, its successor may consider any glaring charges and may, if justified, order an inquiry. Otherwise, each Ministry will become a law unto itself and the corrupt conduct of its Ministers will remain beyond scrutiny." It was further observed: "It cannot be stated sufficiently strongly that the public life of persons in authority must never admit of such charges being even framed against them. If they can be made then an inquiry whether to establish them or to clear the name of the person charged is called for. If the charges were vague or speculative suggesting a fishing expedition we would have paused to consider whether such an inquiry should be allowed to proceed. A perusal of the grounds assures us that the charges are specific, and that records rather than oral testimony will be used to establish them.... Finally it is argued that the action is mala fides. This can only be decided if it can be held that the allegations were false. The Commission will first find the facts. Whether they lead to the conclusion that the inquiry was justified or it was malicious, cannot be said just now, when there are only allegations and recriminations but no evidence. If the charges have been made maliciously or falsely, we are sure the Commission will say so, where necessary. We cannot anticipate the inquiry and hold one ourselves."

In *Nadendla Bhaskara Rao* v. *Government of Andhra Pradesh*,[306] the petitioner, inter alia, contended that in appointing the Commission of Inquiry against him, the respondent acted

306. AIR 1989 Andhra Pradesh 186.

mala fide and the real purpose of appointing the Commission was to bring down the image of the petitioner in the public esteem and to wreak vengeance on account of the bitter political rivalry existing between the parties. It was found that this Commission had been appointed for the reason that an earlier Commission appointed for the same purpose could not proceed with the inquiry. However, in a petition challenging the appointment of the earlier Commission, it was held that the appointment of that Commission was not actuated by mala fides. In view of this, it was held that what was good in respect of the earlier Commission was equally good for the second Commission appointed subsequently to inquire into the same matter. In this case, the petitioner alleged that having resigned from the Chairmanship of the earlier Commission, the Judge in question recommended the Government to appoint one of his acquaintances as Commission of Inquiry for the obvious purpose of exercising influence over the thinking of that acquaintance. The Court found some credence to this when it noticed that the copy of appointment letter was endorsed to the Chairman of the earlier Commission. However, the Court held that this vitiated the appointment of that acquaintance as the Commission.

Where due procedures have been followed and a statement has been made by the Chief Minister of the State in the Legislative Assembly about the formation of the Commission, no mala fide can be imputed on any individual. Such suggestion of mala fide also cannot be accepted as no individual has been impleaded by name in the case.[306a]

Constitution of Commission

On the reading of Section 3(2) it is clear that the Act does not lay down the minimum number or presence of any member obligatory. The sub-section only suggests that a Commission may consist of one or more members. Since the Section does not lay down that there shall be a minimum of two members, the concept of joint responsibility and decision cannot be read in

---

306a. *T. Chitra* v. *The Chief Secretary to the Government, Government of Tamil Nadu and Another* (2008) 1 MJ 422; MANU/TA/9409/2007.

Section 3(2) of the Act. Sub-section (3) read with sub-section (2) makes it clear that the appropriate Government may fill any vacancy which may have arisen. The word 'may' in the Act occurring in Section 3 cannot be read as 'shall' because it will mean the re-writing of sub-section (2) so as to read—'that a Commission shall consist of not less than two members'. Apart from this, the word 'may' cannot be read as 'shall' for the reason that there is no legal obligation on the Government to appoint a Commission of Inquiry at all. The opinion of the Government regarding the necessity of appointing a Commission is subjective opinion. It does not create a legal obligation for the Government nor a legal right in a citizen. Therefore, no mandamus can be issued for directing the Government to appoint a Commission. So also the Government cannot be directed to disband or not a Commission under Section 7 of the Act. The Government cannot also be compelled either to accept or not to accept the report. This being the scheme of the Act, no legally enforceable duty can be read in sub-section (3) of Section 3 by construing the word 'may' as 'shall'.[307]

Reconstitution of Commission

Section 3, as it was originally enacted in 1952, consisted of two sub-sections, namely (1) and (2). Thus, there was no provision for filling up any vacancy in the consideration of a Commission. The present sub-section (3) dealing with filling up of any vacancy in a Commission was inserted in the Act in 1971. However, even before the insertion of sub-section (3), and in the absence of any provisions in this regard, vacancies arising in such a Commission were duly filled in by appointing another person. Thus, by a notification, dated 11-12-1956, the Central Government appointed a Commission consisting of Justice S.R. Tendolkar as Chairman with two other members, whose validity came up for consideration before the Supreme Court in the case of *Rama Krishna Dalmia* v. *S.R. Tendolkar*.[308] Later on, Justice S.R. Tendolkar resigned from the Chairmanship of the Commission

---

307. *(Mrs.) Kiran Bedi* v. *Delhi Administration*, 1989 (2) Delhi Lawyer 190.

308. AIR 1958 SC 538.

and Vivian Bose was appointed as its Chairman on 28-8-1958.[309] It may, thus, be seen that even prior to insertion of sub-section (3), the Governments were indeed exercising powers to fill in any vacancy in a Commission set up under the Act. However, filling up a vacancy is not the same thing as replacing an existing person in a Commission.

In *Lal Krishna Advani* v. *State of Bihar*,[310] a three-member Commission replaced a single-member Commission. Under Section 3 of the Act, the State Government appointed a Commission, known as the Bhagalpur Riot Commission. Initially Hon'ble Mr. Justice Ram Nandan Prasad, a retired Judge of the High Court, was appointed as the sole member of the Commission. But subsequently by a notification, dated 20-9-1993, Hon'ble Mr. Justice Ram Chandra Prasad Sinha and Hon'ble Mr. Justice S. Shamsul Hasan, both retired Judges of Patna High Court were also appointed. Two separate inquiry reports were submitted by the Commission, i.e. one signed by the two members, namely Hon'ble Ram Chandra Prasad Sinha and Hon'ble S. Shamsul Hasan on 11-2-1995 and other by Hon'ble Ram Nandan Prasad, Chairman of the Commission on 28-9-1995. A writ petition was filed seeking expunction of certain remarks against the petitioner in the report of the two Members of the Inquiry Commission for the reason of, inter alia, non-compliance with the requirement of Section 8(B) of the Act. The question of validity of the reconstituted Commission was, however, not raised though the Apex Court had earlier decided such a related question in 1993.[310a]

Under notification dated 6-3-2002, the Gujarat State Government appointed a Commission of Inquiry under the Act of 1952 consisting of Mr. Justice K.G. Shah, retired Judge of the High Court of Gujarat to inquire into and report on "the incident of setting on fire some coaches of Sabarmati Express train near Godhra Railway Station on 27-2-2002 and subsequent incidence of violence in the State of Gujarat in the aftermath

---

309. *M/s Allen Berry & Co. Pvt. Ltd.* v. *Vivian Bose*, AIR 1960, Punjab 86.

310. AIR 1997 Patna 15.

310a. *State of Madhya Pradesh* v. *Ajay Singh*, AIR 1993 SC 825.

and adequacy of administrative measures taken to prevent and deal with the disturbance in Godhra and subsequent disturbance in the State". Subsequently, vide Government notification dated 21-5-2002 issued by the State of Gujarat in Legal Department; the aforesaid Commission was reconstituted by converting the Single Member Commission into two Members Commission headed by Mr. Justice G.T. Nanavati, retired Judge of the Hon'ble Supreme Court as the chair-person and Mr. Justice K.G. Shah, retired Judge of the High Court of Gujarat as a member. Later on, the Central Government appointed a High Level Committee, headed by a retired Supreme Court Judge, Mr. Justice U.C. Benerjee, to inquire into the same incident and suggest safety measures to prevent recurrence of such incidents. The provisions of the Commissions of Inquiry Act, 1952 were extended to the Committee in terms of Section 11 of that Act. The appointment of the Committee was challenged before the Gujarat High Court. One of the grounds of challenge was the Central Government did not have power and jurisdiction to appoint the Committee so long as the State Commission was functioning. By grant of interim relief, a Single Judge of that High Court restrained the implementation of the Committee's report in any manner.[310b] This was upheld by a Division Bench of that High Court in a Letters Patent appeal filed by Union of India.[310c] However, neither before the Single Bench nor before the Division Bench, the validity of the reconstituted State Commission was raised. If the validity of the State Commission could be successfully challenged on the ground of lack of necessary jurisdiction and power of the State Government in reconstituting the Commission, could the validity of the Central Government's Committee have been assailed as has been done in this case? The matter is yet to be finally disposed of on merits, as the Union of India is understood to have filed a Special Leave Petition in the Supreme Court against the judgment of the Gujarat High Court. It will be interesting to watch as to how the matter is dealt with

310b. *Nilkanth Tulsidas Bhatia* v. *Union of India*, Dates 7.3.2006 (Unreported).

310c. *Union of India* v. *Nilkanth Tulsidas Bhatia*, (2006) 2 GLR 952.

before the Apex Court, especially in view of the Supreme Court's decision in the case of *State of Madhya Pradesh* v. *Ajay Singh*,[311] which is discussed below in details.

The question "whether in the scheme of the Commissions of Inquiry Act, the power "to add to, amend or vary" any notification given by Section 21 of the General Clauses Act[312] is available to reconstitute a Commission of Inquiry constituted under Section 3 of the Commissions of Inquiry Act by replacing the sole member appointed initially with another person during the availability of the sole member initially appointed?" came up for consideration before the Hon'ble Supreme Court in the case of *State of Madhya Pradesh* v. *Ajay Singh*.[313] In other words, whether the appropriate Government after constituting the Commission under Section 3 of the Act is empowered to reconstitute the Commission substituting another person as the sole member in place of the initial appointee. It was held in this case that the power under Section 3(3) of the Commissions of Inquiry Act, 1952 was not available to the State Government in the facts of the case to appoint any other person replacing the existing one as the sole member of the Commission of Inquiry. The power under sub-sections (1) and (2) of Section 3 read with Section 21 of the General Clauses Act or even Sections 14 or 16 thereof was also not available for this purpose. While holding as above, the Honb'le Apex Court, inter alia, observed as follows:[314]

> The power of the Government to appoint a Commission of Inquiry and name the person or persons constituting it is in sub-sections (1) and (2) of Section 3. Sub-section (2) merely

311. AIR 1993 SC 825; (1993) 1 SCC 302.

312. The General Clauses Act, 1897, Section "21. Power to issue, to include power to add to, amend, vary or rescind, notifications, orders, rules or bye-laws—where, by any Central Act or Regulation, a power to issue notifications, orders, rules or bye-laws is conferred, then that power includes a power, exercisable in the like manner and subject to the like sanction and conditions, if any, to add to, amend, vary or rescind any notifications, orders, rule or bye-laws so issued."

313. AIR 1993 SC 825; (1993) 1 SCC 302.

314. *Ibid.*, pp. 836-39.

confers the power in the Government to appoint a Commission consisting of one or more members and provides that if there be more than one member of the Commission, then one of them may be appointed Chairman of the Commission. It is not as if sub-section (1) deals with mere appointment of a Commission of Inquiry without clothing it with its personnel and the power to appoint the member/members thereof is to be found only in sub-section (2). That apart, there is nothing in any of these provisions to suggest that the Government has the power to reconstitute the Commission after its appointment by replacing the existing sole member with another person. Sub-section (3) deals expressly with the Government's power to fill any vacancy which may have arisen since the constitution of the Commission. The question of replacement of a member appointed initially is obviously beyond its scope.

Sub-section (3) inserted by amendment in Section 3 of the Commissions of Inquiry Act, 1952 is a clear indication of the limit and extent to which the power of reconstitution of the Commission can be exercised by the Government after the Commission has been constituted. As the Law Commission's report itself indicates, this amendment became necessary to provide expressly in the statute for the Government's power to fill any vacancy after the initial constitution. Whatever may have been the position prior to insertion of sub-section (3) in Section 3, there can be no doubt that after its insertion, the scheme of enactment excludes the power of reconstitution of the Commission in a manner not expressly provided therein. In view of sub-section (3), it is not permissible to construe sub-sections (1) and (2) of Section 3 in any other manner. If the scheme of the enactment gave such wide power to reconstitute a Commission after its initial constitution and permitted replacement or substitution of the existing member of a Commission with another person sans sub-section (3) of Section 3, the power to fill any vacancy was not required to be provided separately and expressly. The mere fact that such a provision was considered necessary and has been enacted by inserting sub-section (3) is sufficient to negative such a contention. It is also significant that in the amendment so made the power is limited only to filling any vacancy without conferring any power to reconstitute the Commission by replacement or substitution of the existing member which indicates that no such power of replacement or substitution of the existing member was contemplated in the scheme of the Act or intended to be conferred on the Government even after the amendment. Section 8A was simultaneously inserted by amendment to provide that the procedure does not require interruption of the inquiry by reason of change in the constitution of the Commission due to filling any vacancy or decrease in the number of members. The expression "or by any other reason" in sub-section (2) of Section 8A cannot be widened to include the reason of reconstitution of the Commission by replacement or substitution of the existing member since that power is not available to the Government in the scheme of the Act and, therefore, this expression in Section 8A(2) cannot be read as conferring any additional power or giving any such indication. The expression "or by any other reason" following "vacancy having been filled" in Section 8A(2) must, therefore, mean any other reason, such as decrease in the number of members, when the initial number is more than one, and the vacancy remains unfilled. It cannot mean substitution of the existing member with another person, since no such power exists. Section 8A(2) is not the source of an additional power but merely an indication of the power to reconstitute the Commission. The indication is of the power of reconstitution being available only in the manner indicated.

In this context, reference to Section 7 of the Commissions of Inquiry Act, 1952 is also apt. This provision lays down that the Commission would cease to exist when the appropriate Government by notification declares that "the continued existence of the Commission is unnecessary". Such a notification issued under Section 7 in the event of the continued existence of the Commission becoming unnecessary has the effect of rescinding the notification issued under Section 3 of the Act constituting the Commission. The enactment, therefore, also provides in Section 7 the only situation in which the Government can rescind the notification issued under Section 3 constituting the

Commission. To the extent to which express provision is made in the enactment, it is common ground, Section 21 of the General Clauses Act, 1897 cannot be invoked.

Section 21 of the General Clauses Act can be invoked only if, and to the extent, if any, the context and the scheme of the Commission of Inquiry Act so permits. The general power in Section 21 of the General Clauses Act is "to add to, amend, vary or rescind any notifications", etc. In the context of reconstitution of the Commission, the power to fill any vacancy in the office of a member of the Commission is expressly provided in sub-section (3) of Section 3 of the Commission of Inquiry Act. Similarly, the power to discontinue the existence of the Commission when it becomes unnecessary can be exercised by issue of a notification in accordance with Section 7 of the Act which results in rescinding the notification issued under Section 3 constituting the Commission. Thus, the power to rescind any notification conferred generally in Section 21 of the General Clauses Act is clearly inapplicable in the scheme of the Commission of Inquiry Act which expressly provides for the exercise of this power in relation to a Commission constituted under Section 3 of the Act. The only material, remaining general powers in Section 21 of the General Clauses Act are the power to 'amend' or 'vary' any notification. The extent to which the constitution of the Commission can be amended or varied by filling any vacancy in the office of a member as provided in the Commissions of Inquiry Act is also obviously excluded from the purview of Section 21 of the General Clauses Act which cannot be invoked for this purpose.

The surviving question, therefore, is: Whether there is power to reconstitute the Commission by replacement or substitution of the existing member, though not provided in the Commissions of Inquiry Act by invoking the residuary power to amend or vary any notification under Section 21 of General Clauses Act? In the first place, in a case like the present where the scheme of the Commissions of Inquiry Act does provide for amendment and variation of the notification issued under Section 3 for the purpose of reconstitution of the Commission in the manner indicated, even that power to amend or vary any notification by virtue of Section 21 of the General Clauses Act must be taken as excluded by clear implication in the sphere of reconstitution of the Commission. Moreover, the power to amend or vary cannot include the power to replace or substitute the existing composition of the commission with an entirely new composition. The fact that the time specified in the initial notification for completing the task of the Commission is enlarged by subsequent notification and this is done in exercise of the general power available under the General Clauses Act to extend time, does not support the argument that the general power under Section 21 of the General Clauses Act is also available to reconstitute the Commission by replacement or substitution of its sole member. The aid of Section 21 of the General Clauses Act for enlargement of time does not conflict with the context or scheme of the Commissions of Inquiry Act.

The context as well as the scheme of the Commissions of Inquiry Act, 1952 clearly indicate that Section 21 of the General Clauses Act, 1897 cannot be invoked to enlarge the Government's power to reconstitute the Commission constituted under Section 3 of the Act in a manner other than that expressly provided in the Commissions of Inquiry Act. There being no express power given by the Commissions of Inquiry Act to the appropriate Government to reconstitute the Commission of Inquiry constituted under Section 3 of the Act by replacement or substitution of its sole member and the existence of any such power being negatived by clear implication, no such power can be exercised by the appropriate Government. The scheme of the enactment is that the appropriate Government should have no control over the Commission after its constitution under Section 3 of the Act except for the purpose of filling any vacancy which may have arisen in the office of a member of the Commission apart from winding up the Commission by issuance of a notification under Section 7 of the Act if the continued existence of the Commission is considered unnecessary. The vacancy in the office of a member of the Commission may arise for several reasons, including resignation by the member, when the Government's power to fill the vacancy under Section 3(3) of the Act can be exercised. Even though a case of implied resignation creating an implied vacancy was set up by the State of Madhya Pradesh before the High Court, that stand was rightly abandoned before the Apex Court.

There is no doubt that the rule of construction embodied in Section 21 of the General Clauses Act cannot apply to the provisions of the Commissions of Inquiry Act, 1952 relating to reconstitution of a Commission constituted thereunder since the subject-matter, context and effect of such provisions are inconsistent with such application. Moreover, the construction made by the Apex Court best harmonises with the subject of the enactment and the object of the legislation. Restoring public confidence by constituting a Commission of Inquiry to investigate into a "definite matter of public importance" is the purpose of such an exercise. It is, therefore, the prime need that the Commission functions as an independent agency free from any governmental control after its constitution. It follows that after appointment, the tenure of members of the Commission should not be dependent on the will of the Government, to secure their independence. A body not so independent is not likely to enjoy the requisite public confidence and may not attract men of quality and self-respect. In such a situation, the object of the enactment would be frustrated. This aspect suggests that the aforesad construction apart from harmonising the provisions of the statute, also promotes the object of the enactment while the construction to the contrary frustrates both.

It may be useful to refer in this regard the provisions of Section 3(3)(b) of the Jammu and Kashmir Commissions of Inquiry Act, which expressly provides for increase in the number of members of a Commission set up under that Act.

The question that now arises is what will be status of a reconstituted commission. Whether such a reconstituted commission will be void ab initio? Or, it will not be treated as a commission constituted under Section 3 of the Act at all. While holding that the appropriate Government does not have powers under the Act to reconstitute a Commission thereunder, the Supreme Court did not deal with the question of status of reconstituted Commission under the Act. The Act does not contain any provision in this regard. There are no penal consequences for reconstituting a Commission that has been set up under Section 3 of the Act. Since the Commissions constituted under the Act are in the nature of fact-finding bodies and their reports are not enforceable on their own and are not otherwise binding on the Government, it appears that a reconstituted Commission may not be void ab initio. At best, a reconstituted Commission may not be treated as the one having been duly set up under the Act and as such, would not be a Commission for the purposes of the Act. If such a Commission has not completed its functions and submitted its report, it may be possible to have a writ of prohition issued against it at the instance of an aggrieved person, restraining it from further functioning. But where it has already submitted its report, nothing further worthwhile can be done and the report of such a Commission can be viewed as of any other fact-finding body.

Inquiry Need not Necessarily Precede by a Preliminary Inquiry

In *Sri Narayanadoss Mahant and Another* v. *Sri T. Neeladri Rao and Another*,[315] it was contended that the Special Officer should have held a preliminary inquiry as to whether the Mutt is a public religious institution before proceeding to act under the notifications issued by the Government, and only then, he would have had jurisdiction to conduct an inquiry into the affairs of the Mutt. Negating this contention, the Court held that "Neither Section 3 of the Act nor the notifications contemplate such a preliminary investigation by the Special Officer. The Officer was acting on information which more than 'prima facie' showed that the Mutt is a public Mutt, and he had also information that the affairs of the Mutt were being grossly mismanaged by the petitioner."

It is, however, open to the appropriate Government to institute a preliminary inquiry to examine the available materials to see if a prima facie case is made out for appointment of a Commission of Inquiry which itself would thoroughly go into

315. AIR 1959 Andhra Pradesh 148.

all the allegations by following the principle of natural justice as is applicable to the fact and circumstances of a particular case. Such an inquiry that the appropriate Government may make to reach the ultimate decision is essentially administrative in nature and not a quasi-judicial inquiry in which any of the parties has the right of hearing.[316]

In *P.R. Nayak* v. *Union of India*,[317] it was contended that the Parliamentary Committee on Public Undertakings had gone into the whole matter and had recommended disciplinary action against delinquent officers and, therefore, no definite matter of public importance survived to justify the appointment of the Commission. On facts, the Court held that the Committee gave no definite findings and it only made a recommendation to the Government to verify and investigate the various matters referred to it. It is true that in some parts of the report recommendation was made to take suitable action against certain named and unnamed officers but it would be straining the language too much to say that even for this purpose no further inquiry or investigation by an independent body was called for. In view of the fact that aspersions were cast by the Committee in its report not only against certain officers but also against the Government, the Government were, in the opinion of the Court, not only justified in the circumstances of the case but acted fairly in deciding that an inquiry into the matters referred to by the Parliamentary Committee should be made not by the Government itself but by an independent body constituted under the Act to find the relevant facts which could be implemented by governmental action. Accordingly, it was held that it could not be said that no definite matters of public importance survived after the report of the Parliamentary Committee and in fact there was eminent justification for the appointment of an independent Commission under the Act to find facts with respect to these matters.

---

316. *Dr. Harekrushna Mahtab* v. *The Chief Minister of Orissa and Others*, AIR 1971 Orissa 175.

317. ILR (1973) I Delhi 747.

Notification under the Section is not Bad for Excessive Delegation

A notification for setting up a Commission of Inquiry under Section 3 is not bad on account of delegation of essential legislative function. Assuming that there is delegation of legislative function, the Act having laid down its policy, such delegation of power, if any, is not vitiated at all, for the legislation by the delegatee will have to conform to the policy so laid down by the Act.[318]

Limits of Executive Power

Where a Commission of Inquiry has been set up by the Government pursuant to the recommendations made by the Parliamentary Committee on Public Undertakings to verify and investigate the subject matters under reference, the legality of the establishment of the Commission can not be assailed on the ground of exceeding limits of executive powers of the Government. The Government in such a case does what the Committee wants it to do, namely, to verify and investigate into various matters dealt with by the Committee. The effect of the terms of reference in this case is not to inquire into the correctness of the conclusions of the Committee. The question of the Government exceeding the limits of its executive power does not arise.[319] However, a notification appointing a Committee, in exercise of the executive of the Government, to monitor the investigation of criminal cases relating to criminal offences, which had been committed during the riots that had taken place after assassination of Smt. Indira Gandhi on 31-10-1984 was quashed for being contrary to the provisions of the Delhi Police Act as well as the Code of Criminal Procedure.[320] Accordingly, it was held that the power of superintendence vested in the Lt. Governor over the police by virtue Section 4 of the Delhi Police

---

318. *Ram Krishna Dalmia and Others* v. *Shri Justice S.R. Tendolkar and Others*, AIR 1958 SC 538, p. 554.
319. *P.R. Nayak* v. *Union of India*, ILR (1973) I Delhi 747.
320. *Brahma Nand Gupta* v. *Delhi Adminitration and Others*, 1989 (4) Delhi Lawyer (DB) 94.

Act could not have been delegated to the Committee. The Lt. Governor also could not have been appointed the Committee with the powers of investigation or direct control over investigation and registration of cases or power of superintendence over police and prosecuting agency. The decision whether to register an FIR, how to proceed with the investigation, are different steps in the course of investigation. The power of monitoring which has been conferred on the Committee by the impugned notification is, in fact, a power of investigating and this power cannot be vested in anyone who is not otherwise, in law, entitled to investigate. It may, thus, be seen that the executive powers should be exercised in conformity with the law.

Notification not Conforming to Article 77

Whether a notification issued under Section 3 of the Act will stand vitiated if it has not fulfilled the requirements of Article 77 of the Constitution of India? This question came up for consideration before the Court in the case of *M. Karunanidhi* v. *Union of India*.[321] Under Article 77, all executive action of the Government of India shall be expressed to be taken in the name of the President. Clause (2) of this Article further provides that orders and other instruments made and executed in the name of the President shall be authenticated in such manner as may be specified in rules to be made by the President and the validity of an order or instrument which is so authenticated shall not be called in question on the ground that it is not an order or instrument made or executed by the President. Article 77(3) enables the President to make rules for the more convenient transaction of the business of the Government of India and for the allocation among Ministers of the said business. In this case, the notification was made by the Cabinet Secretariat in its Department of Personnel and Administrative Reforms, signed by an officer of the rank of the Secretary to the Government of India and issued in the name of the Central Government. The notification was not authenticated in terms of Article 77(2). It was, therefore, contended that the notification was bad. The Court did not accept this contention for the reason that the

321. AIR 1977 Madras 192.

provisions of Article 77 are directory and not mandatory. In support of this view, the Court relied on the case of *State of U.P.* v. *O.P. Gupta*,[322] wherein the Supreme Court, while dealing with an order made by the Government of United Provinces, signed by the Chief Secretary, held that the provisions of Article 166(1) and (2) are directory and not mandatory and substantial compliance with those provisions was sufficient. Article 166 corresponds to Article 77 and requires all executive action of the State Government be expressed in the name of the Governor and its authentication in the prescribed manner. It was further held that the courts were entitled to presume that the official acts were done in a proper manner. Where necessary, the Government could lead evidence to prove that the proceedings were taken according to the requirements of the Constitution and the rules.[323] However, where the evidence in a case does not show that the Order appointing the Commission of Inquiry has been issued, signed or authenticated as required under the Constitution and the rules framed thereunder and the Order has also not been issued in the name of the concerned Constitutional authority, say, the Governor, the notification issued in consequence thereof cannot be sustained. Reference in this regard may be made to the case of *P.K. Kunju* v. *State of Kerala*,[324] wherein the notification was purported to be signed by the Special Secretary, under the superscription: "By Order of the Governor". The contention that a Special Secretary was not a Secretary to the Government and did not fit in with any of the labels[325] specifically mentioned

---

322. AIR 1970 SC 679.

323. *Ram Krishna Dalmia* v. *Justice S.R. Tendolkar*, AIR 1958 SC 538; *State of Karnataka* v. *Union of India*, AIR 1978 SC 68; *Orient Paper Mills* v. *Union of India*, AIR 1979 Calcutta 114.

324. AIR 1970 Kerala 252.

325. Under Rule 12 of the Rules of Business, framed under clauses (2) and (3) of Article 166, every order or instrument of the Government of the State shall be signed by a Secretary, an Additional Secretary, Joint Secretary, a Deputy Secretary, an Under Secretary or an Assistant Secretary or by such Officer as may be specifically empowered in that behalf and such signature shall be deemed to be the proper authentication of such order or instrument.

in Rule 12 of the Rules of Business, did not appeal to the Court. The Court observed that by reason of his "speciality" he did not lose his general brand as a Secretary to Government. However, the file containing the original order signed by the Special Secretary could not be produced to satisfy the Court as to the compliance with the constitutional requirements. It was, inter alia, contended that although the original order had in fact not been signed by the Special Secretary, it had nevertheless been properly and validly issued by the Chief Minister within whose allotted sphere the matter stood, according to the Rules of Business framed under Article 166(2) and (3) of the Constitution, and consistent with Article 154. This contention too did not find favour with the Court as even in such a case the proceeding must have been signed and authenticated by the Chief Minister. As the original of the order was not produced, it could not be said to have been authenticated and signed by the Chief Minister by order of the Governor. Furthermore, production of a draft notification with some unidentified and undated initials and an endorsement that 'this order may issue' but without any one's signature, could not, in the Court's view, amount to a signature or authentication of the original order/notification by the Chief Minister. At best, the Court opined that this could only amount to an order of the Chief Minister, approving the draft put up to him and directing its issue. Accordingly, the Court held that there was no valid notification appointing the Commission of Inquiry.

Fixation of Time in the Notification is Essential

Section 3 of the Act lays down that the notification appointing a Commission of Inquiry should specify the functions and the time within which those functions should be performed, and the Commission shall make the inquiry and performs the functions accordingly. It is, therefore, necessary to fix a time in the notification setting up a Commission of Inquiry within which that Commission is required to complete its report. However, the defect is curable by issue of a subsequent notification. There is nothing to prevent the Government from issuing a fresh notification appointing a Commission and fixing a time. If this can be done, then there is no reason why the same result cannot be achieved by the combined effect of two notifications. In any case the amending notification may be read as a fresh notification within the meaning of Section 3 of the Act, operative at least from the date of the later notification.[326] However, till the defect is cured, the Commission is debarred from functioning under the notifications notwithstanding the fact that the notifications themselves are not invalid. The Commission would be, so to speak, in a state of suspended animation.[327]

There is no warrant for the proposition that the time initially fixed cannot be extended from time to time. Section 21 of the General Clauses Act provides that the power to issue includes the power, inter alia, to amend any notifications or orders, etc. Therefore, the extension of time from time to time would be in exercise of this power to amend. The Government considers the request of a Commission for extension of time and it is upon consideration of such request the extension is given. It may be that the prolongation of the inquiry may cause hardship to the persons appearing before it either voluntarily or in response to notices under Section 8B of the Act. But such delays are inevitable in view of the nature of the terms of reference and the scope of the inquiry.[328]

Since the Court has no power to direct the Government to appoint a Commission under the Act, in the same vein, the Court cannot compel the Government to extend the term of that Commission either.[329]

The requirement of Section 3 in respect of fixed time limit, in the order appointing a Commission of Inquiry, within which the Commission should submit its report, does not apply to inquiring authorities not set up under the Act.

Although fixation of time within which the Commissions should submit their reports is an essential requirement for their

---

326. *P.R. Nayak* v. *Union of India*, ILR (1973) I delhi; 747, pp. 753-54.
327. *Sri Narayanadoss Mahant and Another* v. *Sri T. Neeladri Rao and Another*, AIR 1959 Andhra Pradesh 148.
328. *P.R. Nayak* v. *Union of India*, ILR (1973) I Delhi 747.
329. *Jan Sangharsh Manch* v. *State of Gujarat*, AIR 1998 Gujarat 133.

valid appointment under the Act, yet seldom such reports are submitted in time. Recently, the Liberhan Commission, probing the Babri Masjid demolition case, has been given three-month extension.[330] When it was set up in December 1992, the Commission headed by former Andhra Pradesh High Court Chief Justice Manmohan Singh Liberhan, was given three months to finalise its report. Since then, its term has been extended from time to time and the previous extension was till March 31, 2007. While notifying the last extension, the Government had directed the Commission to submit its report on or before March 31, indicating that it would provide additional manpower if needed. The Commission, however, could not submit its report though it had completed the deposition of the last witness in June 2006. The Liberhan Commission ultimately submitted its report to the Government on 30 June 2009 almost after 17 years of its establishment. Its tenure has been extended 48 times. It held 399 sittings. This is the longest Commission of Inquiry in the history of independent India, on which the government spent over Rs. 8.15 crore until the month before it submitted its report.[330a] The delay in the submission of the report attracted wide-spread criticism in the media.[330b] The criticism of delay in the submission of the report by the Liberhan Commission has been very aptly summed up in the following comment: "If anything, the Liberhan Commission should serve as a model for the future is as to how a commission of inquiry should not be."[330c] Just how long a commission continue? Some commissions are open-ended. For example, Balakrishna Eradi, at 87, is still the chairperson of the commission

330. *Indian Express*, dated 05-04-2007: "Liberhan Commission gets 3-month extension".

330a. "17 Years, 48 Extensions—That's What Liberhan Commission Took to Complete its Probe, *The Indian Express*, July 1, 2009.

330b. M.J. Akbar, "Does Justice Matter After 17 years—The Siege Within," *Times of India*, July 5, 2009; "Self Indicted—Can There be any Excuse for Justice Liberhan to have Taken so long to Submit Babri Report?" Editorial, *The Indian Express*, July 1, 2009, p. 10.

330c. "Organiser—View from the RIGHT Liberhan Commission," *The Indian Express*, July 9, 2009.

on sharing of the Ravi-Beas river water between Punjab and Haryana. Eradi has been holding the post since 1986, surely a record of sorts.[330d]

There may or may not be valid justification for such delays. Strictly speaking, such delay may not even be legally open to any objection in a given case. Nonetheless, the fact remains that if Inquiry Commissions take inordinate and unduly long time in completing their assigned tasks, it may seriously affect their credibility as well as utility and casts doubts on their legitimacy as a tool of information gathering and a part of decision-making process. Many a times, legal proceedings are initiated in Courts in respect of matters even before inquiry in respect thereto is completed by Commissions of Inquiry appointed for that purpose. One may wonder as to what justification would be there for the continuance of such an Inquiry Commission especially when the subject of inquiry has been taken to the Court for adjudication or, as the case may be, trial. It is true that the Courts, while dealing with such cases, will determine the rights and liabilities of the parties involved or the guilt of the accused persons facing trial in such cases. Nevertheless, there may still be certain aspects pertaining to the subject of such an inquiry that may escape judicial consideration in the Court cases and, to that extent, a Commission of Inquiry appointed under the Act in the matter would still be rendering useful job. Notwithstanding that, it would be imperative for all the Commissions of Inquiry to complete their inquiries most expeditiously and at the earliest. Any undue delay in such cases may, at times, frustrate the very purpose of their appointment and seriously jeopardize the efficacy as well as the adequacy of the august institution of the Inquiry Commissions.

The Supreme Court in *Maneka Gandhi* v. *Union of India*[331] has adversely commented upon the delay-aspect in the submission of their reports by Commissions of Inquiry. In this case, the

330d. Coomi Kapoor, "A Commission is Forever," *The Indian Express*, July 10, 2009, p. 10.

331. (1978) 1 SCC 248, p. 317, para 38.

passport of the petitioner was impounded by the Central Government, under Section 10(3)(c) of the Passport Act, in the interests of the general public. This was assailed by the petitioner on several grounds one of which was that the impugned Order was voilative of Article 19(1)(a) or Article 19(1)(g). In this regard, the Court observed that "if impugned Order impounding the passport of the petitioner were voilative of her right to freedom of speech and expression or her right to carry on her profession as a journalist, it would not be saved by Article 19(2) or Article 19(6), because the impounding of the passport for an indefinite length of time would clearly constitute an unreasonable restriction." The Union responded to this by contending that though the period for which the impugned Order was to operate was not specified in so many terms, it was clear that it was intended to be coterminous with the duration of the Commission of Inquiry, since the reason for impounding was that the presence of the petitioner was likely to be required in connection with the proceedings before the Commission of Inquiry and the term of the Commission of Inquiry being limited upto December 31, 1977, the impounding of the passport could not continue beyond that date and, hence, it would not be said that the impugned Order was to operate for an indefinite period of time. This, however, did not find favour with the Court especially having regard to the general practice of non-submission of reports by the Commission of Inquiry within their originally stipulate time periods. Accordingly, their Lordship observed: "Now it is true that the passport of the petitioner was impounded on the ground that her presence was likely to be required in connection with the proceeding before the Commission of Inquiry and the initial time limit fixed for the Commission of Inquiry to submit by the Government was 31-12-1977, but the time limit could always be extended by the Government and the experience of several Commissions of Inquiry set up in this country over the last twenty-five years shows that hardly any Commission of Inquiry has been able to complete its report within the originally appointed time. Whatever might have been the expectation in regard to the duration of the Commission of Inquiry headed by Mr. Justice Shah at the time when the impugned Order was made, it is now clear that it has not been possible for it to complete its labours by 31-12-1977 which was the time limit originally fixed and in fact its term has been extended upto 31-5-1978. The period for which the passport is impounded cannot, in the circumstances, be said to be definite and certain and it may extend to an indefinite point of time. This would clearly make the impugned Order unreasonable.[332]

Another related aspect in this regard is that of Commission's proceedings after the expiry of the time fixed in the notification setting up that Commission and before issue of further notification extending the term of the Commission. Normally, a Commission will cease to exist by afflux of time on the expiry of its term stipulated in the notification under which it is constituted. As such, the Commission is not expected to hold any further proceedings after the expiry of its term. However, issue of notification extending the term of the Commission takes time and quite often issued after the expiry of the previous term of the Commission. Once such a notification is issued, all proceedings held during the intervening period stand regularized. A one-man Commission headed by retired Justice A.N. Gupta was appointed to inquire into the alleged anomalies in the computerized draw of lots for the allotment of 1250 plots in Noida on July 2, 2005. The Commission was set up on July 14, 2005 and given 90 days time to submit its report. Its tenure was last extended to October 31, 2006. But the Commission continued to conduct hearings in February 2007, i.e. four months after its tenure expired. Sources in the State Government stated that the

332. The learned Attorney General, appearing on behalf of the Central Government, made a statement that in case the decision to impound the passport of the petitioner is confirmed by the Central Government after hearing the petitioner, the duration of the impounding will not exceed a period of six months from the date of the decision that may be taken on the petitioner's representation. The Court found this very reasonable and expressed the hope and trust that in future impounding of passport would be for a specified period of time which is not unreasonably long, even though no contravention of fundamental right might be involved.

panel was unlikely to get more time to finish its probe.[333] If that be so, the proceedings and the resultant report would be ultra vires the powers if the Commission as it ceased to legally exist after expiry of its term and further consequences would follow accordingly. But if the term of the Commission is further extended, then all such proceedings will get regularized. In such a case, it will be open to the Commission in law to proceed on the basis of such proceedings notwithstanding the procedural irregularity. The proceedings and the the ultimate report of the Commission will not be vitiated on this count. However, any inordinate delay in the submission of its report by a commission of inquiry strikes at the very root of the purpose and the validity of the setting up that commission. As stated earlier, such inquiries are essentially a tool of information gathering for taking sound decisions in a given matter. Therefore, any undue delay in the submission of the inquiry report causes more harm than its intended use and benefit and throws serious doubts on the very necessity, utility and validity of the institution of inquiry commission itself. "For one, setting a precedent for unending inquiries encourages the political leadership[333a] to postpone any tough decisions by sending them off to an interminable commission. But there's yet another concern. Events like the Babri demolition—and the Gujarat and Bombay riots, and the assassination of Rajiv Gandhi—need to be followed by fact-finding, by sifting the rumours from the truth, by a mechanism of accountability that prevents people's characters being mauled by the Chinese whispers of gossip as well as ensuring that those who bear responsibility can't get away by saying "If there was evidence, wouldn't I have been indicted?' Since Shah Commission probed the Emergency of 30 years ago—had its final report "restricted"[333b] such that, possibly, no complete version

333. As reported in *Hindustan Times*, February 28, 2007, p. 5, titled "Probe into Noida plot scam going nowhere".

333a. For that matter, administrative authority/leadership as well.

333b. A commission report is no longer restrictive after amendment of Section 3 in 1990.

survives—India's commissions of inquiry have failed at this basic function."[333c]

Delay in Instituting Inquiry

Delay by itself would not make an inquiry illegal. In the case of *M. Karunanidhi* v. *Union of India*,[334] one of the grounds on which institution of inquiry was challenged was that over two years had elapsed between the date when the allegations were made originally and the date of the ordering the Inquiry. This, however, did not find favour with the Court, as in the Court's view, there might have been several reasons for the inquiry being postponed.

Can a Commission of Inquiry Suggest Measures to be Taken by the Appropriate Government?

An inquiry necessarily involves investigation into facts and necessitates the collection of material facts from the evidence adduced before or brought to the notice of the person or body conducting the inquiry and the recording of its findings on those facts in its report cannot but be regarded as ancillary to the inquiry itself, for the inquiry becomes useless unless the findings of the inquiring body are made available to the Government which set up the inquiry. It is equally ancillary that the person or body conducting the inquiry should express its own view on the facts found by it for the consideration of the appropriate Government in order to enable it to take such measure as it may think fit to do. The whole purpose of setting up of a Commission of Inquiry consisting of experts will be frustrated and the elaborate process of inquiry will be deprived of its utility if the opinion and the advice of the expert body as to the measures the situation disclosed calls for cannot be placed before the Government for consideration notwithstanding that doing so cannot be to the prejudice of anybody because it has no force of its own. The recommendations of a Commission of Inquiry

---

333c. "Self Indicted—Can There be any Excuse for Justice Liberhan to have Taken so Long to Submit the Babri Report," Editorial, *The Indian Express*, July 1, 2009, p. 10.

334. AIR 1977 Madras 192.

are of great importance to the Government in order to enable it to make up its mind as to what legislative or administrative measures should be adopted to eradicate the evil found or to implement the beneficial objects it has in view. From this point of view, there can be no objection even to the Commission of Inquiry recommending the imposition of some form of punishment which will, in its opinion, be sufficiently deterrent to delinquents in future. But seeing that the Commission of Inquiry has no judicial powers and its report will purely be recommendatory and not effective proprio vigore and the statement made by any person before the Commission of Inquiry is, under Section 6 of the Act, wholly inadmissible in evidence in any future proceedings, civil or criminal, there can be no point in the Commission of Inquiry making recommendations for taking any action "as and by way of securing redress or punishment" which refers to wrongs already done or committed, for redress or punishment for such wrongs, if any, has to be imposed by a Court of law properly constituted exercising its own discretion on the facts and circumstances of the case and without being in any way influenced by the view of any person or body, howsoever august or high powered it may be. Accordingly, a clause in the notification, setting up a Commission of Inquiry, which called upon the Commission to make recommendations about the action to be taken "as and by way of securing redress or punishment", was held to be not necessary for or ancillary to the purposes of the Commission and was directed to deleted being outside the scope of the Act.[335]

In *G.S. Harnal* v. *Union of India and Others*,[336] the terms of reference of the Commission, inter alia, included the following clauses, namely,

> "(iv) to advise on whether there has been any negligence or carelessness on the part of the refinery management and staff in the discharge of their prescribed duties;

---

335. *Ram Krishna Dalmia* v. *Justice S.R. Tendolkar*, AIR 1958 SC 538, pp. 546-47.

336. ILR (1971) II Delhi 129.

(v) arising out of (iv): to recommend further action, if any, that must be taken;"

These clauses were objected to on the ground that these could not have been validly referred to the Commission under Section 3 of the Act and in support of this; the decision of the Supreme Court in *Ram Krishna Dalmia* v. *Justice S.R. Tendolkar and Others*[337] was relied on. Negating this contention, the Court observed that the impugned clauses of the terms of reference of the Commission did not ask the Commission to recommend action as and by way of securing redress or punishment. They merely asked the Commission to advice whether there had been negligence on the part of the Refinery management and the staff and to recommend further action, if any. This was held to be perfectly legal and within the scope of the authority of the Government acting under Section 3 of the Act. The Court observed that the Supreme Court has actually gone and held that such a Commission can even be asked to recommend the imposition of some form of punishment, which will deter such delinquents in future. The Court, therefore, did not find any merit in the objection of the petitioners against these terms of reference.

On the other hand, in *State of Jammu and Kashmir* v. *Bakshi Gulam Mohammad*,[338] the notification setting up the Commission of Inquiry, was challenged, inter alia, on the ground that it did not mention anything about the steps to be taken to prevent the recurrence of the lapses in future. The Court observed that before facts were found steps could not be thought of, for the steps had to suit the facts. The inquiry proposed in this case will, in the course of finding out the lapses alleged, find out the process as to how they occurred and it is only after the process is known that steps can be devised to meet them.

Whether Commission of Inquiry can be Appointed for Inquiring into the Conduct of an Individual or Company?

Section 3, which permits a Commission of Inquiry to be appointed, is wide enough to cover an inquiry into the conduct

337. AIR 1958 SC 538; (1959) SCR 279.

338. AIR 1967 SC 122.

of any individual. There is no force in the contention that the conduct of an individual cannot possibly be a matter of public importance especially when as a result of such conduct public funds have been alleged to be frittered away.[339]

In State of *Jammu and Kashmir* v. *Bakshi Gulam Mohammad*,[340] it was contended, based on Section 10 of J&K Commissions of Inquiry Act, 1962,[341] that an inquiry may be made under the Act into the conduct of a person only incidentally, that is to say, it can be made only when that becomes necessary in connection with an inquiry into something else. It was, therefore, contended that an inquiry, which was directly into the conduct of Bakshi Ghulam Mohammad was outside the scope of the Act. These contentions did not find favour with the Supreme Court. Their Lordships observed: "It could not be natural reading of the Act to cut down the scope of S. 3 by an implication drawn from S. 10. We also think that this argument is ill founded for we are unable to agree that S. 10 does not apply to a person whose conduct comes up directly for inquiry before a Commission set up under S. 3. We find nothing in the words of S. 10 to justify that view. If a Commission is set up to inquire directly into the conduct of a person, the Commission must find it necessary to inquire into that conduct and such a person would, therefore, be one covered by S. 10. It would be strange indeed if the Act provided for rights of a person whose conduct incidentally came to be enquired into but did not do so in the case of persons whose conduct has directly to be inquired into under the order setting up the Commission. It would be equally strange if the Act contemplated the conduct of a person being inquired into incidentally and not directly. What can be done indirectly should obviously have been considered capable of being done directly."[342] The Court further held that the

339. *P.R. Nayak* v. *Union of India*, ILR (1973) I Delhi 747.

340. AIR 1967 SC 122.

341. Sub-sections (1) and (2) of Section 10 of the J&K Commissions of Inquiry Act, 1962 correspond to Sections 8B and 8C of the Commissions of Inquiry Act, 1952 respectively.

342. AIR 1967 SC 122, p. 129.

notification was not violative of Article 14 of the Constitution as the individual whose assets were to be inquired into, was a class by himself and the classification had a rational connection with the setting up of the Commission for the object was to find out whether the wealth had been acquired by him by the abuse of official position.

In *Ram Krishna Dalmia* v. *Justice S.R. Tendolkar*,[343] the notification appointing Commission of Inquiry was challenged on the ground, inter alia, that a Commission of Inquiry could not be appointed under the Act to inquire into the conduct of an individual person or company. It was pointed out that the Act, by Section 3, empowered the appropriate Government in certain eventualities to appoint a Commission of Inquiry for the purpose of making an inquiry into any definite matter of public importance and for no other purpose. The contention was that the conduct of an individual person or company could not possibly be a matter of public importance and far less a definite matter of that kind. This contention, however, did not find favour with the Supreme Court. Hon'ble S.R. Das, CJ observed as follows:

> We are unable to accept this argument as correct. Widespread floods, famine and pestilence may quite easily be a definite matter of public importance urgently calling for an inquiry so as to enable the Government to take appropriate steps to prevent their recurrence in future. The conduct of villagers in cutting the bunds for taking water to their fields during the dry season may cause floods during the rainy season and we see no reason why such unsocial conduct of villagers of certain villages thus causing floods should not be regarded as a definite matter of public importance. The failure of a big bank resulting in the loss of the life savings of a multitude of men of moderate means is certainly a definite matter of public importance but the conduct of the persons in charge and management of such a bank which brought about its collapse is equally a definite matter of public importance. Widespread dacoities in particular parts of the country is no

343. AIR 1958 SC 538.

doubt, a definite matter of public importance but we see no reason why the conduct, activities and modus operandi of particular dacoits and thugs notorious for their cruel depredations should not be regarded as definite matters of public importance urgently requiring a sifting inquiry. It is needless to multiply instances. In each case the question is: Is there a definite matter of public importance which calls for an inquiry? We see no warrant for the proposition that a definite matter of public importance must necessarily mean only some matter involving the public benefit or advantage in the abstract, e.g. public health, sanitation or the like or some public evil or prejudice, e.g., floods, famine or pestilence or the like. Quite conceivably the conduct of an individual persons or companies or a group of individuals or companies may assume such a dangerous proportion and may so prejudicially affect or threaten to affect the public well-being as to make such conduct a definite matter of public importance urgently calling for a full inquiry. Besides, S. 3 itself authorizes the appropriate Government to appoint a Commission of Inquiry not only for the purpose of making an inquiry into a definite matter of public importance but also for the purpose of performing such functions as may be specified in the notification. Therefore, the notification is well within the powers conferred on the appropriate Government by S. 3 of the Act and it cannot be questioned on the ground of its going beyond the provisions of the Act.[344]

In the aforesaid case, the notification setting up the Commission of Inquiry has been challenged on the ground, among others, that the petitioners and their companies have been arbitrarily singled out for the purpose of hostile and discriminatory treatment and subjected to a harassing and oppressive inquiry. The Court, inter alia, observed that "(I)t is true that the notification primarily or even solely affects the petitioners and their companies but it cannot be overlooked that Parliament having left the selective application of the Act

344. AIR 1958 SC 538, p. 544.

to the discretion of the appropriate Government, the latter must of necessity take its decision on the materials available to it and the opinion it forms thereon. The appropriate Government cannot in such matters be expected to sit down and hold a judicial inquiry into the truth of the materials brought before it, and examine the informants on oath in the presence of the parties who are or may be likely to be affected by its decision. In matters of this kind the appropriate Government has of necessity to act upon the information available to it. It is the best judge of the reliability of its source of information and if it acts in good faith on the materials brought to its notice and honestly comes to the conclusion that the act and conduct of the petitioners and the affairs of their companies constitute a definite matter of public importance calling for an inquiry with a view to devise measures for preventing the recurrence of such evil, this Court, not being in possession of all the facts will, we apprehend, be slow to adjudge the executive action to be bad and illegal. We are not unmindful of the fact that a very wide discretionary power has been conferred on the Government and, indeed, the contemplation that such wide powers in the hands of the executive may in some cases be misused or abused and turned into an engine of oppression has caused considerable anxiety in our mind. Nevertheless, the bare possibility that the powers may be misused or abused cannot *per se* induce the Court to deny the existence of the powers. It cannot be overlooked that Parliament has confided this discretion, not to any petty official but to the appropriate Government itself to take action in conformity with the policy and principle laid down in the Act. As this Court has said in *Matajog Dobey* v. *H.C. Bhare*,[345] "a discretionary power is not necessarily a discriminatory power and that abuse of power is not to be easily assumed where the discretion is vested in the Government and not in a minor official" We feel sure, however, that if this law is administered by the Government "with an evil eye and an unequal hand" or for an oblique or unworthy purpose the arms of this Court will be long enough to reach it and to strike down such abuse with a heavy hand".

345. 1955-2 SCR 925, p. 932; ((S) AIR 1956 SC 44, p. 48). (O).

Reference was made in this case to the several matters enumerated in the five clauses set out in the first preamble to the notification and it was urged that those matters did not at all disclose any intelligible differentia on the basis of which the petitioners and their companies could be grouped together as a class. On the part of the Union of India reference was made to the affidavits affirmed by Shri H.M. Patel, the Principal Secretary to the Finance Ministry of the Government of India purporting to set out in detail as the background thereof, the circumstances which led to the issue of the impugned notification and the matters recited therein and the several reports referred to in the said affidavit. Learned counsel for the petitioners took the objection that the reference could not be made to any extraneous matter and that the basis of classification must appear on the face of the notification itself. The Court held that the classification must not always appear on the face of the notification itself and that reference can be made to any extraneous materials. There can be no objection to the matters brought to the notice of the Court by the affidavit of Shri H.M. Patel being taken into consideration along with the matters specified in the notification in order to ascertain whether there was any valid basis for treating the petitioners and their companies as a class by themselves. It was then urged that even if such extraneous matter is taken into consideration, no intelligible criteria could therefrom be deduced which might be taken to distinguish the petitioners and their companies from other persons and their companies. The Court observed: "It is sufficient for our present purpose to say that the facts disclosed on the face of the notification itself and the facts which have been brought to our notice by the affidavits afford sufficient support to the presumption of constitutionality of the notification. There being thus a presumption of validity in favour of the Act and the notification, it is for the petitioners to allege and prove beyond doubt that the other persons or companies similarly situate have been left out and the petitioners and their companies have been singled out for discriminatory and hostile treatment. The petitioners have, in our opinion, failed to discharge that onus."[346]

346. AIR 1958 SC 538, pp. 550-53.

Can a reference to the Commission into the conduct of an individual government servant be said to be discriminatory because there are other recognized procedures for examining such a conduct? This contention came up for consideration before Delhi High Court in *P.R. Nayak* v. *Union of India*.[347] It was alleged in this case that if the Government had felt it necessary to take any action against any officers of the government undertakings concerned for their lapses and dereliction of duty, inquiries, preliminary or otherwise, could be held through the agency of the Central Vigilance Commissioner, the Central Bureau of Investigation, the Public Servants (Inquiries) Act, 1850 and the Government Servants Discipline, Appeal and Control, Rules etc., and, therefore, the appointment of the Commission in exercise of its executive power and its investment with powers under the Act would, in the circumstances, discriminatory. It was pointed out that while the inquiry under the Act is public, a disciplinary inquiry against an officer except under the Public Servants (Inquiries) Act, 1850, would not be open to public gaze; a lawyer has a right to appear before the Commission but not before the disciplinary authority; the public has no say before the disciplinary authority; no evidence has to be given by the officer in the preliminary inquiry in disciplinary proceedings while the defence is to be disclosed at the preliminary stage in the proceedings before the Commission and the proceedings of the Commission were bound to be long drawn process. The Court did not examine this contention as in its opinion the dominant purpose of appointing the Commission was not to hold an inquiry into the conduct of the petitioner and other government officers. Accordingly, the Court held that there was no question of discrimination by referring the matter for investigation to the Commission which is only a fact-finding body and whose findings have no effect proprio vigore.

However, a view can be taken that even if the dominant purpose of the inquiry by the Commission had been the conduct of a Government servant, yet that would not have made any material difference for what has to be seen is the object of inquiry.

---

347. ILR (1973) I Delhi 747.

If the object has been the ascertainment of the facts, the same could have been legitimately referred to a Commission of Inquiry. If the object, on the other hand, is to take some punitive action for the alleged misconduct of a delinquent officer, then recourse cannot be had to a Commission of Inquiry for this purpose. In such a case, recourse may have to be taken to the relevant recognized procedures through the appropriate agency. As has been observed by the Delhi High Court in another case,[348] the crux of the distinction between a fact-finding inquiry and a disciplinary inquiry is that the former does not compel any action and does not impose any punishment; the latter necessarily results in action or punishment. Therefore, the former cannot be quashed while the latter can be quashed.

Nonetheless, it has now been finally settled that a Commission of Inquiry can be validly constituted to inquire into the conduct of an individual or group of individuals where such conduct has assumed such a dangerous proportion and prejudicially affected or threaten to affect public well-being so as to make such conduct a definite matter of public importance for the purposes of Section 3 of the Act.[349]

Amount Spent on Inquiry-allowable Business Expenditure

It is well-settled that the deductibility of expenditure in prosecuting a civil proceedings does not depend on the final outcome of the proceedings, but on whether it is honesty incurred to promote the interest of the business. The essential test which has to be applied is whether the expenses were incurred for the preservation and protection of the assessee's business from any such process or proceedings which might have resulted in the reduction of its income and profits, and whether the same were actually and honestly incurred.[350] No distinction can be made

348. *G.S. Harnal* v. *Union of India*, ILR (1971) II Delhi 129, p. 142.

349. *Shri Ram Krishna Dalmia* v. *Shri Justice S.R. Tendolka*, 1959 SCR 279; *P.V. Jagananth Rao* v. *State of Orissa*, 1968 (3) SCR 789; *Krishna Ballabha Sahay* v. *Commission of Inquiry*, 1969 (1) SCR 387; *The State of Jammu and Kashmir* v. *Bakshi Gulam Mohammad*, AIR 1967 SC 122; *P.R. Nayak* v. *Union of India*, ILR (1973) I Delhi 747.

350. *Birla Cotton Spinning and Weaving Mills Ltd.* v. *Commissioner of Income-tax*, West Bengal, 82 ITR 166.

between civil and criminal litigation if it is incurred for the purpose of the business.[351] In *Parshva Properties Ltd.* v. *Commissioner of Income-tax*,[352] Sabyasachi Mukharji, J, culled out the following principles from the case law in connection with the deductibility of expenditure incurred for defending criminal and other prosecutions, viz.

> (1) The question of deductibility of expenditure of this nature must depend on the purpose and the nature of the expenditure incurred, (2) in order to determine whether the expenditure was deductible or not, it is necessary to find out in what capacity the expenditure was incurred, (3) the ultimate result or decision on which the expenses were incurred does not in any way affect the question of allowability of the expenditure. The aim and purpose of incurring the expenditure should also be examined, and (4) but a penalty for not following the law is not an expenditure which can be said to be incurred by the assessee in the course of his business.

Where a Commission of Inquiry into the administration of the affairs of the assessee had been ordered and the assessee had been required to produce certain documents, the assessee could not sit tight but in its own interest had to respond and co-operate with the Commission of Inquiry. This would be necessary to protect its own reputation and its business. The aim of incurring such expenditure was motivated by commercial expediency and the purpose was to protect the credit of the company and its assets. The moneys were spent for safeguarding and saving the business and keeping it on a sound footing. The expenses were incurred by the assessee in its business or trading capacity and were for the purpose of the business and for the payment of a penalty for infraction of the law. The money spent in connection with the investigation by the Commission of Inquiry was expenditure honestly incurred for the preservation and protection of the assessee's business. The expenses so incurred by the assessee on account of the Commission of Inquiry would

351. *C.I.T.* v. *Dhanrajgiriji Raja Narasingirji* (1973) 91 ITR 544.
352. 104 ITR 631.

be allowable expenditure. So would be the case with the expenses of the law department or the amount spent by the law department of the assessee in connection with the Commission of Inquiry.[353]

Inquiry into Matters that are Subjudice in Court Cases

Quite often, directions are sought from Courts for restraining Commissions of Inquiry from commencing or proceeding with inquiries till Court cases involving the petitioners are concluded as the subject-matter of the inquiries and the cases are the same. In other words, the contention in such cases is that the subject of inquiry is subjudice and if it were allowed to continue, that would prejudice the trial of the case in which the petitioner is involved. The cases[354] cited in support of such a contention, lay down the proposition that any parallel inquiry conducted by an officer with regard to a matter which is subjudice is bound to interfere with the even and ordinary course of justice. There can be no quarrel with regard to this proposition. In order to deal with this contention, it is necessary to examine the question, whether the subject-matter of the inquiry before the Commission of Inquiry, and the subject-matter of the judicial proceedings or investigation, are such that it can be held that the proceedings before the two authorities are parallel proceedings or that the subjects to be dealt with by them overlap each other. Having regard to the aim of the inquiry by the Commission and the subject-matter of the judicial proceedings or, as the case may be, police investigation, it seems that the subject-matter of inquiry by the two authorities is entirely different and such subject-matter does not overlap each other to such an extent as to hold that the two inquiries before the two authorities will be parallel in nature.[355] A Commission of Inquiry under the Act is not conducting any parallel inquiry into a matter, which has become or may become subjudice by the trial of the petitioners. The

353. *South Asia Industries (P) Ltd.* v. *The Commissioner of Income-tax*, New Delhi, ILR (1981) I Delhi 196.

354. *The King* v. *Parmanand* AIR 1949 Pat 222; *D.J. Shield* v. *Ramesam* AIR 1955 Andhra 156.

355. *Gokulananda Roy* v. *Tarapada Mukharjee and Others*, AIR 1973 Cal 233.

apprehension felt by the petitioners in such cases is unfounded and based on a total misconception of the purpose and scope of the enquiry entrusted to a Commission. The definite matter of public importance for which a Commission is set up is not the conduct or activity or acts of omission or commission of any individual. It is not necessary to stress that the inquiry, which the Commission is going to hold, is not an inquiry by a Civil or Criminal Court and the proceedings thereof are not judicial proceedings of a Court of law. The Commission has not been asked to give a decision as to the respective rights and liabilities of any person or to punish any wrong. In an inquiry of this nature, there is no issue between the parties for the Commission to decide and no defendant or an accused person to be tried. There is no 'lis'. The procedure is inquisitional rather than accusatorial. The Commission has been appointed to find the facts relating to the matters it has to enquire into.[356]

The Commission is not making an adjudication. Its order is not enforceable *proprio vigore*. It is a fact-finding body. It would elaborately inquire and investigate whether the allegations on which the Government had prima facie satisfaction were true. If the allegations are found true, Government might take such actions, either civil or criminal, as are legally tenable. If the Government ultimately takes such action on the report of the Commission, the decision in the civil suit would stand in the way.[357] Moreover, on the principle enunciated in *Secretary of State* v. *Mark & Co.*[358] Act vests the Commission with exclusive jurisdiction to make the inquiry if the necessary conditions exist and such jurisdiction cannot be ousted by institution of a suit even on identical matters.

In *Md. Ibrahim Khan* v. *Susheel Kumar*,[359] the Court made the following observations:

---

356. *Puhupram and Others* v. *State of Madhya Pradesh and Others*, 1968 MPLJ 629.

357. *P.V. Jagannath Rao* v. *State of Orissa* (1968) 34 Cut LT 666, p. 712.

358. AIR 1940 PC 105.

359. AIR 1983 AP 69.

It is true that the only power of the Commission is to enquire and make a report and embody therein its recommendations. The Commission has no power of adjudication of any questions of title or dispute and pass a decree which can be enforced proprio vigore. There is no charge as such against any person; nor is there any accused or accusor. There is neither a plaintiff nor a defendant. There are no pleadings raising issues to be tried. No one is punished. No serious disability or disqualification is incurred by the findings. The enquiry made by the Commission differs from a criminal trial. The Commission is only a machinery set up to enquire into a definite matter of public importance and to make a report so as to enable the Government to take such action as the Government may deem fit. Therefore, there is no definite judgment in the enquiry, nor is there any usurpation of judicial functions. Accordingly, the Court held that the grievance of the petitioner that the Commission is going to inquire and decide questions of title of immovable property is wholly unfounded.

There is another aspect of this matter, namely whether Court has powers to restrain proceeding of a Commission of Inquiry by injunction on the ground of threatened contempt. The contention that has been made in such cases is that if the inquiry before the Commission were allowed to be proceeded with, reports of the proceedings before the Commission would be published from day to day and such publication is bound to interfere with the course of justice. Accordingly, it has been argued in such cases that Courts have jurisdiction to restrain proceedings that would involve a contempt of Court. The fact that the Commission has not made its report or is yet to commence its proceedings is not material. These contentions have found favour with the Courts in some of the cases. Reference in this regard may be made to one such case, namely, *Dwijendra Mohan Banerjee* v. *State of West Bengal and Others*[360] wherein the Court observed: "(T)his court ought not to stay its hands

360. (1966-67) (Vol. LXXI) 71 CWN 312.

and allow the proceedings before the Commission of Inquiry to commence and then proceed to deal with the parties for contempt of court.... The authorities to which reference has been made earlier in this judgment make it quite clear that publicity with regard to matters pending before the court which would have the effect of prejudicing the public at large against the parties to the proceedings before a court, must be stopped and punished. If such publicity can be punished by the court on the ground of contempt it can, in my view, be stopped as well and must be so stopped, be restraining the parties from proceeding with the enquiry before the Commission of Inquiry."[361]

This case was, however, distinguished subsequently in *Gokulananda* v. *Tarapada*[362] on the ground that there was no denial by the State Government that the terms of reference of the Commission of inquiry involved in investigation into matters which were the subject-matter of the writ petition. Notwithstanding this, the later judicial trends do not support this contention even if the matter under inquiry before the two authorities is parallel and overlapping. In *Gokulnanda* v. *Tarapada*,[363] the Calcutta High Court observed: "On the law as it stands now, there can be hardly any doubt that where a Commission of Inquiry has been appointed to inquire into matters of public importance there will not be any contempt of Court, even though the matters which are to be inquired into by the Inquiry Commission are the same, as those which are pending in a litigation before the Civil or Criminal Courts. It is now well settled that since the Commission of Inquiry, in conducting the inquiry is performing a statutory duty, although such inquiry may be parallel in nature, the question of contempt of Court would not arise merely because of the pendency of identical questions before a Court of Law, Civil or Criminal."

The matter seems to have been finally settled by the Supreme Court in *Sammbhu Nath* v. *Kedar Prasad Sinha and Others*.[364]

361. Case-law on the subject discussed.

362. AIR 1973 Calcutta 233.

363. *Ibid.*

364. AIR 1972 SC 1515.

In this case, the publication of the notification appointing Commission of Inquiry in the press during the pendency of certain criminal revision petitions was assailed on the ground of contempt of Court, alleging that the publication, inter alia, related to a matter which was the subject-matter of criminal revision petitions in the High Court and had the result of interfering with the course of justice and prejudicing the mankind against the two applicants. The learned judge who dealt with the application found the appellant guilty of contempt of Court, because it was he who had handed over the offending matter to the press for publication in the newspaper. The editor as also the printer and publisher too were found guilty because of the publication of the news item in the paper. However, the contemners were let off with a warning as the contempt, in the opinion of the High Court, was of a technical nature. The three contemners filed appeal against this in the Supreme Court by special leave. Discussing the law relating to contempt of Court in details, the Hon'ble Supreme Court held that the subject-matter of inquiry before the Commission and the question for decision which was the subject of criminal revision petitions were distinct and separate and not identical matters, the publication of the notification appointing the Commission in press did not amount to contempt of Court, particularly when the notification was published in whole and not in part. The Apex Court went a step further and observed: "It may be that some of the matters which were connected with the criminal revision petitions were the subject of inquiry by the Commission of Inquiry, but that would not attract liability for contempt of Court." In the case of *P.V. Jagannath Rao* v. *State of Orissa*[365] the appellant had challenged notification issued under Section 3 of the Commissions of Inquiry Act appointing a Commission of Inquiry to inquire into certain allegations against persons who had held the offices of Chief Ministers and Ministers in Orissa. An argument was advanced in that case that one of the items of charges, which were to be inquired into by the Commission, was the subject-matter of an appeal pending in the

365. AIR 1969 SC 215; (1968) 3 SCR 789.

High Court. Question arose in that context whether the setting up of the Commission of Inquiry by the State Government or the continuation of the inquiry by the Commission would be tantamount to contempt of Court. This Court held that the above acts would not constitute contempt of Court and observed:

> It was pointed out by this Court in *Shri Ram Krishna Dalmia* v. *Shri Justice S.R. Tendolkar*[366] that the inquiry cannot be looked upon as a judicial inquiry and the order ultimately passed cannot be enforced proprio vigore. The inquiry and the investigation by the Commission do not therefore amount to usurpation of the function of the Courts of law. The scope of the trial by the Courts of law and the Commission of Inquiry is altogether different. In any case, it cannot be said that the Commission of Inquiry would be liable for contempt of Court if it proceeded to inquire into matters referred to it by the Government Notification. In appointing a Commission of Inquiry under Section 3 and in making the inquiry contemplated by the notification, the Commission is performing its statutory duty. We have already held that in the appointing of the Commission of Inquiry the Government was acting bona fide. It is, therefore, not possible to accept the argument of the appellants that the setting up of the Commission of Inquiry by the State Government or the continuance of the inquiry by the Commission so constituted would be tentamount to contempt of Court.

On the other hand, in *Brijpal Dass* v. *Justice Shri B. Beri*,[367] the Court did not consider it proper to adjudicate certain issues for the reason that the same were subjudice before the Commission.

Inquiry Pending Investigation

The scope of inquiry by a Commission and that of a criminal trial being entirely different, the pendency of the police investigation in order to track the real offenders for the purpose

366. AIR 1956 SC 538; (1959) SCR 279.

367. 1981 ILR 31 Rajasthan 361.

of trial as accused will not stand as a legal bar to the appointment of Commission with regard to the circumstances mentioned in certain items of the notification (i.e. items (a) and (b)) under which certain persons, including the deceased, sustained injuries (item (a) of the notification) and certain other deceased person disappeared and whose body recovered subsequently (item (b) of the notification). There is no prosecution of anybody before a Commission, nor is there any accused as such to defend himself, and there is no charge of any criminal offence against anybody. The Commission is required to collect facts fairly to all concerned in the best possible manner and advised the Government with its findings. It will be ultimately for the Government, after perusal of the report of the Commission, to decide whether it will accept the findings of the Commission and take appropriate measures as advised or even otherwise.[368]

In *M. Karunanidhi* v. *Union of India,*[369] it was, inter alia, contended that the Tamil Nadu Public Men (Criminal Misconduct) Act, 1973 was in the statute book, and no enquiry could be ordered in respect of the misconduct of a Minister of a State under any other enactment. The Court found this submission untenable in view of the amended provision in Section 29 of the Act according to which the provisions of the Act of 1973 were in addition to and not in derogation of any other law for the time being in force. The Court, therefore, held that an inquiry under the Commissions of Inquiry Act, 1952 was not barred by the existence of the Tamil Nadu Public Men (Criminal Misconduct) Act, 1973.

It will be expedient to refer to the case of *Peoples Union for Democracy Rights and Another* v. *Ministry of Home Affairs*[370] wherein the petitioners prayed, inter alia, for the relief, namely, that by an appropriate writ, order or direction appoint a Commission of Inquiry to carry out an investigation into the role of the police and political interference in the carnage/riots

---

368. *Manabendra Sarkar* v. *State of Assam and Others*, AIR 1974 Gauhati 46.

369. AIR 1977 Madras 192.

370. AIR 1985 Delhi 268.

in Delhi. Apart from the practical difficulties in carrying out parallel investigation by the Court by appointing Commissioner to investigate, the Court dealt with the moot question, viz. is it open to the Court to interfere with the investigation which was still going on.

The investigation is a matter for the police under the Code of Criminal Procedure. J.L. Kapur, J. in the case of *State of West Bengal* v. *S.N. Basak*,[371] observed as under:

> Section 154 deals with information in cognizable offences and S. 156 with investigation into such offences and under these sections, the police has the statutory right to investigate into the circumstances of any alleged cognizable offence without authority from a Magistrate and this statutory power of the police to investigate cannot be interfered with by the exercise of power under S. 439 or under the inherent power of the Court S. 561A, when there was no case pending at the time excepting that the person against whom the investigation has started had appeared before the Court, had surrendered and had been admitted to bail.

The Court must realize that under the scheme of the Code, the work of investigation has been entrusted to the police and nobody else. It is not even subject to the normal supervisory power of the Court.

In *State of West Bengal* v. *Sampat Lal*[372] the Calcutta High Court appointed a DIG CBI, as special officer for conducting investigation into the death of two young persons on the allegations that the State Government was not doing their duties and were treating the case of murder as case of suicide. State of West Bengal came up in appeal to the Supreme Court wherein Ranganath Misra, J. made the following observations, namely:

> The next aspect to be considered is whether it is open to the Court to interfere with the investigation which is still proceeding. It has been conceded before us and rightly in

371. AIR 1963 SC 447.

372. AIR 1985 SC 195; (1985) I SCC 317.

our view, that investigation is a matter for the police under the scheme of the Code. Judicial opinion seems to be settled and we have several authorities of this Court where interference by the Court into police investigation has not been approved.... The functions of the judiciary and the police are complementary, not overlapping, and the combination of individual liberty with a due observance of law and order is only to be obtained by leaving each to exercise its own function, always, of course, subject to the right of the Court to intervene in an appropriate case when moved under Section 491 of the Criminal Procedure Code to give directions in the nature of habeas corpus. In such a case as the present, however, the Court's functions begin when a charge is preferred before it, and not until then.... The investigation in the present case is still pending as we were told at the Bar. It is quite likely that some day, and we hope and trust that there would be no further delay, the Court of competent jurisdiction would be in seisin of the matter and would be called upon to decide whether it was a case of murder or suicide. We have, therefore, thought it proper exercise of discretion not to enter into the facts and express any opinion one way or the other so as to prejudice the trial that might take place. It is sufficient to indicate that there is residuary jurisdiction left in the Court to give directions to the investigating agency when it is satisfied that the requirements of the law are not being complied with and investigation is not being conducted properly or with due haste and promptitude. The Court has to be alive to the fact that the scheme of the law is that the investigation has been entrusted to the police and is ordinarily not subject to the normal supervisory power of the Court. We are inclined, on the facts of the case as placed before us to take the view that the materials placed before the Court did not justify an exception to be made to the rule indicated by this Court and the appointment of a Special Officer was not called for at this stage.

In view of the legal position as above, the Delhi High declined[372a] to interfere with the investigation that was still giving on and dismissed the prayer for the issuance of an appropriate Writ, order or direction for appointing a commission of Inquiry to inquire into the allegations that were subject of police investigation. While doing so, the Court also observed: "An inquiry by this Court by appointing Commissioner will not reveal more. No new facts will be unearthed but the inquiry will be exploited by communalist of all groups to project themselves as spokesman for one community. There will be the charges, counter-charges real or imaginary. Any enquiry by the Court will not alleviate the feelings of riots striken people but would rather exacerbate them.... The refusal by the Government to appoint a Commission of Inquiry is a political decision. The Courts should never be resorted to for political games by one party or the other. People have great faith and trust in the justice which is administered in the institutions known as 'Courts'. Even a person when he is sent to the gallows, the society accepts and respects verdict of the Court. If the Court starts entering into the political arena directly or indirectly, expressly or impliedly, they will cause serious damage to the institution of judiciary.... In 'public interest litigation', the Courts by and large meant for enforcement of fundamental rights by giving effective relief. No effective relief can be given in terms of prayer (a)."

Inquiry vis-à-vis Action under Other Statutes

Apart from the pending cases and investigations referred to hereinbefore, quite often inquiries under the Commissions of Inquiry Act are opposed and challenged on the ground that the subject-matter of inquiry is covered under a given statute. In this regard, it is necessary to have proper and correct understanding of the nature and extent of inquiry under the Act vis-à-vis the action that can be taken under any other law, which are quite often in addition to and not in derogation of other law for the time being in force. In *U. Dakshinamoorthy* v. *Commission of*

372a. *Peoples Union of Democratic Rights and Awther* v. *Ministry of Home Affainrs*, AIR 1985 Delhi 268.

Inquiry,[373] a Commission of Inquiry was appointed to inquire and report into an incident at a given police station on certain day, involving cross complaints of assault by a police officer and an advocate. The petitioner, an advocate other than one whose conduct was subject of inquiry, filed the writ petitions, contending, inter alia, that 'misconduct' on the part of the advocate concerned was not a definite matter of public importance; the police officer involved in the incident had already complained to the Bar Council of the State and thereby submitted to the jurisdiction of the Bar Council; and the Advocates Act being a special Act providing for remedy for certain liabilities, including disciplinary inquiry into any misconduct of a member advocate and penalties therefor in Section 35 thereof and, hence, the remedy provided by the statute alone must be followed and it was not competent to follow any other course. Accordingly, it was contended that the Commission of Inquiry could not be constituted to inquire into such alleged misconduct of the advocate, which fell within the exclusive jurisdiction of the Tribunals constituted under the Advocates Act. While dismissing these contentions, the Court observed that "the Commission of Inquiry is purely a fact-finding Commission as it has not the moorings of a Court as it is popularly understood, nor are there two persons placed on either side to place their views on a given subject, nor is there a lis in issue before it." On a comparison of the provisions of the two statutes, the Court further observed: "It is therefore clear that the functions of the Commission of Inquiry so far as the latter part of clause 2(ii) of the reference is concerned (i.e. any misconduct on the part of the named advocate) and those of the Bar Council, are mutually exclusive, and one is independent of the other. Whilst a Commission of Inquiry only finds facts, and is interdicted from rendering a decision on such found facts, the Bar Council has a statutory right to act on such information and take such action as is necessary under Section 35 of the Advocates Act, by referring the matter, if it has reason to believe that the Advocate has been guilty of professional or other misconduct,

373. AIR 1980 Madras 89 (FB).

to the disciplinary committee for necessary action. If this dichotomy is borne in mind, then the contention that the Commission has no jurisdiction to go into the question whether there has been any misconduct on the part of the Advocate will not arise at all."[374]

Bias

The Act and the rules made thereunder do not provide any qualifications for being appointed as a Commission of Inquiry. The general principles as are applicable to constitution of administrative bodies are applicable to such Commissions as well. Thus, a Commissioner should not be judge in his own cause. He should also not suffer from the infirmity of being biased.

The rule against the bias is an offshoot of the principle of natural justice. Bias by interest which disqualifies a Judge falls into two broad classes:

(A) Where the Judge has a pecuniary interest in the subject-matter of the litigation;

(B) Where from kindred or other cause the Judge may have a bias in favour of one of the parties.[375] This rule is based on the maxim 'Nemo judex in causa sua', which means that no man can be a Judge in his own cause. Professor Wade elucidated the principle as follows: 'Nemo judex in re sua' 'A Judge is disqualified from determining any case in which he may be, or may fairly be suspected to be, biased. So important is this rule that Coke supposed that it should prevail even over an Act of Parliament.'[376] Massey in his treatise on Administrative Law has neatly described the principle

374. Since the petitions were dismissed on merits, the Court did not consider the point as to whether the petitioner was not an aggrieved person entitled to invoke the jurisdiction of the High Court under Article 226 of the Constitution.

375. *Constitutional Law of India* by H.M. Seervai, 3rd Edition, Volume II, para 16, p. 118.

376. *Administrative Law* by H.W.R. Wade, Sixth Edition, p. 473.

of bias in the following words: "Personal bias arises from a certain relationship equation between the deciding authority and the parties which incline him unfavourably or otherwise on the side one of the parties before him."[377]

Lord Hewart, C.J. founded the rule in *Rex* v. *Sussex*[378] thus:

...a long line of cases shows that it is not merely of some importance but is of fundamental importance that justice should not only be done, but should manifestly and undoubtedly be seen to be done.

The learned Chief Justice observed:

Nothing is to be done which creates even a suspicion that there has been an improper interference with the course of justice.

Slade, J., speaking of the *Queen's Bench Division*, in *R.* v. *Camborne Justices*,[379] expressed his concern in this regard that its continued and inappropriate application may lead to the erroneous impression that it is more important that justice should appear to be done than that it should in fact be done. The application of this rule has been aptly described by Garner[379a] as under:

The natural justice 'bias' rule looks to external appearance rather than to proof of actual improper exercise of power. If the reasonable observer would have the requisite degree of suspicion of bias in the decision maker then that decision can be challenged. It is a matter of courts ensuring that 'justice is seen to be done'.

The rule against bias is an intrinsic requirement of the administration of justice. Breach of this rule disqualifies a Judge/Arbitrator to adjudicate the dispute before him and if the Judge/Arbitrator had already adjudicated upon it, renders the

377. *Administrative Law* by I.P. Massey, 3rd Edition, p. 151.

378. (1924) 1 KB 256.

379. (1954) 2 All ER 850, p. 855.

379a. *Garner's Administrative Law*, Seventh Edition.

adjudication null and void. The rule against bias applies with all vigour to Courts and Tribunals, judicial proceedings and quasi-judicial proceedings; and also to those who are entrusted with the duty of adjudicating the rights of the parties, like arbitrators, is universally accepted principle.[380]

Bias may be against a person or may be in respect of a question for consideration. Objection to the appointment of a person as Commission of Inquiry should be raised at the earliest opportunity. If it is not done, it may be construed as waiver of right, if any, to challenge the participation of the person in the inquiry.[381] It is no doubt true that when allegations of personal bias are made against a person functioning as an authority or Tribunal, it is desirable that affidavit should be filed by the person concerned.[382] Even if a person is held to be biased, the report of the inquiry will not be vitiated if there are other members of the Commission of Inquiry who are not so biased.[383]

The approach to the question whether a Tribunal is biased is laid down by the Supreme Court in *Manak Lal* v. *Dr. Prem Chand*[384] where it is observed: "It is well settled that every member of a tribunal that is called upon to try issues in judicial or quasi-judicial proceedings must be able to act judicially; and it is of the essence of judicial decisions and judicial administration that judges should be able to act impartially, objectively and without any bias. In such cases the test is not whether in fact a bias has affected the judgment; the test always is and must be whether litigant could reasonably apprehend that a bias attributable to a member of the tribunal might have operated against him in the final decision of the tribunal. It is in this sense

380. *K. Vijaya Bhaskar Reddy* v. *Government of Andhra Pradesh and Others*, AIR 1996 AP 62.

381. *Manak Lal* v. *Dr. Prem Chand* (1957) SCR 575.

382. *Dr. Ku. Sneh Rani Jain* v. *The State of M.P.*, 1978 Lab IC NOC 43. In this case, it was held, on facts, that the allegations of bias resting on the ground of relationship with the student were not substantiated although the Commissioner had filed no affidavit.

383. *G.S. Harnal* v. *Union of India and Others*, ILR (1971) II Delhi 129.

384. 1957 SCR 575.

that it is often said that justice must not only done but must also appear to be done."

What is the test of bias? Where the bias is pecuniary bias, slightest interest of the adjudicator in the subject-matter of litigation would disqualify the Judge. The classical illustration of this type of bias is the case of *Dimes* v. *Grand Junction Canal Propretary*.[385] There the House of Lords, presided by Lord Cottenham, rendered the decision in favour of the respondent-company. After Lord Cottenham ceased to be the Lord Chancellor, that decision was challenged before the House on the ground that Lord Cottenham was a shareholder of that company. The House of Lords set aside its earlier judgment on the ground of pecuniary interest of the Lord Chancellor although it was admitted that the interest could not have influenced the judgment in the remotest degree.

The other category of bias is personal bias, which is also termed by Garner[386] as 'appearance of bias'. For this category of bias the test laid down by Lord Heward, C.J., is:

> Nothing is to be done which creates even any suspicion that there has been an improper interference with the course of justice.[387]

In *Metropolitan Properties Co. (F.G.C.) Ltd.* v. *Lannon*,[388] Lord Justice Edmund Davies elucidated the test as follows:

> With profound respect to those who have propounded the 'real likelihood' test, I take the view that the requirement that justice must manifestly be done operate with undiminished force in cases where bias is alleged and that any development of the law which appears to emasculate that requirement should be strongly resisted.... But I cannot bring myself to hold that a decision may properly be allowed to stand even although there is reasonable suspicion of bias on the part of one or more members of the adjudicating body.

---

385. (1852) 3 HLC 759.

386. *Garner's Administrative Law*, Seventh Edition.

387. *K. Vijaya Bhaskar Reddy* v. *Governmet of A.P.*, AIR 1996 A.P. 62.

388. (1969) 1 KB 577.

In *Ranjit Thakur* v. *Union of India*,[389] the Supreme Court applied the test of 'real likelihood of bias' to mean whether a reasonable person, in possession of relevant information, would have thought that bias was likely and whether the authority concerned was likely to be disposed to decide the matter only in a particular way. Their Lordships observed that what was relevant was the reasonableness of the apprehension in that regard in the mind of the party and pointed out that the proper approach for the Judge was not to look at his own mind and ask himself, however, honestly, "Am I biased? but to look at the mind of the party before him. The question in that case arose under the Army Act, 1950 where the decision of the Court-martial was questioned as being biased. The appellant before the Supreme Court was punished for violating the norms for presenting representations to higher officer. While serving the sentence he was again tried for disobeying a lawful command given by his superior officer. The Court-martial consisted of the fourth respondent therein and two others. About the fourth respondent, the appellant had sent representations complaining illtreatment. The proceedings were challenged on the ground of bias on the part of the fourth respondent. The Supreme Court held that the presence of the fourth respondent in the Court-martial rendered the proceedings coram non-judice and the judgement a nullity.

Explaining the 'real likelihood test', Mathew J., speaking for the Supreme Court in *S. Parthasarthi* v. *State of A.P.*,[390] observed that the Court must look at the impression which other people have and that follows from the principle that justice must not only be done but seen to be done; there must be real likelihood of bias and that surmises and conjectures would not be enough.

Justice Thakkar vividly summarizes the test thus:

> Reasonable apprehension in the mind of a reasonable man is necessary. Such reasonable apprehension must be based on cogent materials. Again, there must be reasonable evidence

389. AIR 1987 SC 2386: (1987) 4 SCC 611.
390. AIR 1973 SC 2701: 1973 Lab IC 1607.

to satisfy that there was a real likelihood of bias. Vague suspicions of whimsical, capricious and unreasonable people should not be made the standard to regulate normal human conduct.

It follows that in determining the question of personal bias the Court should see whether there is undisputed material which is likely to give rise to reasonable apprehension of bias in the mind of the person complaining of bias taking care that apprehension is not vague, whimsical or capricious suspicion. The Court will have to satisfy itself of three things before recording a finding of bias against the authority, viz.:

(i) there is uncontroverted and undisputed material;

(ii) the material is such as is likely to give rise to reasonable apprehension in the mind of the person complaining of bias; and

(iii) the apprehension is not a vague, whimsical or capricious suspicion.

In *Gullapalli Nageswara Rao* v. *State of Andhra Pradesh*,[391] it was held that two well-settled principles of the doctrine of bias that applied equally to judicial as well as quasi-judicial tribunals, were,—(1) that no man shall be a judge in his own cause and that (2) justice should not merely be done but must also appear to be done. It was further held that any kind of bias in a judicial authority, whether financial or other, for or against any party, or any position that might impute bias, must disqualify him as a judge. The same idea was expressed by the Supreme Court in *The Andhra Pradesh State Road Transport Corporation, Hydrabad and Another* v. *Sri Satyanarayana Transports (Private) Ltd., Guntur and Others*,[392] as follows:

It is an elementary rule of natural justice that a person who tries a cause should be able to deal with the matter before him objectively, fairly, and impartially.... In dealing with cases of bias, it is necessary to remember that 'no one can act in a judicial capacity if his previous conduct gives ground

391. (1960) 1 SCR 580.

392. AIR 1965 SC 1303.

for believing that he cannot act with an open mind'. The broad principle which is universally accepted is a person trying a cause even in quasi-judicial proceedings, must not only act fairly, but must be able to act above suspicion of unfairness. The use of the word 'bias' should be confined to its sphere. Its proper significance is to denote a departure from the standard of even-handed justice which the law requires from those who occupy judicial office or those who are commonly regarded as holding a quasi-judicial office, such as an arbitrator.

It is a cardinal principle of natural justice that a person must not be a judge in his own cause. Besides, if he has a pecuniary interest in the case brought before him, or is hostile to a party whose case he is called upon to try, that would introduce the infirmity of bias and would disqualify him from trying the case. These principles of natural justice, which are the essence of all judicial and quasi-judicial decisions, have been made applicable to administrative acts as well. Thus, in *A.K. Kraipak* v. *Union of India*,[393] the Supreme Court observed:

> Till very recently it was the opinion of the courts that unless the authority concerned was required by law under which it functioned to act judicially there was no room for the application of the rules of natural justice. The validity of that limitation is now questioned. If the purpose of the rules of justice is to prevent miscarriage of justice one fails to see why those rules should not be made applicable to administrative enquiries.

This view has been expressed in *Re Pergamon Press Ltd.*,[394] wherein Sachs, L.J. observed as follows:

> The nature of the proceeding, the purposes for which the reports may be used, the matter which may be found in them and the extent of the publication be respectively as described, it seems to me,...very clear that in the conduct of the proceedings there must be displayed that measure of

393. AIR 1970 SC 150.

394. 1970 All ER 535.

natural justice which Lord Reid in *Ridge* v. *Baldwin*,[395] described as 'insusceptible of exact definition but what a reasonable man would regard as fair procedure in particular circumstances'. To come to that conclusion it is, as recent decisions have shown, not necessary to label the proceedings 'judicial', 'quasi-judicial', 'administrative' or 'investigatory'; it is the characteristics of the proceedings that matter, not the precise compartment or compartments into which they fall and one of the principal characteristics of the proceedings under consideration is to be found in the inspectors' duty, in their statutory fact-finding capacity to produce a report which may be made public and may thus cause severe injury to an individual by its findings.

Again, in this case, Lord Denning M.R., observed:

They must be masters of their own procedure. They should be subject to no rules save this: they must be fair.

In view of these decisions, it seems to be the consensus of judicial opinion both in this country as well as England, that rule of 'fair play in action' must be observed by all authorities, judicial, quasi-judicial or administrative.[396] When a Court, judicial authority, quasi-judicial authority or a statutory authority or any other authority takes a decision which has civil consequences and/or affects the rights of a person, the doctrine of bias would apply. This being the position in law with regard to application of rule against bias, can the same principle be extended to the proceedings before the Commission of Inquiry under the Act, whose function is to collect facts, record findings and give recommendations which cannot be enforced proprio vigore? This question can be looked at from two angles; the first is the object and the purpose of the enquiry contemplated under the Act and the second is the rights of the person whose conduct and/or reputation is involved in the enquiry. Though the proceedings under the Act are inquisitorial, yet for limited purposes the Commission is treated as Civil Court under sub-

395. (1964) AC 40.

396. *The Statesman Ltd.* v. *The Fact Finding Committee*, AIR 1975 Calcutta 15.

section (4) of Section 5 of the Act and the proceedings are treated as judicial proceedings provided a notification is issued under sub-section (1) of Section 5 applying sub-sections (2) to (5) to the proceedings before a Commission. Further, in the procedure laid down by the Commission under Section 8 of the Act it is provided that the procedure prescribed in the Code of Civil Procedure, as far as may be, will be followed and that the principles of natural justice are applicable to the proceeding before the Commission and the question of contravention of those principles has to be decided in the light of the terms of reference to the Commission, provisions of the Act, the rules made thereunder and the procedure settled by the Commission.[397]

It is pertinent to note here the modern equivalent of the principles of natural justice epitomized by Lord Denning in *B. Surinder Singh Kanda* v. *Government of the Federation of Malaya*.[398] The learned Law Lord observed thus:

> .... The rule against bias is one thing. The right to be heard is another. Those two rules are the essential characteristics of what is often called natural justice. They are the twin pillers supporting it. The Romans put them in the two maxims: Nemo judex in causa sua: and Audi alteram partem. They have recently been put in the two words, Impartiality and Fairness.

---

397. In Administrative Law by D.D. Basu, Third Edition 1993, p. 313, the author has expressed a view, relying on *State of Jammu & Kashmir* v. *Bakshi Gulam Mohammed*, AIR 1967 SC 122, namely, "There is no question of invoking the rule of natural justice except insofar as they are incorporated in the Act itself in Ss. 8B, 8C of the Act or in the Rules made thereunder." However, the Andhra Pradesh High Court expressed a different view in this regard in *K. Vijaya Bhaskar Reddy* v. *Government of Andhra Pradesh,* when Quadari, J. said that "having gone through the judgment in *Bakshi Gulam Mohammed's* case, referred to supra, carefully, we are unable to say that the Supreme Court laid down therein that the rules of natural justice do not apply to the proceedings before the Commission of Inquiry".

398. (1962) AC 322.

From the aforesaid, it follows that wherever the principles of natural justice are attracted the duty to act impartially and fairly automatically follows. From the point of view of public confidence as well as from the point of view of protection of rights of the category of persons dealt with in Sections 8B and 8C of the Act, the impartiality of the Commission is of paramount importance. It is but just and proper to allow such persons to raise the plea of rule against bias to have the satisfaction that the proceedings are conducted impartially, which will commensurate with the spirit of the Act and will also inspire confidence in the public about the enquiry conducted by the Commission, rather than to preclude them from raising the plea of bias. Giving our most anxious consideration to this question we are inclined to think that allowing persons envisaged in Section 8B to raise the plea of bias which is but a concomitant of the rule of natural justice before the Commission of Inquiry would be in tune with the spirit and the object of the Act.[399]

The question of bias has to be decided from the point of view of the person who alleges it and it is to be determined whether there is reasonable justification for such person to apprehend a biased approach by the authority concerned or that he will not get even-handed justice with an open mind. Thus, if the subject-matter of the terms of reference to the Commission was the same as the subject-matter of the preliminary inquiry against the petitioner, it might be possible to contend that the Commission would be biased and prejudiced in the future conduct of the Commission against the petitioner having come to the conclusion, even though prima facie, against him while holding the preliminary inquiry. The ultimate result will, in any case, turn out to be on the emergence, or, as the case may be, absence of any reasonable justification underlying apprehension of bias as may have been entertained by the petitioner. Accordingly, the fact that the task of framing charges against the petitioner for the disciplinary inquiry was performed by the Commission, cannot by itself justifiably give rise to an

399. *K. Vijaya Bhaskar Reddy* v. *Government of Andhra Pradesh*, AIR 1996 AP 62, p. 70.

apprehension of bias. It is normal for judicial officers in criminal trials to frame charges without there being any possibility of attack on the basis of bias or prejudice against such judicial officers. The findings reached by the Commission in the preliminary inquiry should not be such as to the expression of its opinion or determination of the guilt or otherwise of the petitioner. With a view to avoid any such controversy in this regard, it is normal and proper procedure not to entrust the task of framing charges for a departmental inquiry against an official of the Government to the Commission which is inquiring into the connected matter. However, there is no absolute embargo. Where there is reasonable justification for doing so in the facts and circumstances of a given case, it may not be open to contend in law that the Commission cannot be entrusted with both the functions. Furthermore, the fact that the person who is appointed as the Commission of Inquiry, has been consulted prior to his such appointment with regard to definite matters of public importance, cannot indicate either any mala fides of the Government or a non-application of mind. Where the Government has formed its opinion about the existence of the definite matters of public importance which necessitated the inquiry and having framed the terms of reference which it intend to be incorporated in the proposed notification, it sent the same to the Commission just prior to its appointment and, in fact, made additions of certain terms of reference to the terms of reference initially referred, indicate that there has been application of such mind.[400]

In *V. Narayana Rao* v. *State of A.P.*,[401] while dealing with the charge of bias levelled against Mr. Muralidhara Rao, heading a one-man Commission of Inquiry, the Court observed that "while it is true that he traveled beyond the scope of reference and while reading of his report discloses his devotion and dedication to the cause of upliftment of backward classes, there is no material to hold that the was either biased in favour of backward classes or biased against other classes".

---

400. *P.R. Nayak* v. *Union of India*, ILR (1973) I Delhi 747.

401. AIR 1987 A.P. 53: 1987 Lab. IC 152.

'Recently, all three members of the Justice N.N. Mathur Commission resigned in the wake of the Rajasthan High Court issuing notices to the two members, former Chief Secretary Inderjeet Khanna and retired Indian Police Service Officer H.N. Meena, in response to a public Writ by two persons challenging their integrity. The same petitioners had earlier challenged the locus standi of the Mathur Commission as well on which the Division Bench of the High Court, on January 4, had questioned the government's intention in setting up an inquiry of that kind. An inquiry into the Raje regime's acts of omission and commission, including alleged malpractices involving 22000 crore, was among the promises made by the Congress to the public in its election campaign. Accordingly, Justice N.N. Mathur, along with other two members, was appointed as a committee by the Congress Government in Rajasthan almost a year ago. It was not constituted under the Commissions of Inquiry Act, 1952.[401a] Since all the members of the Commission resigned, the challenge to the appointment of the members on the ground of integrity no longer survives for consideration, resulting in the deprivation of further judicial input in the matter. The principles governing the suspect matter are, however, otherwise well established as elaborated above.

Motive in Accepting Commission's Report or Otherwise—Irrelevant

In *V. Narayana Rao* v. *State of A.P.*,[402] it was, inter alia, alleged by the petitioners that the Government which was not anxious to implement or act upon the Commission's report suddenly thought of accepting it in undue haste for extraneous considerations with oblique motives and not out of any genuine concern for backward classes in view of impending meet of backward classes under the chairmanship of the opposition leader to press for acceptance of the Commission's recommendations and, as such, was bad being mala fides. It was further contended that the Government apprehended that the

401a. See "Mathur panel members resign", *The Hindu*, January 16, 2010, p. 5.

402. AIR 1987 AP 53; 1987 Lab. IC 152.

Backward Class voters, which were its mainstay and the principal vote bank, might slip away from it and transfer their loyalties to the opposition party and evidently, the impugned action was taken by the Government with the intention of taking the wind out of the sails of the opposition. Dismissing these contentions, the Court observed as follows:

> In a democracy where political parties form the Governments and Oppositions there is nothing unusual in each of them trying to win the people to its side and in taking measures to ingratiate themselves with voters. In such a situation, the motives or good faith are not really relevant. In a democracy, the Government may take a measure, under public pressure, under Opposition's pressure or otherwise, which it may not really believe in. But that is neither here nor there. In law, the motives have no relevance on the question of legality. Indeed a responsible Government is supposed to be responsive to the demands of the Opposition and the people. Wherever they see justification in their demands, they are expected to concede them. In such a case it cannot be said that the action is vitiated by extraneous considerations or political motives. No one can say that since the Government has delayed a particular measure, or because the Opposition is about to start a campaign or agitation to compel it to take that measure, the Government shall not take that measure and allow the Opposition to mount the agitation. The charge of mala fides is in the context misconceived.

The Court distinguished the cases cited by the petitioners in support of the proposition that 'where a statutory authority acts out of considerations not germane or relevant under the statute, the action is bad'. The Court did not see any analogy between those cases and the one under its consideration and observed: "So far as the statutory authorities are concerned, it goes without saying that the action be taken by them under a statute, should be for reasons germane to the statute and conceived to serve the purpose of the statute. But here is an action, which is not only a policy measure, but partly a political decision as well."

Appointment of a High Court Judge as Commission of Inquiry

Under Section 3 of the Commissions of Inquiry Act, 1952, the appropriate Government is empowered to appoint a Commission "for the purpose of making an enquiry into any definite matter of public importance". The State Government is not fettered in any manner in selecting the person or persons for appointment on the Commission.

Quite often, high-level judicial inquiries by sitting High Court Judges are instituted. Such appointments are neither in breach of any law nor that of the provisions of the Commissions of Inquiry Act, 1952. Such an appointment will also not be vitiated for the reason of a Judge having been retired before submission of the Inquiry Report.[403]

In *Samaruram Holiram* v. *B.K. Chaudhury*,[404] the appointment of a High Court Judge as a Commission of Inquiry came to be challenged as ultra vires the powers of the State Government. In this case, it was urged that since a Judge of a High Court is not under the control of the State Government and can only perform such other functions as he may undertake at the request of the President, the State Government was not competent to appoint a High Court Judge as a member of the Commission nor was the Judge entitled to accept the appointment without reference to the President. Rejecting the contention, a Division Bench of the Nagpur High Court held that "a Judge of a High Court is competent to act on a Commission at the request of a State Government, even though the permission of the President has not been obtained. Absence of such permission may, if the work is done to the exclusion of his own duty as a Judge, only affect the period of his actual service but not his appointment as a member of a Commission". It was further observed that from Article 217, it follows that, in the absence of termination of his office in the manner laid down in the proviso to Article 217(1) of the Constitution, he does not cease to be a Judge of the High Court, even though he may undertake

403. *Sardar Malkeet Singh* v. *State of U.P.*, AIR 1993 All 343.

404. AIR 1953 Nagpur 331.

certain functions outside the scope of his duties as a Judge. If he undertakes to discharge those functions at the request of the President, the time spent by him in their performance shall be counted as "actual service" under para 11(b)(i) of Part D of Second Schedule of the Constitution, for which he would be entitled to allowance at the rate specified in para 10. Para 11(b)(i), thus, only defines what period shall be counted as actual service for which allowances would be payable, and does not import any restriction on a Judge to take up or discharge functions as are not expressly, or by necessary implication, prohibited by the Constitution. Furthermore, the provision in Article 221 for the protection of the rights of Judge of a High Court cannot be read as entailing any restriction on his voluntarily undertaking any other functions. If by agreeing to perform a function his allowances are affected, it is nobody else's concern. Nor can the request made to him to undertake the function be called in question simply because his allowances have been affected.

Often times, Judges of High Courts are appointed under the Commissions of Inquiry Act to head Commissions for various purposes. These Commissions are temporary affairs and many a time their sittings are not continuous. A Judge of the High Court when he is appointed to head a Commission of this kind does not demit his office as a Judge and when the Commission is not sitting he is entitled to sit as a Judge of the High Court. It is only where a Judge of the High Court is appointed to another post, which is a whole time post that it may be said that on such appointment he can no longer work as a Judge of the High Court for the time being though even in such a case, when the work is over, he reverts as a Judge of the High Court without fresh appointment. Such, for example, was the case of the Income-tax Investigation Commission where the appointments were whole time and a Judge of the High Court appointed as a member of the Investigation Commission could not at the same time work as a Judge of the High Court. But Judges appointed to head Commissions under the Commissions of Inquiry Act stand in a different position altogether. These Commissions are not whole time posts and their sittings are not even continuous.

In such a case, a Judge appointed to head a Commission of Inquiry remains as part of the High Court and if the Commission of Inquiry is not working continuously he is entitled to sit and act as a Judge of the High Court in the intervals. Where a Judge heads temporary Commissions of Inquiry under the Commissions of Inquiry Act, he remains a part of the High Court and is entitled to sit and act as a Judge of the High Court whenever he thinks fit. The appointment of a Judge as Commission of Inquiry does not deprive him of the rights and privileges of a Judge of the High Court. Whenever he finds time to attend to his duties as a Judge of the High Court while acting as a Commission of Inquiry, he can do so.[405]

Notwithstanding the competence of the appropriate Government to appoint Judges as Commissions of Inquiry, the fact remains as to whether this would be proper and desirable, especially in view of the imperative need to maintain independence of judiciary. It has been said that though the appointment of sitting Judges on the verge of retirement and retired Judges as Inquiry Commissions by the Executive may be justified, yet it may strike at the root of an independent judiciary in the absence of effective and meaningful consultative process for selecting the right incumbent(s). Though this practice has an advantage of utilizing the talents of experiences hands, it has one disadvantage, as it is capable of misuse by making the appointment(s) based on political patronage. A Judge on the verge of retirement may at least contemplate the chances of being appointed a Commission after retirement. It is not to stress that these appointments do have any impact on all Judges. But at least some of them might be interested. To say that some may be interested and their independence might be affected is not intended to cast aspersion on the judiciary as a whole. It is a possibility with potential for the destruction of the independence of judiciary. There may be temptations lurking in these appointments with possibilities of adversely affecting the independence of judiciary.[406]

---

405. *Alok Kumar Roy* v. *Dr. S.N. Sarma*, AIR 1968 SC 453, p. 455; 1968 MPLJ 552.

406. *Nixon M. Joseph and Another* v. *Union of India and Others*, AIR 1998 Kerala 385.

As far back as 1989-90, the Arrears Committee, which was constituted by the Government of India on the recommendation of the Chief Justices' Conference, emphasized the need for reappraisal insofar as appointment to Judges as Commissions under the Commissions of Inquiry Act, 1952 was concerned. The Committee recommended amendment of the Act to provide for appointment of Retired Judges as Commissions under the Act on the advice of the Chief Justice. Paras 9.19 and 9.20 of the Report of the Arrears Committee 1989-90, dealing with appointment of Judges as Commissions under Act, read as follows:

"Need for Reappraisal Emphasised

The demand for appointment of Judges of the High Courts and the Judges of the Supreme Court under the Commissions of Inquiry Act is ever on the increase. Solutions to several problems that confront the Nation are sought to be found by appointing Judges of the High Courts or the Judges of the Supreme Court as Commissions under the Commissions of Inquiry Act. Many of the issues which are referred to such commissions, it is a matter of common knowledge, are not of such magnitude or importance requiring the attention of the Judges of the superior Courts. The work of these commissions takes several months and sometimes years depriving the High Courts/Supreme Court their valuable services, which we cannot afford to lose with the problem of mounting arrears staring in our eyes. Unlike a judicial verdict, the report of a Commission of inquiry does not result in resolving the problems. Further steps have to be taken for that purpose. The opinion of the Commission is also not binding on the Government which appoints such Commissions. It is a matter of common knowledge that though commissions are appointed with great amount of enthusiasm and expectation after the report are submitted by the Commissions, there is hardly anything done in most of the cases to give effect to the views expressed or the recommendations made. Many such reports lie only collecting dust in the offices. Another curious thing which we have noticed is that after a Judge of a High Court submits his report it is announced that it is being scrutinised by a Committee of officials and many times it is on the advice of the committee of such officials it is decided as to which of the recommendations of the commission deserve to be implemented and which not. We often find allegations being made against the Judges appointed as Commissions, their reports criticized as being biased or rendered with a view to favour one or the other. The manner in which this machinery has been utilized has to a considerable extent, affected the image of the Judges of the High Court and the Supreme Court. The bed rock of the judiciary is the confidence of the people. Appointment of Judges of the High Courts and the Supreme Court as Commissions and the manner in which their reports have been dealt with have to some extent contributed to affecting the confidence of the people. Is it, therefore, not a very useful exercise to draw the Judges from the High Courts and the Supreme Court for appointment as such Commissions when their services are badly needed in the Courts for tackling the problem of arrears? It is no doubt true that the increasing demand for appointment of Judges as Commissions of Inquiry is an indication of the confidence of the people in the Judiciary. It is also true that when there is a paramount need for the services of Judges in the interest of the Nation, we should not be found wanting in offering our services. But are we really in a position to spare the services of the Judges? Arrears are mounting, the required number of posts of Judges are not sanctioned and those sanctioned are also not promptly filled up. When such is the acute problem of the judiciary itself, we should give serious thought to this problem.

Appointment of Retired Judges on the Advice of the Chief Justice Recommended

When a large number of retired Judges, who are in good health and mentally alert are available in the country their services can be utilized for appointment of Commissions rather than sitting Judges of the High Courts. Appointment of sitting Judges of High Courts should be made only under exceptional circumstances. The sitting Judges are appointed as Commissions of Inquiry on the advice of the Chief Justice and with the consent of the Judge concerned. This ensures that the person appointed as the Commission is not the nominee of the government. In order to inspire the confidence of the people, it is desirable that the choice of the personnel of the commission is not left to the executive discretion of the Government. This problem can be solved by suitably amending the Commissions of Inquiry Act making provision to the effect that a Commission under the Commissions of Inquiry Act should be appointed only with the consent or concurrence of the Chief Justice. Thus, even if a retired Judge is to be appointed as a Commission, it should be done in accordance with the advice of the Chief Justice. This will ensure the confidence of the people in the Commission without at the same time denuding the High Courts of the services of the sitting Judges of the High Courts. This will go a long way in tackling the problem of arrears in our courts."

Guidelines for Appointment of Judges as Commissions

The question whether a sitting Judge of the High Court can be appointed to a Commission, came up for consideration before the Apex Court in the case of *T. Fenn Walter and Others* v. *Union of India and Others*.[407] When the petition came up for hearing and disposal, the Court was no longer concerned with the reliefs sought for in the writ petition as the Judge resigned from the post of President of the State Consumer Disputes Redressal Commission, Pondicherry, on the filing of the writ petition. However, the Apex Court dealt with the matters in details on merits for the reason that the matter was of some constitutional importance, as sitting judges were quite often appointed to various posts and Tribunals and whether they could still discharge the duties as sitting Judges was a vexed question. In this regard, the Court referred to the Constituent Assembly debates and observed as follows:

> While considering Article 103 of the Draft Constitution, one of the Hon. Members of the Constituent Assembly suggested that there should be a new Article, namely, Article 103A to the effect that a person who is holding or has held office of a Judge of the Supreme Court shall not be eligible

407. 2002(5) SCALE 185.

for appointment to any office of emoluments under the Government of India or State other than that of the Chief Justice of India or the Chief Justice of a High Court. Various opinions were expressed by the Members of the Constituent Assembly. Replying to the various suggestions, Dr. B.R. Ambedkar stated as follows:

I understand to be the idea underlying this particular amendment. For the purpose of understanding the main idea underlying this amendment, I think we have to take up three different cases. One case is the case of a Judge of the Supreme Court who has been appointed to an executive office with no right of reversion to the Supreme Court. This is one case. The second case is the appointment of a Supreme Court Judge after he has held that post to an executive office of a non-judicial character. The third case is the case of a executive office of a Supreme Court Judge being given or assigned duties of a non-judicial character with the right to revert to the Supreme Court. I understand that—my friend Dr. Sen may correct me if I am wrong—this amendment refers to the third proposition, viz., the assignment of a Supreme Court Judge to non-judicial duties for a short period with the right for him to revert to the Supreme Court. With regard to the first case that I mentioned, viz., the appointment of a Supreme Court Judge to an executive office provided the Supreme Court Judge resigns his post as a Judge of the Supreme Court, I do not see any objection at all, because he goes out of the Supreme Court altogether.

With regard to the second case, viz., the assignment of duties to a Supreme Court Judge who has retired, we have just now disposed of it. There ought to be no limitation at all.

With regard to the third case, I think it is a point, which requires consideration. We have had two cases in this country. One was the case, which occurred during the war when a Judge of the Federal Court was sent round by the then Government of India on diplomatic missions. We have also had during the regime of this Government the case where the Chief Justice or a Judge—I forget now, of one of the High Courts, was sent out on a diplomatic mission. On both occasions there was some very strong criticism of such action. My Friend, Mr. Chimanlal Setalvad, came out with an article in the Times of India criticizing the action of the Government. Personally I share those sentiments.

In view of the fact that there are many Statutes enacted by the Parliament which provide for a sitting Judge of the High Court to be appointed either as the President, Chairman, or Vice Chairman of any Tribunal or Commission, it cannot be said that a sitting Judge of a High Court shall neither be appointed to any other post nor shall be assigned any other judicial or quasi-judicial work. But, invariably, in all cases, the Chief Justice of the concerned High Court would be consulted in case the appointment is sought of a sitting Judge. Normally, a Judge who is to retire from service shortly may be desirous of accepting any other assignment either as a Chairman, Vice Chairman or a Member of any Commission or Tribunal. But if a sitting Judge is appointed to a regular post of Chairman, Vice Chairman or Member or a Tribunal and the decision of that authority is subjected to judicial review of the High Court, it may not be an ideal situation. Under the Constitution of India, security of judicial tenure has been provided to the Judges of the superior Courts and they could be removed only as per the provisions prescribed under Article 124(4) of the Constitution on account of the proved misbehaviour or incapacity. Sometimes, the sitting Judge who is appointed to the post of Chairman, Vice Chairman or Member of any Tribunal or Commission would be liable to be removed by the appointing authority. This also is not desirable in view of the Constitutional position being occupied by the Judge.

Quite often sitting judges are appointed as Inquiry Commissions. Generally it may not create any difficulty if the inquiry itself can be conducted without prejudice to other judicial work as a Judge of the superior Court. However, the appointment of Judges to head or chair Commission of Inquiry or to perform other non-judicial work would create unnecessary burden on the Judges and it would affect the administration of justice. The work of these commissions takes considerable time and there are several instances where the work of the Commission continued for years. If sitting Judge is appointed, considerable time is lost and the Judge would not be in a position to attend to his regular judicial work. In view of the mounting arrears of cases in superior Courts, it would be difficult to lend services of a Judge for such Commission work. Moreover, the report of the Commission of Inquiry is often stated to have only recommendatory value and the opinions expressed therein are ignored and no follow-up actions are being taken by the Government. In some matters, when political issues are also involved, even impartiality and objectivity of the Court may sometimes be questioned due to some extraneous and oblique motives. The public image and prestige of the Court as guardian of the Constitution and rule of law has to be maintained. It is desirable that the Judges are not subjected to unwanted criticism on account of appointment as the Inquiry Commission. The image and the authority of the Court, which is of utmost importance, have to be upheld. Justice Harlan F. Stone in a letter as far back as in 1953 wrote: "It has been a long tradition of our Court that its members do not serve on committees or perform other services not having a direct relationship to the work of the Court."[408] Keeping in view all these aspects, the appointment of a sitting Judge as a Commission of Inquiry has to be made only on rare occasions if it becomes necessary for the paramount national interest of the country.

When a sitting Judge is appointed to another post, which is whole-time and if the decision taken in that capacity is subject to judicial review, it may not be in the best interests of the independence of the judiciary. Sometimes, the additional post held by the Judge may not be of equivalent status or may be under different situations, which may even spell out a master and servant relationship between the Judge and the appointing authority. Even though this may not create any conflict of duty or interest, in these days of multifarious litigation, it is always desirable for the Judge of the superior judiciary to keep away from areas of controversy so that the public confidence in our system is not hampered in any way.

---

408. *Harvard Law Review* (Vol. 87, 1953-54).

Having regard to various constitutional issues, the Hon'ble Supreme Court formulated some broad guidelines as to the manner in which the appointment of a sitting Judge of High Court to a Commission should be dealt with. These guidelines are as follows:[409]

(1) Appointment of a sitting Judge to the following offices may not be objectionable:

  (a) As a Commission of inquiry under the Commissions of Inquiry Act.

  (b) Judicial office which is of such a high character and where it has to be filled up by a sitting Judge to fulfill the requirement of law, e.g. under Article 262 of the Constitution of India which provides for adjudication of any dispute with respect to the use, distribution or control of water or any inter-State river or river-valley, read with Inter State Water Disputes Act, 1956.

  (c) Where expertise and experience of a sitting Judge is required to discharge the functions, a sitting Judge may be appointed, for example, as a Member of the Finance Commission or Law Commission.

(2) Appointment of sitting Judge to a Tribunal is not desirable where the adjudicating members are composed of other members who are not Judges or qualified to be appointed as Judges, such as bureaucrats, revenue officials, etc.

(3) So also, appointment of sitting Judge to a Judicial Tribunal is not desirable where the statute or the rules and regulations framed therein contemplate provisions for removal from such office or other disciplinary action by any authority.

(4) When a sitting Judge is appointed to a post or Tribunal, he shall be amenable to the disciplinary jurisdiction only in the manner provided for in Article 124(4) of the Constitution of India if he is a Judge of the

409. *T. Fenn Walter* (*supra*), pp. 191-92.

Supreme Court or in the manner provided for in proviso (b) to Article 217(1) read with Article 124(4) of the Constitution of India if he is a Judge of a High Court.

(5) Where the post may not be a whole-time post but the nature of duties are such that his order as a Tribunal or Commission would be subjected to the supervisory jurisdiction of the High Court under Articles 226, 227, a sitting Judge of the High Court may not be appointed to such post, but if the sitting Judge concerned has only a short period to retire from service, he may be appointed, but after accepting the full-time post, he shall not sit as a Judge and discharge duties and function (both judicial and administrative) as a sitting Judge of High Court, even though he may not demit office consequent on his appointment to a full-time post.

(6) When the Chief Justice of a High Court is consulted for appointment of a sitting Judge as Member, Chairman, Vice Chairman or President of any Court, Commission or Tribunal and it is a whole-time post, the Chief Justice shall bear in mind the relevant circumstances and shall not compromise the dignity of the office of the sitting Judge and shall strive to preserve the independence of judiciary.

(7) When a sitting Judge who has only a short period to retire from service is appointed to a post, he shall express his willingness to relinquish the remaining tenure as a Judge and then only his service shall be made available for such a post.

On 27 November 2006, the Supreme Court scrapped all Commissions of Inquiry headed by sitting Judges of High Courts and directed that no sitting Judge of any High Court will be appointed to head an Inquiry Commission as it affects judicial work. The order came from a Bench of Justices Arijit Pasayat and S.H. Kapadia after the Court was informed by the Additional Solicitor General, Gopal Subramanium, that none of the chief secretaries of the States had furnished data regarding sitting High Court Judges heading Commissions of Inquiry. The Bench, however, clarified that the order will not be applicable to those Commissions of Inquiry who are at the fag end of their task and only need to prepare and submit reports. It also strongly disapproved of the tendency of State Governments to appoint sitting Judges of High Court to head inquiry panels despite an earlier order of the Apex Court against such appointments. The Apex Court observed that sitting High Courts Judges were supposed to hold judicial inquiries only in matters of national and public importance and it was not proper on the part of the State Governments to frequently appoint them to head inquiries into trivial and local issues.[410] The Apex Court's rationale is simple: why appoint sitting Judges when they are already overburdened with cases? When many retired Judges of High Courts are in good health, the State Governments would do well to make use of their wisdom and experience in heading Inquiry Commissions. Undoubtedly, the Apex Court was forced to disband the probe panels due to the lackasaisical attitude of the State Governments. It is common knoweledge that most probe panels were appointed for political reasons. The State Governments used to appoint them on any issue, citing "public importance". In fact, appointment of a sitting Judge for a probe panel had become a simple affair. All that a State Government needed to do was to take the consent of the Chief Justice of the

410. *Hindustan Times*, New Delhi, Tuesday, November 28, 2006—"IN THE SUPREME COURT No Sitting HC Judge can head probe panel", p. 13. Earlier, the issue was raised by the ASG during the hearing of a PIL, on ragging menace and the Court had asked the Centre to seek information from the States and Union Terrirories on the number of sitting Judges heading Commissions of Inquiries. The Court expressed its displeasure when the ASG said that not a single State or Union Territory had till date responded to the request for details in this regard. "Left hanging—in Orissa—Justice A.S. Naidu Commission of Inquiry, which is probing the police firing at Kalinga Nagar in January this year in which 12 tribal protesters were killed; Justice P.K. Mohanty Commission of Inquiry, which is probing the stampede inside the Puri Jagannath temple in which four devotees were killed;—in Bihar—Justice Chandramauli Kumar Prasad Commission of Inquiry, which is probing the circumstances that led to the assault on Additional District Judge D.N. Barai in Bhagalpur Civil Court in 1997.

High Court concerned. Moreover, such Commissions took a very long time to submit their reports to the Governments. Even so, their recommendations were very rarely implemented. Consequently, precious time and energy of the sitting High Court Judges were wasted in the whole exercise. The Apex Court has not only put a cap on such appointments but also wants to know from the States how many reports have been implemented so far. It would be interesting to wait for their response on this matter of far reaching importance.[411]

Even as demands are being made by political parties for appointment of sitting Judges to Commissions of Inquiry, the Supreme Court declined to reconsider its order that no sitting Judge of any High Court be so appointed, and, if any judge was already appointed he could not continue. A Bench consisting of Justice Ajit Pasayat and Justice D.K. Jain passed this order[412] while rejecting an application filed by Orissa to allow the Commission, headed by a sitting High Court Judge, to continue to probe the Kalinga Nagar Police firing. The Government submitted that Justice A.S. Naidu was appointed considering the serious problem highlighted in the letter of the Chief Minister to the Chief Justice of the High Court. The Chief Justice suggested the name of Justice Naidu for the Commission which was sitting only on Saturdays, Sundays and other Court holidays. Writing the judgment, Justice Pasayat said that from a reading of the letters of the Chief Minister of Orissa and the Chief Justice of the Orissa High Court, nowhere it appeared that either the State Government or the Chief Justice considered the matter to be of paramount national interest to warrant the appointment of a sitting Judge of a High Court as Commission.[413] Even the notification dated 4 February 2006, appointed the Commission, did not indicate it to be of paramount national interest. Though

411. "Not at courts' cost Retired judges can head inquiry commissions", Editorial, *The Tribune*, 30 November 2006.

412. *University of Kerala* v. *Council, Principals' Colleges, Kerala & Ors.* 2007 (5) SCALE 406.

413. *Times of India*, New Delhi, 16 April 2007, reported as "Sitting judges cannot be appointed to probe panels".

it was strenuously urged by the learned counsel for the applicant—State that the Commission was only permitted to work on holidays, the Court was of the view that it really was of no consequence. As noted in *T. Fenn Walter's* case[414] the considerations have to be of several aspects including the administrative "paramount national interest" angle. Accordingly, the Court observed: "That does not appear to be a factor considered when the request was made for appointment of a sitting Judge as the Commission and the reply of the Chief Justice of the High Court accepting the prayer. It could not be shown to us as to how the issues being enquired into by the Commission are of paramount national interest. Further the stand that the Commision was required to give recommendation on various other aspects like industrialization, etc. is really of no consequence. It is not known as to on what basis a sitting Judge appointed as a Commission, can throw light on the broader issues like industrialization, etc. In any event, the parameters of enquiry do not include these aspects."[415] From this observation, it follows that there has to be clear evidence either in the notification appointing a sitting High Court Judge as the Commission or in other material relating to appointment of such a Commission that the subject of inquiry has been of paramount national interest warranting appointment of a sitting High Court Judge as the Commission. However, where there is such evidence on the records of the case based upon which the appropriate Government has formed its opinion as to nature of the subject of inquiry being of paramount national importance, it will not be open to the Court to sit in judgment in the matter. The Court should not usurp to itself the executive function of the appropriate Government and substitute its own opinion with that of the appropriate Government. The scope of judicial review in such cases is a limited one and would be confined to ascertain if there is some evidence to support the view of the appropriate Government that the subject of inquiry being of paramount national importance warranting appointment of a

414. (2002) (6) SCC 184.

415. *University of Kerala* v. *Council, Principals' Colleges, Kerala & Ors.*, 2007 (5) SCALE 406, p. 409.

sitting Judge of a High Court. Of course, such an appointment would invariably be made with the concurrence of the Chief Justice of the concerned High Court. The fact that the appropriate Government considered the subject of inqury being of paramount national importance, does not make it incumbent upon the Chief Justice to recommend the name of a sitting Judge of the High Court in all cases. Even when the appropriate Government is of the opinion that the subject of inquiry is of paramount national importance that may warrant appointment of a sitting Judge of the High Court as the Commission, the Chief Justice will be well within his right to decline to recommend the name of a sitting Judge of the High Court for any reason. In any case, it has to be borne in mind that the appointment of a sitting Judge as a Commission should be more by way of an exception rather than a general rule and all the concerned authorities are expected to work responsibly in unison and harmony with each other.

Status of Commission Manned by a Judge

The appointment of a Judge of the High Court to a Commission of Inquiry does not alter the status of the Commission or equates it with the High Court itself. The Judge of a High Court, who is appointed to a Commission of Inquiry, does not carry with him all the jurisdiction and powers of the High Court when he discharges his functions as the Commission of Inquiry. The proceedings before the Judge, who constitutes the Commission of Inquiry, are not proceedings of the High Court. The expression "actual service" of a Judge of a High Court as defined in paragraph 11(b)(i) of the Second Schedule to the Constitution, envisages the possibility of a Judge of a High Court being entrusted with functions other than judicial and quasi-judicial functions. Quite obviously that definition is not intended to confer any jurisdiction on the High Court in relation to the performance of such other functions as a Judge of that High Court may, at the request of the President, undertake to discharge. In the definition of "actual service" of a Judge of a High Court, no distinction is drawn between the various classes of "such other functions as a Judge may, at the request of the President, undertake to discharge", that is, between judicial functions, quasi-judicial and functions other than judicial and quasi-judicial functions. Even if it is judicial or quasi-judicial work that a Judge of a High Court undertakes, if that work is unconnected with the jurisdiction of the High Court, the fact that he holds the office of a Judge of that High Court cannot make that a work of that High Court and within its jurisdiction. Accordingly, any contempt committed in relation to such proceedings before a Commission would certainly be contempt of that Commission. True, it would also be in contempt of the learned Judge who presides over that Commission. But nonetheless it is only contempt of the Commission and not contempt of the High Court. When a Judge of the High Court is appointed as Commission of Inquiry, he has not the powers of a Judge of that Court to punish persons for contempt of the Commission under Article 215 of the Constitution.[416]

Equality in Remuneration to Members of Commissions

In *M.L. Jain* v. *Union of India*,[417] the petitioner was appointed a member of a Committee to inquire into cases of certain riots on 23 February 1987 and the terms of appointment provided for fixation of lump sum honorarium. Subsequently, the Government issued guidelines, vide Government of India's O.M. dated 8 October 1987, regulating remuneration, i.e. salary and allowances, payable to retired Supreme Court and High Court Judges appointed on Commissions/Committees of Inquiry or re-employed on whole time basis by Government of India. Initially, the term of the Committee was for six months and, honorarium, therefore, was fixed for six months. The term of the Committee had to be extended on account of injunction issued by Delhi High Court restraining the Committee from functioning. The Committee remained in existence until the notification, under which it was appointed, was quashed by the High Court on 4 October 1989. The petitioner claimed remuneration under the aforesaid Government of India's O.M. of 8 October 1987. The respondents relied on the terms of

416. In the matter of Mr. Hayles, Editor of *The Mail* and another, AIR 1955 Madras 1 wherein similar observations were made in respect of a High Court Judge appointed as Industrial Tribunal.

417. AIR 1993 SC 1150.

appointment providing for lump sum honorarium and were willing to pay accordingly. The High Court dismissed the petition. On appeal by special leave under Article 136 of the Constitution of India, the respondents were directed to pay to the petitioner in terms of O.M. dated 8 October 1987, after adjusting the payment already made of the originally stipulated honorarium, especially in view of the fact that those who worked as full time members of the other committees were paid salary and allowances in terms of the said O.M. and no explanation whatsoever had been given by the respondents as to why the petitioner/appellant was not paid similarly as per the guidelines contained in the said O.M. It may be pertinent to note the following observations made by the Apex Court in this case, viz.: "We are unable to understand as to how the Committee could transact any work after the High Court quashed it out of existence w.e.f. 4 October 1989. We are also unable to understand as to how the Committee could function at all from 24 December 1987 when the High Court had injuncted it from functioning. We will, however, presume that since the Committee continued to exist, the appellant was tied up with it and as has been stated by him in his further affidavit, the Committee did its work till it was quashed." Accordingly, the respondents were directed to make payment up to 4 October 1987, on which day the High Court quashed the notification under which the Committee was appointed.

Delay or Inaction on Inquiry Report

Although the report of a Commission of Inquiry is not binding on the Government, yet the Government is expected to take its action, whatever it may be, on such a report. Any undue delay or inaction of such a report will negate the very purpose of the constitution of a Commission of Inquiry. When for decades the Government failed to take notice of the Reports of Commissions of Inquiry headed by former Judges of Supreme Court or High Courts, the very purpose for setting up such Commissions gets frustrated and the argument that such commissions are appointed only as an eye-wash, acquires credibility. It is appropriate that when in a matter of 'definite public importance', a Commission of Inquiry is appointed under the Commissions of Inquiries Act, 1952, the State Government should examine the report expeditiously and decide what action, if any, is required to be taken on that report promptly. To keep a report pending for years together and, as, in this case, for a decade, does no credit to anybody. Reports of Commissions of Inquiry should not be allowed to gather dust for years together as it reflects adversely on the utility of such commissions and would affect the credibility of the entire exercise.[418]

Non-placing of Commission's Report before Legislature

Sub-section (4) of Section 3 requires the appropriate Government to lay before each House of Parliament or, as the case may be, the Legislature of the State, any report of the Commission made under sub-section (1) along with a memorandum of the action taken thereon, within a period of six months of the submission of the report by the Commission to the appropriate Government. Amending Act 79 of 1971 originally introduced this sub-section into the Act. According to the objects and reasons appended to the Amending Bill, this sub-section was introduced "in the light of the experience gained indicating that many Government do not place the Commission's report before the Assembly at all though they relate to important issues of national interest. It was thought necessary to compel the Government to place the report before the Parliament or the appropriate State Legislature together with a memorandum of action thereon, within a period of six months from the date of submission of the report".[419]

Soon after the assassination of Smt. Indira Gandhi, the Government of India by notification dated 20-11-1984 constituted a Commission under the Commissions of Inquiry Act, 1952. The Commission was presided over by Mr. Justice M.P. Thakkar, a sitting Judge of the Supreme Court. The Commission framed regulations under Section 8 of the Act in regard to the procedure for enquiry and regulation 8 framed

---

418. *Fazalur Rehman and Others* v. *State of U.P. and Others*, AIR 1999 SC 3460.

419. *V. Narayana Rao* v. *State of A.P.*, AIR 1987 AP 53; 1987 Lab IC 152.

therein reads: "In view of the sensitive nature of enquiry the proceedings will be in camera unless the Commission directs otherwise." This regulation, thus, made it clear that the proceedings of the Commission will be ordinarily in camera. It would only be in public if the Commission so directs. Recording of evidence and the proceedings of the Commission had in fact been in camera throughout and even the report, interim and the final report. And then also it was stated by the Commission itself to be confidential. Under the Act as it stood before the amendment which was done by the Ordinance No. 6 of 1986 normally the Government was supposed to place the report of the Commission under Section 3 sub-clause (4) of the Act before the House of the People within six months of the submission of the report by the Commission but the Government did not do that. The steps were taken to amend the Commissions of Inquiry Act and on May 14, 1986 the President of India promulgated an Ordinance No. 6 of 1986 namely Commission of Inquiry (Amendment) Ordinance, 1986 by which sub-sections (5) and (6) were introduced to Section 3 as follows:

> 5. The provisions of sub-section (4) shall not apply if the appropriate Government is satisfied that in the interest of the sovereignty and integrity of India, the security of the State, friendly relations with foreign States or in public interest, it is not expedient to lay before the House of People or, as the case may be, the Legislative Assembly of the State, the report or any part thereof, of the Commission on the inquiry made by the Commission under sub-section (1) and issues a notification to that effect in the Official Gazette.
>
> *Explanation.* For the purpose of sub-section (5), "report" includes an interim report and all proceedings of a Commission.
>
> 6. Every notification issued under sub-section (5) shall be laid before the House of People or, as the case may be, the Legislative Assembly of the State, if it is sitting, within seven days of its re-assembly, and the appropriate Government shall seek the approval of the House of the People or, as the case may be, the Legislative Assembly of the State, to the notification by a resolution moved within a period of fifteen days beginning with the day on which the notification is so

laid before the House of the People or, as the case may be, the Legislative Assembly of the State and if the House of the People or, as the case may be, the Legislative Assembly of the State makes any modification in the notification or directs that the notification should cease to have effect, the notification shall thereafter have effect only in such modified form or be of no effect, as the case may be.

In pursuance of this amendment on May 15, 1986 the Central Government issued a notification under sub-section (5) of Section 3 stating "The Central Government, being satisfied that it is not expedient in the interest of the security of the State and in the public interest to lay before the House of People, the report submitted to the Government on 19-11-1985, and 27-2-1986, by Justice M.P. Thakkar, a sitting Judge of the Supreme Court of India appointed under the notification of the Government of India, in the Ministry of Home Affairs No. SO 867(B), dated the 20th Nov. 1984 thereby notifies that the said report shall not be laid before the House of People." It is interesting that on 20-8-1986, Ordinance No. 6 was replaced by Commission of Inquiry (Amendment) Act, 1986 (Act No. 36 of 1986) with retrospective effect. The said notification dated May 15, 1986 was also got approved by the House of People as required under sub-section (6) of Section 3. Accordingly, the reports of the Commission were not laid before the House.[420]

Sub-sections (5) and (6), which were inserted into the Act as aforesaid in 1986, were omitted from the Act 1990. The Commissions of Inquiry (Amendment) Bill, 1989 (Bill No. 97 of 1989), which later on became the Commissions of Inquiry (Amendment) Act, 1990 (Act 19 of 1990), stated the objects and reasons underlying these amendments as follows:

"Statement of Objects and Reasons

Sub-section (4) of Section 3 of the Commissions of Inquiry Act, 1952 casts an obligation on the appropriate Government to lay the report of the Commission of Inquiry appointed

420. *Kehar Singh* v. *The State* (Delhi Admn., AIR 1988 SC 1883, pp. 1899-90).

under sub-section (1) thereof before the House of People or, as the case may be, the Legislative Assembly concerned, together with a memorandum of action taken thereon, within a period of six months of the submission of the report. However, in 1986, section 3 had been amended so as to provide therein that under certain circumstances the report of the Commission of Inquiry may not be so laid.

2. A Commission of Inquiry is always set up for the purpose of making an inquiry into any definite matter of public importance. As such, the report submitted by such a Commission should not be withheld from the House of the People or the Legislative Assembly under any circumstances and the public should have access to information which is of vital importance and interest to them. It is felt that the amendment made in 1986 should be done away with.

3. The Bill seeks to achieve the above object."

The Act, however, does not provide for the consequences for any failure to lay the report of a Commission in compliance with the requirements of this sub-section. Recently, the report of the National Commission for Religious and Linguistic Minorities, headed by former Chief Justice of India, Justice Ranganath Misra, in cold storage for the past two years, was tabled in both Houses of Parliament on December 18, 2009. The report was initially circulated in May 2007 in view of the controversy which it had provoked, several of its copies had been withdrawn and the report has since been effectively missing from public view.[420a] Whether circulation of the report, even before laying it on the floors of both Houses of Parliament, is a breach of the Parliament privileges, is a debatable question. But it is certainly an impropriety on the part of the government to do so.

In *V. Narayana Rao* v. *State of A.P.*,[421] the State Government failed to place the report on the floor of the Legislature for a period of approximately four years. The question arose whether

420a. See "After two years, Ranganath report tabled", *The Indian Express*, December 19, 2009, p. 6.

421. AIR 1987 AP 53; 1987 Lab IC 152.

on this account the report should be treated as non est or void and whether it should be held that the action taken by the Government thereon was incompetent and invalid. The Court held: "The provision is not mandatory. There is no other provision in the Act which provides for the consequence that flows from the non-observance of the requirements of sub-s. (4). Evidently, this sub-section was conceived as a check upon the Government inaction, or deliberate suppression of the report before the Parliament/Legislative Assembly along with the Memorandum of action taken by it thereon. But, if we hold that non-placing of the Report or non-observance of the time-limit prescribed in the sub-section results in rendering the very Report void, and that, on that account, the Government is precluded from taking any action on the basis of such Report, it would amount to placing a premium upon the delay or default on the part of the Government and would not serve the purpose of the sub-section. It is one thing to say that on account of this lapse of time the Report has lost its relevance or validity in a given case or that the relevant circumstances have undergone such a change that the Report is no longer relevant, or of any use, and quite a different thing to say that the report is rendered void after the period of six months on the ground of non-compliance with the said sub-section. In case of non-observance of the said sub-section it is always open to any member of Parliament/Legislature, or any Opposition party/group to question the Government as to why the Report of the Commission is not placed before the House, and also regarding the action taken by the Government on such Report."

It was further held in this case that in view of the fact that the Government took action on the report on the day it was scheduled to be placed before the legislative assembly and thereby pre-empting any discussion or debate in the House upon the said report and the memorandum of action, it could be held that such action was not liable to be quashed especially when the assembly did not disapprove the report or the action thereon. In the circumstances, it was held, the Legislature must be deemed to have approved the action taken by the Government on the report.

Laying of Report of Commission before Legislature to which Act is not Applicable or whose Appointment is Found to be Void Ab Initio

The question whether the report of a Commission appointed in exercise of executive power or whose appointment has been found to be illegal and void ab initio, is required to be laid before the Parliament or, as the case may be, the State Legislature in terms fo Section 3(4) of the Act, came up for consideration before the High Court of Gujarat in the case of *Union of India* v. *Nilkanth Tulsidas Bhatia*.[422] A Division Bench that High Court, comprised of M.S. Shah and Sharad D. Dave, JJ., observed: "In the first place, the above provisions[423] are applicable to the report of the Commission appointed under Section 3(1) of the CoI Act and not to the report of a Committee. Admittedly, what the Railway Administration of the Central Government had appointed on 4-9-2004 was a Committee and not a Commission under Section 3(1) of the CoI Act. Assuming that the Committee by whatever name called was an authority contemplated by Section 11 of the CoI Act, the proviso to Sub-section (1) of Section 3 applies in either case whether what is appointed is a Commission under Section 3(1) of the CoI Act or is an authority (by whatever name called) referred to in Section 11 of the Act.... (T)he embargo that when the Commission appointed by the State Government to inquire into the same matter is functioning, the Central Government cannot appoint another Commission or Committee to inquire in the same matter—this embargo applies irrespective of the fact whether the appointment of the Commission/Committee by the Central Government is on the formation of the necessary opinion by the Central Government itself or even under a resolution in that behalf passed by the Parliament. Once the appointment of the Committee made on 4-9-2004 is found to be illegal and void ab initio, the question of laying the report of the Committee before the Parliament cannot arise nor can the Railway Administration be permitted to go ahead with giving publicity

---

422. (2006) 2 GLR 952.

423. Section 3(4) of the Commissions of Inquiry Act, 1952.

to the report of such Committee. Once the strong prima facie case is made regarding not merely illegality in appointment of the Committee, but also total lack of jurisdiction to make such appointment, the question of making the report available to Parliament for discussion would not arise even if the Committee were appointed pursuant to a resolution of the Parliament."[424]

Powers of Commission.

4. The Commission shall have the powers of a Civil Court, while trying a suit under the Code of Civil Procedure, 1908, in respect of the following matters, namely:

(i) [425][summoning and enforcing the attendance of any person from any part of India] and examining him on oath;

(ii) requiring the discovery and production of any document;

(iii) receiving evidence on affidavits;

(iv) requisitioning any public record or copy thereof from any court or office;

(v) issuing commissions for the examination of witnesses or documents;

(vi) any other matter, which may be prescribed.

Objects and Reasons

Section 4 of the Act authorizes the Commission to summon and enforce the attendance of any person. It does not, however, specify the territorial jurisdiction for the Commission in this behalf and, consequently, it may be argued that the restrictions under Order XVI, Rule 19 of the Code of Civil Procedure, 1908

---

424. It is understood that the Union of India, in the Ministry of Railway, has preferred a Special Leave Petition in the Supreme Court against this judgment and the matter is yet to attain finality.

425. Subs. by Act 79 of 1971, Section 6 for certain words. Furthermore, as a Commission of Inquiry is not a Court, the question of initiating any proceedings under the Contempt of Court Act in respect of proceedings before a Commission of Inquiry will not arise. This lacuna has now been filled up by Section 10A of the Commission of Inquiry Act providing for penalty for bringing the Commission into disrepute.

would be attracted, since, under Section 4, a Commission, in summoning witnesses, has the same powers as a Civil Court. In view of the different nature of the work assigned to a Commission of Inquiry, it is considered that this restriction should not apply to Commission appointed under the Act. The clause seeks to amend Section 4 suitably so as to empower the Commission to summon and enforce the attendance of any person from any part of India (vide paragraph 27 of the report).[426]

Scope and Ambit of Powers

The section is couched in a very general form and langage. Powers coferred under this section on a Commission of Inquiry are unfettered. Nevertheless, since these powers correspond to the powers of a Civil Court, that too, which such a Court has while trying a suit under the Code of Civil Procedure, 1908, the powers of a Commission of Inquiry ought to be viewed as necessarily being circumscribed in the same manner, to same extent, and subject to the same conditions as is the case with the corresponding powers of a Civil Court. The powers under this section will, therefore, have to be construed, mutatis mutandis, in accordance with the legal principles governing the exercise of corresponding powers by a Civil Court. Thus, though the Commission is given power to summon and examine any person or to produce any document or to requisition any public record, without any condition or fetter, yet any exercise of such powers should be coupled with the belief and satisfaction that witness or document in question may be useful for, or relevant to, the subject-matter of inquiry. It is true that the rules of construction do not warrant any addition or deletion of a word or words that the Legislature has chosen not to add or delete. Also, the dictum of casus omissus mandates against filling up any omission for this is the function of the legislature. But it is equally true that the Act has to be read and construed as a whole and not in piecemeal. Also, a wholesome construction of the Act warrants that similar words and analogous provisions be construed in the

426. Twenty-fourth Report of the Law Commission of India on the Commissions of Inquiry Act, 1952. Notes on Clauses, Clause 6 of the Commissions of Inquiry (Amendment) Bill, 1971.

same manner and in the same sense. Section 5 of the Act deals with additional powers of the Commission. Reading the two Sections together, especially having regard to the object and the scheme of the Act, it appears that the requirement of relevance of any witness or document to the subject of inquiry is deemed to be inbuilt in Section 4.

Nature of Powers

It would appear from Section 4 that it only clothes the Commission with certain powers of a Civil Court but does not confer on it the status of a Court. It is only under sub-section (4) of Section 5 that the Commission is deemed to be a Civil Court and sub-section (5) of that Section imparts to the proceeding before it the character of a judicial proceeding. However, these provisions only create a fiction, which cannot extend beyond the purpose for which it is created.[427]

Section 4 of the Act, no doubt, gives certain powers to the Commission to call for certain documents as provided for by the Code of Civil Procedure. In other words, Section 4 of the Act merely applies certain provisions of the Code of Civil Procedure only for certain purposes. By the application of these provisions, the Commission neither becomes a Court nor do the proceedings before it become judicial proceedings. The proceedings before the Commission cannot be held to be judicial proceedings as defined in Section 1 of the Evidence Act. It is, therefore, manifest that the provisions of the Evidence Act do not in terms apply to the proceedings before the Commission. Section 123 of the Evidence Act is in the nature of an exception to the general rule of admissibility, which is found in the Evidence Act. While the principles of the Evidence Act may be applicable to the evidence produced before the Tribunal, it would not be proper on a parity of reasoning to infer that even the exceptions contained in the Evidence Act would also be applicable. Moreover, in view of Section 5 sub-clause 2 of the Act, it seems that the Act itself has impliedly excluded the application of the Doctrine of

427. *M.V. Rajwade I.A.S., Distt. Magistrate* v. *Dr. S.M. Hassan and Others*, AIR 1954 Nagpur 71.

"Privilege" as embodied in Section 123 of the Evidence Act from the ambit of the jurisdiction of a Tribunal appointed under this Act unless Section 5 sub-clause 2 of the Act is applied by a notification made, by the Government in pursuance of the provisions of Section 5(1) of the Act. In other words, what Section 4 has done, is merely to apply those sections of the Code of Civil Procedure, which relate to the discovery and production of documents. The relevant provision in this regard is contained in Order 11, Rule 14 of the C.P.C. Under this provision what the Court has to do, is to determine whether the document, which it has called for is material to the issue in question, and once it has come to this conclusion it has got an absolute discretion to call for these documents. This discretion given to the Court under Order 11, Rule 14, C.P.C. and other like provisions and has not in fact applied the provisions of the Evidence Act, it is obvious that the Commission has unfettered discretion to allow the production of the documents irrespective of the fact that these documents are privileged or not. Moreover, Section 5(2) of the Act clearly embodies the safeguard mentioned in Section 123 of the Evidence Act. Under Section 5, sub-clause (1), of the Act, the Government has been given discretion to apply all or any of the provisions of sub-sections 2, 3, 5 and 6 of the Act. The position, therefore, is that the Commission enjoys unfettered powers to order for the production of documents, which have to be exercised only in accordance with the provisions of the C.P.C. and no provisions of any other law. Thus, what the Legislature has done, is to exclude for the time being the operation of the "Doctrine" of privilege as embodied in Section 123 of the Evidence Act from the ambit of the proceedings, which a Commission has to hold under the Act. The Legislature has, however, fully empowered the Government to intervene in the proceedings if it thinks that a claim of privilege has to be raised and this can be done by applying the provision of Section 5, sub-clause (2) of the Act. Under sub-section (2) of Section 5 of the Act, it has been laid down that a Commission shall have the power to require any person to produce the necessary information subject, however, to any privilege which may be claimed by him, under any law for the time being in force. The privilege contemplated by this sub-section is, undoubtedly, the privilege contained in Section 123 and other allied sections of the Evidence Act. It is obvious that unless sub-section (2) is made applicable by the Government under Section 5(1) of the Act, the Commission has got unfettered powers in asking for the production of documents. By exercising these powers the Commission also suffers from a serious infirmity namely that it has no power to grant the claim of privilege if it is raised by a party to the proceedings. Sub-section (2) enlarges the powers of the Commission in this respect that the Commission is invested with powers to grant privilege if claimed by any person under any law for the time being in force, which includes the Evidence Act. Thus, sub-section (2) does confer additional powers on the Commission and it cannot be said that by putting this interpretation, the powers of the Commission are reduced. The Act has, thus, deliberately excluded the application of the claim of privilege as contained in Section 123 of the Evidence Act and other sections by giving the right to enforce this claim to the Government, if necessary, by application of Section 5(2) of the Act.[428]

On 21-8-1989, the Judicial Committee, presided by Justice D.P. Wadhwa, directed CBI to produce on affidavit copies of statement of certain persons, if any, recorded under Section 161, Cr.P.C. or though not recorded under Section 161, Cr.P.C. but recorded in case dairies.[429] This was objected to by the CBI in a writ petition before Delhi High Court[430] wherein it was, inter alia, submitted that under Section 172(2), Cr.P.C., a police diary could not be used as an evidence. It was further submitted that the investigation was going on and would only be completed by submission of the report under Section 173, Cr.P.C. Supply

428. *State of Jammu and Kashmir* v. *Anwar Ahmed Aftab and Others*, AIR 1965 Jammu and Kashmir 75.

429. Order of Goswami Wadhwa Commission of Inquiry as reported in 1989 (3) Delhi Lawyer 277.

430. *Union of India through Director, Central Bureau of Investigation, N. Delhi* v. *Delhi Bar Association and Others*, 1989 (3) Delhi Lawyer (DB) 306.

of copies of the statements at that stage was beyond contemplation of the provisions of Cr.P.C. and might prejudicially affect the prosecution of some advocates named as accused in the FIR. Under Section 175, Cr.P.C., the copies could only be supplied after the filing of the complaint under Section 173. The impugned order was, thus, assailed as being without jurisdiction and competence and amounted to interference in the statutory powers of the police to investigate. Disclosure of statements during investigation would have wide ramifications and to do so even through a collateral proceeding would jeopardize the entire concept of criminal investigations under Cr.P.C. Negating these contentions, the Court observed that the decision of the Supreme Court in *Khatri and Others* v. *State of Bihar and Others*[431] was a complete answer to the objections raised by the CBI. In this case, the Supreme Court, inter alia, observed that "the provisions of the Criminal Procedure Code are applicable where an offence under the Indian Penal Code or under any other law is being investigated, inquired into, tried or otherwise dealt with. Accordingly, bar under Sections 162 and 172 of the Code of Criminal Procedure would not be attracted to writ proceedings under Article 32 or Article 226 or to civil proceedings. Applying the ratio of the Supreme Court decision, the bar under Sections 161, 162, 172 and 173 or other provisions of Chapter XII, Cr.P.C. would not apply against any production of the statements or police diaries ordered to be produced by Commission/Committee of Inquiry. "It is not a criminal court nor even a civil court. There is no 'inquiry' or 'trial' of an 'offence' before a Committee acting under the Commissions of Inquiry Act. It is merely a fact-finding body whose function is to establish truth on matters of public importance through all relevant material. Even the Evidence Act is not applicable to these proceedings. It has all the powers of summoning the witnesses and production of documents similar to the civil court. But a Commission/Committee is the master of its own procedure."

---

431. AIR 1981 SC 1068.

Extent of Powers

The power of the Commission to call upon any person to appear as a witness under Section 4 of the Act, which in terms is very wide and is not circumscribed by fetters of stage. In *Smt. Kiran Bedi* v. *Committee of Inquiry*,[432] the respondent opposed the direction of the Committee of Inquiry for calling of persons covered under Section 8B of the Act at the end and at that stage such person even at the risk of not producing his defence, for some reason, chooses not to appear as a witness, the Committee would be deprived of knowing the facts in the knowledge of such person and such a course would obviously hamper the enquiry. Negating this contention, the Court observed that the apprehension seems to be more imaginary than real inasmuch as the Commission would have power under Section 4 to call such person as a witness even at that stage.

In *Sri Narayanadoss Mahant and Another* v. *Sri T. Neeladri Rao and Another*,[433] the summons issued by the Special Officer acting as the Commission of Inquiry, was challenged on account of its form. It was urged that the summons should have specified the particular documents or account books which had to be produced by the petitioner instead of requiring him to produce 'all the documents, accounts and other materials in your custody, control, possession or power relating to the above Institution'. The Court observed that "the Special Officer was trying to find out in what manner and to what extent there had been mismanagement of the properties of the Mutt, and in the nature of things he could not have furnished a list of documents and accounts to be produced by the petitioner. The petitioner was asked to produce all documents, etc. relating to the Mutt and under Section 4(b) of the Act, the Commission of Inquiry has the power to require the discovery and production of any document. The summons did mention, however, that the documents and accounts of the Mutt were necessary in connection with the inquiry 'touching the administration, management and present condition of the endowments of Sri Hathiramjee Mutt, Tirupathyu'.

---

432. AIR 1989 SC 714.

433. AIR 1959 Andhra Pradesh 148.

In *M/s. Allen Berry & Co.* v. *Vivian Bose*,[434] it was contended on behalf of the petitioners that all the documents which were in the possession of the Commission should be shown to the petitioners and they should be allowed their right of inspection not only for the purpose of contradicting any material that might appear against them but also for the purpose of putting forward such material as might be in their favour. In this regard, the Court observed: "It is for the Commission to decide what to do in this matter and it has been indicated in its orders to what extent and how the inspection of the records will be allowed. The Commission has made it quite clear that at later stages any documents that are sought to be used against the petitioners or are considered material will be shown to those interested to prepare their defences. That will include matters in their favour just as much as are against them. The procedure indicated by the Commission in the matter of inspection of documents appears to be quite just and it is not for us to decide at what particular stage or stages and what particular documents should be shown to the petitioners. The claim of the petitioners for a general and roving discovery is not sustainable even if the Code of Civil Procedure were to apply."[435]

Right to Cross-examine Witnesses

Section 4(c) of the Act does not confer a right on a party appearing before the Commission to require a witness giving evidence by an affidavit to be produced for his cross-examination. The Commission would, of course, permit cross-examination in a case where it thinks that necessary. He can always file affidavits of his own denying the allegations made in affidavits filed on behalf of other party. If the evidence on both sides is tendered by affidavits, no one should be at any special disadvantage.[436]

Right to Allow Inspection of Documents

In *State of Rajasthan* v. *Justice B.P. Beri*,[437] it was contended by the petitioner that while Section 4(d) of the Act authorized

---

434. AIR 1960 Punjab 86.

435. *Ibid.*, p 94.

436. *State of Jammu and Kashmir* v. *Bakshi Gulam Mohammad*, AIR 1967 SC 122, p. 133.

437. AIR 1968 Rajasthan 77.

the Commission to requisition any public record, it did not authorize it to permit inspection of such record or documents by other persons. It was emphasized that the production of documents is one thing and its inspection is quite a different thing regarding which the Commission has no power. This, however, did not find favour with the Court. The contention was repelled by making the following observations, namely: "It is true that section speaks of certain powers to be utilized for the purpose of enforcing attendance of persons, their examination, discovery and production of documents or requisition of any public record but it cannot be overlooked that the relevant documents are produced for the purpose of collecting facts and evidence so that the Commission may be able to perform its main function as a fact finding body effectively. It can undoubtedly seek the assistance of all those who have volunteered to assist the Commission in the discharge of its functions pursuant to the general notice issued by it.... We do not think the Commission is precluded from seeking the aid of such persons for getting at the truth if it considers it necessary that the relevant documents should be perused by such persons.... We are not satisfied that by the impugned order any of the legal rights of the petitioners have been infringed nor are we satisfied that impugned order was one passed without jurisdiction or there was otherwise any apparent error on the face of the record so as to justify the exercise of our extraordinary powers under Article 226 of the Constitution."

Public Document

The term 'public documents' has not been defined in the Commissions of Inquiry Act. Although the provisions of the Evidence Act, 1872 are not applicable to the proceedings of a Commission of Inquiry, yet it will be useful to refer to Section 74 of this Act as it defines the term 'public documents'. Section 74 of the Evidence Act, 1872 reads as follows:

"74. Public documents.—The following documents are public documents:

(1) Documents forming the acts or records of the acts—

(i) of the sovereign authority,

(ii) of official bodies and tribunals, and

(iii) of public officers, legislative, judicial and executive, of any part of India or of the Commonwealth, or of a foreign country;

(2) Public records kept in any State of private documents."

Section 75 of the Evidence Act further provides that all other documents are private.

A definition of the term can also be found in the Public Records Act, 1993, which has been enacted to regulate the management, administration and preservation of public records of the Central Government, Union Territory Administration, public sector undertakings, statutory bodies and corporations, commissions and committees constituted by the Central Government or a Union Territory Administration and matters connected therewith or incidental thereto. Section 2 of the Act is a definition clause. Clause (e) of this section defines the term 'public records'. The definition is, however, an inclusive definition. Section 2(e) of this Act reads as follows:

"'public records' includes—

(i) any document, manuscript and file;

(ii) any microfilm, microfiche and facsimile copy of a document;

(iii) any reproduction of image or images embodied in such microfilm (whether enlarged or not); and

(iv) any other material produced by a computer or by any other device, of any records creating agency."

Section 2(f) of this Act defines 'records creating agency' as follows:

"(f) records creating agency includes—

(i) in relation to the Central Government, any ministry, department or office of that Government;

(ii) in relation to any statutory body or corporation wholly or substantially controlled or financed by the Central Government or commission or any committee constituted by that Government, the offices of the said body, corporation, commission or committee;

(iii) in relation to a Union Territory Administration, any department or office of that Administration;

(iv) in relation to any statutory body or corporation wholly or substantially financed by Union Territory Administration or commission or any committee constituted by that Administration, the offices of the said body, corporation, commission or committee.

Section 35 of the Evidence Act, 1872 provides for relevancy of an entry in public record or an electronic record made in performance of duty. Accordingly, an entry in any public or other official book, register or record or an electronic record, stating a fact in issue or relevant fact, and made by a public servant in the discharge of his official duty, or by any other person in performance of a duty specifically enjoined by the law of the country in which such book, register, or record or electronic record is kept, is itself a relevant fact.

Under Section 77 of the Evidence Act, certified copies of public documents can be produced in proof of the contents of the public documents or parts of the public documents of which they purport to be copies. Such certified copies can be marked as exhibit under Order 13, Rule 1 of the Code of Civil Procedure. No suspicion can be attached to certified copies of public documents such as records of the Government or records of judicial proceedings. Such copies may, therefore, be received in evidence even though they were not produced at the first hearing under Order 13, Rule 2, C.P.C. Section 76 of the Evidence Act further provides for grant of certified copies of a public document by the public officer having custody of such public documents, to any person, on demand, who has a right to inspect such documents. However, this will be on payment of fee in terms of that section. The section further provides the manner of certification. Section 79 of the Evidence Act provides for presumption as to genuineness of certified copies. The copies of public documents are as good as original documents in cases mentioned in Section 78A of the Evidence Act.

The priniciple of public documents being admissible generally is "that it should be public inquiry, a public document and made by a public officer". It must be made "for the purpose of the public making use of it, and being able to refer to it".[438]

The term "public records and documents" is used in two senses. In the first sense it has reference to the mode of providing the document; in the second, to what the document proves. In the first sense it includes all documents, which are of such a public nature that production of the original is excused, and proof by copies is admitted. In this sense, wills deposited in the Probate Court, and Pleadings and affidavits filed in the superior Courts are public documents.

In the second sense, public documents are those documents which are evidence generally, and not merely as against the parties thereto, of the facts stated therein. Thus, a register of marriages is good evidence of the fact and date of marriages registered therein. Most documents, which are public in this sense, are public in the first sense also. But the converse is by no means true.[439]

Commissions of Concurrent Jurisdiction

The Act does not envisage multiple commissions functioning simultaneously in respect of the same subject-matter. Nonetheless, in law, it is possible to hold different inquiries into the same event or incident but for different objects and purposes. In such a case, there may be possibility of overlapping in their respective scope of inquiries to certain extent. Thus, Justice M.L. Jain Commission of Inquiry was constituted under the Act with the mandate to make an inquiry with respect to, inter alia, the chain of events leading, and all the facts and circumstances relating, to the assassination of Shri Rajiv Gandhi at Sriperumbodur (other than the matters covered by the terms of reference for the Commission of Inquiry headed by Shri Justice J.S. Verma).[440] Similarly, both the Central Government and the Gujarat State Government appointed Justice U.C. Banerjee Commission and

438. per Lord Blackburn in *Sturla* v. *Freecia*, 1880 5 AC 643.

439. Ency. of the Laws of England cf. Advanced Law Lexicon, P. Ramanatha Aiyar, 3rd Edition, 2005, p. 3846.

440. *Ram Jethmalani* v. *Subramaniam Swamy*, AIR 2006 Delhi 300.

Justice Nanavati Commission respectively to inquire into the incident of firing of certain coaches of Sabarmati Express at Godhara though purported to be for different purposes with purportedly different terms of references.[441] In such cases, a question may arise as to whether a Commission of Inquiry can issue summons to another Commission of Inquiry to produce its records and documents pertaining to the same incident/event under its inquiry. Rule 7 of the Commission of Inquiry (Central) Rules, 1972 provides that the report of a Commission and the papers relating to its secretariate, its establishment matters and all other matters handled by or in the Commission including evidence tendered before the Commission shall be preserved intact by the Commission and shall be remitted with the report of the Commission. Since such records are public records, the provisions of Section 4(d) are applicable to requisition of such public records by a Commission of Inquiry. There would be no difficulty where the inquiry whose records are requisitioned has been completed and the report along with other related records have been submitted to the appropriate Government. The concerned department/office of that Government may be called upon to furnish such records/documents as the Commission consider useful and relevant to its inquiry. Difficulties may, however, arise where the two Commissions may be still working simultaneously in respect of the same incident or event, though, for different objects and purposes. Since the subject-matters of inquiries of two Commissions can never be the same and identical in law, theoretically speaking, there is not likely to be an occasion to call for the records of the inquiry of one Commission by another Commission. But as stated above, the two Commissions may come to inquire the same incident or event though for different objects and purposes, there may be overlapping of the two inquiries to some extent. The question

441. The legality of the Central Commission was successfully challenged in Gujarat High Court in the case of *Nilkanth Tulsidas Bhatia* v. *Union of India* (SB)(2006)(unreported) and *Union of India* v. *Nilkanth Tulsidas Bhatia* (2006) 2 GLR 952(DB). It is understood that the Union of India has preferred a special leave petition against the said judgment and the matter is yet to attain finality.

may then arise if, in such a case, one Commission can invoke its powers under Section 4 read with Section 5, as the case may be, to call upon another Commission to furnish its records or the documents in its possession where that Commission is of the opinion that the documents filed with another Commission inquiring the same incident/event may be useful for, and relevant to, the inquiry it is making. Further question that may arise in this regard is what if the other Commission fails to comply with such a requisition for any reason, especially when the provisions of Section 5 have been made applicable to such a Commission seeking information from another Commission. In such a case, can the Commission that has failed to comply with the requisition of its records by other Commission be proceeded against, in law, for such non-compliance? Where the Commission seeking information is in possession of the complete details of the required documents and the persons who have filed them with the other Commission, there may not be any difficulty in procuring these documents directly from the persons who have filed these with the other Commission by summoning them to do so. Where it is not so, the Commission may not be left with any option but to call upon the other Commission to furnish the required documents and records. If the Commission seeking information from another Commission is of the view that the records of the other Commission or the documents that the other Commission may be having in its possession relating to the incident/event common to both the inquiries, would be useful for, and relevant to, its inquiry, will it be open in such a case to the Commission to requisition from the other Commission all such records as may be having any bearing on the incident/event that is inquired into, without specifying in any manner what and which these records are? Normally, any request for information/documents concerning the subject of inquiry, ought to be, and would always be, respected and complied with by the Commission from whom the requisition is sought, if it has such information/documents especially having regard to the comity of bodies having concurrent jurisdiction. However, difficulties may arise in the absence of details of the requisitioned documents. In the absence of such details, it may not be feasible for the requisitioning Commission to specify the particular documents/records that are required to be filed with it. Of necessity, such a requisition may have to be couched in general terms, referring to all such documents/records that the requisitioned Commission may be having in its possession pertaining to or having bearing on, the incident/event under inquiry. The requisitioned Commission may feel that the compliance with the requisition from another Commission at the given stage may prejudice, or be of detriment to, its own inquiry. Or, the records may be too voluminous and unwieldy to be so provided and there may be practical and genuine difficulties in providing their copies to any one. In such cases where the requisitioned Commission is of the considered opinion that it might not be possible for it to comply with such a requisition from another Commission for the time being, it may inform the requisitioning Commission accordingly, with due respect and courtesy as is expected from among bodies having concurrent jurisdiction. Normally, it is expected that the requisitioning Commission will respect the views of the requisitioned Commission and will not proceed further in the matter. This is specially so as the two inquiries are independent of each other and are expected to proceed in their respective domain without unduly encroaching upon the jurisdiction of the other Commission. However, if any such Commission persists in compliance with its requisition by other Commission, and consequently the matter is unduly precipitated; there may not be any escape from invoking the writ jurisdiction of the Court as the ultimate arbiter in the matter.

There may be cases where the records pertaining to the subject of inquiry by a Commission may be in judicial custody pursuant to Court's directions in the matter. Thus, in the case of the Commission set up to inquire into the alleged anomalies in the computerized draw of lots for the allotment of 1250 plots on July 2, 2005. On July 24, 2006, the Supreme Court in this case directed[442] that all records related to the case would be kept

---

442. Reported in *Hindustan Times*, February 28, 2007 as 'Probe into Noida scam going nowhere'.

with the Registrar of the High Court. One may question whether an inquiry Commission in such a case could not even have access to the material related to the case that is in judicial custody. In other words, the question may arise whether the Commission of Inquiry can call upon the Registrar of the High Court to produce before it the records relating to the subject of inquiry. There does not seem to be any bar to this except that there may be certain procedural changes from the ordinary course followed in such cases such as leave of the Court for such production. Where the Court is otherwise seized of the Commission's proceedings, it may issue necessary directions on its own subject to which the Commission can have access to the relevant records that are entrusted to such judicial custody. In other cases, the officer concerned may place the case for necessary leave and such further directions as may be considered proper and necessary in the matter. A person who may be acting in terms of the Court's directions will enjoy immunity against any penal action for non-compliance with the Commission's requisition, if any.

Writ Jurisdiction and the Commission

The general principle underlying the basis of the Court's jurisdiction by way of writs is most precisely stated by Atkin, L.J., in *R.* v. *Electricity Commrs.*[443] The passage from this judgment which has been relied upon in all subsequent decisions, both in England and India, runs thus:

> ...the operation of the writs has extended to control the proceedings of bodies who do not claim to be, and would not be recognized as, Courts of Justice. Wherever any body of persons having legal authority to determine questions affecting the rights of subjects, and having the duty to act judicially, act in excess of their legal authority they are subject to the controlling jurisdiction of the King's Bench Division exercised in these writs.

The expression "any body of persons" includes not only inferior Courts in the strict sense but also a person, body or authority

443. (1924) 1 KB 171.

having the duty to act judicially. The bodies of persons to whom a writ can be issued need not necessarily be statutory bodies.[444]

The observation of Atkin, L. J., was construed in some of the subsequent decisions as treating the condition "having the duty to act judicially" as mandatory. In *R.* v. *Legislative Assembly of the Church Assembly*,[445] Lord Hewart, C. J., observed that it is not enough that a body should have the legal authority to determine questions affecting the rights of subjects but there must be superadded to that characteristic the further characteristic that the body has the duty to act judicially. This observation was disapproved by the House of Lords in *Ridge* v. *Baldwin*.[446] After citing the passage from the judgment of Lord Radcliff in *Nakkuda Ali's* case,[447] which quoted the judgments of Atkin, L. J. and Lord Hewart, C. J., Lord Reid observed thus:

> Of course if it were right to say that Lord Hewart's gloss on Atkin L. J., stated 'a general principle that is beyond dispute, the rest would follow'. But I have given my reasons for holding that it does no such thing, and in my judgment the older cases certainly did not 'illustrate' any such general principles...they contradict it. No case older than 1911 was cited in Nakkuda'a case on this question, and this question was not only one of several difficult questions which were argued and decided. So I am forced to the conclusion that this part of the judgment in Nakkuda's case was given under a serious misapprehension of the effect of the older authorities and therefore cannot be regarded as authoritative.

---

444. *Dr. Harekrushna Mahtab* v. *The Chief Minister of Orissa and Others*, AIR 1971 Orissa 175; *R.* v. *Criminal Injuries Compensation Board*, Ex parte Lain, (1967) 2 QBD 864; The D.F.O., *South Kheri* v. *Ram Sanehi Singh* 1970 SCD 181.

445. (1928) 1 KB 411.

446. 1964 AC 40.

447. (1963) 1 QB 539.

Ridge v. *Baldwin*[448] has been consistently accepted as laying down good law by the Supreme Court.[449] The statute or the administrative order creating the authority may either expressly or by necessary implication lay down that the enquiry would be one of quasi-judicial in nature in which principles of natural justice would be followed. But the converse is not true. In other words, the absence of such a prescription does not necessarily lead to the conclusion that the proceeding is not quasi-judicial. The duty to act judicially is to be inferred from the nature of the power and it is not required to be superadded by any provision of law granting the power. The choice of a high judicial authority for an enquiry cannot invest the inquiry with an impress of being quasi-judicial. The status and qualification of the person entrusted with the inquiry would not determine its intrinsic character. Even purely administrative inquiries can be entrusted to such persons. An administrative inquiry is not converted into a quasi-judicial one merely because the inquiring authority has examined, or promised to examine, certain persons. This can be done even in an administrative inquiry wherein the inquiring authority has a wide discretion to examine or not to examine any of the concerned persons.[450]

The true test for the application of writs is whether a body, though set up by the Government in exercise of its powers under a statute, discharges statutory functions or not. It has been laid down by the Supreme Court in *Praga Tools Corporation* v. *C.A. Imanual*,[451] that a mandamus lies to secure the performance of a public or statutory duty in the performance of which the one who applies for it has a sufficient legal interest. Further, it has been observed that it is not necessary that the person or the authority on whom the statutory duty is imposed need be a public official or an official body. A mandamus can issue, for

448. (1964) AC 40.

449. *Associated Cement Companies Ltd.* v. *P.N. Sharma*, AIR 1965 SC 1595; *Bhagwan* v. *Ram Chand*, AIR 1965 SC 1767.

450. *Dr. Harekrushna Mahtab* v. *The Chief Minister of Orissa and Others*, AIR 1971 Orissa 175.

451. AIR 1969 SC 1306.

instance, to an official of a society to compel him to carry out the terms of the statute under or by which the society is constituted or governed and also to companies or corporations to carry out duties placed on them by the statutes authorizing their undertakings. It is, therefore, apparent from what has been laid down in the aforesaid decision of the Supreme Court that for the purpose of having the performance of statutory duties, a writ in the nature of mandamus will lie. This does not mean that no negative order can be passed directing an authority not to do something. A writ will lie not only for compelling an authority to perform the statutory duties, but also for restraining or prohibiting it from doing something which it is not entitled to do under the law.[452]

Existence of a right is the sine qua non for the issue of a writ of mandamus. In *State of Orissa and Others* v. *Rajasaheb Chandanmull Indrakumar (P) Limited and Another,*[453] a contention was raised that an application under Article 226 does not lie unless the petitioner has a legal right and the Court does not assist the petitioner to continue to do acts forbidden by law. The Supreme Court accepted this argument. In another case,[454] the Supreme Court observed that the condition precedent to the issue of mandamus is that there is one claiming it a legal right to the performance of a legal duty by one against whom it is sought. In support of this view, the Supreme Court relied on the following observations of Bruce J., in *R.* v. *Lewisham Union,*[455] viz. "This Court has never exercised a general power to enforce the performance of their statutory duties by public bodies on the application of anybody who chooses to apply for a mandamus. It has always required that the applicant for a mandamus should have a legal and specific right to enforce the performance of those duties."

---

452. *The Statesman* v. *The Fact Finding Committee*, AIR 1975 Calcutta 15.
453. AIR 1972 SC 2112.
454. *Praga Tools Corporation* v. *Shri C.A. Imanual and Others* (1969) 3 SCR 773.
455. (1897) 1 QB 498, p. 510.

In *State of Orissa* v. *Ram Chandra Dev*,[456] it was held that though the jurisdiction of the High Court under Article 226 is wide in that sense, the concluding words of the Article clearly indicate that before a writ or an appropriate order can be issued in favour of a party, it must be established that the party has a right and the said right is illegally invaded or threatened and that the existence of a right is the foundation of the petition under Article 226. In another case,[457] the Supreme Court observed that in order that a mandamus may issue to compel the respondents do something, it must be shown that the statute imposed a legal duty and the petitioner has a legal right under the statutes to enforce its performance.

In *State of Madhya Pradesh* v. *Bhailal Bhai*,[458] the Supreme Court has held that where there has been a threat only and the right has not been actually infringed an application under Article 226 would lie and the Courts would give necessary relief by making an order in the nature of injunction. In order to maintain an application under Article 226, it is not necessary for the petitioner to show that he has already suffered an actual injury; apprehension of injury or threat of injury is enough.[459] Therefore, it is not correct to say that so long the right is not actually infringed or a party does not actually suffer a writ petition will not be maintainable at his instance.[460]

In *Orient Paper Mills* v. *Union of India*,[461] the Court observed:

> It is not correct to say that there could be injury only if there is trial or punishment. If the entire proceeding is found to be without jurisdiction and the conditions precedent for

---

456. AIR 1964 SC 685.

457. *Dr. Rai Shivendra Bahadur* v. *The Governing Body of the Nalanda College* (1962) Supp. 2 SCR 144.

458. AIR 1964 SC 1006.

459. *Ram Krishna* v. *Union of India*, AIR 1969 Calcutta 18; *Bengal Immunity Co.* v. *State of Bihar*, AIR 1955 SC 661; *Kochuni* v. *State of Madras*, AIR 1959 SC 725.

460. *The Statesman* v. *The Fact Finding Committee*, AIR 1975 Calcutta 15.

461. AIR 1979 Calcutta 114.

appointing the Commission under Section 3 of the Act were not fulfilled as alleged by the petitioner, in that case subjecting the petitioner to such a proceeding itself is a substantial injury. In *Gulab Kanwar* v. *Enforcement Officer*,[462] this Court observed: It will be unjust to compel the petitioner to appear before the authorities in respect of the proceedings which I have held to be initially void. If the petitioner can satisfy the court that the subject-matter of the inquiry is not a definite matter of public importance, in that case the Commission shall have no power to inquire into the matters with respect to which the requisitions have been sent by the Commission.

In such a case, a writ petition will lie under Article 226(1)(b) of the Constitution.

It is implicit in the exercise of the extraordinary jurisdiction that the relief asked for must be one to enforce a legal right and that the existence of the right is the foundation of the exercise of jurisdiction of the Court under Article 226 of the Constitution. The right that can be enforced under Article 226 of the Constitution shall ordinarily be the personal or individual right of the petitioner himself, though in the case of some of the writs like habeas corpus or quo warranto this rule may have to be relaxed or modified.[463]

In *Bhagwat Dayal Sharma* v. *Union of India*,[464] the petitioner disclosed his interest in filing the petition for a writ of mandamus directing the Union Government to appoint a Commission of Inquiry to inquire into the allegations made by against certain political personalities, by stating that he was a citizen of India, a tax-payer and a member of the Rajya Sabha representing the State of Haryana and a former Chief Minister of that State and, thus, vitally interested to see that the powers vested in any Minister in the State were not abused for self aggrandisement

462. AIR 1977 Calcutta 383.

463. *Calcutta Gas Company (Proprietary) Ltd.* v. *State of West Bengal*, AIR 1962 SC 1044.

464. ILR (1974) I Delhi 847.

and the Administration of the State run honestly and cleanly and further that the Ministers at the Centre were not conniving with Ministers in the State to perpetrate the region of corruption, nepotism, terrorism and enrichment at the cost of public. On the allegation made in the petition, it was prayed that a writ in the nature of mandamus or any other appropriate writ, direction or order be issued to the respondents directing, inter alia, the Central Government to appoint a Commission of Inquiry under Section 3 of the Commissions of Inquiry Act, 1952, to inquire into the charges contained in the memoranda dated October 27, 1971 and February 24, 1972 against Shri Bansi Lal, the then Chief Minister of Haryana. The question of locus standi was considered by Delhi High Court on the assumption—without going into the validity of the allegations in that behalf—that the various matters in respect of which allegations were made in the petition were 'definite matters of public importance' within the meaning of Section 3 of the Act. On this question, the Court observed, the matter had to be determined from the point of view whether the petitioner had a legal right to the relief with a corresponding duty obligation on the Government to give that relief. The Court further observed that all that petitioner had stated was that he was a citizen, a tax-payer, a member of the Rajya Sabha and a former Chief Minister of the State of Haryana. In essence his status was no better than of a member of the public. Counsel for the petitioner had used, during his arguments, high-sounding words and phrases relating to democracy, integrity, corruption, nepotism, terrorism, enrichment at the cost of the public and the spirit of the Constitution to urge that every citizen had a right to see that those in power were not corrupt. These expressions might be used on and from other platforms but they were not relevant in a Court of law, which is concerned with rights and obligations arising out of the Constitution and the laws. The petitioner had clearly no right under the statute, namely, the Commissions of Inquiry Act, 1952 and, therefore, no locus standi to move the petition for a writ of mandamus. Accordingly, the petition was dismissed in limine.

The term 'rights' has, however, been given a broad interpretation in the context the expression "to determine questions affecting the rights of subjects" as laid down by Atkin L.J.[465] The rights affected may appertain to personal liberty or status or they may be of a proprietary, fiscal or contractual nature and they are not necessarily 'rights' in the strict jurisprudential sense of attributes to which correlative duties are annexed; but in a wider sense which include the clearly defined interest of the subject.[466] Thus, where the petitioner as the secretary of the Hojai Citizens' Association and as representative of a substantial section of the people, has entered appearance before the Commission of Inquiry appointed under Section 3 of the Act and his memorandum on behalf of the association has been accepted by the Commission, his application under Article 226, challenging the appointment of the Commission, cannot be dismissed on the ground that he has no locus standi to make the application nor any legal right of his has been affected.[467]

If any administrative order adversely affects any right or interest, then the principles of natural justice must be observed in the inquiry unless the statute either expressly or by necessary implication prohibits it.[468] In such cases there is a duty to act judicially. In *A.K. Kraipak* v. *Union of India*,[469] the Supreme Court laid down the following proposition:

> For determining whether a power is an administrative power or a quasi-judicial power one has to look to the nature of the power conferred, the person or persons on whom it is conferred, the framework of the law conferring that power, the consequences ensuing from the exercise of that power and the manner in which that power is expected to be exercised.

---

465. *R.* v. *Electricity Commrs.* (1924) 1 KB 171.
466. *Seervai Constitutional Law of India*, p. 606, which has extracted the aforesaid passage from Judicial Review of Administrative Action by S.A. Smith. Cf Dr. Herekrushna Mahatab the Chief Minister of Orissa, AIR 1971 Orissa 175.
467. *Manabendra Sarkar* v. *State of Assam and Others*, AIR 1974 Gauhati 46.
468. *Ridge* v. *Baldwin* 1964 AC 40.
469. AIR 1970 SC 150.

Their Lordships further said:

> The concept of rule of law would lose its validity if the instrumentalities of the State are not charged with the duty of discharging their functions in a fair and just manner. The requirement of acting judicially in essence is nothing but a requirement to act justly and fairly and not arbitrarily or capriciously. The procedures which are considered inherent in the exercise of a judicial power are merely those which facilitate if not ensure a just and fair decision. In recent years the concept of quasi-judicial power has been undergoing a radical change. What was considered as an administrative power some years back is now being considered as a quasi-judicial power.

In *Dr. Harekrushna Mahtab* v. *The Chief Minister of Orissa and Others*,[470] the power conferred upon the inquiring authority was merely for preliminary verification of the allegations made. The verification was with the object of seeing whether prima facie it was based on reliable materials which would justify the appointment of a Commission of Inquiry. The inquiry did not affect the rights or interest of the persons concerned. The recommendations of the inquiring authority would result only in the appointment of a Commission of Inquiry which itself would be a fact-finding body and would enquire whether the allegations were true or not. The ultimate findings of the Commission of Inquiry were not enforceable proprio vigore. It was, therefore, held that such an administrative inquiry did not affect any interest or right of the persons concerned. It was contended that the inquiry affected the petitioner inasmuch as his reputation had been assailed, his career and status had been jeopardized, he stood the risk of facing a Commission of Inquiry relating to events dated back to 1956 resulting in great harassment and trouble and incurring large expenses to defend himself and his completed and finalised income tax proceedings were sought to be reopened. The Court did not see any force in this contention and observed that if at all, the petitioner's reputation had been affected by the allegations themselves. By the acts of the inquiring

470. AIR 1971 Orissa 175.

authority none of these consequences ensued. Even if the report of this inquiry was accepted, a Commission of Inquiry would be appointed. In the inquiry the petitioner's stand might be redeemed. The harmful rumours about him would get killed and public confidence might be restored in him. What would ultimately he held by the Commission of Inquiry, it was difficult to predict. But the position was clear that no harm was caused to his reputation by the action of the inquiring authority. At best, the aforesaid apprehensions might be the indirect and very remote effect of the inquiring authority's report which was intended only for testing the allegations themselves and that for the limited purpose of finding out a prima facie case for a further probe. The analogy was more or less with an inquiry under Section 202, Criminal Procedure Code. Investigation into a complaint could not be said to affect the person complained against in any manner. The nature of the power conferred upon the Inquiring authority in the case was to find out whether a further probe was to be made into the allegations and whether in the public interest, a Commission of Inquiry should be established. The effect of the exercise of the power was either to have or not to have a further probe by appointment of a Commission of Inquiry. The conclusion of the inquiring authority was expressed in a report. He determined no rights nor the guilt or innocence of any one. He did not even initiate any proceedings which had to be left to the ordinary criminal procedure. Thus, by the inquiry so conducted, the rights and interest of the petitioner were not affected and as otherwise no duty was laid on the inquiring authority to act judicially, the question of conducting the inquiry in accordance with the principles of natural justice did not arise. The exercise of the power so conferred upon the inquiring authority did not necessitate an inquiry in accordance with the principles of natural justice. Even otherwise on facts, the Court found that the inquiring authority acted in a fair and just manner. On such a conclusion, a writ of certiorari, it was held, could not be issued.

Although the report of the Commission of Inquiry has no legal force proprio vigore and as such there is no scope for quashing such a report by issue of writ of certiorari, yet the

Court may consider issuing a writ of mandamus forbearing the Government from taking an action solely on the basis of the report if the same is vitiated by the violation of any statutory provision such as Section 8B of the Act. A writ of certiorari will also lie to quash the memorandum of charge based solely on the finding rendered by the Commission of Inquiry in violation of Section 8B. Accordingly, the charge was quashed without prejudice to the right of the State to initiate fresh proceedings if the charge can be established by other materials independent of the finding of the Commission.[471]

It may also be useful to refer to the following observations of the Supreme Court[472] in this regard, viz.: "It may not be necessary for a person to wait till certain action is initiated by the Government considering the report of the Inquiry Commission where the observations made by the Commission are such which militate against the reputation of a person and particularly without giving any chance to such a person to explain his conduct. It would be open for him to move the Court for deletion of such remarks made against him violating the provisions of Section 8B of the Act."

The Supreme Court further said: "The Government actually takes action or it does not or the fact the report is yet to be considered from that angle, cannot be a reason to submit that it won't be appropriate stage to approach the Court. There may be occasions where after consideration of report the Government may not decide to take any action against the person concerned, yet, the observation and remarks may be such which may play upon the reputation of the person concerned and this aspect of the matter has been fully taken care of under clause (b) of Section 8B of the Act. It is not, therefore, necessary that one must wait till a decision is taken by the Government to take action against the person after consideration of the report. We have already dealt with the point about the right to have and protect one's reputation. We, therefore, find no force in the

471. N. *Manoharan* v. *State of Tamil Nadu*, AIR 1981 Madras 147.

472. *State of Bihar* v. *Lal Krishna Advani and Others*, AIR 2003 SC 3357, p. 3361.

submission that the respondent No. 1 had approached the Court at premature stage."

It is well settled that the writ jurisdiction of the Court has to be exercised according to certain well-established principles; and one of such principles is that the High Court sitting in writ jurisdiction is not an appellate Court, which should substitute its own opinion for the opinion of the Tribunal concerned. There must be an error of law apparent on the face of the record in order to attract this jurisdiction. This must be a clear and speaking error and not an error which appears in drawing inferences or which involves appreciation of documentary evidence. Where the Commission has jurisdiction to hold whether or not the documents are relevant and the Commission has held that the documents are relevant and has given reasons for the same, it is not for the High Court, sitting in writ to determine the propriety or otherwise of the reasons given by the Commission.[473]

In *Kaushalya Devi* v. *Bachittar Singh*,[474] the Supreme Court made the following observations:

> This Court had occasion again to consider the question of the extent of the High Court's powers to interfere on a writ of certiorari in *Nagendra Nath Bora* v. *Commr. of Hills Division*.[475] It was pointed out in that case that the principle underlying the jurisdiction to issue a writ or order of certiorary was no more in doubt; but the real difficulty arose, as it often did, in applying the principle to the particular facts of a given case. It was also pointed out that the High Court has exercised its supervisory jurisdiction in that case in respect of errors which could not be said to be errors of law apparent on the face of the record; if at all they were errors in appreciation of documentary evidence or affidavits, errors in drawing inferences or omissions to draw inferences. In

---

473. *State of Jammu and Kashmir* v. *Anwar Ahmed Aftab and Others*, AIR 1965 Jammu and Kashmir 75.

474. AIR 1960 SC 1168.

475. 1958 SCR 1240: AIR 1958 SC 398.

other words, it was further observed, these were errors, which a Court sitting as a Court of appeal, only, could have examined and, if necessary, corrected. In the present case, also we feel, with respect that what the High Court has done is to correct what may be errors in appreciation of documentary evidence or errors in drawing inferences. We are, therefore, of opinion that there was no error of law apparent on the face of the record in this case which would justify interferences by the High Court with the order of the Deputy Custodian General.

In *Satyanarayan Laxminarayan Hegde* v. *Mallikarjun Bhavanappa Triumale*,[476] their Lordships made the following observations:

An error which has to be established by a long drawn process of reasoning on points where there may conceivably be two opinions can hardly be said to be an error apparent on the face of the record. As the above discussion of the rival contentions show the alleged error in the present case is far from self-evident and if it can be established, it has to be established, by lengthy and complicated arguments. We do not think that such an error can be cured by a writ of certiorary according to the rule governing the powers of the superior Court to issue such a writ.

Another well settled principle is this regard is that where a part of cause of action arises within the jurisdiction of a particular Court, that Court gets the jurisdiction to entertain an application under Article 226 of the Constitution.[477]

The discretionary and extraordinary jurisdiction of the Court is not to be exercised at the instance of a person who is not vigilant in the vindication of his rights. The Court has denied relief to those who have not acted promptly or properly even when a legal cause of action is discernible. When the agent of a candidate sought to stultify the election proceedings virtually on the eve of the election, the Court declined to investigate his

---

476. AIR 1960 SC 137.

477. *Orient Paper Mills* v. *Union of India*, AIR 1979 Calcutta 114.

grievance having regard to such conduct that disentitles relief to a party in proceedings under Article 226 of the Constitution.[478] The Court declined to entertain and adjudicate the matter in proceedings under Article 226 of the Constitution when the petitioner had not brought to the notice of the Commission the alleged departure from the provisions of the reference order or the violation of the principles of natural justice.[479]

In writ petitions, the petitioners are seeking extraordinary remedies which are in the discretion of the Court. In exercising this discretion, the Courts are guided mainly by considerations of fair play and justice.[480] Thus, if there is alternative remedy, the Court may refuse to grant relief. Unexplained and unreasonable delay in filing a writ petition may also disentitle the petitioner to any relief at the hands of the Court. However, delay of four years was held to be not very fatal where jurisdiction of the Commission to inquire into the matters had been challenged. Moreover, the question of delay would not arise where a writ of prohibition was asked for. Furthermore, it is well settled that by acquiescence no jurisdiction can be conferred in a case where there is inherent lack of jurisdiction. If the petitioner can satisfy the Court that the appointment of Commission is without jurisdiction in that case, their acquiescence might not itself be a bar for denying the relief asked for.[481]

At times, the question of necessary parties to a writ petition against an order of a Commission of Inquiry assumes importance. In *Md. Anis Khan* v. *T.L.V. Aiyar*,[482] the Full Bench of the High Court held that before a contrary order could be passed, the parties who had been benefited by the impugned order should have been impleaded. In this case, the Inquiry Commission refused to conduct inquiry against a number of persons mentioned

478. *Mathew* v. *Election Commissioner of India*, AIR 1982 Kerala 265; 1982 Kerala LT 479.

479. *S.V. Purushothaman* v. *State of Kerala*, AIR 1983 Kerala 118, p. 123.

480. *G.S. Harnal* v. *Union of India and Others*, ILR (1971) II Delhi 129.

481. *Orient Paper Mills* v. *Union of India*, AIR 1979 Calcutta 114, p. 121.

482. AIR 1970 Patna 334.

by the petitioner. This was done while giving a ruling on a preliminary issue relating to the interpretation of a general/ residuary clause in the terms of reference to the Commission. The inquiry in this case was against six-named persons. The clause in question, namely clause (d), reads as "Whether, besides the persons above-named, any other person or persons or persons holding official position, either as a member of the Council of Ministers or otherwise, during any of the aforesaid periods, made illegal gains or indulged in corruption, favouritism, abuse of power or other malpractices in like manner as aforesaid." The question that arose was whether the Commission was required to inquire into and report as to all matters of corruption, favouritism, abuse of power, etc. of all persons holding official positions in the State during the specified periods or only in respect of such acts, which also involved one or more of the six specified persons for, in the absence of such a linkage, the charge would fall outside the said clause. The Commission adopted the latter view and held, vide the impugned order, that it was necessary that one or more of the six persons named in para 1 of the notification constituting the Commission, should be involved in the act that is sought to be inquired into. While passing this order, the Commission neither had before it the persons against whom the inquiry was sought by the petitioner nor had given them any hearing. The Full Bench observed, "At the stage at which the Commission was considering the various affidavits filed under clause (d) of paragraph 4, it may not have been necessary to hear the parties affected, but after the impugned order was passed by the Commission, the persons who will be affected by the reversal of the order ought to have been impleaded in this court, so that they would have had an opportunity of supporting the order."[483] The Court did not appreciate the petitioner's contention that the concerned persons who were not before the Court might yet be allowed to be impleaded at that stage. In the circumstances where the petitioner had not indicated the details of the names and the addresses of the persons whom he wanted to implead, and no application had been filed making

483. AIR 1970 Patna, p. 337 (para 4).

this prayer and giving the names and addresses of the persons, it would not be possible for the Court to pass an effective order for impleading any persons at the instance of the petitioner of the writ case.

It is now well settled that a party seeking for a writ in the nature of mandamus must prove that he demanded justice from the authority responsible for the performance of duties and that the demand was refused. The demand must be made to the proper authority and not to an authority that is not in position to perform its duty in the manner as demanded. The underlying principle is that "as a general rule the order will not be granted unless the party complained of has known what he was required to do, so that he had the means of considering whether or not he should comply".[484] This aspect is very aptly illustrated by the case of *Statesman* v. *Fact Finding Committee*.[485] In this case, the claim of the petitioners was that the Committee should not act and they prayed for a writ in the nature of mandamus commanding the respondents to forbear from taking steps or proceedings whatsoever pursuant to or under the resolution of the Government and from requiring the petitioners to answer the questionnaire issued by the Committee. The petitioners did not claim the rescission, cancellation or withdrawal of the said resolution under which the Committee was constituted. It was held that the prayer, which had been made by the petitioners, was directly concerned with the actions of the Committee. The Government had nothing to do with the questionnaire issued by the Committee. In these circumstances, it could not be held that the Government was the proper authority to whom a demand for justice should have been made. The proper authority was the Committee and the petitioners had rightly made a demand for justice from the Committee. It was further held that demand for justice was not a matter of form but it was a matter of substance. Applying this principle in the facts of the case, the Court held that proper and sufficient demand for justice had been made in the case.

484. Article 198, *Halsbury's Laws of England*, Volume 11, Third Edition, p. 106.

485. AIR 1975 Calcutta 15.

It is well-established principle that the Court normally would be slow to issue writ of mandamus to compel any person or authority, charged with the duty to perform any act to, to do such act unless it is satisfied on the pleading and the evidence in support thereof that the party seeking that relief had earlier made a specific request in that behalf to such person or authority, and that person or authority had declined or refused to comply with that request. The absence of pleadings, much less evidence, that there was such an earlier demand to and refusal by the respondents to order an inquiry into the allegations made by the appellant/petitioner would be an additional ground why the Court could not have granted the relief sought besides the long and unjustifiable delay in invoking the writ jurisdiction of the Court.[486]

"There cannot be any doubt that proceedings before such a Commission have to be reviewed in the white light of highest moral standards. The necessity to preserve the purity of the proceedings before a Commission cannot be over-emphasised. It would be desirable that situations of possible conflict between public duty and professional involvement are avoided. The observations of the Supreme Court of India in decisions dealing with such Commissions of Inquiry have emphasised the necessity for such guarded action in the matter of the appointment of and functioning by Commissions; for, otherwise, as has been pointed out by the Supreme Court 'the public is not likely to repose its confidence in such a Tribunal...'"—vide AIR 1967 SC 122.[487] It is not without significance that many of the Commissions have referred to in the fore of their reports the words of Lord Scarman regarding the objectives of such Commissions of Inquiry. The words are worthy of recapitulation in this context:

> In all countries, certainly in those, which enjoy freedom of speech and a free press, moments occur when; allegations and rumours circulate causing a nation-wide crisis of confidence in the integrity of public life or about other

---

486. *Rajendran* v. *Home Secretary*, AIR 1983 Kerala 59.

487. *The State of Jammu and Kashmir and Others* v. *Bakshi Gulam Mohammad and Another*, AIR 1967 SC 122.

matters of vital public importance. No doubt this rarely happens, but when it does it is essential that public confidence should be restored, for without it no democracy can long survive. This confidence can be effectively restored only by thoroughly investigating and probing the rumours and allegations so as to search out and establish the truth. The truth may show that the evil exists, thus enabling it to be rooted out, or that there is no foundation in the rumours and allegations by which the public has been disturbed. In either case, confidence is restored.

A question may arise whether a writ of certiorari will issue even if the Commission departs from an ideal conduct or a prescribed norm. The observations of the Australian High Court in *Queen* v. *Collins*,[488] indicates that curial intervention is not justified in such circumstances. It observed:

> ...it will not legally affect the rights of the applicant; with or without such a report, and even, no doubt, in direct opposition to any recommendations in it, the Minister might, in his absolute discretion take action...or might decide to take no action at all...and it is only the degree of likelihood of that intervention occurring in a sense adverse to the applicant's interests which is increased by the actual nature of the Commission's recommendation. That cannot, in my view, suffice to justify curial intervention, by means of certiorari, in the case of Royal Commission whose sole function is to inquire and report to the Executive the result of its inquiries, whose mode of conducting its inquiry is entirely unfettered, either by statute or by executive direction, and whose report neither directly affects rights nor is a condition precedent to the affecting of them. It accordingly becomes unnecessary to examine the particular grounds upon which the applicant relies or to determine whether, if there be errors of law disclosed, there exists anything in the nature of a record upon the face of which they appear.

Having regard to the conduct of the petitioner in this case, the Court did not proceed to deal with the question and observed:

488. 50 ALJR 471.

Whether the observations contained therein are distinguishable from the facts of the case, or whether the view still holds good, regard being had to the winds of change in the administrative law, is also a matter which does not arise for determination now, in view of my declining to consider such issues having regard to the conduct of the petitioner. The Royal Commission on Tribunals of Inquiry, 1966 (United Kingdom) considered whether there should be any statutory rules of procedure for Commission. It observed:

> Any alleged failure to comply with the rules might be brought up for review by prerogative writ to the High Court and the inquiry thereby delayed or frustrated.[489]

The above observations may indicate that review by prerogative writ by High Court would be available when there has been non-compliance with the rules of procedure prescribed for the Commission. Whether that is equally applicable if there is a departure from the terms of reference order is yet another question which might arise for adjudication in appropriate cases. It is not necessary to deal with these aspects in this writ petition in the light of the conclusion reached by me earlier."[490]

Hearing Before Issue of Rule Nisi

In *M. Karunanidhi* v. *Union of India*,[491] the petitioner's counsel submitted that without issuing rule nisi, the counsel for the Central Government (i.e. the respondent) should not be heard. Dismissing this submission, the Court observed: "We are not aware of any such rule. In order to verify the facts, it has been the practice of this court to ask the Government Pleader or the Central Government counsel to state the facts or refer to relevant documents so that the court would be able to know whether the allegations made in the petition are true or not, even before admitting the petition. The court is not precluded

---

489. *The Commissions of Inquiry Act, 1952* by K.A. Ramasubramaniam, p. 82.

490. *S.V. Purushothaman* v. *State of Kerala and Others*, AIR 1983 Kerala 118, pp. 124-25.

491. AIR 1977 Madras 192.

from getting facts from the opposite side at the time of admission stage. Though the procedure as to entering caveat is not followed in this court, hearing the other side before admission is not unusual."

Withdrawal of Petition

Once rule has been issued under Article 226 it has either to be made absolute or discharged. The proceedings in writ jurisdiction may be civil proceedings but they are proceedings in the realm of public law. Even in certiorari, especially when there is no compromise, once rule nisi has been issued it has to be made absolute if there is no valid return by the end of the day. Where there is a return all that the Court is called upon to decide is whether it is a valid return. If it is valid, the rule must be discharged. If it is not valid, the rule has to be made absolute. In an appropriate case leave may be granted but where the Court feels that the judicial process has been abused or the application for leave to withdraw is not bona fide, leave has to be refused and judgment pronounced. Where the request for withdrawal is a belated one and not accompanied with any reasonable explanation/justification for delay, the same may not be viewed as bona fide and accordingly, the Court will decline to grant leave to withdraw the petition and, instead, proceed to judgment on merits.[492]

Additional Powers of Commission.

5. (1) Where the appropriate Government is of opinion that, having regard to the nature of the inquiry to be made and other circumstances of the case, all or any of the provisions of sub-section (2) or sub-section (3) or sub-section (4) or sub-section (5) should be made applicable to a Commission, the appropriate Government may, by notification in the Official Gazette, direct that all or such of the said provisions as may be specified in the notification shall apply to that Commission and on the issue of such a notification, the said provisions shall apply accordingly.

(2) The Commission shall have power to require any person, subject to any privilege which may be claimed by that person under any law for the time being in force, to furnish information

492. *Dhirendra Brahmachari* v. *Union of India*, AIR 1979 NOC 91 (Delhi).

on such points or matters as, in the opinion of the Commission, may be useful for, or relevant to, the subject matter of the inquiry [493][and any person so required shall be deemed to be legally bound to furnish such information within the meaning of section 176 and section 177 of the Indian Penal Code].

(3) The Commission or any officer, not below the rank of a gazetted officer, specially authorized in this behalf by the Commission may enter any building or place where the Commission has reason to believe that any books of account or other documents relating to the subject-matter of the inquiry may be found, and may seize any such books of account or documents or take extracts or copies therefrom, subject to the provisions of Section 102 and Section 103 of the Code of Criminal Procedure, 1898, in so far as they may be applicable.

(4) The Commission shall be deemed to be a Civil Court and when any offence as is described in Section 175, Section 178, Section 179, Section 180 or Section 228 of the Indian Penal Code is committed in the view or presence of the Commission, the Commission may, after recording the facts constituting the offence and the statement of the accused as provided for in the Code of Criminal Procedure, 1898, forward the case to a magistrate having jurisdiction to try the same and the magistrate to whom any such case is forwarded shall proceed to hear the complaint against the accused as if the case had been forwarded to him under Section 482 of the Code of Criminal Procedure, 1898.

(5) Any proceeding before the Commission shall be deemed to be a judicial proceeding within the meaning of sections 193 and 228 of the Indian Penal Code.

Objects and Reasons

This clause seeks to amend sub-section (2) of Section 5 of the Act casting an obligation on the person required by the Commission to furnish any information under the sub-section, to furnish such information (vide paragraph 28 of the Report).[494]

---

493. Ins. by Act 79 of 1971, Section 7.

494. Twenty-fourth Report of the Law Commission of India on the Commissions of Inquiry Act, 1952. Notes on Clauses, Clause 7, the Comissions of Inquiry (Amendment) Bill, 1971.

STATE AMENDMENTS

Madhya Pradesh

For Section 5, substitute the following:

5. Additional Powers of Commission: (1) Where the State Government is of opinion that having regard to the nature of the Inquiry to be made and other circumstances of the case, all or any of the provisions of sub-section (2) or sub-section (3) or sub-section (4) or sub-section (5) or sub-section (6) or sub-section (7) should be made applicable to Commission, the State Government may, by notification shall apply to that Commission and on the issue of such a notification, the said provisions shall apply accordingly.

(2) The Commission shall have power to require any person, subject to any privilege which may be claimed by that person under any law for the time being in force, to furnish information on such points or matters as, in the opinion of the Commission, may be useful for or relevant to, the subject-matter of the inquiry and any person so required shall be bound to furnish such information.

(3) The Commission or any officer, not below the rank of a gazetted officer, specially authorized in this behalf by the Commission may enter any building or place where the Commission has reason to believe that any books of account or other documents relating to the subject-matter of inquiry, may be found, and may seize any such books of account or documents or take extracts or copies therefrom, subject to the provisions of Section 102 and Section 103 of the Code of Criminal Procedure, 1898 (Act V of 1898), in so far as they may be applicable.

(4) The Commission shall be deemed to be a Civil Court and when any offence as is described in Section 175, Section 178, Section 179, Section 180 or Section 228, of the Indian Penal Code, 1860 (Act XLV of 1860), is committed in the view or presence of the Commission, the Commission may, after recording the facts constituting the offence and the statement of the accused as provided for by the Code of Criminal Procedure, 1898 (Act V of 1898), forward the case

to a magistrate having jurisdiction to try the same and the Magistrate to whom any such case is forwarded shall proceed to hear the complaint against the accused as if the case had been forwarded to him under Section 482 of the Code of Criminal Procedure, 1898 (Act V of 1898).

(5) If any person, by words either spoken or intended to be read, makes or publishes any statement or does any other act which is calculated to bring the Commission or any members thereof into disrepute, he shall be punishable with simple imprisonment which may extend to two years or with fine or with both.

(6) The provisions of Section 198(B) of the Code of Criminal Procedure, 1898 (Act V· of 1898), shall apply in relation to an offence under sub-section (5) as they apply in relation to an offence referred to in sub-section (1) of the said section 198(B), subject to the modification that no complaint in respect of such offence shall be made by the Public Prosecutor except with the previous sanction of the State Government.

(7) Any proceeding before the Commission shall be deemed to be judicial proceeding within the meaning of Sections 193 and 228 of the Indian Penal Code, 1860 (Act XLV of 1860).[495]

West Bengal

In its application to West Bengal, to Section 5 add as under—

"Explanation.—For the purpose of this sub-section, any police officer of or above the rank of Inspector of Police shall be deemed to be a gazetted officer."—W.B. Act 49 of 1980, Section 3 (24-1-1981).

West Bengal

S. 5AA.

In its application to the State of W.B., after Section 5, Section 5AA inserted:

---

495. Commission of Inquiry (Madhya Pradesh Amendment) Act, 1966 (29 of 1966), Section 2 (22-10-1966).

5AA. Power to authorize a Commission to try certain offences summarily: (1) Where the person or, as the case may be, one at least of the persons constituting a Commission appointed by the State Government is a person who is holding or has held the office of a Judge of the Supreme Court or of a High Court or any other judicial office not lower in rank than that of a Sessions Judge and the State Government is of opinion that, having regard to the nature of inquiry to be made and other circumstances of the case, the provisions of this section should be made applicable to such Commission, the State Government may, by notification in the Official Gazette, direct that the provisions of this section shall apply to that Commission and on the issue of such a notification, the said provisions shall apply accordingly.

(2) If at any stage of a proceeding before the Commission it appears to the Commission that any person appearing in such proceeding had knowingly or wilfully given false evidence or had fabricated false evidence with the intention that such evidence should be used in such proceeding, the Commission may, if satisfied that it is necessary and expedient in the interest of justice that the person should be tried summarily for giving or fabricating, as the case may be, false evidence, take cognizance of the offence and may, after giving the offender a reasonable opportunity of showing cause why he should not be punished for such offence, try such offender summarily, so far as may be, in accordance with the procedure prescribed of summary trials under the Code of Criminal Procedure, 1973 and sentence him to imprisonment for a term which may extend to three months, or to fine which may extend to five hundred rupees, or to both.

(3) When any such offence as is described in Section 175, Section 178, Section 179 or Section 180 of the Indian Penal Code is committed in the view or presence of the Commission, the Commission may cause the offender to be detained in custody and may, at any time on the same day, take cognizance of the offence and, after giving the offender a reasonable opportunity of showing cause why he should

not be punished under this section, sentence the offender to simple imprisonment for a term which may extend to one month, or to fine which may extend to five hundred rupees or to both.

(4) In every case tried under sub-section (3), the Commission shall record the facts constituting the offence with the statement (if any) made by the offender as well as the finding and the sentence.

(5) Any person convicted on a trial held under sub-section (2) or sub-section (3) may appeal to the High Court and the provisions of Chapter XXIX of the Code of Criminal Procedure, 1973, shall so far as they are applicable, apply to appeals under this section and the Appellate Court may alter or reverse the finding, or reduce or reverse the sentence appealed against.

(6) The provisions of this section shall have effect notwithstanding anything contained in the Code of Criminal Procedure, 1973 or in sub-section (4) of Section 5 but nothing in this section shall affect the power (if any) of the Commission to proceed under sub-section (4) of section 5 in respect of any offence, where it does not choose to proceed under this section.

(7) Words and expressions used in this section and not defined in this Act shall have the same meanings as in the Code of Criminal Procedure, 1973.[496]

Vires of the Section

The constitutional validity of sub-section (3) of Section 5 of the Act was challenged in *Sri Narayanadoss Mahant and Another* v. *Sri Neeladri Rao and Another*[497] on the ground of conferring an uncontrolled and arbitrary power of entry and seizure and being violative of the fundamental rights of the petitioner guaranteed by Articles 25 and 26 of the Constitution. Negating the contention, the Court observed that "sub-section (3) of

496. The Commission of Inquiry (West Bengal Amendment) Act, 1974 (51 of 1974), Section 6 (12-12-1974).

497. AIR 1959 Andhra Pradcsh 148.

Section 5 of the Act gives only a limited power to the authorized officers to enter any building or place where the Commission of Inquiry has reason to believe that any books of account or other documents relating to the subject matter of the inquiry may be found; and the search and seizure of books of account or documents can be done only after observing the formalities prescribed by Sections 102 and 103 of the Code of Criminal Procedure. Under Section 103 a search shall be made in the presence of two or more respectable inhabitants of the locality; a list of all things seized in the course of such search and of the places in which they are respectively found, shall be prepared by the officer conducting the search and shall be signed by the witnesses; and further, the occupant of the place searched or some person in his behalf shall, in every instance, be permitted to attend during the search, and a copy of the list prepared under the section, signed by the said witnesses, shall be delivered to such occupant or person. The power of search and seizure is thus hedged in by several restrictions and safeguards. Moreover in a search conducted under Section 5(3) of the Act, there is little danger of the search party interfering with the worship in the religious institution or violating the sanctity of the inner sanctuary, for it can hardly ever happen that books of account and documents relating to the management of a religious institution, would be kept in the sanctum sanctorum. Thus the right of entry, search and seizure, conferred by Section 5(3) of the Act, does not violate the sanctity of the institution nor is it likely to wound religious sentiments. That power is not unbridled and unregulated power."[498]

Section 5(2) of the Act compels a man on peril of prosecution under Sections 176 and 177 of Indian Penal Code to furnish information which is useful or relevant in the inquiry.[499] In view of the provisions of Sections 4 and 5 of the Act, on the petitioner declining to give testimony on oath, the Commission was held to have acted legally and within its jurisdiction in lodging a complaint against him for committing offences under Sections

498. AIR 1959 Andhra Pradesh, pp. 152-53.

499. *(Mr.) Bansi Lal* v. *State and Another*, ILR (1981) I Delhi 715.

178 and 179, I.P.C. It was then the duty of the Magistrate to inquire into the complaint. No doubt a person to whom a notice is issued under Section 8B has the option not to produce evidence in what may be called his defence but that is something quite distinct from declining to take oath when called upon by an authority entitled to do so and when the person is required to give evidence is present before that authority. In order to complete the investigation the Commission could summon the petitioner and inasmuch as the petitioner was present before the Commission he could be called upon to give testimony on oath. On his declining to do so the Commission chose to lodge a complaint under Sections 178 and 179, I.P.C. It was held there was no violation of Article 14 of the Constitution.[500]

Applicability to Deemed Commissions

On issue of a notification under Section 11 of the Act, an inquiring authority, other than a Commission set up under Section 3 of the Act, is deemed to be a Commission appointed under Section 3 for the purposes of the Act. The question whether by applying all the provisions of the Act by a notification under Section 11, any separate and distinct directions as contemplated by sub-section (1) of Section 5 are necessary to confer powers on the Commission of, inter alia, seizure, came up for consideration before Delhi High Court in *P.R. Nayak* v. *Union of India*.[501] The Court, however, did not give any definite answer to this question, as the Court did not find, on facts of that case, any seizure made by the Commission as was alleged by the petitioner.

The question was, however, answered in the affirmative by the Calcutta High Court in *The Statesman* v. *The Fact Finding Committee*[502] in the following terms, viz.:

> It is manifestly clear from Section 11 that the Central Government has been invested with the powers under that

---

500. *Dhirendra Brahmachari* v. *Union of India*, AIR 1979 NOC 91 (Delhi).

501. ILR (1973) I Delhi 747.

502. AIR 1975 Calcutta 15.

Section for the purpose of conferring on the authority set up for the purpose of making an inquiry into any definite matter public importance, the status of a Commission of Inquiry under Section 3. The Government may direct that all the provisions or any of the provisions of the Act will apply to that authority. Even if the Government directs that a single provision will apply to that authority still that authority by virtue of the deeming provisions contained in Section 11 will be deemed to be a Commission appointed under Section 3. The operation of the provisions of sub-sections (2) to (5) of Section 5 depends upon the provision of sub-section (1), namely, on the issue of a notification by the Government under sub-section (1). Sub-section (1) prescribes the mode for bringing into operation the provisions of sub-sections (2) to (5). These sub-sections will not have any existence apart from sub-section (1). Even where a direction is made under Section 11 that all the provisions will apply, a further notification has to be issued under sub-section (1) of Section 5 for the purpose of conferring the powers under these sub-sections upon the authority to be deemed a Commission under Section 11. The respective considerations which are to be made by the Government under sub-section (1) of Section 5 and those under Section 11 are different. Under Section 11 what is to be considered by the Government is whether all or any of the provisions of the Act should be made applicable to the authority other than a Commission appointed under Section 3. Under sub-section (1) of Section 5, the Government has to consider the nature of the inquiry to be made and also other circumstances of the case. The powers under sub-sections (2), (3) and (4) are additional powers which are not vested in the Commission of Inquiry after it is appointed under Section 3. After the appointment of a Commission of Inquiry under Section 3, the Government has to further consider whether it will confer on the Commission of Inquiry the additional powers under sub-sections (2), (3) and (4) of Section 5. There is no indication in Section 11 that the Government can invest such an authority with the powers under sub-sections (2),

(3) and (4)) without a further notification under sub-section (1). I am not impressed with the contention made on behalf of the respondents that the word 'provisions' in Section 11 means and should be read as 'powers'. In the instant case, sub-section (1) has been excluded and, accordingly, it must be held that sub-sections (2), (3) and (4) have not been and cannot be applied to the Committee. It is impossible to think that while in the case of a Commission of Inquiry appointed under Section 3 a notification under sub-section (1) of Section 5 is required to be made for the purpose of conferring on the Commission the powers under sub-sections (2), (3) and (4) no notification under sub-section (1) will be necessary for conferring such powers on the authority other than a Commission appointed under Section 3. The provisions of sub-section (1) upon which the operation of the provisions of sub-sections (2), (3) and (4) depends, have been excluded. I am, therefore, of the view that the provisions of sub-sections (2), (3), (4) and (5) have not been legally and validly applied to the Committee and as such the Committee does not possess any powers under those sub-sections. It is not disputed that the petitioners have been asked to answer the questionnaire in the purported exercise of the alleged power of the Committee under sub-section (2) of Section 5. In view of my finding that the Committee does not possess powers under sub-sections (2), (3) and (4) it cannot direct the petitioners to answer the questionnaire.[503]

It is clear from the aforesaid that such separate and distinct directions in terms of sub-section (1) of section 5 are necessary in order to confer additional powers, including that of seizure, on a deemed Commission in the same manner in which these are conferred on a Commission otherwise set up under Section 3 of the Act.

Commission of Inquiry—Whether a Court

The question whether a Commission under the Act is a Court or not, came up for consideration, in the context of

503. Para 66, p. 42.

Contempt of Court Act, in the earlier years of its operation. The Act has been amended in 1971 so as to expressly provide in Section 10A for penalty for acts calculated to bring the Commission or any member thereof into disrepute. Nonetheless, the earlier case law on the subject provides an insight into the nature of legal fiction created in sub-section (4) of Section 5, whereunder the Commission is deemed to be a Court.

The term "Court" has not been defined in the Contempt of Courts Act, 1952. Section 3 of the Indian Evidence Act, 1872 defines a "Court" as including all Judges and Magistrates, and all persons, except arbitrators, legally authorized to take evidence. This definition, however, has been held to be not exhaustive but framed only for the purpose of Indian Evidence Act and is not be to be extended where such an extension is not warranted.[504] Sections 19 and 20 of the Indian Penal Code, 1860 define the words "Judge" and the "Court of Justice" as under:

> Section 19: "Judge"—The word "Judge" denotes not only every person who is officially designated as a Judge, but also every person, who is empowered by law to give, in any legal proceeding, civil or criminal, a definitive judgment, or a judgment which, if not appealed against, would be definitive, or a judgment which, if confirmed by some other authority, would be definitive, or who is one of a body of persons, which body of persons is empowered by law to give such a judgment.
>
> Section 20: "Court of Justice"—The words "Court of Justice" denote a Judge who is empowered by law to act judicially alone, or a body of Judges which is empowered by law to act judicially as a body, when such a Judge or body of Judges is acting judicially.

The pronouncement of a definitive judgment is, thus, considered the essential sine qua non of a Court and unless and until a binding and authoritative judgment can be pronounced by a person or a body of person it cannot be predicated that he or they constitute a Court.[505]

---

504. *Brajnandan Sinha* v. *Jyoti Narai* (1955) 2 SCR 955.

505. *Brajnandan Sinha* v. *Jyoti Narain* (1955) 2 SCR 955, p. 962.

Coke on Littleton and Stroud defined the word "Court" as a place where justice is judicially administered.

According to Stephen,[506] "In every Court, there must be at least three constituent parts—the 'actor', 'reus' and 'judex': the 'actor' or plaintiff, who complains of an injury done; the 'reus' or defendant, who is called upon to make satisfaction for it; and the 'judex' or judicial power, which is to examine the truth of the fact, and to determine the law arising upon that fact, and if any injury appears to have been done, to ascertain, and by its officers to apply, the remedy."

In *Mahabaleswarappa* v. *Gopalaswami*,[507] Curgenven J., after reviewing several authorities observed:

> To summarise the effect of these decisions it would seem that we have to look, not to the source of a tribunal's authority, or to any peculiarity in the method adopted of creating it (though it is undoubtedly a consideration that it derives its powers mediately or immediately from the Crown) but to the general character of its powers and activities. If it has power to regulate 'legal rights by the delivery of definitive judgments', and to enforce its orders by legal sanctions, and if its procedure is judicial in character, in such matters as the taking of evidence and the administration of the oath, then it is a court.

These observations were approved in *Hari Charan* v. *Kaushi Charan*[508] and also in Deputy Commr., Goalapara v Upendra Saran.[509] The least that is required of a Court is the capacity to deliver a "definitive judgment", and unless this power vests in a tribunal in any particular case, the mere fact that the procedure adopted by it is of a legal character and it has the power to administer an oath will not impart to it the status of a Court.[510]

---

506. *Stephen's Commentaries on the Laws of England*, 6th Edn., p. 383.
507. AIR 1935 Madras 673.
508. AIR 1940 Calcutta 286.
509. AIR 1950 Assam 25.
510. *M.V. Rajwade* v. *Dr S.M. Hassan*, AIR 1954 Nagpur 71.

The Privy Council in the case of *Shell Co. of Australia* v. *Federal Commissioner of Taxation*[511] defined "Judicial Power" as follows:

> Is this right? What is "judicial power"? Their Lordships are of opinion that one of the best definitions is that given by Griffith, C.J. in *Huddart, Parker & Co.* v. *Moorehead*[512] where he says: "I am of opinion that the words 'judicial power' as used in section 71 of the Constitution mean the power which every sovereign authority must of necessity have to decide controversies between its subjects, or between itself and its subjects, whether the rights relate to life, liberty or property. The exercise of this power to give a binding and authoritative decision (whether subject to appeal or not) is called upon to take action.

Their Lordships further enumerated[513] certain negative propositions in relation to this subject:

"1. A tribunal is not necessarily a Court in this strict sense because it gives a final decision;
2. Nor because it hears witnesses on oath;
3. Nor because two or more contending parties appear before it between whom it has to decide;
4. Nor because it gives decisions which affect the rights of subjects;
5. Nor because there is an appeal to a Court;
6. Nor because it is a body to which a matter is referred by another body."[514]

An administrative tribunal may act judicially but still remain an administrative tribunal as distinguished from a Court, strictly so called. Mere externals do not make a direction to an

511. (1931) AC 275, p. 295.
512. (1909) 8 CLR 330, 337.
513. *Ibid.*, p. 297.
514. *Rex* v. *Electricity Commissioners* (1924) 1 KB 171.

administrative officer by an ad hoc tribunal an exercise by a Court of Judicial power.[515]

The same principle was reiterated by the Supreme Court in *Bharat Bank Limited* v. *Employees of Bharat Bank Ltd.*[516] and *Maqbool Hussain* v. *The State of Bombay*[517] where the test of a judicial tribunal as laid down in a passage from *Cooper* v. *Wilson*[518] was adopted by the Apex Court:

> A true judicial decision presupposes an existing dispute between two or more parties, and then involves four requisites: (1) The presentation (not necessarily orally) of their case by the parties to the dispute; (2) if the dispute between them is a question of fact, the ascertainment of the fact by means of evidence adduced by the parties to the dispute and often with the assistance of argument by or on behalf of the parties on the evidence; (3) if the dispute between them is a question of law, the submission of legal arguments by the parties; and (4) a decision which disposes of the whole matter by a finding upon the facts in dispute and an application of the law of the land to the facts so found, including where required a ruling upon any disputed question of law.

Maqbool Hussain's case, above referred to, was followed by the Supreme Court in *A.A. Venkataraman* v. *The Union of India and Another*[519] where a Constitution Bench of the Supreme Court also laid down that both finality and authoritativeness were the essential tests of a judicial pronouncement. It is clear, therefore, that in order to constitute a Court in the strict sense of the term, an essential condition is that the Court should have, apart from having some of the trappings of a judicial Tribunal, power to give a decision or a definitive judgment which has

---

515. *Shell Co. of Australia* v. *Federal Commissioner of Taxation* (1931) AC 275, p. 298.
516. (1950) SCR 459.
517. (1953) SCR 730.
518. (1937) 2 KB 309, 340.
519. (1954) SCR 1150.

finality and authoritativeness which are the essential tests of a judicial pronouncement.[520]

Under sub-section (4) of Section 5, the Commission is deemed to be a Court. Sub-section (5) of Section 5 imparts to the proceeding before it the character of a judicial proceedings. However, these provisions only create a fiction, which cannot extend beyond the purpose for which it is created. The purpose for which the fiction has been created is to be gathered from what follows after the words, which create the fiction. Applying this test, it would appear that the purpose for which the fiction is created in sub-section (4) of Section 5 of the Commissions of Inquiry, 1952 is to be inferred from the words that follows the expression "the Commission shall deemed to be a Civil Court". It would not be correct to contend that the above expression is full and complete in itself and what follows it only denotes the limitation on the full-fledged status and powers of a Civil Court that the Commission would otherwise have possessed. If that was the intention of the Legislature, the sentence would have been completed after the words "Civil Court" and what follows it would have been the subject of a separate sub-section or sentence. It is, therefore, clear that under the Commissions of Inquiry Act, 1952, the Commission is fictionally a civil Court only for the purpose of the contempt punishable under Sections 175, 178, 179, 180 and 228 of the Indian Penal Code, 1860, subject to the condition that it has not the right itself to punish the contemners, a right which other Courts possess under Section 480 of the Code of Criminal Procedure, 1898. Similarly it follows that the fiction relating to the proceedings before the Commission is confined to the offences that are punishable under Sections 193 and 228 of the Indian Penal Code, 1860, referred to in sub-section (5) of the Act, and does not extend beyond this limit. Accordingly, a Division Bench of Nagpur High Court held in *M.V. Rajwade* v. *Dr. S.M. Hassan*[521] that the Commission of Inquiry presided over by a High Court Judge was not a Court within the meaning of the Contempt of Courts Act, 1952.

---

520. *Brajnandan Sinha* v. *Jyoti Narain* (1955) 2 SCR 955, pp. 963-64.

521. AIR 1954 Nagpur 71.

An enquiry under the Commissions of Inquiry Act, 1952 is of wholly different character. There is no accuser, no accused and specific charges for trials; nor is the Government, under the law, required to pronounce, one way or the other, on the findings of the Commission. In *re Maharaja Madhava Singh*,[522] was a case of the Commissioners appointed by the Viceroy and Governor-General in Council for the purpose of enquiring into the truth of a certain imputation against the Maharajah, in which their Lordships of the Privy Council observed:

> It is sufficient to say that the Commission in question was one appointed by the Viceroy himself for the information of his own mind, in order that he should not act in his political and sovereign character otherwise than in accordance with the dictates of justice and equity, and was not in any case a Court, or, if a Court, was not a Court from which an appeal lies to His Majesty in Council.

In *Dr. Baliram Waman Hiray* v. *Mr. Justice B. Lentin and Others*,[523] the Court made the following observations:

> A Commission of Inquiry is not a Court properly so called. A Commission is obviously appointed by the appropriate Government 'for the information of its mind' in order for it to decide as to the course of action to be followed. It is therefore a fact-finding body and is not required to adjudicate upon the rights of the parties and has no adjudicatory functions. The Government is not bound to accept its recommendations or act upon its findings. The mere fact that the procedure adopted by it is of a legal character and it has the power to administer an oath will not impart to it the status of a Court.

In *Virindar Kumar Satyawadi* v. *State of Punjab*,[524] a three-Judges Bench speaking through Venkatarama Ayyar, J. relying upon the celebrated decision of the House of Lords in *Shell Co.*

522. 32 Calcutta 1 (PC); 31 Ind. App. 239 (PC).

523. AIR 1988 SC 2267; (1988) 4 SCC 419.

524. AIR 1956 SC 153.

of Australia v. *Federal Commissioner of Taxation*,[525] explaiend the legal connotation of the term 'Court' in these words:[526]

> What distinguishes a Court from a quasi-judicial tribunal is that it is charged with a duty to decide disputes in a judicial manner and declare the rights of parties in a definitive judgment. To decide in a judicial manner involves that the parties are entitled as a matter of right to be heard in support of their claim and to adduce evidence in proof of it. And it also imports an obligation on the part of the authority to decide the matter on a consideration of the evidence adduced and in accordance with law. When a question therefore arises as to whether an authority created by an Act is a Court as distinguished from a quasi-judicial tribunal, what has to be decided is whether having regard to the provisions of the Act it possesses all the attributes of a Court.

It is a familiar feature of modern legislation to set up bodies and tribunals, and entrust them with work of a judicial, quasi-judicial administrative character, but they are not Courts in the accepted sense of that term though they may possess, as observed by Lord Sankey, L.C. in *Shell Co. of Australia's* case,[527] some of the trappings of a Court, Venkatarama Ayyar, J. in *Virindar Kumar Satyawadi*[528] has referred to several decisions of the Courts in England and Australia as to what are the essential characteristics of a Court as distinguished from tribunals exercising quasi-judicial functions.

It would not be correct to contend that the legal fiction contained in the first part of sub-section (4) is complete in itself and, therefore, a Commission of Inquiry must, by reason of the legal fiction contained therein, be deemed to be a Civil Court 'for all purposes'. The argument fails to take note of the fact that the words 'for all purposes' are not there in the first part of

525. 1931 AC 275.

526. *Virindar Kumar Satyawadi* v. *State of Punjab*, AIR 1956 SC 153, p. 157.

527. *Supra*.

528. *Supra*.

sub-section (4) and the Court cannot in the guise of interpreting the provision, supply any causus omissus. The first part of sub-section (4) merely provides by the legal fiction that a Commission of Inquiry shall be deemed to be a Civil Court and it stops there. We are quite clear that the first part cannot be read in isolation but must take its colour from the context in which it appears. It would not be correct to contend that the fiction created by the first part by the words "shall be deemed to be a Civil Court" is full and complete in itself. The purpose and object of the legal fiction created by the first part of sub-section (4) is reflected in the second. A Commission of Inquiry is, therefore, fictionally a Civil Court for the limited purpose of proceeding under Section 482 of the old Code or under Section 346 of the present Code. A fortiori, the legal fiction contained in sub-section (5) of Section 5, which relates to the proceedings before the Commission is necessarily confined to offences that are punishable under Sections 193 and 228 of the Indian Penal Code and does not extend beyond that.

In view of the aforesaid, it follows that the decision of the Nagpur High Court in *M.V. Rajwade's* case[529] and that of the Madhya Pradesh High Court in *Puhupram*[530] lay down the correct law. The least that is required of a Court is the capacity to deliver 'definitive judgment', and merely because the procedure adopted by it is of a legal character and it has power to administer an oath will not impart to it the status of a Court. That being so, it must be held that a Commission of Inquiry appointed by the appropriate Government under Section 3(1) of the Commissions of Inquiry Act is not a Court for the purposes of Section 195 of the Code.[531]

A Commission of Inquiry under the Act is, thus, obviously appointed by the appropriate Government "for the information of its own mind", in order that it should not act, in exercise of its executive power, "otherwise than in accordance with the

529. AIR 1954 Nagpur 71.

530. 1968 MPLJ 629.

531. *Dr. Baliram Waman Hiray* v. *Mr. Justice B. Lentin* and others AIR 1988 SC 2267, p. 2285.

dictates of justice and equity". It is a fact-finding body meant only to instruct the mind of the Government without producing any document of a judicial nature.[532] It is not possible to accede to the contention that the Commission is a Civil Court by virtue of the deeming provision contained in sub-section (4) of Section 5 of the Act.[533] The legal fiction in this regard cannot be extended beyond its intended purpose. Had it been a Court in its own right, there would not been any necessity for applying the legal fiction to it.

Duty to Furnish Information

Sub-section (2) of this section enjoins upon any person who is required by the Commission to furnish information as is, in the opinion of the Commission, useful or relevant to the subject of enquiry, to be legally bound to furnish such information within the meaning of Section 176 and Section 177 of the Indian Penal Code, 1860. Failure to furnish information required by the Commission within the stipulated period would constitute offences punishable under these sections of the Code.[534]

Privilege against Furnishing Information

Duty to furnish information in terms of Section 5(2) is subject to any privilege which may be claimed under any law for the time being in force. In *Orient Paper Mills* v. *Union of India*,[535] it was held that a decision of the Cabinet related to the affairs of Cabinet in determination and execution of public policies and for non-production of the same privilege could be claimed under Section 123 of the Evidence Act. In this case, the Court observed: "The first clause of Section 162 of the Evidence Act requires that a witness summoned to produce a document must bring it to the Court and then raise an objection against either its production or its admissibility. An objection to the production or admissibility of evidence specified in Section 162 of the Evidence Act relates to all claims of privilege provided by

---

532. M.V. *Rajwade* v. *Dr. S.M. Hassan*, AIR 1854 Nagpur 71.
533. *Allen Berry & Co.* v. *Vivian Bose*, AIR 1960 Punjab 86, p. 90.
534. *Statesman* v. *Fact Finding Committee*, AIR 1975 Calcutta 15, p. 24.
535. AIR 1979 Calcutta 114.

the relevant sections of Chapter IX of Part III of the Act. Section 123 is only one of such privileges. So the jurisdiction given to the Court to decide the validity of the objections covers not only the objection raised under Section 123 but to all other objections as well."

The Court further observed:

> It is well settled that the privilege should not be claimed under Section 123 because it is apprehended that the document if produced would defeat the defence raised by the State. In the supplementary affidavit when privilege is claimed concerning a particular document, the Court has to determine the character or class of the document. If it comes to the conclusion that the document does not relate to the affairs of the State then it should reject the claim for privilege and direct its production.

Limit of Delegation in Section 5(3)

In *Allen Berry & Co.* v. *Vivian Bose*,[536] Investigating Officers were appointed by the Commission to collect material and record statements of persons who volunteered to appear as witnesses and these Investigating Officers would then submit reports. This, it was contended, was contrary to the well-known maxim delegata potestas non potest delegare. Negating the contention, it was held that the maxim could possible have no applicability to the facts of the case. It was pointed out that admittedly the Commission had only appointed Inspectors to collect certain material and record only those statements which were volunteered by the witnesses. That had been done essentially to assist and help the Commission in the collection of material, which it was physically impossible for the Chairman and the Members of the Commission to do collectively or individually. It was true as stated in Broom's *Legal Maxims*,[537] that an individual clothed with judicial functions could not delegate the discharge of these functions unless he was expressly empowered to do so but although a deputy could not transfer his entire powers to another, yet a deputy having general powers might in

536. AIR 1960 Punjab 86.

537. Page 571, Tenth Edition.

general constitute his servant or bailiff for the purpose of doing some particular act provided of course that such act be within the scope of his own legitimate authority. The other maxim on which reliance had been placed in this connection was the one stated in Broom's *Legal Maxims*,[538] expressio unius est exclusio alterius, meaning that the express mention of one thing implies the exclusion of another. It was contended that Section 5(3) of the Act indicated the limit of delegation, which could be made by the Commission of its powers and functions and, therefore, it should be implied that delegation of other functions was completely excluded. As the Court came to the conclusion on facts that there was no delegation of any functions in the case, the applicability of the maxim could not be invoked. Moreover, this point had not been shown to have been raised before the Commission. These aspects have now been specifically provided in Sections 5A and 5B, which have been inserted in the Act in 1988.

Power of Commission to utilize the services of certain officers and investigation agencies for conducting investigation pertaining to inquiry.

[539][**5A.** (1) **The Commission may, for the purpose of conducting any investigation pertaining to the inquiry, utilise the services:**

(a) **in the case of a Commission appointed by the Central Government, of any officer or investigating agency of the Central Government or any State Government with the concurrence of the Central Government or the State Government, as the case may be; or**

(b) **in the case of a Commission appointed by the State Government, of any officer or investigation agency of the State Government or Central Government with the concurrence of the State Government or the Central Government, as the case may be.**

---

538. Page 443, *ibid.*

539. Ins. by Section 8, Act 79 of 1971.

(2) For the purpose of investigating into any matter pertaining to the inquiry, any officer or agency whose services are utilized under sub-section (1) may, subject to the direction and control of the Commission:

(a) summon and enforce the attendance of any person and examine him;

(b) require the discovery and production of any document; and

(c) requisition any public record or copy thereof from any office.

(3) The provisions of Section 6 shall apply in relation to any statement made by a person before any officer or agency whose services are utilized under sub-section (1) as they apply in relation to any statement made by a person in the course of giving evidence before the Commission.

(4) The officer or agency, whose services are utilized under sub-section (1), shall investigate into any matter pertaining to the inquiry and submit a report thereon (hereafter in this section referred to as the investigation report) to the Commission within such period as may be specified by the Commission in this behalf.

(5) The Commission shall satisfy itself about the correctness of the facts stated and the conclusions, if any, arrived at in the investigating report submitted to it under sub-section (4), and for this purpose the Commission may make such inquiry (including the examination of the person or persons who conducted or assisted in the investigation) as it think fit.]

Objects and Reasons

This clause seeks to insert a new Section 5A in the Act. Under this new Section, a Commission appointed by the Central Government is empowered to utilise the services of any officer or investigation agency of the Central Government or, with the concurrence of the State Government concerned, the services of any officer or investigating agency of that State Government.

Correspondingly, a Commission appointed by a State Government may utilise the services of any officer or investigating agency of the State Government or with the concurrence of the Central Government, the services of any officer of investigating agency of the Central Government. Provision has also been made to the effect that for the purposes of such investigations any officer or investigating agency whose services are utilized may, subject to the direction and control of the Commission, summon and enforce the attendance of any person and examine him; and requisition any public record or copy thereof from any office. The officer or agency, whose services are utilized, shall after investigating into any matter pertaining to an inquiry submit report thereon to the Commission within such period as may be specified by the Commission in this behalf. The section further provides that Commission shall satisfy itself about the correctness of facts stated and the conclusions, if any, arrived at in the report and for this purpose the Commission may make such inquiry (including the examination of the person or persons who conducted, or assisted in, the investigation) as it deems fit (vide paragraph 17 of the report).[540]

[541] [Power of Commission to appoint assessors

5B. The Commission may, for the purpose of conducting any inquiry, appoint persons having special knowledge of any matter connected with the inquiry as assessors, to assist and advise the Commission in the inquiry and the assessors shall be entitled to such traveling and other expenses as may be prescribed.]

Objects and Reasons

Opportunity is being availed of to give effect to the recommendations of the Committees on Subordinate Legislation of both the Houses of Parliament to the effect that the Commissions of Inquiry Act should be amended to make specific provision for the appointment of assessors and for the payment

540. Twenty-fourth Report of the Law Commission of India. Notes on Clauses, Clause 8, the Commissions of Inquiry (Amendment) Bill, 1971.

541. Ins. by Act 63 of 1988, Section 2.

of travelling allowance and dearness allowance to assessors and witnesses. Such a provision at present exists in the Commissions of Inquiry (Central) Rules, 1972, made under the Act.[542]

Statements made by persons to the Commission.

6. No statement made by a person in the course of giving evidence before the Commission shall subject him to, or be used against him in, any civil or criminal proceeding except a prosecution for giving false evidence by such statement:

Provide that the statement—

(a) is made in reply to a question which he is required by the Commission to answer, or

(b) is relevant to the subject matter of the inquiry.

Rule of Privilege

Section 6 of the Act embodies 'the rule of qualified privilege'. The High Court of Delhi in the case of *Ram Jethmalani* v. *Subramaniam Swamy*[543] has very elaborately dealt with the rule of privilege. In order to have correct and better understanding of the origin and the ambit of the rule, it will be expedient to refer, in extenso, the relevant extracts of that judgment.

Origin of the Rule of Absolute Privilege

The origin of the rule of absolute privilege could easily be traced to judicial proceedings in a Court of law. Needless to state, of the many fundamental rights enshrined to the citizens in various democratic countries of the world, primacy has been accorded to right to justice. On grounds of public policy, absolute immunity from liability was conceived of for Judges, counsel and witnesses for the reason it was felt that during judicial proceedings in Court, every participative player must be free from the fear of being harassed by an action or allegation, whether true or false that he acted with malice.

In India and most of the democratic countries, a second specie of absolute privilege finds mentioned under the

542. Paragraph 2 of the Statement of Objects and Reasons, the Commissions of Inquiry (Amendment) Bill, 1988.

543. AIR 2006 Delhi 300.

Constitution or Parliamentary traditions. Under our Constitution, vide Articles 105(2) and 194(2) provisions have been made giving complete immunity to the statements made by Members of Parliament and State Legislatures respectively, in course of proceedings of the House.

This status was, however, denied to tribunals not being at par with Courts. Proceedings before tribunals which had all the trapping of a Court were alone held eligible to be entitled for absolute privilege.[544]

In *Lincoln* v. *Deniels*,[545] absolute privilege against liability for defamation that attaches to proceedings before a Court of justice was extended to disciplinary proceedings before Benchers of an Inn of Court for the reason; disciplinary powers of the Benchers were held derived from the Judges. Additionally, it was held that while exercising power, the Benchers act judicially. Distinction was drawn in respect of direct complaints to the Bar Council which may lead to disciplinary proceedings before the Benchers on the ground that the Bar Council is a distinct body deriving authority from the general meeting of the members and not from the Benchers.

Nature of Commissions' Proceedings and the Application of the Rule

Decisions in *Ram Krishna Dalmia* v. *Justice S.R. Tendolkar*,[546] *P.V. Jagannath Rao* v. *State of Orissa*,[547] and *Dr. Baliram Waman Hiray* v. *Justice B. Lentin*[548] have held that proceedings before a Commission of Inquiry under the Commissions of Inquiry Act, 1952, notwithstanding having powers of a Civil Court by virtue of Section 4 of the Act, cannot be equated with judicial proceedings in a Court of law.

A Commission under the Commissions of Inquiry Act, 1952 is appointed by the appropriate Government for the information of the mind of the Government in order for it to decide the

544. *Addis* v. *Crocker*, 1960 (2) All ER 629.

545. (1961) 3 All ER 740.

546. AIR 1958 SC 538.

547. AIR 1969 SC 215.

548. AIR 1988 SC 2267: 1988 (4) SCC 419.

course of action to be followed. It is a fact-finding body and is not required to adjudicate upon the rights of the parties and has no adjudicatory power. The Government is not bound to accept its recommendations or act upon its findings. Mere fact that the procedure adopted by it is akin to a procedure at a civil trial and it has the power to administer oath would not impart the commission with the status of a Court.

Way back in the year 1935, in *William Francis O'Conor* v. *Gordon Waldron*,[549] Lord Atkin held that notwithstanding the fact that a Commissioner appointed under the Combines Investigation Act had attributes similar to those of a Court of justice, proceedings before it canot be equated as judicial proceedings in a Court of law.

Nature of Absolute Privilege

The issue of absolute privilege has remained a subject-matter of considerable debate. Is absolute privilege absolute in the sense of being infinite? As late as 1998, it was held in *Waple* v. *Surey County Council*[550] as follows:

> The absolute privilege which applies to statements made in the course of judicial proceedings and in the documents made in such proceeding, would only be entitled where it was strictly necessary to do so in order to protect those who were to participate in the proceedings from being sued themselves.

The decision brings out that absolute privilege is not absolute in the context of being infinite. Even when the occasion is privileged, one gets no licence to utter irrelevant and scandalous things unrelated to the proceedings. If what is stated is necessary to relevant to the proceedings, immunity would be absolute.

Kinds of Privilege

In *Panday Surinder Nath Sinha* v. *Bageshwari Prasad*,[551] distinction between absolute and qualified privilege was brought out as under:

---

549. AIR 1935 PC 3.

550. 1998 (1) All ER 625.

551. AIR 1961 Patna 164.

(i) In absolute privilege, it is the occasion which is privileged and when once the nature of the occasion is shown, it follows, as a necessary inference, that every communication on that occasion is protected, in qualified privilege, the occasion is not privileged, until the defendant has shown how that occasion was used. It is not enough to have an interest or a duty in making a statement the necessity of the existence of an interest of duty in making the statement complained of, must also be shown.

(ii) In absolute privilege, the defendant gets absolute exemption from liability; in a qualified privilege, the defendant gets a conditional exemption from liability.

(iii) In absolute privilege, the defendant is exempted from liability even when there is malice on his part; in qualified privilege, the defendant is exempted from liability only when there is no malice on his part.

(iv) In absolute privilege, statements are protected in all circumstances, irrespective of the presence of good or bad motives, in qualified privilege, even after a case of qualified privilege has been established by the defendant, it may be met by the plaintiff proving in reply improper or evil motive on the part of the defendant, in which case defence of qualified privilege vanishes and the plaintiff succeeds.

(v) In absolute privilege as well as in qualified privilege, the defendant has to prove his plea of privilege, but with this difference that in absolute privilege the defence is absolute and irrefutable by plaintiff, whereas in qualified privilege the defence is not absolute but rebutable by the plaintiff.

Onus of Proof

Generally, the onus to prove a fact is on the person who asserts it unless the law provides otherwise. Gatley on Libel and Slandar[552] has opined that where a defendant alleges that the

552. 10th Edition, vide para 27.18.

words complained of were published on a privileged occasion, he must specify the circumstances he relies on in support of that contention. The learned author has further opined that where a defence of absolute privilege is set up, it is for the defendant to allege and prove all such facts as are necessary to bring the words complained of within the privilege, unless such facts are disclosed in the statement of case, or otherwise admitted before or at the trial of the occasion.[553]

Qualified Privilege and Malice

Qualified privilege may be defeated and its protection destroyed by proof of express malice. But how is express malice to be established?

In *Laughton* v. *Bishop of Sodor*,[554] in a charge to his clergy in convocation, the Bishop opined, in a rather harsh language, upon a speech made by a Barrister who had been instructed to oppose a bill before the House of Keys, promoted by Government, and which vested additional Ecclesiastical patronage in the Bishop and in which the conduct of the Bishop was attacked and unworthy motives were attributed to the Bishop. What was spoken by the Bishop was sent to a newspaper for publication.

Sir Robert Collier delivering judgment in the Judicial Committee dealing with the question whether in spite of occasion being privileged, there was express malice, that is to say, defence was actuated by motive of personal spite or ill will, independent of the occasion opined:

> Some expressions here used undoubtedly go beyond what was necessary for self-defence, but it does not, therefore, follow that they afford evidence of malice for a jury. To submit the language of privilege communcation to a strict scrutiny, and to hold all excess beyond the absoloute exigency of the occasion to be evidence of malice would be to effect greatly limit, if not altogether defeat, that provision which the law throws over privileged communications.

553. 10th Edition, vide para 13.4.

554. (1872) LR 4 PC 495.

In *Adam* v. *Ward*,[555] plaintiff, an officer in the cavalry regiment was subsequently elected a Member of Parliament. In a speech in the House of Commons, he charged the General Commanding the brigade of which his late regiment formed part, of sending confidential reports to headquarters on officers under his command containing willful and deliberate misstatements. The General referred the matter to the Army Council. Secretay to Council wrote a letter to the General vindicating against the charge made by the plaintiff. Letter contained defamatory statements about the plaintiff. The letter was sent to the press for publication. Plaintiff brought the action.

Lord Loreburn observed[556] as under:

> Language has been used in some cases which seems somewhat to confuse the two separate points, namely, whether the defendant has gone beyond the privilege which the occasion creates, and whether the defendant has forfeited the privilege by malice. Excess of privilege in part of a defamatory publication may of course be evidence of malice as to the whole of it, but the two things are different. The one is a matter for the Judge; the other is matter for the jury. And observations made by the Judges in directing juries as to what is evidence of malice are not necessarily applicable when they have to rule as to excess of privilege. But I agree that in ruling upon that subject a Judge may well think that a man is justified in inculpating his accuser in order more effectively to exculpate himself, and also may well think that the defendant has not exceeded the privilege when he has expressed himself with some warmth under real provocation, though no one can be justified in using such an occasion beyond the reasonable limits of self-defence.

Lord Dunedin observed[557] as under:

---

555. 1917 AC 309.

556. *Ibid.*, p. 321.

557. 1917 AC 327.

> If the defamatory statement is quite unconnected with and irrelevant to the main statement which is ex-hypothesis privileged then I think it is more accurate to say that the privilege does not extend thereto than to say though the result may be the same, that the defamatory statement is evidence of malice. But when the defamatory statement is, so to speak, part and parcel of the privileged statement and relevant to the discussion, then I think the first way is the true way to put it, and under it will also range all the cases where the express malice is arguable from the too great severity or redundancy of the expressions used in the privileged document itself. In short, I adopt the law as laid down by Lord Esher M.R. in (1895) 2 QB 156, p. 170. The learned Judge there says...in this case there was no evidence of such malice. That being so, the defendants have proved that the occasion was privileged and there was no evidence of malice in the mind of anybody to rebut that privilege, and the defence stands good. But then the jury was asked to find, and have found, that the privilege was acceded. There may be an excess of the privilege in the sense that something has been published which is not within the privileged occasion at all, because it can have no reference to it.

Lord Atkin, reviewing the charges including the decisions in *Laughton's* case[558] observed as under:

> These authorities, in my view, clearly establish that a person making a communication on a privileged occasion is not restricted to the use of such language merely as is reasonably necessary to protect the interest or discharge the duty which is the foundation of his privilege; but that, on the contrary, he will be protected, even though his language should be violent or excessively strong, if, having regard to all the circumstances of the case, he might have honestly and on reasonable grounds believed that what he wrote or said was true and necessary for the purpose of his vindication, though in fact it was not so.

---

558. *Laughton* v *Bishop of Sodor* (1872) LR 4 PC 495.

The Division Bench of Bombay High Court, in *Janardan Karandikar* v. *Ramchandra Tilak*,[559] taking note of the decision in *Laughton's* case[560] and *Adam's* case,[561] dealing with a privileged occasion applied the test adopted by Lord Dunedin[562] by going into the language used in the context of it being "too great severity or redundancy in the expression used".

In the context of the constitutional protection of freedom of speech and freedom of the press, the US Supreme Court, in *New York Times Company* v. *Sullivan*,[563] rendered an important decision pertaining to libel. The question before the Court was of the rule of liability in an action brought by a public official against critics of his official conduct which action tended to abridge the freedom of speech of the press that was guaranteed by the 1st and the 14th amendments. The Constitutional Bench opined that such an action was maintainable provided the official established that statements were made with actual malice.

What is actual malice? A statement made with knowledge that it was false or with reckless disregard of whether it was false or not constitutes actual malice as explained in *Sullivan's* case.[564] The decision in *Sullivan's* case additionally highlighted the issue that an injunction would not lie against intended publications, remedy was, to establish actual malice if aggrieved and obtained redressal by way of pecuniary damages.

Actual malice would be evidenced by ill will, evil or corrupt motive, intention to injure, hatred, enmity, hostility, or spite. In *Garrison* v. *Louisiana*,[565] the US Supreme Court defined reckless disregard in making statements with a high degree of awareness of their probable falsity as proof of actual malice. In

559. AIR 1947 Bomaby 209.

560. *Laughton* v. *Bishop of Sodor* (1872) LR 4 PC 495.

561. *Adam* v. *Ward*, 1917 AC 309.

562. *Ibid.*

563. 376 US 254.

564. *Ibid.*

565. 379 US 64.

St. Amant v. *Thompson*,[566] the test applied was whether the defendant entertained serious doubts as to the truth of the statements. In *Cortis Publishing Company* v. *Butts*,[567] the US Supreme Court suggestd that a defendant's good faith in publishing defamatory falsities will be unlikely to prove persuasive where the story (1) is fabricated by the defendant, (2) is the product of his imagination, (3) is based wholly on unverified information. Nor will they be likely to prevail when the publisher's allegations are so inherently improbable that only a reckless man would have put forth the same in circulation or where there are obvious reasons to doubt the veracity of the informant or the accuracy of his reports.

In *St. Amant* v. *Thompson*,[568] a note of caution was inserted: mere negligence of the defendant in failing to discover the falsity of his statement is not sufficient to show actual malice.

The Hon'ble Supreme Court in *R. Rajagopal* v. *State of Tamil Nadu*[569] noted decision in *Sullivan's* case.[569a] This case involved the question concerning the freedom of press vis-à-vis the right of privacy of the citizens of the country and also the question at to the parameters of the right of the press to criticize and comment on the acts and conduct of public officials. After referring to the principles emerging from the United States and English decisions including *Sullivan's* case, the Court dealt with the question as to how far these principles were relevant under our constitutional system. In this context, the Court observed: "(W)e must remember that our society may not share the degree of public awareness obtaining in United Kingdom or United States. The sweep of the First Amendment to the United States Constitution and the freedom of speech and expression under our Constitution are not identical though similar in their major premises. All this may call for some modification of the principles

566. 390 US 727.

567. 388 US 130.

568. 390 US 727.

569. (1994) 6 SCC 632.

569a. 376 US 254.

emerging from the English and United States decisions in their application to our legal system." Accordingly, the Court set out certain broad principles, keeping in mind the above considerations. Before stating these principles, it will be expedient to refer in brief the factual matrix in the context of which the Court evolved these principles.

In this case, the first petitioner who was the editor, printer and publisher of a weekly magazine, intended to publish the autobiography of a condemned prisoner. The autobiography sets out the close nexus between the condemned prisoner and several IAS, IPS and other officers. Before commencing the serial publication of the autobiography in the magazine, petitioner announced that the magazine would be coming out with the sensational life history of the condemned prisoner.

The State brought an action for injunction. On the issue whether the State could maintain an action for injunction and whether public officers who apprehended that they may be defamed can also seek an injunction and what were the rights of the parties, the Hon'ble Supreme Court summarized the legal position in India as under:

(1) The right to privacy is implicit in the right to life and liberty guaranteed to the citizens of this country by Article 21. It is a "right to be let alone". A citizen has a right to safeguard the privacy of his own, his family, marriage, procreation, motherhood, child-bearing and education among other matters. None can publish anything concerning the above matters without his consent whether truthful or otherwise and whether laudatory or critical. If he does so, he would be violating the right to privacy of the person concerned and would be liable in an action for damages. Position may, however, be different, if a person voluntarily thrusts himself into controversy or voluntarily invites or raises a controversy.

(2) The rule aforesaid is subject to the exception, that any publication concerning the aforesaid aspects becomes unobjectionable if such publication is based upon public records including Court records. This is for the

reason that once a matter becomes a matter of public record, the right to privacy no longer subsists and it becomes a legitimate subject for comment by press and media among others. We are, however, of the opinion that in the interests of decency (Article 19(2)) an exception must be carved out to this rule, viz., a female who is the victim of a sexual assault, kidnap, abduction or a like offence should not further be subjected to the indignity of her name and the incident being publicized in press/media.

(3) There is yet another exception to the rule in (1) above-indeed; this is not an exception but an independent rule. In the case of public officials, it is obvious, right to privacy, or for that matter, the remedy of action for damages is simply not available with respect to their acts and conduct relevant to the discharge of their official duties. This is so even where the publication is based upon facts and statements which are not true, unless the official establishes that the publication was made (by the defendant) with reckless disregard for truth. In such a case, it would be enough for the defendant (member of the press or media) to prove that he acted after a reasonable verification of the facts; it is not necessary for him to prove that what he has written is true. Of course, where the publication is proved to be false and actuated by malice or personal animosity, the defendant would have no defence and would be liable for damages. It is equally obvious that in matters not relevant to the discharge of his duties, the public official enjoys the same protection as any other citizen, as explained in (1) and (2) above. It needs no reitration that judicially, which is protected by the power to punish for contempt of Court and Parliament and Legislatures protected as their privileges are by Articles 105 and 194 respectively of the Constitution of India, represents exception to this rule.

(4) So far as the Government, local authority and other organs and institutions exercising governmental power

are concerned, they cannot maintain a suit for damages for defaming them.

(5) Rules 3 and 4 do not, however, mean that Official Secrets Act, 1923 or any similar enactment or provision having the force of law does not bind the press or media.

(6) There is no law empowering the State or its officials to prohibit or to impose a prior restraint upon the press/media.

Following observations in the decision in *Sullivan's* case[569b] was noted and relied upon by their Lordships of the Supreme Court:

> Authoritative interpretations of the First Amendment guarantees have consistently refused to recognize an exception for any test of truth—whether administered by Judges, Juries or Adminstrative Officials—and especially one that puts the burden of proving the truth on the speaker.
>
> * * *
>
> A Rule compelling the critic of official conduct to guarantee the turth of all his factual assertions and to do so on pain of libel judgments virtually unlimited in amount—leads to..."self-censorship". Allowance of the defence of truth, with the burden of proving it on the defendant, does not mean that only false speech will be deterred. Even Courts accepting this defence as an adequate safeguard recognized the difficulties of adducing legal proofs that the alleged libel was true in all its factual particulars.... Under such a rule, would be critics of official conduct may be deterred from voicing their criticism, even though it is believed to be true and even though in fact true, because of doubt whether it can be proved in Court or fear of the expense of having to do so. They tend to make only statements which 'steer far wider of the unlawful zone'.... The rule thus dampens the vigor and limits the variety of public debate. It is inconsistent with the First and Fourteenth Amendments.

569b. *New York Times Company* v. *Sullivan*, 376 US 254.

> The constitutional guarantees require, we think, a federal rule that prohibits a public official from recovering damages for a defamatory falsehood relating to his official conduct unless he proves that the statements was made with 'actual malice'—that is, with knowledge that it was false or with reckless disregard of whether it was false or not.

A word on the issue of fair comment. The expession is a misnomer in the context it is used. Law does not necessarily require that the comment be reasonable or fair in the ordinary sense. Law requires the opinion to be honestly held. If a fact alleged is true, it is bound to be a fair comment. If on a given fact a person forms an opinion which every ordinary man may possibly form, howsoever strong, exaggerated or prejudiced are the views expressed; it would be a case of fair comment.

In the decision reported as *Telnikoff* v. *Maturevitch*,[570] it was held that if the defendant can show as an objective matter that the opinion was one which could be honestly held, he does not have to prove that he in fact held it. Rather it is then for the claimant to prove as part of his allegation of malice that the defendant did not in fact honestly hold the view.

In *Broadway Approvals Ltd., and Another* v. *Odhams Press Ltd. and Another*,[571] it was held that an honest and fair expression of opinion on a matter of public interest is not actionable even though it may be untrue and not established at a trial.

In the opinion of Lord Nicholls sitting as a Judge of the Court of Final Appeal of Hongkong in *Tsc Wai Paul* v. *Chang*,[572] it was held:

> To summarise in my view a comment which falls within objective limits of the evidence of fair comment can loose its immunity only by proof that the defendant did not genuinely hold the view that he expressed. Honesty of the belief is the touchstone.

---

570. (1991) 4 All ER 817.
571. (1965) 2 All ER 523.
572. (2001) EMLR 777.

To succeed in a plea of fair comment, the defendant must establish that the statement was a comment and not a fact. Thereafter, the defendant must establish that the comment had a sufficient factual basis (i.e. the comment must be based on facts which are themselves sufficiently true). He must additionally establish that the comment was one, which an honest person could hold (this is an objecive test, not to be confused with reasonableness). And finally, that the subject-matter of the comment was in public interest.

Whether the statement is a fact or a comment can be a very difficult distinction as invariably the two are mixed up. A guiding principal could be culled from the decision reported as *Clarke* v. *Norlon*,[573] wherein it was observed:

> More accurately it has been said that the success of comment is something which is or can be reasonably be inferred to be a deduction, inference, conclusion, criticism, remark, observation etc.

Defamation is a public communication which tends to injure the reputation of another. What statements are defamatory and the span of defences varies from jurisdiction to jurisdiction but there is common agreement in all jurisdictions that statements that are unflattering, annoying, irksome, embarrassing or hurt one's feelings are not actionable. Common element in all jurisdictions is the potential to injure the reputation.

Since law of defamation, by making actionable certain utterances, runs counter to another widely accepted legal tenet—the right to freedom of expression, the two have been harmonized by judicial process so that an individual's right of privacy and protection of honour and reputation is preserved and at the same time the public interest in free speech is also protected.

The pendulum between reputation and expression has swung back and forth through history, but a body of positive jurisprudence evidenced by the decision in *Sullivan's* case[574] has developed. However, the case law developed around political

---

573. (1910) VLR 494.

574. *New York Times Company* v. *Sullivan*, 376 US 254.

speeches may be noted. The aim of the law was to see that there was no chilling effect. If a person is under a fear of being sued, he may not express himself freely on public issues and this would chill the public debate. Decision in *Sullivan's* case as followed by the Supreme Court of India in *R. Rajagopal's* case[575] highlighted that Government nor Government Officials, if criticized in discharge of their duties, could bring no action for injunction and could not chill a public debate. Subject to establishing actual malice, action could be brought by Government official if his personal reputation was damaged. However, no action could be brought in relation to loss of reputation to the office.

Traditional defences to an action for defamation have now become fairly crystallized and can be compartmentalized in three compartments: truth, fair comment and privilege. Truth, or justification, is a complete defence. The standard of proof of truth is not absolute but is limited to establishing that what was spoken was 'substantially correct'. Fair comment offers protection for the expression of opinions. Standard of proof is not that the Court has to agree with the opinion, but is limited to determine whether the views could honestly have been held by a fair-minded person on facts known at the time. Unlike defence of truth, defence based on fair comment can be defeated if the plaintiff proves that the defamer acted with malice. Similar is the situation whether the defence is of qualified privilege. Privilege is designed to protect expression made for the public good. Protection of qualified privilege is lost if actual malice is established. In public interest, absolute privilege is a complete defence. Rationale of absolute privilege being restricted to Court proceedings or proceedings before Tribunals which have all the trappings of a Civil Court and Parliamentary proceedings is that if threat of defamation suits loom large over the head of lawyers, litigants, witnesses, Judges and Parliamentarians it would prohibit them from speaking freely and public interest would suffer.

---

575. AIR 1995 SC 264: (1994) 6 SCC 632.

Conditions for Applicability of the Section

Bare reading of this section reveals that before it is invoked it must be shown that (a) civil or criminal proceedings have been launched against the applicant on the basis of the statement made by the defendant/accused in the course of giving his evidence before the Commission; (b) the statement was made in reply to a question which he was required to answer by the Commission; and (c) such statement was relevant to the subject-matter of the inquiry. If these conditions are not fulfilled, the protective umbrella provided under this section cannot be availed. Further, this protection is also not available against the prosecution of such witness for giving false evidence.[576]

This section applies only to statements made in reply to a question which a person was required by the Commission to answer or which were relevant to the subject-matter of the enquiry. The remaining provisions of the section may be analyzed as containing three propositions, viz.:

(1) No statement made by a person in the course of the evidence given by him shall subject him to any civil or criminal proceeding.

(2) No statement made by a person in the course of giving evidence before the Commission shall be used against him in any civil or criminal proceeding.

(3) Notwithstanding these two propositions, the person making the statement was liable to prosecution for giving false evidence by such statement.[577]

Where averments made in the plaint clearly revealed that the cause of action was being claimed by the plaintiff against the defendant on the basis of the "written submission" filed by the defendant before the Commission and not on the basis of the statement made by the defendant during the course of his evidence before the Commission and there was nothing record to show that the written submissions were filed by the defendant

576. *Ram Jethmalani* v. *Subramaniam Swamy*, AIR 2006 Delhi 300, p. 306.

577. *The State of Maharashtra* v. *Ibrahim Mohd. Hussein Maddu and Others*, 1978 Cri.L.J. 1157.

in reply to any question by the Commission which the defendant was bound to answer and that the offending portion of the written submission against the plaintiff was in any way relevant to the inquiry before the Commission, it was held, in an action for damages for libel, the basic ingredients for the applicability of Section 6 of the Act were not fulfilled.[578]

Nature of Protection under the Section

Section 6 gives protection to persons making statements before the Commission in reply to questions asked by the Commission or relevant to the matter of enquiry, so that the persons making the statements will state the truth, the whole truth and nothing but the truth before the Commission, unhampered by any fear, that they would thereby render themselves liable to civil or criminal proceedings or to some prejudice or detriment as a result of the statements made before the Commission.[579]

Section 6 is, thus, intended to encourage people to come forth and give evidence before a Commission without being apprehensive of civil or criminal liability because of their giving evidence before a Commission. This section lays down that no statement made by a person in the course of giving evidence before the Commission shall subject him to or be used against him in any civil or criminal proceedings. It, however, envisages a limited prosecution for giving false evidence. That apart, the consequences of any statement made before the Commission are far more perilous than civil or criminal proceedings. It may result in public condemnation "without trial, without appeal and without redress". The Royal Commission in its report on Tribunals of Inquiry, 1966 observed:[580]

> It is true that a Tribunal does not hold a trial but only investigates and reports. Nevertheless reputation and careers

578. *Ram Jethmalani* v. *Subramaniam Swamy*, AIR 2006 Delhi 300, p. 307.

579. *The State of Maharashtra* v. *Ibrahim Mohd. Hussein Maddu and Others*, 1978 Cri.L.J. 1157.

580. Para 39.

may depend upon their findings, e.g. in the Budget Leak Tribunal which was held in public, the Tribunal found that there had been an unauthorized disclosure by Mr. J.H. Thomas to Sir Alfred Butt of information relating to the budget and that use was made by Sir Alfred Butt of that information for private gain; thus ended both their political careers.

The publicity however which such hearings usually attract is so wide and so overwhelming that it would be virtually impossible for any person against whom an adverse finding was made to obtain a fair trial afterwards.

There in U.K., such Tribunals are set up upon a resolution of both Houses of Parliament and so far no person has been prosecuted upon their findings and yet the Commission advised that because of the inquisitorial nature of the proceedings and consequent pain which they may cause to individuals, Tribunal should be set up as sparingly as possible.[581]

But, here in India, Commissions are galore; their findings do hardly end anybody's public career. Prosecutions are launched as easily as they are withdrawn.[582]

The question for consideration is whether the words "no statement shall be used against him in any civil or criminal proceedings" can be interpreted to mean that the statement cannot be used for any purpose whatever except the one mentioned in Section 6. There is difference of opinion among Courts on this aspect. In *Sohanlal* v. *State*,[583] a single Judge of the Bombay High Court observed that, in the first place, if it was the object of the Legislature that the statement of a person made before a Commission should not be used for any purpose whatever in a subsequent civil or criminal proceeding, the Legislature could have said so clearly. The very fact that the Legislature has not chosen to say so is very significant. The

581. Para 64.

582. *(Mr.) Bansi Lal* v. *State*, ILR (1981) I Delhi 715, p. 728.

583. AIR 1965 Bombay 1: 1964 Maharashtra LJ 525.

material words are "against him". The question for consideration is whether the use of a statement made before a Commission as an earlier statement to contradict a later statement, as provided for by Section 145 of the Evidence Act, would amount to a "use against the person making the said statement." When a statement made by a witness before a Commission is used as an earlier statement for contradicting the witness under Section 145 of the Evidence Act, it cannot be said that such use is against him. The purpose of using an earlier statement under Section 145 of the Evidence Act is to show that the witness is unreliable and that the Court should not believe him. Such use under Section 145 of the Evidence Act, does not amount to "use against the witness", as contemplated by Section 6 of the Commissions of Inquiry Act, 1952. The use of an earlier statement before a Commission for the purpose mentioned in Section 145 of the Evidence Act, would be helpful to a Court which has to decide whether the witness concerned should be believed or not. In enacting Section 6 of the Act, the Legislature could not possibly intend to lay down that a statement of a witness made before a Commission could never subsequently be shown to be inaccurate, wrong or false, except in a prosecution against that witness mentioned in the said section. The expression "No statement...shall subject him to" clearly indicates that a statement made before a Commission could not be made the basis of a civil or criminal proceeding against the person making that statement, i.e. no civil or criminal liability could arise out of such statement, the only exception being the one mentioned in Section 6 itself. The latter part, viz. "No statement...shall be used against him" only lays down that in any other civil or criminal proceeding the statement, even though not the sole basis of that proceeding, shall not be used so as to fasten any civil or criminal liability on the person making the statement, of course, subject to the exception mentioned in Section 6. Dreading Section 6 as a whole, it is clear "that it merely lays down that a statement made by a person before a Commission would not expose the person making that statement to any civil or criminal action, which would render him liable on account of that statement, subject to the only exception mentioned in that section. Thus, the statements made by the prosecution witnesses before the Commission, can be used by the defence for the purpose mentioned in Section 145 of the Evidence Act.[584]

On the other hand, a different view was taken in *Puhupram* v. *State of Madhya Pradesh*.[585] The observations made by a Division Bench in this regard may be usefully referred to, viz. "The language of Section 6 is plain enough to show that no statement made by a person before a Commission of Inquiry can subject him to, or be used against him in, any civil or criminal proceeding except in a prosecution for giving false evidence before the Commission. In the case of *Ram Krishna Dalmia*,[586] the Supreme Court has observed that 'the statement made by any person before the Commission of Inquiry is, under Section 6 of the Act, wholly inadmissible in evidence in any future proceedings, civil or criminal' (underlining is ours). We are aware of a decision of a learned single Judge of the Bombay High Court in *Sohanlal* v. *State*[587] holding that where incidents in respect of which the accused are being prosecuted in a criminal trial have been the subject-matter of an inquiry by a Commission of Inquiry appointed under the Act, the statements made by the prosecution witnesses before the Commission can be used by the defence for the purpose mentioned in Section 145 of the Evidence Act, 1872. The learned single Judge took the view that such a use of the statements for the purposes of Section 145 of the Evidence Act does not constitute use of the statements against the person making the statement. With all due deference to the learned single Judge, we do not find ourselves in agreement with this view especially in view of the observations of the Supreme Court in *Ram Krishna Dalmia's* case[588] that statements under Section 6 of the Act are wholly inadmissible in evidence in any future proceeding, civil or criminal. It is not necessary for the petitioners to participate in the inquiry held by the Commission

584. *Sohanlal Pahladraj Vaid* v. *State*, AIR 1965 Bombay 1.

585. 1968 MPLJ 629.

586. AIR 1958 SC 538, p. 544.

587. AIR 1965 Bombay 1.

588. AIR 1958 SC 538.

if they think that their participation will prejudice the criminal trial. No doubt, the Commission has the power of summoning and enforcing the attendance of any person. But it is reasonable to think that the Commission, constituted as it is by one of the Judges of this Court, will not compel the petitioners or any of the persons standing trial to give evidence and, thus, will not give a chance to them to complain that they have been prejudiced in the criminal trial by being forced to give evidence before the Commission."[589]

The Bombay High Court reiterated its earlier view in the case of *State of Maharashtra* v. *Mohd. Hussein Maddu*[590] wherein the case of *Puhupram* v. *State of Madhya Pradesh*[591] was noted but distinguished for the reason that the decision of Madhya Pradesh High Court in that case was obiter. In that case, it was pointed out, the Court was not called upon to decide the question as to whether a statement made before the Commission could be used in the cross-examination of the prosecution witnesses. That was a case in which the petitioners applied to the High Court for stay of the enquiry against them before the Commission till the conclusion of criminal cases instituted against them in respect of offences under Sections 148, 149, 120B and 302, I.P.C. during the pendency of the enquiry before the Commission. One of the apprehensions of the petitioners was that they would be compelled to make statements, which would be made use of against them in the criminal case which necessarily is a contest between the accused and the State. The Division Bench observed as follows:[592]

> It is not necessary for the petitioners to participate in the inquiry held by the Commission if they think that their participation will prejudice the criminal trial. No doubt, the Commission has the power of summoning and enforcing the attendance of any person. But it is reasonable to think

---

589. *Puhupram* v. *State of Madhya Pradesh*, 1968 MPLJ 629, p. 632.

590. 1978 Cri.L.J. 1157.

591. 1968 MPLJ 629.

592. *Ibid.*, p. 632.

> that the Commission, constituted as it is by one of the Judges of this Court, will not compel the petitioners or any of the persons standing trial to give evidence and thus will not give a chance to them to complain that they have been prejudiced in the criminal trial by being forced to give evidence before the Commission.

The Bombay High Court agreed with the above observations of the Madhay Pradesh High Court, as they were concerned with the possible use of the statements made by the petitioners-accused against the accused. They rightly held, the Bombay High Court observed, that the use of such statements in the criminal case against the petitioners must be barred under Section 6 of the Act. But the bar could not be extended to the use of such statements for the purposes of cross-examination under Section 145 of the Evidence Act. The Bombay High Court very aptly illustrated the import of Section 6 of the Act in the following words:

> The first rule in Section 6 prohibits a suit being filed against a person, say X, who may have made a statement before the Commission "I burnt the house of A". A cannot file a suit against such person relying on that statement before the Commission. A also cannot file a suit for damages against the person without making use of the statement and then produce such a statement under S. 145 in the suit, as the use of such a statement would be 'against' the person within the meaning of S. 6. The Parliament never intended, in our opinion, to bar such statements being produced by way of cross-examining under S. 145 the person making the statements, if at all such statements are relevant or otherwise admissible. The bar is only to prevent use of statement to support some claim against him. There is no bar to the use of such statements in proceedings against third persons in which such person is examined as a witness as in the present case before us. The very fact that the third rule in S. 6 permits prosecution of such person for giving false evidence by making such statement before the Commission, manifestly indicates that the whole purpose of enacting S. 6 was to enable the person making the statement before the

Commission to be unhampered by any adverse pending or impending or likely civil or criminal proceedings against himself, or by proceedings in which he was likely to be prejudiced in some manner other than prosecution for giving false evidence when making such statement before the Commission.

The Court further observed:

Whether a particular statement made by a witness before the Commission is used "against him" will depend on the prejudice or detriment caused or likely to cause to the person in civil or criminal proceedings or otherwise. It must, therefore, necessarily depend on the facts and circumstances relating to the use or intended use. Whether any particular prejudice or detriment can be said to result from the use of the statements will also depend on facts. Mere cross-examination under S. 145 can at the most expose this statement. That does not render the use of the statement "against him" in law because law requires him to tell the truth, the whole truth and nothing but the truth before the Commission also and implies that he will be prosecuted for perjury if he tells lies.

Accordingly, the Court held that "the bar under the said words (i.e. "against him") can apply only when there is some sort of legal contest between the witness to whom the statement is intended to be put under S. 145 and some other person in civil or criminal proceedings (other than proceedings against the witness for perjury committed by such statements) which may result in some detriment or prejudice to the witness in such proceedings, pending or impending. The bar cannot be attracted in a case of using the statement under S. 145 for contradicting the witness and thereby discrediting his veracity. Private interest of a person in the witness box to be not discredited must be overridden by the public interest in discovering the truth in a Court of Justice."

The judgment of the Bombay High Court in State of *Maharashtra* v. *Ibrahim Mohd. Hussein Maddu*[593] was followed

593. 1978 Cri.L.J. 1157.

by Gauhati High Court in *State of Assam* v. *Suprabhat Bhadra*.[594] In this case, the Court accordingly held that "Section 6 of the Act does not inhibit use of the statement made by a witness before a Commission in a subsequent civil, criminal or other proceeding for the purpose of contradicting the witness. The use of the statement for corroboration is not visualized by Section 145 of the Evidence Act, but if any other statute permits it, Section 6 of the Act does not stand in the way. The statement would not, however, be usable against the witness in any prosecution of perjury for having given false evidence in the subsequent proceeding."[595]

In this regard, the following observations made by Kerala High Court in *Natarajan Narayana Kurup* v. *The State*,[596] may also be referred to, viz.:

> There is nothing in S. 6 which prohibits the use of statements made before the Commission of Inquiry to contradict or discredit the witness in any subsequent proceedings. A previous statement when used to contradict a witness under S. 145 of the Evidence Act, unlike an admission does not become substantive evidence but merely serves the purpose of throwing doubt on his veracity. Such use will not subject the concerned person to any civil or criminal proceeding except a prosecution for giving false evidence. Section 8B which was incorporated in 1971 reinforces the conclusion that S. 6 bars the use of statements made by a person before the Commission only in civil or criminal proceedings involving that person and does not bar their use for impeaching the credibility of a person in a proceeding wherein he figures as a witness. As the bar under S. 6 does not extend to the use of such statements to impeach the creditability of the witnesses as provided in S. 145 of the Evidence Act, the creditability of those witnesses that had appeared before the Commission earlier has to be decided taking into account

594. 1982 Cri.L.J. 1672.

595. *Ibid.*, pp. 1674-75.

596. 1982 Cri.L.J. NOC 69 (Ker).

the conflicting stand taken by them before the Commission of Inquiry.

This aspect can be said to have been finally settled by the Hon'ble Supreme Court in *Kehar Singh* v. *State*.[597] In order to have better appreciation and understanding of the subject, it will be useful to refer the relevant extracts of the judgment as follows:

> On analysis of the provision, it will be found that there are restrictions on the use of a statement made by a witness before the Commission. First is "shall subject him to...any civil or criminal proceedings except a prosecution for giving false evidence by such statement". This, in my opinion, is the first restriction. The second restriction, according to me, is spelt out from the words "or be used against him in any civil or criminal proceedings". Thus if we examine the two restrictions stated above it appears that a statement given in a Commission cannot be used to subject the witness to any civil or criminal proceedings nor it can be used against him in any civil or criminal proceedings and in my opinion it is in the context of these restrictions that we will have to examine the provisions of the Evidence Act which permit the use of a previous statement of a witness and for what purpose. Section 145 read with S. 155(3) and S. 157 are the relevant provisions of the Evidence Act. S. 145 reads:
>
> Cross-examination as to previous statements in writing.—A witness may be cross examined as to previous statements made by him in writing or reduced into writing and relevant to matters in question, without such writing being shown to him, or being proved; but if it is intended to contradict him by the writing, his attention must, before the writing can be proved, be called to these parts of it which are to be used for the purpose of contradicting him.

This provision permits that a witness may be cross-examined as to the previous statement made by him in writing or reduced to writing relevant to the matters in question without such

597. (1988) 3 SCC 609: AIR 1988 SC 1883.

writing being shown to him or being proved. But if it is intended to contradict him by the writing his attention must be drawn to these parts of the writing, and it can be proved. A witness could be cross-examined on the previous statement but if a contradiction is sought to be proved then that portion of the previous statement must be shown to him and proved in due course.

Section 155 of the Evidence Act provides for the use of a previous statement to impeach the credit of a witness. Section 155 reads:

> 155. Impeaching credit of witness—The credit of a witness may be impeached in the following ways by the adverse party or, with the consent of the Court, by the party who calls him:
>
> (1) by the evidence of persons who testify that they, from their knowledge of the witness, believe, to be unworthy of credit;
>
> (2) by proof that the witness has been bribed, or has (accepted) the offer of a bribe, or has received any other corrupt inducement to give his evidence;
>
> (3) by proof of former statements inconsistent with any part of this evidence which is liable to be contradicted;
>
> (4) when a man is prosecuted for rape or an attempt to ravish, it may be shown that the prosecutrix was of generally immoral character.

This section provides that the credit of a witness may be impeached in the following ways by an adverse party with the consent of the Court by the party who calls him and the third sub-clause refers to a former statement which is inconsistent with the statement made by the witness in evidence in the case and it is permissible that the witness be contradicted about that statement. The third provision is Section 157, which provides for the use of a previous statement for corroboration. It reads:

> 157. Former statements of witness may be proved to corroborate later testimony as to same fact. In order to corroborate the testimony of a witness, any former statement

made by such witness relating to the same fact, at or about the time when the fact took place, or before any authority legally competent to investigate the fact, may be proved.

A perusal of these three sections clearly indicates that there are two purposes for which a previous statement can be used. One is for cross-examination and contradiction and the other is for corroboration. The first purpose is to discredit the witness by putting to him the earlier statement and contradicting him on that basis. So far as corroboration is concerned it could not be disputed that it is none of the purposes of the defence to corroborate the evidence on the basis of the previous statement. Section 145, therefore, is the main section under which relief was sought by the accused. The use for which the previous statement was asked for was to contradict him if necessary and if it was a contradiction then the earlier statement was necessary so that the contradiction be put to the witness and that part of the statement can be proved.

To my mind, there could be no other purpose for which the appellants could use the previous statements of those witnesses. Contradiction could be used either to impeach his credit or discredit him or to pull down or bring down the reliability of the witness. These purposes for which the previous statements are required could not be said to be purposes, which were not against the witnesses. The two aspects of the restrictions, which Section 6 contemplates and have been discussed earlier, are the only two aspects which could be the result of the use of these statements. I cannot find any other use of such previous statements in criminal proceedings. It is, therefore, clear that without going into the wider questions even a plain reading of Section 6 as discussed above will prohibit the use of the previous statements at the trial either for the purposes of cross examination to contradict the witness or to impeach his credit. The only permissible use, which has been provided under Section 6, which has been discussed earlier and, therefore, the Courts below were right in not granting the relief to the accused.

The report of the Commission was also prayed for although learned counsel could not clearly suggest as to what use report of the Thakkar Commission could be to the accused in his defence. The report is a recommendation of the Commission for consideration of the Government. It is the opinion of the Commission based on the statements of witnesses and other material. It has no evidentiary value in the trial of the criminal case. The Courts below were also justified in not summoning the reports.[598]

Protection under Article 20(3)

Section 6 gives the immunity, which is complete to the statements made by any person while giving evidence before the Commission. Section 6, however, does not cover the case of production of an incriminating document and gives no immunity with regard to the same. Section 6 of the Act will be operative only after a statement has been made or a document has been produced. But the inhibition in Article 20(3) of the Constitution of India against testimonial compulsion extends to the very first stage and the person accused of an offence cannot be compelled to state a fact or produce a document, which may tend to incriminate him. The moment such compulsion is exercised he can claim the immunity. Article 20(3) is in the following terms: "No person accused of any offence shall be compelled to be a witness against himself." The question in this regard is whether Article 20(3) of the Constitution can or cannot be invoked by the witnesses who are examined by the Commission. The question has been answered in the negative by the Andhra Pradesh High Court in *Suryanarayana* v. *Vijaya Commercial Bank Ltd.*,[599] wherein it has been held that the immunity granted by Article 20(3) does not extend to civil proceedings. In a subsequent decision of a Division Bench of the Calcutta High Court, *Collector of Customs* v. *Calcutta Motor and Cycle Co.*,[600] it has been laid down that the protection afforded by Article 20(3) is available to a person accused of an offence not merely with respect to the evidence to be given in the Courtroom in the

---

598. *Kehar Singh and Others* v. *The State (Delhi Admin.)*, AIR 1988 SC 1883, pp. 1901-02: (1988) 3SCC 609, pp. 645-47.

599. AIR 1958 AP 756.

600. AIR 1958 Calcutta 682.

course of a trial but also at previous stages, if a formal accusation had been made of the commission of an offence which might in the normal course result in prosecution. In coming to this conclusion, the Division Bench referred to and relied to a great extent on the decision in *M.P. Sharma* v. *Satish Chandra*[601] wherein Jagannadhadas J. observed as follows: "Analysing the terms in which this right has been declared in our Constitution, it may be said to consist of the following components: (1) It is a right pertaining to a person "accused of an offence"; (2) It is a protection against "compulsion to be a witness"; and (3) It is a protection against such compulsion resulting in his giving evidence "against himself".... Broadly stated the guarantee in Article 20(3) is against "testimonial compulsion". It is suggested that this is confined to the oral evidence of a person standing his trial for an offence when called to the witness-stand. We can see no reason to confine the content of the constitutional guarantee to this barely literal import. So to limit it would be to rob the guarantee of its substantial purpose and to miss the substance for the sound as stated in certain American decisions.... Considered in this light, the guarantee under Article 20(3) would be available in the present cases to these petitioners against whom a First Information Report has been recorded as accused therein. It would extend to any compulsory process for the production of evidentiary documents which are reasonably likely to support a prosecution against them."[602] It was held, however, that the searches, which had been ordered, did not attract the immunity granted by Article 20(3) as that were not tantamount to compelled production within the meaning of Article 20(3).

In *M/s Allen Berry and Co. Private Ltd. and Another* v. *Vivian Bose and Others,*[603] a Division Bench of the Punjab High Court concurred with the views of the Calcutta High Court on this question. In this case, the Court, inter alia, has observed that although the immunity under the Constitution is complete but under Section 6 of the Act it is a limited and narrow one.

---

601. AIR 1954 SC 300: 1954 SCR 1077.

602. *Ibid*., pp. 303-04.

603. AIR 1960 Punjab 86.

The inhibition in Article 20(3) is a part of the fundamental rights. It extends to the very first stage and the person accused of an offence cannot be compelled to state a fact or produce a document, which may tend to incriminate him. The moment such compulsion is exercised he can claim the immunity. Section 6 will merely render his statement immune but will not afford protection against such compulsion to give self-incriminating answers or to produce self-incriminating documents. For these reasons it is not possible to accede to proposition that the immunity under Section 6 of the Act is co-extensive with the one under Article 20(3) of the Constitution and was a complete substitute for the prohibition enjoined by Article 20(3). The Court further held that witnesses who appear before it if and when the occasion arises could invoke Article 20(3) in the proceedings before the Commission.

"Against"—Needs to be Liberally Construed

Having regard to the broader object underlying the Commissions of Inquiry Act, 1952, that is to say, to inform the mind of the appropriate Government of the true facts through the instrumentality of the Commissions' reports and also the purpose of providing protection under Section 6 to persons appearing before the Commissions appointed under the Act to ensure that they speak the truth, it will be proper and necessary to liberally construe the word "against" in that section so as to further, rather than hamper, the realization of these object and purpose.

The Act gives power to the Commissions appointed thereunder to regulate their own procedure and also to decide whether to sit in camera or in public. A Commission appointed under the Act does not decide any dispute. There are no parties before the Commission. There is no lis. The Commission is not a Court except for a limited purpose. The procedure of the Commission is inquisitorial rather than accusatorial. The Commission more often may have to give assurance to persons giving evidence before it that their statements will not be used in any subsequent proceedings except for perjury. Without such an assurance, the persons may not come forward to give statements. If persons have got lurking fear that their statements given before the Commission are likely to be used against them or utilized for productive use on them in any other proceeding, they may be reluctant to expose themselves before the Commission. Then the Commission would not be able to perform its task. The Commission would not be able to reach the nuggests of truth from the obscure horizon. The purpose for which the Commission is constituted may be defeated.

The Court should avoid such construction to Section 6 which may stultify the purpose of the Act. Section 6 must on the other hand, receive liberal construction so that the person deposing before the Commission may get complete immunity except in a case of prosecution for perjury. That is possible if the word "against" used in Section 6 is properly understood. The meaning given in Black's Law Dictionary[604] supports such construction:

> "Against—Adverse to, contrary.... Sometimes meaning 'Upon', which is almost synonymous with word 'on'...."

Apart from that, it may also be noted that Section 6 contains only one exception. That is prosecution for giving false evidence by such statement. When the Legislature has expressly provided a singular exception to the provisions, it has to be normally understood that other exceptions are ruled out.

This view gets confirmation from the report of the Royal Commission on Tribunals of Inquiry (1966). It will be useful to refer to the relevant provisions of the English statutes, which are not materially dissimilar to our Act. There are two English statutes, which may be looked into in this regard, namely, (i) The Special Commission Act, 1888; and (ii) The Tribunals of Inquiry (Evidence) Act, 1921.

Section 9 of the Special Commission Act, 1988 provides:

> 9—A witness examined under this Act shall not be excused from answering any question put to him on the ground of any privilege or on the ground that the answer thereto may criminate or tend to criminate himself. <u>Provided that no evidence taken under this Act shall be admissible against any</u>

604. Page 57.

> person in any civil or criminal proceeding except in the case of a witness accused of having given false evidence in any inquiry under this Act...." (Emphasis supplied)

Section 1(3) of the Tribunals of Inquiry (Evidence) Act, 1921, provides:

> A witness before any such tribunal shall be entitled to the same immunities and privileges as if he were a witness before the High Court or the Court of Session.

Section 9 of the Special Commission Act, 1888 protects the witness in every respect except in a prosecution for giving false evidence by such statement. It provides that the evidence given by him shall be inadmissible in any civil or criminal proceedings. Section 1(3) of the Tribunals of Inquiry (Evidence) Act, 1921 provides only a limited or partial immunity to a witness. It is similar to the immunity afforded to a witness before the High Court or the Court of Session.

In 1966, the Royal Commission on Tribunals of Inquiry was constituted under the Chairmanship of the Rt. Hon'ble Lord Justice Salmon. The Commission was appointed to review the working of the Tribunals of Inquiry (Evidence) Act, 1921, and to consider whether it should be retained or replaced by some other provision. The Commission was also authorized to suggest any changes in the Act as are necessary or desirable; and to make recommendations. The Royal Commission in its report[605] recommended:

> (vii) Further Immunity:
>
> 63. Section 1(3) of the Act of 1921 provides that a witness before any Tribunal shall be entitled to the same immunities and privileges as if he were a witness before the High Court or the Court of Session. This means that he cannot be sued for anything he says in evidence e.g. if he says "A is a liar. His evidence is untrue." A cannot sue him for defamation. It does not mean however that his answer as a witness cannot be used in evidence against him in any subsequent civil or criminal proceedings. We consider the witnesses'

605. Para 63 of the Report.

> immunity should be extended so that neither his evidence before the Tribunal, nor his statement to the Treasury Solicitor, nor any documents he is required to produce to the Tribunal, shall be used against him in any subsequent civil or criminal proceedings except in criminal proceedings in which he is charged with having given false evidence before the Tribunal or conspired with or procured others to do so. This extension of the witness's immunity would bring the law in this country into line in this respect with similar provision in the legislation of Canada, Australia and India and indeed with S. 9 of the Special Commission Act, 1888. It would also, in our view, be of considerable assistance in obtaining relevant evidence, for persons may be chary of coming forward for fear of exposing themselves to the risk of prosecution or an action in the civil courts. Moreover, the suggested extension of the immunity would make it difficult for a witness to refuse to answer a question on the ground that his answer might tend to incriminate him. Thus not only would the witness be afforded a further measure of protection but the Tribunal would also be helped in arriving at the truth.

The Royal Commission appears to have thoroughly examined the provisions as to immunity to witnesses in the legislations of Canada, Australia and India and Section 9 of the Special Commission Act, 1888. The Commission has stated that the immunity provided to witnesses under Section 1(3) of the Act, 1921 is insufficient for the purpose of advancing the object of the Act. It should be extended so that the statement of a witness before the Tribunal shall not be used against him in any subsequent civil or criminal proceedings except in a prosecution for perjury by giving false evidence before the Tribunal. The extension of such immunity, according to the Royal Commission, would bring Section 1(3) of the Act, 1921 into line with the similar provisions in the legislations of Canada, Australia and India. The legislation in India is the Commissions of Inquiry Act, 1952. It is apparent that the Royal Commission was of opinion that Section 6 of Indian Act provides complete protection to witnesses in terms of Section 9 of the Special Commission Act, 1888. It means that the statement given before a Commission shall not be admissible against the person in any subsequent civil or criminal proceeding save for perjury.

There is, therefore, much to be said for the observation made in *Dalmia's* case[606] and indeed that is the proper construction to be attributed to the language of Section 6 of the Act. This view was affirmed and re-emphasised by the Supreme Court in the case of *Kehar Singh* v. *State (Delhi Administration).*[607] While doing so, the Supreme Court approved the case of *Puhupram* v. *State*[608] and overruled the decisions in *Sohanlal* v. *State,*[609] *State of Maharashtra* v. *Ibrahim Mohd*[610] and *State of Assam* v. *Suprabhat Bhadra.*[611]

[612]**[Persons not obliged to disclose secret process of manufacture of goods in certain cases.**

6A. Except in cases where a Commission is expressly required to inquire into the process of manufacture of any goods, nothing in this Act shall be deemed to compel any person giving evidence before the Commission to disclose any secrete process of manufacture thereof.]

Objects and Reasons

This clause seeks to insert a new Section 6A in the Act. This new section provides, in the interest of trade, that nothing in the Act would render it compulsory for any person giving evidence before the Commission to disclose any secret process of manufacturing of any goods, except in cases where the Commission is expressly required to inquire into the process of manufacture of any goods (vide paragraph 32 of the Report).[613]

---

606. AIR 1958 SC 538.

607. AIR 1988 SC 1883, pp. 1946-48: (1988) 3 SCR 609, pp. 719-22.

608. 1968 MPLJ 629.

609. AIR 1965 Bom 1: 66 Bom LR 353: 1965 (1) CriLJ 10.

610. 1978 CriLJ 1157.

611. 1982 CriLJ 1672.

612. Ins. by Act 79 of 1971, Section 9.

613. Twenty-fourth Report of the Law Commission of India on the Commissions of Inquiry Act, 1952. Notes on Clauses, Clause 9, the Commissions of Inquiry (Amendment) Bill, 1971.

[614] [Commission to cease to exist when so notified.

7. (1) The appropriate Government may, by notification in the Official Gazette, declare that—

(a) a Commission (other than a Commission appointed in pursuance of a resolution passed by[615] (each House of Parliament or, as the case may be, the Legislature of the State) shall cease to exist, if it is of opinion that the continued existence of the Commission is unnecessary;

(b) a Commission appointed in pursuance of a resolution passed by [16](each House of Parliament or, as the case may be, the Legislature of the State) shall cease to exist if a resolution for the discontinuance of the Commission is passed by [16](each House of Parliament or, as the case may be, the Legislature of the State).

2. Every notification issued under sub-section (1) shall specify the date from which the Commission shall cease to exist and on the issue of such notification, the Commission shall cease to exist with effect from the date specified therein].

Objects and Reasons

In view of the recommendations of the Joint Committee to divest the Government of the power to discontinue a Commission of Inquiry before it has submitted its report, the clause seeks to amend Section 7 of the Act suitably so as to ensure that a Commission appointed in pursuant to a resolution by the House of People or the Legislative Assembly of a State, shall not cease to exist until a resolution for the discontinuance of the Commission has been passed by the House of the People or, as the case may be, the Legislative Assembly of the State.[616]

---

614. Subs. by Section 10, *ibid.*, for Section 7.

615. Subs. by Act 19 of 1990, Section 3.

616. Notes on Clauses, Clause 10, the Commissions of Inquiry (Amendment) Bill, 1971.

Nature and Applicability of the Section

Under Section 7(1)(a) of the Act, the Government has ample discretion to discontinue the inquiry if it is of opinion that continuance of the said inquiry is wholly unnecessary.

Section 3 of the Act enjoins the Government to specify the time within which a Commission has to submit its report. According to the section, a notification appointing the Commission should specify the functions and the time within which those functions should be performed and the Commission shall make the inquiry and perform the functions accordingly. If the Commission does not perform the functions within the time specified in the notification, the Commission cannot have the functions continued after the expiry of the period. In other words, on the expiry of the term the Commission automatically ceases to exist. Once the Commission ceases to exist by efflux (sic) of time there was no necessity for the Government to notify the cessation of the Commission under Section 7 of the Act. Section 7(1)(a) of the Act states that the appropriate Government may, by notification in the Official Gazette, declare that a Commission shall cease to exist, if it is of opinion that the continued existence of the Commission is unnecessary. Sub-section (2) of Section 7 of the Act provides that the notification should specify the date from which the Commission shall cease to exist. Notification under Section 7 of the Act is contemplated only in the case of a Commission, which is continued to exist. If the Commission had ceased to exist on the expiry of the term for which it is appointed, Section 7 of the Act cannot apply. In the case of a Commission which is having continued existence the Government needs to issue a notification under Section 7 of the Act declaring that it ceased to exist from a particular date. In other words, notification under Section 7 of the Act is not warranted in relation to a Commission, which is not having continued existence as in the case of the term of the Commission having expired. In *Jan Sangharsh Manch* v. *State of Gujarat*,[617] the term of the Commission expired on 30-6-1997. Since the Government has not extended its term, it automatically ceased

617. AIR 1998 Gujarat 133.

to exist with effect from 30-6-1997. The Commission did not continue to exist after 30-6-1997. In such a situation, there was no necessity for the Government to issue a notification under Section 7 of the Act on 2-9-1997. If any such notification is issued, it has only to be ignored.

In *State of Gujarat* v. *Consumer & Education Research Centre*,[618] the Government of Gujarat constituted an inquiry in 1979 commonly known as "Machu Dam II Inquiry" and appointed a sitting Judge of the High Court as the Commission of Inquiry. Subsequently, by the order impugned the inquiry was discontinued as the Government thought that it was wholly unnecessary. Reasons for this were stated in the notification. There was nothing on record to show any collateral considerations for issuing the impugned notification. The High Court did not find any factual mala fide for discontinuing the Commission but struck down the impugned order on the ground that it was tainted with legal malice. On appeal, the Supreme Court set aside the order of the High Court, as the Apex Court did not find any shred of legal malice in the order passed by the Government. Nor the Court saw any reason or justifiable cause to come to a finding that the order of the Government was influenced by collateral considerations.

Procedure to be followed by the Commission.

8. The Commission shall, subject to any rules that may be made in this behalf, have power to regulate its own procedure [including the fixing of places and times of its sittings and deciding whether to sit in public or in private].[619]

Objects and Reasons

Clause 11 seeks to make consequential amendment to Section 8 of the Act. Clause 12 seeks to insert three new Sections 8A, 8B and 8C of the Act. The new Section 8A provides that an inquiry shall not be interrupted by reason of any vacancy in, or change in the constitution of the Commission. Under new Section 8B, a Commission of Inquiry is required to give to every person,

---

618. AIR 1984 SC 652.

619. Certain words omitted by Section 11 of Act 79 of 1971.

whose conduct the Commission considers it necessary to inquire into, and to every person whose reputation, in the opinion of the Commission, is likely to be prejudicially affected by the inquiry, a reasonable opportunity of being heard in the inquiry and to produce evidence in his defence.

A new Section 8C confers on the appropriate Government and on persons whose conduct the Commission considers it necessary to inquiry into or whose reputation, in the opinion of the Commission is likely to be prejudicially affected by the inquiry, the right to cross-examine witnesses and to be represented before the Commission by a legal practitioner or, with the consent of the Commission, by any other person.[620]

Role of Government

In *Maneka Gandhi* v. *Union of India*,[621] the passport of the petitioner was impounded as the Central Government was of the opinion that the presence of the petitioner was likely to be required before the Commission of Inquiry that the Government had appointed. The petitioner challenged this on the ground, inter alia, that the passport could not be impounded on the basis of mere opinion of the Central Government as it was for the Commission of Inquiry, and not the Central Government, to decide whether presence of the petitioner was required or not. The Court found this argument without force and observed as follows:

> It is true that ultimately it is for the Commission of Inquiry to decide whether the presence of the petitioner is likely to be required in order to assist it in its fact finding mission, but the Central Government which has constituted the Commission of Inquiry and laid down its terms of reference would certainly be able to say with reasonable anticipation whether she is likely to be required by the Commission of Inquiry. Whether she is actually required would be for the Commission of Inquiry to decide, but whether she is likely

---

620. Notes on Clauses, Clauses 11 and 12, the Commissions of Inquiry (Amendment) Bill, 1971.

621. (1978) 1 SCC 248.

to be required can certainly be judged by the Central Government. When the Central Government appoints a Commission of Inquiry, it does not act in a vacuum. It is bound to have some material before it on the basis of which it comes to a decision that there is a definite matter of public importance which needs to be inquired into and appoints a Commission of Inquiry for that purpose. The Central Government would, therefore, be in a position to say whether the petitioner is likely to be required in connection with the proceeding before the Commission of Inquiry. It is possible that ultimately when the Commission of Inquiry proceeds further with the probe, it may find that the presence of the petitioner is not required, but before that it would only be in the stage of likelihood and that can legitimately to be left to the judgment of the Central Government.

Extent of Commission's Powers

Section 8 gives the Commission power to regulate its own procedure subject to any rules made under the Act. The Commission may, thus, decide its own procedure. But, while doing so, it cannot go behind the rules made under the Act. This section has, therefore, to be read in the light of such rules.[622]

The Commission of Inquiry, under Section 8 of the Act, has full power and jurisdiction to fix its own place of sittings. The Commission can pass fresh orders from time to time in different circumstances in regard to the place of sitting, etc. It is not possible to bind the Commission to fix its place of sitting at any particular place alone. The best course open to the affected persons would only be to approach the Commission itself in case of any difficulty.[623] The Court cannot issue mandamus to shift the venue. So far as the venue is concerned, it is the statutory power of the Commission/Committee of Inquiry under Section 8 to do so. No one can demand a venue of their choice

---

622. *State of Jammu and Kashmir* v. *Bakshi Gulam Mohammad*, AIR 1967 SC 11, p. 133.

623. *Sardar Malkeet Singh* v. *State of U.P.*, AIR 1993 Allahabad 343.

on the ground of Articles 14 and 21. This is clearly impressible in law.[624]

In *S.V. Purushothaman* v. *State of Kerala*,[625] the State Government passed an order[626] on 5-8-1982, whereunder Justice P. Narayana Pillai, a former Judge of Kerala High Court, was appointed as Commission. The terms and conditions of reference included, inter alia, the following clauses, viz.:

4. Venue of Sittings: The sittings of the Commission would be at the conference hall of the Inspection Bungalow of the Kerala State Electricity Board near Bharath Tourist Home, Eranakulam.
5. The Additional Advocate General is directed to be present at all the sittings of the Commission with the connected Government records of enquiry considered by the Commission to be relevant.
6. The Secretary, Kerala State Electricity Board is directed to be present at all the sittings of the Commission with the records of the Kerala State Electricity Board connected with the inquiry and considered to be relevant.

The petitioner took objection to the venue of the sitting of the Commission and the presence of the Additional Advocate General. The objection to the venue was that it was absolutely under the control of the counter-petitioner, the Minister for Electricity, and that he was afraid to attend the sittings of the Commission. According to him, it was unfair to so fix the venue, "when other suitable accommodations in Government buildings are available in plenty". He demurred to the presence of the Additional Advocate General for the reason that it was an unprecedented conduct on the part of the Government viewed in the light of the 'several commissions' appointed in the past "for making enquiries into similar allegations of misconduct and corruption against

624. *Kiran Bedi* v. *Delhi Administration*, 1989 (2) Delhi Lawyer 190.

625. AIR 1983 Kerala 118.

626. Ext. P-3.

Ministers and for other purposes". The Court did not find any substance in these grievances and observed as under.

Fixing of the venue of the Commission in the Conference Hall of the Inspection Bungalow of the Electricity Board will not in any way adversely affect a fair and proper inquiry by a Commission of the stature of the 3rd respondent. There is no reasonable basis for the petitioner to be apprehensive about that venue. Merely because the Commission holds its inquiry in the Conference Hall of the Inspection Bungalow of the Electricity Board, the place does not become insecure or unsafe either for the petitioner or for his witnesses. The allegation that the Minister and his men could have control over the place or intimidate the witnesses for the petitioner if the Commission holds the inquiry in that Conference Hall cannot be accepted without sufficient materials or evidence justifying such an apprehension. The petitioner would have it that the Government fixed the venue, without leaving it to the Commission to decide such venue after ascertaining the convenience of parties. I may point out in this connection that the order[627] passed by the Commission (and produced along with a memo by the Government Pleader on 13-10-1982) would indicate that the venue was so fixed on the basis of the desire expressed in that behalf by the Commission. The Commission has pointed out the reasons, which impelled it to fix such a venue having regard to the convenience of the parties participating in the inquiry. The reasons so given by the Commission are indeed weighty. Even otherwise, the unfounded apprehension on the part of the petitioner regarding the safety and security of himself and his witnesses is no ground whatever to quash the Government order.

The other reason put forward for quashing the Government order is the provision in Clause 5 of Ext. P-3. It may be noted that under that clause the Additional Advocate General was only directed to be present at the sitting of the Commission with the connected records of the inquiry

627. Ext. X-1.

considered by the Commission to be relevant. This stands in contradistinction to Clause 6 of that order whereunder the Secretary of the Board is to be present at the sitting of the Commission with the records of the Board connected with the inquiry and considered to be relevant. Under Clause 5 it is entirely for the Commission to consider the relevance of connected Government records for the inquiry. The Additional Advocate-General is only to be present, with the Government records so considered by the Commission to be relevant. Such mere presence of the Additional Advocate-General for the purpose of facilitating an easy and expeditious handing over of the Government records cannot in any way subvert the objective of the inquiry. If such a senior law officer is directed to be present at the inquiry for the purpose of passing over to the Commission such records as the Commission considered as relevant for the inquiry that would only aid the inquiry and expedite it. That can hardly be a reason for quashing the Government order.

Section 8 of the Act, thus, confers very wide powers on the Commission to regulate its own procedure and that is subject only to any rules made under Section 12 of the Act. The so-called Rules made by the Commission itself in exercise of its own powers under Section 8 of the Act are nothing but broad principles which the Commission has formulated for its own guidance and for the information of all concerned. These are not such hard and fast rules as cannot be varied or departed from by the Commission. Any departure from the so-called rules made by the Commission will not necessarily amount to illegality. Furthermore, where the Commission has reserved to itself the power to amplify the rules of procedure as it deemed fit, then changing the rules in itself is not violative of the principles of natural justice. The Court will not interfere in exercise of its extraordinary jurisdiction where the dispute between the parties is as to the stage at which inspection of documents is to be given and all that the petitioners want is that inspection of documents be given to the persons concerned after they had filed their statement of facts.[628]

628. *State of Rajasthan* v. *Justice B.P. Beri*, AIR 1968 77.

However, where the directions given by a Commission of Inquiry or the procedure followed by it is inconsistent with the normal principles, which should guide any Commission of Inquiry, the same are liable to be interfered with appropriately by the Court. In *Sarjerao Kondiba Sagar* v. *P.G. Karnik*,[629] a Commission of Inquiry was appointed to inquire into the incidents of violence leading to firing by the police and to determine whether the firing justified or not and whether excessive or otherwise. In the course of inquiry, a question arose as to who would lead the evidence first. The Commission directed that the parties who claimed that the firing was unnecessary or that it was excessive should lead their evidence first and that the officers who resorted to the firing will lead their evidence later on. These directions were challenged as being contrary to all established principles of natural justice and contrary to the intent and purpose of the inquiry directed to be held under the notification constituting the Commission. A Division Bench of the Bombay High Court observed: "The Commission of Inquiry has been ordered to be held for the main purpose of determination by the Commissioner about the question of the firing being justified or not and whether excessive or otherwise. The background of the inquiry is the fact of the incidents of violence having taken place and incidents of firing having taken place. In ordinary circumstances, in an inquiry of the above nature having regard to the Governmental and public interest, the first principle which may be noticed by any Commission of Inquiry would be that unless there was proper justification for the purpose firing cannot be undertaken by the police. Even when it is undertaken, it should be limited to the requirements of protection of public interest and it should not be excessive. Prima facie, all relevant facts justifying the resort to firing would be and should be within the knowledge of the officers involved in the incidenr and/or commencement of the firing. Ordinary public would be divided on this question. Some would support the case of the police and some would support the case of the other political parties. The main facts proving that the firing was justified and

629. AIR 1973 Bombay 171.

was not excessive are liable to be put forward on behalf and/or by the officers of the police involved in the incident of firing and those others who support the case of the officers in that connection. The case that the firing was justified and was not excessive, that would be made in chief, would have to be destroyed largely by cross-examination of such evidence and to some extent by positive counter-evidence, which may be led on behalf of the interested political parties and/or public. Apparently in the directions, which he gave the learned Commissioner has failed to appreciate the above position. His directions are accordingly inconsistent with the above normal principles which should guide any Commission of Inquiry." The directions given by the Commissioner were accordingly set aside.

In *Sardar Malkeet Singh* v. *State of U.P.*,[630] the Allahabad High Court dissented from the decision of the Bombay High Court in Sarjerao Kondiba Sagar case.[631] The legal position is that the Evidence Act does not apply, nor any question of placing burden of proof on any party arises in proceedings before a Commission of Inquiry. On the facts of the case, the Allahabad High Court held that "so far the observation made by the Commission in the order, Annexure 2, observing 'Since burden is on the affected persons to show that...' is concerned, it is true, the word 'burden' has been used in the order, but it does not mean that the Commission has placed the burden of proof upon the petitioners or upon the affected persons. Inquiry by a Commission under the Commissions of Inquiry Act does not culminate into any decision. There are no parties before it, nor there is any 'lis' between the parties.... In a proceeding where there are no parties to the proceedings having any lis between them which is to be decided, in our view, question of burden of proof loses its importance. Both parties are aware of the matter. Whatever facts both parties place before the Commission in the shape of evidence including affidavits and statements, etc. the Commission of Inquiry has to consider that material and record its findings. These findings are neither a

630. AIR 1993 Allahabad 343.

631. AIR 1973 Bombay 171.

'decision' nor they are enforceable...." In the above circumstances, the mere use of the word 'burden' in the order Annexure 2 passed by the Commission is of no significance or consequence.

The Court further observed that the Commission has also been given power to frame its own rules and procedure. It has discretion to require any party to adduce evidence first. Much significance cannot be attached to order in which the facts are placed before the Commission by different parties. Such things have relevance in judicial proceedings where there are contesting parties, one seeking relief against the other and the Court has to pass an enforceable decree against one of them. The nature of proceeding before the Commission of Inquiry is entirely different. The Commission of Inquiry has to look into the facts that are put by different parties and members of the public, etc. and it has only to ascertain the facts in the mater and forward its report containing findings to the Government. It is for the Government to decide what measures or action it has to take, if at all. In case, judicial proceedings are initiated in any Court of law, in pursuance of the report, then question of proof and burden of proof, etc. will arise in the judicial proceedings and the persons proceeded against will have all benefits, if any of the procedural law, or that of the provisions of the Evidence Act.[632]

In *P.R. Nayak* v. *Union of India*,[633] the petitioner contended that he would be seriously prejudiced in his defence before the Commission that was set up pursuant to the recommendations of the Parliamentary Committee because it would involve the frank discussion of the report of the Committee and that was likely to involve him in contempt of Parliament particularly when in-camera proceedings had been refused by the Commission. The Court was not satisfied that any of the defence of the petitioner was such as was likely to involve him the contempt of Parliament. The Court observed: "The mere fact that the Commission rejected the petitioner's prayer to hold its proceedings in-camera would not be a justification for saying that the

---

632. *Sardar Malkeet Singh* v. *State of U.P.*, AIR 1993 Allahabad 343.
633. ILR (1973) I Delhi 747.

Commission should be restrained from continuing its proceedings because in some remote and undisclosed contingencies something that may be said by a party before it may involve such party in contempt of Parliament."[634]

In *S.V. Purushothaman* v. *State of Kerala*,[635] the Commissioner issued notice dated 13-8-1982 to the petitioner, directing him to appear for the hearing fixed on 6-9-1982, at the Conference Hall of the Inspection Bungalow of the Kerala Electricity Board. On that day the petitioner appeared along with his counsel and filed a petition,[636] supported by an affidavit,[637] objecting to the venue of the sitting of the Commission and the presence of the Additional Advocate General at the sittings of the Commission. It was alleged that the Commission was not even prepared to receive the petition and insisted that the petition should be withdrawn. According to the petitioner, the Commission did not call upon the respondent Minister to file his statement nor did he call for the production of the documents referred to in the complaint. The petitioner further alleged that he was not given an opportunity to adduce evidence. In the words of the petitioner: "But he (Commission) straightway asked the petitioner's advocate to argue the case on merits." According to the petitioner, when the advocate pleaded his inability to argue the case the Commission insisted on having it on the very next day but ultimately posted it to 13-9-1982. The petitioner contended: "In view of the aforesaid attitude taken by the 3rd respondent the petitioner felt apprehensive about the impartiality of the Commissioner and the petitioner was forced not to participate in the proceedings of the Commission." He filed a petition[638] before the Commission on 8-9-1982, which after narrating some of the facts alluded to above, expressed his decision not to participate in the proceedings of the Commission.

---

634. ILR (1973) I Delhi 771.
635. AIR 1983 Kerala 118.
636. Ext. P-5.
637. Ext. P-6.
638. Ext. P-7.

The Commission proceeded with the enquiry, though the petitioner and his advocate had withdrawn from it. Thereupon, the petitioner filed a writ petition in the High Court, praying, inter alia, "to issue of a writ in the nature of mandamus directing respondent No. 1—State—to withdraw the appointment of 3rd respondent as Commissioner and to make a fresh appointment preferably of a sitting Judge of the High Court to examine the prima facie case of the allegations contained in petition[639] and/or refer these allegation to a Commission of Inquiry under the Commission of Inquiry Act without delay." The Court did not find any substance in this prayer in the facts of the case. The Court observed: "It is not necessary for the purpose of the writ petition to go into the details of what had happened on 6-9-1982 before the Commission of Inquiry. It is admitted by the petitioner himself that the Commissioner had adjourned the further hearing to 13-9-1982. The petitioner did not participate in the hearing on that day. He withdrew from the Commission by submitting petition (Ext. P-7) on 8-9-1982. There was no basis, on that day, for the petitioner to be reasonably apprehensive about the impartiality of the Commission or to withdraw from the inquiry. The only two reasons put forward in purported justification of his doubting the impartiality of the Commission and the propriety of the inquiry, as indicated in Exts. P-5 and P-6 have been found to be untenable and invalid. A person who conducts in such a casual and in such a lighthearted manner before a high-powered commission like the 3rd respondent, who, on his own, withdrew from the further inquiry cannot justifiably seek for a cancellation of the order Ext. P-3 (appointing the Commission) by the Government. It may also be noted that he had not made any representation before the Government for the cancellation of Ext. P-3 before approaching this court with a prayer for a writ of mandamus seeking that relief. There not having been a preceding demand for relief, a prayer for mandamus may not be available at all. Even otherwise, the circumstances of the case are such that the petitioner does not deserve such a relief in these proceedings."

---

639. Ext. P-2.

The Court further observed: "Equally devoid of merit is the prayer for the appointment of a fresh Commission by the very same petitioner and in respect of the very same allegations. It has to be borne in mind that the procedure to be followed in connection with an inquiry entrusted with a Commission is essentially to be laid down by the Commission itself. Normally, the procedure evolved by the Commission would be fair in form and just in its working. Merely because one of the parties in the inquiry is unjustifiably apprehensive about the impartiality of the Commission, it is not obligatory for the Government to cancel the appointment of one Commission and proceed to appoint another in its stead. These grave matters have to be dealt with by all concerned with the great seriousness they require."[640]

[641][Inquiry not to be interrupted by reason of vacancy or change in the constitution of the Commission

8A. (1) Where the Commission consists of two or more members, it may act notwithstanding the absence of the Chairman or any other member or any vacancy among its members.

(2) Where during the course of an inquiry before a Commission, a change has taken place in the constitution of the Commission by reason of any vacancy having been filled or by any other reason, it shall not be necessary for the Commission to commence the inquiry afresh and the inquiry may be continued from the stage at which the change took place.

Construction of the Section

Section 8A cannot be construed to mean that the vacancy shall be filled in by the Government and in the absence of the filling of such a vacancy, the proceedings would be void. The positive wording of Section 8A is contrary even to such a faint

---

640. *S.V. Purushothaman* v. *State of Kerala*, AIR 1983 Kerala 118, pp. 122-23.

641. Ins. by Section 12, Act 79 of 1971.

suggestion. Irrespective of a vacancy, the Commission may act and act legally. This is made clear by the non-obstant clause, viz. "notwithstanding the absence...". Sections 8A (1) and (2) are not meant for the temporary absence such as short-term leave. The language is consistent with Section 3 of the Act where the Act does not oblige the Government to appoint two members as the minimum strength of a Commission. It may also be noted that an inquiry by the Committee in this case is not quasi-judicial in nature.[642]

Persons likely to be prejudicially affected to be heard

8B. If, at any stage of the inquiry, the Commission,-

(a) considers it necessary to inquire into the conduct of any person; or

(b) is of opinion that the reputation of any person is likely to be prejudicially affected by the inquiry,

the Commission shall give to that person a reasonable opportunity of being heard in the inquiry and to produce evidence in his defence:

Provided that nothing in this section shall apply where the credit of a witness is being impeached.

Conditions of Applicability

The use of the word 'or' between Clauses (a) and (b) of Section 8B of the Act makes it clear that Section 8B would be attracted if requirement of either Clause (a) or Clause (b) is fulfilled. Clause (a) of Section 8B applies when the conduct of any person is to be enquired into whereas Clause (b) applies to a case where reputation of a person is likely to be prejudicially affected. Once a Commission or Committee of Inquiry, governed by the provisions of the Act, considers that the conduct of any person among others is to be examined, it will not be open to it to take a stand that Section 8B is not attracted insofar as that

---

642. *Kiran Bedi* v. *Delhi Administration*, 1989 (2) Delhi Lawyer 190. The case of *United Commercial Bank Limited* v. *Their Workmen*, 1971 SCR 380 was distinguished on the ground of the industrial tribunal being quasi-judicial and with reference to the provisions of the Industrial Disputes Act.

person is concerned. Recourse to procedure under Section 8B is not confined to any particular stage. Issue of a formal notice under Section 8B is not sine qua non for attracting its applicability. A case which is otherwise covered under Section 8B, cannot be taken out of its ambit by refraining from issue of notice to the concerned person under this section. Once the Commission or, as the case may be, the Committee decides to enquire into the conduct of any person, it should issue notice under the section to that person.[643]

Reputation—Protection of

It is well settled that when any judicial authority, quasi-judicial authority or any other authority including administrative authority, takes a decision which may have civil consequences and affects right of a person or persons, the principles of natural justice would at once come into play. The role of natural justice requires that a person against whom an allegation is being enquired into has to be given a chance of hearing before he is condemned. It cannot be denied that the reputation of any individual is an important part of the right to life. It is, therefore, in recognition of such importance, the legislatures inserted Section 8B of the Act by virtue of amending Act 79 of 1971. The paramount importance of such requirement can be readily inferred from the judgment in the case of *Smt. Kiran Bedi and Jinder Singh* v. *The Committee of Inquiry*,[644] wherein the following observations were made, viz.:

> The reason for the importance attached with regard to the matter of safeguarding the reputation of a person being prejudicially affected in Clause (b) of section 8-B of the Act is not far to seek.
>
> The following words of caution uttered by the Lord to Arjun in *Bhagwad Gita* with regard to dishonour or loss of reputation may usefully be quoted:

---

643. *Smt. Kiran Bedi and Jinder Singh* v. *Committee of Inquiry*, AIR 1989 SC 714.

644. AIR 1989 SC 714.

> Akirtinchapi Bhutani Kathaishyanti te-a vyayam Sambhavitasya Chakirtir Marandatirichyate" (2.34). (Men will recount thy perpetual dishonour, and to one highly esteemed, dishonour exceedeth death.)

In Blackstone's *Commentary of the Laws of England,*[645] it has been stated that the right of personal security consists in a person's legal and uninterrupted enjoyment of his life, his limbs, his body, his health and his reputation.

In Corpus Juris Secundum,[646] is to be found the statement of law in the following terms:

> It is stated in the definition of Person,[647] that legally the term "person" includes not only the physical body and members, but also every bodily sense and personal attribute, among which is the reputation a man has acquired. Blackstone in his Commentaries classifies and distinguishes those rights which are annexed to the person, jura personarum, and acquired rights in external objects, jura rerum; and in the former he includes personal security, which consists in a person's legal and uninterrupted enjoyment of his life, his limbs, his body, his health, and his reputation. And he makes the corresponding classification of remedies. The idea expressed is that a man's reputation is part of himself, as his body and limbs are, and reputation is a sort of right to enjoy the good opinion of others and it is capable of growth and real existence, as an arm or leg. Reputation is, therefore, a personal right and the right to reputation is put among those absolute personal rights equal in dignity and importance to security from violence. According to Chancellor Kent, "as a part of the rights of personal security, the preservation of every person's good name from the vile arts of detraction is justly included. The laws of the ancients, no less than those of modern nations, made private reputation one of the objects of their protection".

---

645. Vol. 1, IVth Edition, p. 101.

646. Vol. 77, p. 268.

647. 70 C.J.S. p. 688, note 66.

The right to the enjoyment of a good reputation is a valuable privilege of ancient origin and necessary to human society, as stated in Libel and Slander S. 4 and his right is within the constitutional guaranty of personal security as stated in Constitutional Law S. 205, and a person may not be deprived of this right through falsehood and violence without liability for the injury as stated in Libel and Slander S. 4.

Detraction from a man's reputation is an injury to his personality, and thus an injury to reputation is a personal injury, that is an injury to an absolute personal right.

In *D.F. Marion* v. *Davis*,[648] it was held:

The right to enjoyment of a private reputation, unassailed by malicious slander is of ancient origin, and is necessary to human society. A good reputation is an element of personal security and is protected by the Constitution equally with the right to the enjoyment of life, liberty and property.

It can, therefore, be safely gathered that reputation is a part of fundamental right and personal liberty as guaranteed under Article 21 of the Constitution of India. Therefore, having regard to the importance of such a right, Section 8B of the Act casts a mandatory duty on the Commission to give a reasonable opportunity to the person whose conduct or reputation is likely to be prejudiced by such inquiry or the findings recorded therein. Under the safeguards as provided under Section 8B a person whose conduct or reputation is going to be criticized has got a legitimate right to defend his/her case and cross-examine witness before such findings are recorded.[649]

Entitlement to the Benefit of the Section

The entitlement to the benefit of Section 8B would be determined with reference to the fulfillment of the conditions specified therein. If these conditions are satisfied in respect of a person, then, that person would be entitled to the benefit of the section. The fact whether he has been issued notice under the section or not, is not material. Even if the notice has not been

---

648. 55 American LR 171.

649. *Lal Krishna Advani* v. *State of Bihar*, AIR 1997 Patna 15.

issued in a case that will not deprive the person concerned of the benefit of the section if he is otherwise entitled to it. Mere non-issue of a notice under Section 8B ought not to make any difference if one otherwise satisfies the conditions mentioned in Section 8B. The issue of such a notice is not contemplated under Section 8B of the Act. It is enough if at any stage the Commission considers it necessary to enquire into the conduct of any person. Such person would thereafter be governed by Section 8B of the Act. Such a person cannot be subjected to any hostile discrimination by asking him to enter the witness-box at the inception of the hearing whereas other persons who are similarly placed are required to testify at the end of the hearing.[650]

The reason for this has been very aptly elaborated by a Division Bench of Gauhati High Court in a recent judgment[651] in the following words:

> The purpose for which Section 8B has been incorporated in the Act will be defeated if the witnesses of such person to whom such protection under Section 8B has been given, are asked to examine first, as in that case it will amount to denying the opportunity to such person to produce evidence in his defence, because if those witnesses are examined first, then he will have no other witness to adduce in his defence, thereby leaving him in a situation where he cannot defend himself. Such an action would amount to violation of the statutory protection given under S. 8B of the Act as well as would be against the principle of natural justice.

Accordingly, the Division Bench directed that "District Administration has to examine first all its witnesses as required by R. 5(5)(a) of Rules, excluding its witnesses who has/have been cited as witness by any person to whom the protection under S. 8B of the Act is given. Such witnesses falling under S. 8B of the Act are to be examined after the examination of the other public memorialists and other witnesses."

---

650. *Smt. Kiran Bedi and Jinder Singh* v. *Committee of Inquiry*, AIR 1989 SC 714.

651. *District Administration, Tura* v. *Commissioner of Inquiry*, Meghalaya, AIR 2007 (NOC) 275 (Gau).

In *Motahar Hossain* v. *Haratosh Chakrabarty*,[652] issue of notices under Section 8B was challenged on the ground that these were issued without any material and without forming any opinion and without any basis or justification. Upholding this contention and thereupon quashing the notices, the Court observed that "in order to issue a notice at any stage the Commission of Inquiry must be of the opinion that the person to whom the notice is given might be prejudicially affected. There must be prima facie material for formation of the opinion that the person may be prejudicially affected, otherwise the entire world had to be given notice. Section 8B for its observance requires the formation of opinion by the appropriate authority that the reputation of a person to whom the notice is given is likely to be prejudicially affected". Thus, if notices are issued on the basis of certain complaint on the basis of which there could not be any investigation that is likely to prejudicially affect the reputation of the notices, the notices cannot be sustained for the reason of having been issued without any material.

It is for the Commission to satisfy itself whether protection under Section 8B is to be given to any person on the basis of the materials available on its record. The Commission cannot do so mechanically. Therefore, extension of protection under Section 8B to certain Government officials only of District Administration and not to others cannot *per se* be held discriminatory in the absence of similar material available against them as been the case with the officials to whom protection under Section 8B has been extended.[653]

However, it is not necessary that the conditions envisaged in Section 8B should be included in the terms of reference to attract the applicability of the section. Nor the same is required to be reflected in the complaint pursuant to which the Commission of Inquiry has been constituted. If the investigation made by the investigating agency of the Commission reveals that there may be matters in the investigation which may prejudice any person,

652. 84 CWN 560.

653. *District Administration, Tura* v. *Commissioner of Inquiry*, Meghalaya, AIR 2007 (NOC) 275 (Gau).

it would be proper on the part of the Commission to issue notice to that person under Section 8B of the Act. But the Commission must have otherwise been validly constituted under the Act. If the Commission is not so validly constituted, it may vitiate any notice issued under Section 8B to any person as well.[654]

Section 8B requires the Commission to consider, if, at any stage of the enquiry, it considers necessary to enquire into the conduct of any person or is of opinion the reputation of any person is likely to be prejudicially affected by the inquiry, whether the Commission should give to that person a reasonable opportunity of being heard in the enquiry and to produce evidence in his defence. Section 8B, however, makes it unnecessary for the Commission to give such opportunity to a witness where the credit of the witness is being impeached.[655] Both Sections 8B and 8C of the Act spell out that the person referred to in Section 8B is different from the person whose evidence is recorded by the Commission and that such a person is entitled, if he so wishes, to cross-examine a witness, to address the Commission and to be represented by a legal practitioner. However, protection under Section 8B can be given to public memorialist as well if the conditions of applicability of the section are otherwise satisfied.[656]

A person to whom a notice is issued under Section 8B of the Act has the option not to produce any defence but that is something quite distinct from declining by a person to take oath and give evidence when called upon by any authority competent to do so specially when he is present before that authority. Since the petitioner's conduct could be adversely commented upon, he was given an opportunity under Section 8B of the Act, which he could or could not avail as he thought fit. But that does not allow anyone to violate the law or act in a manner, which may

---

654. *Sushil Chandra Chowdhury* v. *Secretary, Chakraborty Commission of Inquiry*, 84 CWN 583, p. 600.

655. *State of Maharashtra* v. *Ibrahim Mohd. Hussein Maddu*, 1978 CriLJ 1157.

656. *District Administration, Tura* v. *Commissioner of Inquiry*, Meghalaya, AIR 2007 (NOC) 275 (Gau).

allegedly be an offence. In *Mr Bansi Lal* v. *State*,[657] the petitioner refused to take oath and give evidence for which he was prosecuted in terms of Section 5(2) of the Act. The Commission was of the view that the Minister's oath (1) did not prohibit him from disclosing the information before a Commission, (2) the Constitution does not provide for any penalty for breach of such oath, (3) the obligation is not absolute as the information can be revealed in due discharge of duties, and (4) disclosure of information before a Commission set up by the government after he has ceased to be a Minister does not amount to breach of oath. The Court did not find anything wrong with this view of the Commission.

However, where there is valid justification for the refusal by the police officials to take oath for cross examination at the stage when they are required to do so, the direction for filing a complaint against the police officials for an offence under Section 178, IPC, would not be proper.[658] In *Smt. Kiran Bedi* v. *Committee of Inquiry*,[659] the Supreme Court considered two propositions in this regard, namely: (1) whether on the belief that they were persons covered by Section 8B of the Act the petitioners could avoid the consequences of Sections 178 and 179, IPC by claiming absolute immunity from binding themselves by an oath or affirmation for answering questions put to them and (2) whether they could avoid those consequences if they had valid justification for refusing to take oath or affirmation without claiming an absolute immunity from binding themselves by an oath or affirmation. Examining the case law on this subject, both in India and abroad, the Court answered the first proposition in the negative and the second proposition in the affirmative. Accordingly, the Court held that in view of the provisions contained in Sections 4 to 6 of the Act and the rules framed thereunder that the petitioners on the belief that they were persons covered by Section 8B could not avoid the

---

657. *(Mr.) Bansi Lal* v. *State*, ILR (1981) I Delhi 715, p. 729.

658. *Smt. Kiran Bedi and Jinder Singh* v. *The Committee of Inquiry*, AIR 1989 SC 714 Case law discussed.

659. AIR 1989 SC 714, p. 727.

consequences of Sections 178 and 179 by claiming absolute immunity from binding themselves by an oath or affirmation for answering questions put to them. The Court further held that a valid justification put forth by the witness can be considered to constitute sufficient ground to make him immune from prosecution. In reaching these conclusions, the Court relied on the case law on the subject. It may be expedient to refer to the same in order to have better understanding of the subject.

In *McGrain* v. *Daugherty*,[660] one of the questions which arose for consideration was whether the Senate—or the House of Representatives, both being on the same plane in this regard—has power, through its own process, to compel a private individual to appear before it or one of its committees and give testimony needed to enable it efficiently to exercise a legislative function belonging to it under the Constitution. It was held that the power of inquiry—with process to enforce it—is an essential and appropriate auxiliary to the legislative function and that the provisions in this behalf are not of doubtful meaning, but "are intended to be effectively exercised, and therefore, to carry with them such auxiliary powers as are necessary and appropriate to that end. While the power to exact information in aid of the legislative function was not involved in those cases, the rule of interpretation applied there is applicable here. A legislative body cannot legislate wisely or effectively in the absence of information respecting the conditions which the legislation is intended to affect or change, and where the legislative body does not itself possess the requisite information—which not in frequently is true—recourse must be had to others who do possess it. Experience has taught that mere requests for such information often are unavailing, and also that information which is volunteered is not always accurate or complete; so some means of compulsion are essential to obtain what is needed. All this was true before and when the Constitution was framed and adopted. In that period, the power of inquiry—with enforcing process—was regarded and employed as a necessary an appropriate attribute of the power to legislate—indeed, was treated as inhering in it.

660. (1926) 71 L. Ed. 580.

Thus, there is ample warrant for thinking, as we do, that the constitutional provisions which commit the legislative function to the two houses are intended to include this attribute to the end that the function may be effectively exercised".

On these findings, with regard to refusal by the witness to appear and testify before the Committee and being attached as a consequence thereof, it was held:

> We conclude that the investigation was ordered for a legitimate object; that the witness wrongfully refused to appear and testify before the Committee and was lawfully attached; that the Senate is entitled to have him give testimony pertinent to the inquiry, either at its bar or before the committee; and that the district court erred in discharging him from custody under the attachment.

In *Uphaus* v. *Wyman*,[661] a witness at an investigation by the Attorney General of the State of New Hampshire, conducted pursuant to a resolution of the State legislature authorizing the Attorney General to determine whether there were subversives within the State, refused to obey a subpoena calling for the production of a list of persons who were guests at a camp operated within New Hampshire by a voluntary corporation of which the witness was executive director. On petition of the Attorney General, the Merrimack County Court called the witness before it and the witness again refused to produce the information, asserting, first, that, by the Smith Act[662] Congress had so completely occupied the field of subversive activities that the States were without power to investigate in that area, and, second, that the due process clause precluded enforcement of the subpoena. The Court rejected the witness argument, and, upon his continued refusal to produce the list, adjudged him in contempt and committed him to jail until he should comply. The Supreme Court of New Hampshire affirmed, and even after remand by the United States Supreme Court it reaffirmed its former decision. On appeal, while affirming the decision of the

661. (1959) 3 Law Ed 2d. 1090.

662. 18 USCs. 2385.

Supreme Court of New Hampshire the United States Supreme Court held that since the Attorney General sought to learn if subversive persons were in the State because of the legislative determination that such persons, statutorily defined with a view toward the Communist Party, posed a serious threat to the security of the State, the investigation was undertaken in the interest of self-preservation and this governmental interest outweighed individual rights in an associational privacy which, however, real in other circumstances were here tenuous at best. It was further held that "the governmental interest in self-preservation is sufficiently compelling to subordinate the interest in associational privacy of persons who, at least to the extent of the guest registration statute, made public at the inception of the association they now wish to keep private. In the light of such a record we conclude that the State's interest has not been 'pressed, in this instance, to a point where it has come into fatal collision with the overriding' constitutionally protected rights of appellant and those he may represent".

In *Sinclair* v. *United States*,[663] it was held:

> Neither Senate Joint Resolution 54 nor the action taken under it operated to divest the Senate or the committee of power further to investigate the actual administration of the land laws. It may be conceded that Congress is without authority to compel disclosures for the purpose of aiding the prosecution of pending suits; but the authority of that body, directly or through its committees, to require pertinent disclosures in aid of its own constitutional power, is not abridged because the information sought to be elicited may also be of use in such suits.

In *Kastigar* v. *United States*,[664] the United States District Court for the Central District of California ordered the petitioners to appear before a grand jury and to answer its questions under a grant of immunity. The immunity was based upon a provision of the Organized Crime Control Act of 1970 stating that neither the compelled testimony nor any information directly or indirectly

663. (1928) 73 Law Ed 692.

664. (1972) 32 Law Ed 2d 212.

derived from such testimony could be used against the witness. Notwithstanding the grant of immunity, the petitioners refused to answer the grand jury's questions and were found in contempt. The United States Court of Appeals for the Ninth Circuit affirmed,[665] rejecting the petitioners' contention that it violated their constitutional privilege against self-incrimination to compel them to testify without granting them transactional immunity from prosecution for any offence to which the compelled testimony might relate.

The United States Supreme Court further held that the power of Government to compel persons to testify in Court or before grand juries and other governmental agencies was firmly established but was not absolute, being subject to a number of exemptions, the most important of which was the Fifth Amendment privilege against self-incrimination. With reference to Federal Statute[666] it was held:

> That a federal statute permitting the government to compel a witness to give testimony, but granting the witness immunity from the use in any criminal case of the compelled testimony or any evidence derived therefrom, does not violate the Fifth amendment privilege against self-incrimination.

In *Brown* v. *Walker*,[667] the question involved was with regard to an alleged incompatibility between that clause of the 5th Amendment to the Constitution, which declares that no person "shall be compelled in any criminal case to be a witness against himself" and the act of Congress of February 11, 1893[668] which enacts that "no person shall be excused from attending and testifying or from producing books, papers, tariffs, contracts, agreements and documents before the Inter-State Commerce Commission, or in obedience to the subpoena of the Commission, on the ground or for the reason that the testimony or evidence, documentary or otherwise, required of him, may tend to

665. *Kastigar* v. *United States* (1971) 440 F2d 954.

666. 18 USCSs. 6002.

667. (1895) 40 Law Ed. 819.

668. 27 Stat. at L. 443.

criminate him or subject him to a penalty or forfeiture. But no person shall be prosecuted or subjected to any penalty or forfeiture for or on account of any transaction, matter, or thing concerning which he may testify, or produce evidence, documentary or otherwise, before said Commission, or in obedience to its subpoena, or either of them, or in any such case or proceeding." It was held:

> It is entirely true that the statute does not purport, nor is it possible for any statute, to shield the witness from the personal disgrace or opprobrium attaching to the exposure of his crime; but, as we have already observed, the authorities are numerous and very nearly uniform to the effect that, if the proposed testimony is material to the issue on trial, the fact that the testimony may tend to degrade the witness in public estimation does not exempt him from the duty of disclosure. A person who commits a criminal act is bound to contemplate the consequences of exposure to his good name and reputation, and ought not to call upon the courts to protect that which he has himself esteemed to be of such little value. The safety and welfare of an entire community should not be put into the scale against the reputation of a self-confessed criminal, who ought not, either in justice or in good morals, to refuse to disclose that which may be of great public utility, in order that his neighbours may think well of him. The design of the constitutional privilege is not to aid the witness in vindicating his character, but to protect him against being compelled to furnish evidence to convict him of a criminal charge. If he secures legal immunity from prosecution, the possible impairment of his good name is a penalty, which it is reasonable he should be compelled to pay for the common good. If it be once conceded that the fact that his testimony may tend to bring the witness into disrepute, though not to incriminate him, does not entitle him to the privilege of silence, it necessarily follows that if it also tends to incriminate, but at the same time operates as a pardon for the offence, the fact that the disgrace remains no more entitles him to immunity in this case than in the other.

It is in this view of the matter and in view of the provisions contained in Sections 4 to 6 of the Act and the rules framed thereunder that the Supreme Court was of the opinion in the case of *Kiran Bedi and Jinder Singh*[669] that the petitioners on the belief that they were persons covered by Section 8B could not avoid the consequences of Sections 178 and 179 by claiming absolute immunity from binding themselves by an oath or affirmation for answering questions put to them. Indeed in this case the petitioners were not asserting that they could not be required at all to appear as a witness before the Committee and make statement on oath. As is apparent from the Supreme Court's earlier order dated 18th August 1988,[670] on behalf of both the petitioners, it was submitted that they did not either wish to delay the proceedings or to show disrespect to the Committee but only wanted to protect their own interest by making the submission which they made before the Committee as per legal advice given to them. According to learned counsel for the petitioners the legal advice given to the petitioners was that since they were persons covered by Section 8B of the Act they were entitled to produce evidence in defence and could as such be called upon to enter the witness box at the end of this inquiry and could not be required to enter the witness box for cross-examination almost as the first two witnesses before the Committee. According to him, the stand taken by the petitioners was that they being covered by Section 8B of the Act their defence would be put to serious jeopardy and will be prejudicially affected if they were required to appear in the witness box for cross-examination at the very inception of the inquiry even before statements of witnesses providing the accusations against the petitioners had been recorded which they were entitled to defend. In this background, the Supreme Court passed on to the second proposition referred to above, namely, whether the petitioners could avoid the consequences contemplated by Sections 178 and 179, IPC by putting forth valid justification for refusing to bind themselves by oath or affirmation even

669. AIR 1989 SC 714.

670. Reported in AIR 1988 SC 2252.

without claiming an absolute immunity from binding themselves by an oath or affirmation.

In *Watkins* v. *United States*,[671] a union officer, appearing as a witness before a sub-committee of the House Committee on Un-American Activities, refused to answer questions as to past Communist Party membership of certain persons, objecting to the questions on the ground of lack of pertinency to the subject under inquiry by the sub-committee. In a prosecution in the United States District Court for the District of Columbia, he was convicted of violating the statute providing for criminal punishment of witnesses before congressional committees who refuse to answer any question pertinent to the question under inquiry, and the conviction was affirmed by the United States Court of Appeals for the District of Columbia Circuit. On certiorari, the United States Supreme Court reversed the conviction. Warren, Chief Justice, speaking for the five members of the Court, ruled that to support a conviction under a statute a congressional investigating committee must, upon objection of a witness on the grounds of pertinency, state for the record the subject under inquiry at that time and the manner in which the propounded questions are pertinent thereto. Consequently refusal to answer a question on the ground that it was not pertinent was found to be a valid justification.

In *Flaxer* v. *United States*,[672] relying on the decision in *Watkins*[673] that the Courts must accord to the defendants every right which is guaranteed to defendants in all other criminal cases it was held that one of these guarantees is proof beyond a reasonable doubt that the refusal of the witness was deliberate and intentional. This decision is, therefore, an authority for the proposition that if the refusal of the witness was not deliberate and intentional but was for a valid cause such refusal could not be made the basis for prosecuting the witness.

671. (1957) 1 Law Ed 2d 1273.

672. (1958) 3 Law Ed 2d 183.

673. *Watkins* v. *United States* (1957) 1 Law Ed 2d 1273.

In *Murphy* v. *Waterfront Commission of New York*,[674] notwithstanding the grant of immunity under the laws of New Jersey and New York, petitioners, as witnesses before the Waterfront Commission of New York Harbor, refused to answer questions on the ground that the answers might tend to incriminate them under federal law, to which the grant of immunity did not purport to extend. Petitioners were thereupon held in civil and criminal contempt of Court. The New Jersey Supreme Court affirmed the civil contempt judgments, holding that a State may constitutionally compel a witness to give testimony, which might be used in a federal prosecution against him. On certiorari, the United States Supreme Court vacated the judgment of contempt and remanded the cause to the New Jersey Supreme Court. It was held:

> ...we hold the constitutional rule to be that a State witness may not be compelled to give testimony which may be incriminating under federal law unless the compelled testimony and its fruits cannot be used in any manner by federal officials in connection with a criminal prosecution against him. We conclude, moreover, that in order to implement this constitutional rule and accommodate the interests of the State and Federal Governments in investigating and prosecuting crime, the Federal Government must be prohibited from making any such use of compelled testimony and its fruits. This exclusionary rule, while permitting the States to secure information necessary for effective law enforcement, leaves the witness and the Federal Government in substantially the same position as if the witness had claimed his privilege in the absence of a State grant of immunity. It follows that petitioners here may now be compelled to answer the questions propounded to them. At the time they refused to answer, however, petitioners had a reasonable fear, based on this Court's decision in *Feldman* v. *United States*,[675] that the federal authorities might use the answers against them in connection with a federal prosecution.

---

674. (1964) 12 Law Ed 2d 678.

675. (1943) 322 US 487.

We have now overruled *Feldman* and held that the Federal Government may make no such use of the answers. Fairness dictates that petitioners should now be afforded an opportunity, in the light of this development, to answer the questions. Accordingly, the judgment of the New Jersey Courts ordering petitioners to answer the questions may remain undisturbed. But the judgment of contempt is vacated and the cause remanded to the New Jersey Supreme Court for proceedings not inconsistent with this opinion.

Accordingly, in the case of *Kiran Bedi and Jinder Singh*, the Supreme Court held that "it is, therefore, clear that a valid justification put forth by the witness was considered to constitute sufficient ground to make him immune from prosecution".[676]

Conduct Includes Misconduct

A plain reading of the section shows that a Commission of Inquiry under the Act can inquire into the conduct of an individual. The antithesis of 'conduct' is misconduct. If conduct can be inquired into, then misconduct, as popularly understood, which means improper conduct, can also be the subject-matter of inquiry by the Commission of Inquiry.[677]

Not Ultra Vires the Constitution

Section 8B of the Act is a provision giving statutory recognition to the rule of natural justice. It cannot be said to be ultra vires the Articles 14, 19, 20(3) and 21 of the Constitution by any stretch of imagination. Indeed this section embodies the principle of justness and fairness and that would be in accordance with the established principles of the rule of law. An option given to a party and a duty imposed on a Commission can, in no way, be unconstitutional. Rule 5(2)(a) of the Rules enables the Commission to call upon any person who in its opinion should be given an opportunity of being heard in the inquiry to furnish to the Commission a statement relating to such matters as may be specified in the notice. So long as the notice is with

676. *Smt. Kiran Bedi and Jinder Singh* v. *The Committee of Inquiry and Another*, AIR 1989 SC 714.

677. *U. Dakshinamoorthy* v. *Commission of Inquiry*, AIR 1980 Madras 89.

regard to matters, which are within the competence of the Commission to inquire into, it cannot be invalid. The principles of the rule of law embodied in Articles 14, 19, 20(3) and 21 of the Constitution do not envisage that an inquiry under a valid law be stultified. Indeed, the power as given by Rule 5(2)(a) is in furtherance of the principles of rule of law and anyone receiving a notice, in order to uphold the rule of law, should comply with it. The notice has to be construed fairly and in accordance with the maxim *ut res magis valeat, quam pareat* (that an act may avail rather than perish). Therefore, the rule cannot also said to be in conflict with Section 8B of the Act.[678]

Nature and Quantum of Hearing to be Given by Commission

The nature of the inquiry made by a Commission of Inquiry is only a fact-finding inquiry. The general rule is well established that in a fact-finding inquiry, there is no person who is in the position of an accused or a defendant. The purpose of the inquiry is only to gather material for the information of the Government or the authority concerned. It is only if the material so gathered discloses a prima facie case against a person that further necessary action will be instituted against him by way of a trial or a disciplinary inquiry. In such an action, he would be in the position of an accused or a defendant and would be given a full opportunity of defending himself. Therefore, no question of giving such an opportunity of defending himself in a fact-finding inquiry arises in such a case.[679]

An exception to this general rule is made in Section 8B of the Act. The reason for this exception can be gathered from the following words of Prof. S.A. de Smith:[680] "Exceptionally, it may be necessary to import the rules of natural justice into the

678. *Dhirendra Brahmachari* v. *Union of India*, AIR 1979 NOC 91 (Delhi).

679. *Amalendu Ghosh* v. *District Traffic Superintendent, North Eastern Railway*, AIR 1960 SC 992: *Champak Lal* v. *Union of India* (1964) 5 SCR 190; *State of U.P.* v. *Akbar Ali Khan*, AIR 1966 SC 1842; *Parry-Jones* v. *Law Society*, (1968) 2 WLR 397; *G.S. Harnal* v. *Union of India and Others*, ILR (1971) II Delhi 129.

680. *Judicial Review of Administrative Action* by Prof. S.A. de Smith, Second Edition, p. 219.

conduct of an inquiry or investigation, the holding of which is not a prerequisite of further proceedings or action. Since the hearings and report of a judicial tribunal of inquiry set up to investigate an alleged public scandal attract a great deal of publicity, it is unfair to deny a person against whom damaging allegations may be made before the tribunal the procedural protection accorded to a defendant in legal proceedings."

The Royal Commission on Tribunals of Inquiry (1966) under Lord Justice Salmon also recommended the grant of a hearing to a person involved in such a statutory inquiry. The same learned Judge in delivering the Lionel Cohen Lectures (1967) on "Tribunals of Inquiry", however, observed that "the Tribunals' Inquiry is inescapably inquisitorial. There is no lis, no plaintiff or defendant, no prosecutor or accused, no charges, indictments or depositions".

The hearing given in a fact-finding inquiry is, therefore, a limited one. It is not as elaborate as is given in a trial or disciplinary inquiry. In *Wiseman* v. *Borneman*,[681] under Section 28 of the U.K. Finance Act, 1960, only a limited hearing was given to an assessee before a statutory authority ascertained the existence of a prima facie case against him. For, the assessee was to get full hearing if on the strength of the prima facie case, action was instituted against him. A unanimous House of Lords held that this was sufficient hearing in the circumstances.

It is implicit in this section that notices thereunder have to be issued in the absence of the person whose conduct is being inquired into or the person whose reputation, in the opinion of the Commission, is likely to be prejudicially affected by the inquiry. The Commission has, therefore, to proceed on the basis of the material before it.[682]

The Commissions of Inquiry (Central) Rules, 1972 provide such a hearing to the persons whose conduct is the subject-matter of inquiry by the Commission. Under these rules, the Commission acts in two stages. The first stage is the invitation

681. (1969) 3 WLR 706.

682. *P.R. Nayak* v. *Union of India*, ILR (1973) I Delhi 747, p. 784.

of statements from persons who, in the opinion of the Commission should be given an opportunity of being heard in the inquiry. Similarly members of the general public acquainted with the subject-matter of the inquiry may also file their statements. Then comes the next stage. If after examining the statement so filed, the Commission thinks it necessary, it may record oral evidence of persons who have filed the statements or of other persons whose evidence is relevant to the inquiry. Some persons including those submitting statement may be prejudicially affected by the inquiry. These persons and those who are examined as witnesses are, therefore, given a full opportunity of defending themselves.[683]

This section incorporates and embodies the rule of natural justice, i.e. not to condemn a person without affording him an opportunity of being heard. It is open to the person to whom a notice is issued not to avail of the opportunity afforded to him to appear and produce evidence in his defence in which case his conduct and reputation will be inquired into in his absence. The language of Section 8B does not suggest that any detailed reasons have to be recorded before issuing the notices and mere issue of notice by itself cannot establish any bias against the notice especially when he himself has been participating in the proceedings before the Commission even before issue of any notice to him.[684]

Section 8B embodies the rule of natural justice, not to condemn a person without affording him an opportunity of being heard. The concept of natural justice includes three main rules: (i) no one should be a judge in his own cause, (ii) *audi alteram partem*, no one should be condemned unheard, and (iii) absence of bias.[685] Opportunity of being heard was initially determined by Rules 4 and 5 of the Central Commission of Inquiry (Procedure) Rules, 1960, but the Parliament enacted these provisions in the Act by an amendment in 1971. The

683. *G.S. Harnal* v. *Union of India*, ILR (1971) II Delhi 129.

684. *P.R. Nayak* v. *Union of India*, ILR (1973) I Delhi 747, p. 784.

685. *A.K. Kraipak* v. *Union of India*, AIR 1970 SC 150.

opportunity envisages under Section 8B of the Act has been spelt out clearly in Section 8C, namely; (i) cross-examination of witnesses, (ii) right to address the Commission, and (iii) representation by a lawyer. Section 8B is an option to the petitioner.[686]

Adequacy of hearing given in a case is a question of fact. If a person, whose conduct is under investigation in an inquiry, is given opportunity to produce evidence or witnesses in his defence and he chooses not to do so, he cannot complain that opportunity of adducing defence has been denied to him. Where the inquiry was against the Refinery, its management and staff, all of them were said to have been put on notice to defend themselves. The statement of the Refinery was regarded as the statement on behalf of the management and the staff as without them, the Refinery was only the site and the factory and, therefore, it was held that hearing was given to the management and the staff of the Refinery when statement on their behalf was filed before the Commission. The members of the management and the staff were free to engage separate counsel for their own defence or examine witnesses for their individual defence. If they did not do so, they could not blame the Commission. The opportunity was given to the Refinery as a whole from the very beginning to defend its management and the staff. It was not necessary that the Commission should individually address members of the management and the staff of the Refinery to avail themselves of such opportunity. By the choice of the Refinery itself the pattern of their defence was that the lawyer of the Refinery defended the management and the staff of the Refinery and no members of the management and the staff made separate arrangements for the individual defence of the officers and, therefore, it was held that hearing was not denied to the petitioners during the inquiry.[687]

Section 8B postulates that depending upon the stage of enquiry at which opportunity is provided to the addressee of the notice necessary information should be furnished in the notice.

---

686. *Mr. Bansi Lal* v. *State*, ILR (1981) I Delhi 715, p. 726.

687. *P.R. Naik* v. *Union of India*, ILR (1973) I Delhi 747.

No pro forma notice is prescribed under the Act. But it appears to be implicit that if the Commission has collected any material, either documents or State witnesses, on the basis of which it formed the opinion, tentatively, that the reputation of any person is likely to be prejudicially affected, a reference to that material should be made in the notice. One cannot be unmindful of the fact that the person who is provided with an opportunity of being heard is given an option to produce evidence in his defence with regard to his reputation which is likely to be prejudicially affected in the enquiry so he should know and be told of the material which was the basis of forming the requisite opinion by the Commission of Inquiry because it was collected behind his back and he has to defend himself with regard to that material and has also to participate in the further enquiry. If the material which formed the basis of opinion by the Commission is not clearly indicated in the notice, the very purpose of giving a reasonable opportunity would be frustrated and the addressee of the notice will be placed in wilderness. Therefore, it becomes necessary to examine the following two aspects, namely,

(i) what material was taken into consideration by the Commission while forming the opinion that the reputation of the petitioners is likely to be prejudicially affected by the enquiry; and

(ii) has that material been referred to in the notices under Section 8B of the Act?

In this regard, the following propositions can be obtained from the case law of the subject of "reasonable opportunity of being heard", viz.:

1. The scope and extent of reasonable opportunity must be judged in the light of the constitution of the statutory body which has to function in accordance with the rules laid down by the Legislature.
2. Whether an opportunity has been afforded and whether that opportunity was or was not reasonable in a given case should be ascertained by the Court on encyclopaedic view of all the material in the case.

3. In every case the minimum requirement of hearing must be satisfied and there must be a fair and honest determination of the question.
4. The test for the minimum requirement is satisfied if the person concerned was given proper opportunity of making a representation or statement that would dissipate the suspicion of the authority competent to take action.
5. Whether the representation dispelled or confirmed, the suspicion was of no consequence.[688]

However, a different view was taken by a Division Bench of Gauhati High Court in *District Administration, Tura* v. *Commissioner of Inquiry, Meghalaya*,[689] when it observed as follows:

> Neither Section 8B of the Act nor any other provision of the Act requires to disclose the materials available on the record of the Commission, on the basis of which the Commission considers it necessary to give the protection under Section 8B of the Act, in the intimation given to such person about giving such protection as discussed above. No notice in fact is required to be issued under Section 8B. What requires to be provided is an opportunity of being heard in the inquiry, which includes the examination of its witnesses in defence. Therefore, non-disclosure of the ground or the particulars of materials available on record of the Commission, which is the basis for giving such protection will not vitiate the order passed by the Commission, because of the right available to such person to inspect records and or to get the copy of the materials from the Commission. Section 8B of the Act only contemplates protection and not accusation.
>
> Further person, who complains about such non-furnishing of materials in the notice and/or non-discloser of grounds in

688. *Dharani Trading Company* v. *State of A.P.* (1974) 2 APLJ 166; *Mohd. Ibrahim Khan* v. *Sushil Kumar*, AIR 1983, Andhra Pradesh 69.

689. AIR 2007 (NOC) 275 (Gau).

such notice, must demonstrate the prejudice caused to him for such non-supply/non-discloser.

The question that arises in the context of the above observations is whether an aggrieved person can be said to have been accorded a reasonable opportunity of being heard if he is given hearing without informing him as to what case he has to meet at the hearing. If the person is kept in the dark as to the allegations levelled against him as, in the opinion of the Commission, such allegations and consequential inquiry may prejudicially affect that person, will it be still necessary for him to prove 'prejudice' specifically on account of non-furnishing of particulars of those allegations and the related material? In such a case, can it not be said that the prejudice resulting from non-furnishing of such particulars is writ large on the face of it? When one is giving hearing in defence, he must know what he is defending. A hearing in order to be reasonable cannot be in vacuum or abstract. It is inherent in the concept of 'defence' that the person must know the case against him which he is called upon to defend. If he is denied that information on the case against him, the hearing, if any, will neither be reasonable nor effective. When law provides for hearing to a person in any case, it does not envisage a perfunctory hearing but a real and effective one. Otherwise, the very purpose of hearing will be negated. With due respect to the Division Bench,[689a] the view propounded by it does not appear to be in conformity with the rationale underlying the requirement of affording reasonable opportunity of being heard in a case.

Form of Hearing

S.A. de Smith in his standard well-known work *Judicial Review of Administrative Action*[690] stated, under the heading 'Form of Hearing', as follows:

689a. *District Administration, Tura* v. *Commissioner of Inquiry*, Meghalaya, AIR 2007 (NOC) 275 (Gah) (DB).

690. 3rd Edition, p. 177.

It must be pointed out, however, that when the words "hearing" or "opportunity to be heard" are used in legislation, they nearly always denote a hearing at which oral submissions and evidence may be tendered. In some legislative contexts the term "hearing" is used in contrast to "inquiry": in practice a hearing may be held in private, though members of the general public are not necessarily excluded; the conduct of both hearings and inquiries in town planning matters is oral and is now governed by similar procedural rules.

In the absence of clear statutory guidance on the matter, one who is entitled to the protection of the *audi alteram partem* rule is now prima facie entitled to put his case orally but in a number of contexts the courts have held natural justice to have been satisfied by an opportunity to make written representations to the deciding body, and there are still many situations where a person will be able to present his case adequately in this way.

Reference may also be made to another passage from that work[691] wherein it is stated:

Refusal to permit cross-examinations of witnesses at an administrative hearing will usually be a denial of natural justice.

But S.A. de Smith again observed in the said work[692] as follows:

Again, deprivation of the opportunity to test evidence by cross-examination is not a violation of natural justice if the tribunal can and does decide merely on the strength of an inspection of oral or written submissions supplemented by its own local or specialized knowledge, or if the proceedings before an investigating body are only for the purpose of collective information....

---

691. 3rd Edition, p. 188.

692. *Ibid.*, p. 189.

In *Halsbury's Laws of England*,[693] under the heading 'Evidence on Affidavit'; the following passage occurs:

> A deponent may be ordered to attend for cross-examination on his affidavit before a Judge, master or examiner of the court and the court may refuse to act on an affidavit where the deponent cannot be cross-examined.

Natural justice is really nothing more than fair play in action. But rules of fair play differ from Court to Court. They certainly do differ in their applicability to different legislative and factual situations. The fundamental rule, to put it in a simple form, is that the citizen should be entitled to a 'hearing' free of bias before any decision, which will prejudicially affect his right, is taken. This rule of fairness does not mean that a citizen should, in all circumstances, be entitled to a traditional, elaborate, time-consuming process of a trial in a law Court; but merely that he should be afforded an opportunity to present his version of the issue in a manner appropriate to the particular exercise of power.[694]

Effect of Denial of Hearing

Fact-finding inquiries have been held in Britain first by Parliamentary Committees from 1660 onwards and then under the Tribunals of Inquiry (Evidence) Act, 1921 and lastly in India under the Commissions of Inquiry Act, 1952. The working of these inquiries has been studied by Royal Commission in 1966, by Prof. G.W. Keeton in his book *Trial by Tribunal* (1960) and by Lord Justice Salmon in his *Lionel Cohen Lectures* (1967). But it has never been suggested that a mere fact-finding inquiry was or should be held to have been vitiated by denial of hearing to persons into whose conduct such inquiry was held. Nor was such a fact-finding inquiry ever quashed.[695]

What is the effect if the concerned person is not given an adequate hearing during the inquiry before the Commission? If that person approached the Court during the pendency of the

---

693. IV Edition, p. 215.

694. *Mohd. Ibrahim Khan* v. *Sushil Kumar*, AIR 1983 Andhra Pradesh 69.

695. *Mohd. Ibrahim Khan* v. *Sushil Kumar*, AIR 1983 Andhra Pradesh 69.

inquiry, the Court would find it easier to direct the Commission to hear the petitioner.[696] A writ of prohibition would more favourably be considered if a fact-finding inquiry is pending.[697] But if such an inquiry is over, the Court would look askance at a prayer that the report of the inquiry should be quashed. The proposition that certiorari goes against the record and may be issued even after the inquiry body has ceased to exist would more properly apply to the report of a disciplinary inquiry committee. It cannot apply to the report of a fact-finding inquiry. For, such a report is only a piece of information which may be read by the Government or by any one else purely as facts. It has no force of itself. The Government is free to take such view of the facts as it deems fit. The formation of a view or opinion by the Government on the basis of such a report is a subjective process. It is an exercise of administrative discretion by the Government. In no sense is the process of forming such an opinion a judicial function. A certiorari to quash is issued against that record which prejudicially affects some person in the sense that some action is taken against the said person on the basis of the said record. The record of the disciplinary inquiry imposing punishment on a person would be such a record.[698]

In taking administrative decision, it is open to the Government to consider other material not included in a judicial or quasi-judicial inquiry. Thus, in addition to the facts ascertained by the Commission of Inquiry, it is open to the Government to consider other facts including other expert advice. The Government is, therefore, not restricted to the report and the proceedings of the Commission of Inquiry in acquainting itself with the subject of inquiry and taking administrative decision thereon. Besides, even if the Government is relying solely on the report and the proceedings of the Commission to arrive at the conclusion that there is a prima facie case for

---

696. *Vallimavil Ammal* v. *The Commission of Inquiry*, ILR (1968) 2 Madras 188.

697. *Judicial Review of Administrative Action* by Prof. S.A. de Smith, Second Edition, p. 218.

698. *G.S. Harnal* v. *Union of India and Others*, ILR (1971) II Delhi 129.

initiating action against certain persons, such a decision exists apart from the report of the Commission as the report cannot even be used as evidence against those persons. Can the Court quash such a decision? Answering this question in the negative, Delhi High Court observed[699] that "just as this Court cannot compel the government to hold a disciplinary inquiry against the petitioners similarly this Court cannot compel the Government not to hold such a disciplinary inquiry against the petitioners. If this is the legal position, it would be perfectly futile for the Court to quash the report of the Commission. Such quashing only kills the action directly based on the report. It cannot affect action which is not compelled by the report but which is based on an independent decision of the Government. This is the crux of the distinction between a fact-finding inquiry and a disciplinary inquiry. The former does not compel any action and does not impose any punishment. The latter necessarily results in action or punishment. Therefore, the former cannot be quashed while the latter can be quashed".

However, the fact remains that under Section 8B of the Act and the rules framed under the said Act, the Commission of Inquiry appointed under the provisions of that Act is bound to give a reasonable opportunity to the person whose conduct is sought to be inquired into and whose reputation is likely to be prejudicially affected by the inquiry. It is a mandatory requirement. Therefore, that portion of the report which deals with the conduct and reputation of the person concerned, without giving him an opportunity of being heard in the inquiry should be taken to be vitiated for violation of Section 8B of the Act. In *N. Manoharan* v. *State of Tamil Nadu*,[700] the State Government appointed a Commission of Inquiry under Section 3 of the Act to inquire into the incidents of beating and ill-treatment alleged to have taken place in the Central Prison, Madras during February 1976. The Commission inquired into the conduct of the appellant as Jail Warden, and gave a finding against him that he took part in the beating of the detenues on

---

699. *G.S. Harnal* v. *Union of India and Others*, ILR (1971) II Delhi 129.

700. AIR 1981 Madras 147.

the night of 2nd February 1976. While recording this finding, the Commission did not give any hearing to him in terms of Section 8B. Based on the said finding, disciplinary proceedings were initiated against him by the State and a charge memo was served upon him by the Enquiry Officer. Though the appellant had originally prayed for a writ of certiorari to quash that portion of the report which affected him, he had subsequently filed a petition for substituting the prayer to mandamus forbearing the respondents from taking any action against him based on the report, which according to him, vitiated by the violation of the statutory provision in Section 8B of the Act. The Court issued a writ of mandamus forbearing the respondents from taking any action against the appellant solely based on the finding of the Commission. In a linked petition,[701] the Court also issued a writ of certiorari, quashing the memorandum of charge that was solely based on the finding of the Commission having been recorded in violation of Section 8B. This was, however, without prejudice to the rights of the respondents to initiate fresh proceedings if the charge could be established by other materials independent of the finding recorded by the Commission in its report.

This matter can be said to have attained finality with the Supreme Court's judgment in the case of *State of Bihar* v. *Lal Krishna Advani*,[702] wherein the following pertinent observations were made, viz.: "One is entitled to have and preserve one's reputation and one also has a right to protect it. In case any authority, in discharge of its duties fastened upon it under the law, traverses into the realm of personal reputation adversely affecting him, must provide a chance to him to have his say in the matter. In such circumstances right of an individual to have the safeguard of principles of natural justice before being adversely commented upon by a Commission of Inquiry is statutorily recognized and violation of the same will to bear the scrutiny of judicial review.... The provision as contained under Section 8B of the Act was brought into the statute book by Amending Act

701. AIR 1981 Madras 147.

702. AIR 2003 SC 3357.

79 of 1971.... Thus the principle of natural justice was got inducted in the shape of statutory provision. It is thus incumbent upon the Commission to give an opportunity to a person before any comment is made or opinion is expressed which is likely to prejudicially affect that person. Needless to emphasise that failure to comply with principles of natural justice renders the action non-est as well as the consequences thereof."

Whether Right to Hearing Includes Right to Cross-examine

Rules of natural justice require that a party against whom an allegation is being inquired into should be given a hearing. It cannot, however, be acceded to that the right to hearing includes right to cross-examine in all cases. That right must depend upon the circumstances of each case and must also depend on the statute under which the allegations are being inquired into.[703] The rules of natural justice vary with the varying constitution of statutory bodies and the rules prescribed by the Act under which they function; and the question, whether or not any rules of natural justice had been contravened should be decided not under any preconceived notion, but in the light of the statutory rules and provisions.[704] In the context of the present Act, it has to be remembered that the statute permits a Commission of Inquiry to be set up for fact-finding purposes. The report of the Commission has no force *proprio vigore*. This aspect of the matter is important in deciding the rules of natural justice reasonably applicable in the proceedings of the Commission of Inquiry under the Act. Though this section gives a right to be heard but Section 8C gives only a restricted right to cross-examine. The latter right is confined only to the witnesses called to depose against the person demanding the right. So the Act does not contemplate a right of hearing to include a right to cross-examination.[705]

---

703. *State of Jammu and Kashmir* v. *Bakshi Gulam Mohammad*, AIR 1967 S C 122.

704. *Nagendra Nath Bora* v. *Commr. of Hills Divisions and Appeals, Assam*, AIR 1958 SC 398, p. 409.

705. *State of Jammu and Kashmir* v. *Bakshi Gulam Mohammad*, AIR 1967 SC 122, p. 133.

Right of cross-examination and representation by legal practitioner.

8C. The appropriate Government, every person referred to in section 8B and, with the permission of the Commission, any other person whose evidence is recorded by the Commission,—

(a) may cross-examine a witness other than a witness produced by it or him;

(b) may address the Commission; and

(c) may be represented before the Commission by a legal practitioner or, with the permission of the Commission, by any other person.

General

Section 8C of the Act confers the right of cross-examination, the right of audience and the right of representation through a legal practitioner on the appropriate Government, on every person referred to in Section 8B and with the permission of the Commission, on any other person whose evidence is recorded by the Commission. Clauses (a) and (b) of Section 8B refer respectively to persons whose conduct the Commission considers it necessary to enquire into and persons whose reputation, in the opinion of the Commission, is likely to be prejudicially affected by the inquiry. It is undeniable that the person whose conduct is being enquired into and he be a Chief Minister or a Minister, the doings of the Government itself are exposed to the fierce light of publicity. But that is a risk which is inherent in every inquiry directed at finding out the truth. It does not, however, justify the specious submission that the inquiry constitutes an interference with the executive functions of the State Government or, that it confers on the Central Government the power to control the functions of the State executive. After all, it is in the interest of those against whom open allegations of corruption and nepotism are made that they should have an opportunity of repelling those allegations before a trained and independent Commission of Inquiry which is not hide bound by the technical rules of evidence. It is only be establishing the truth that the purity and integrity of public life can be preserved and that is the object which the Commissions of Inquiry Act seeks to achieve.[706]

Right to Cross-examination is Circumscribed by the Statutory Provisions

This section provides to a person a limited right to cross-examine only those persons who give viva voce evidence before the Commission against him. If right to cross-examination is viewed as inherent in Section 4(c) in respect of every person who swore an affidavit as to the facts involved in the inquiry, then Section 8C would become superfluous. Order 1, Rule 4 of Code of Civil Procedure states that the evidence of the witnesses in attendance shall be taken orally in open Court. Order 19, Rule 4, CPC reads as:

> Any court may at any time for sufficient reason order that any particular fact or facts may be proved by affidavit, or that the affidavit of any witness may be read at the hearing, on such conditions as the Court thinks reasonable.
>
> Provided that where it appears to the Court that either party bona fide desires the production of a witness for cross-examination, and that such witness can be produced, an order shall not be made authorizing the evidence of such witness to be given by affidavit.

Order 19, Rule 1 has to be read with Order 18, Rule 4. It would therefore appear that Order 19, Rule 1 is intended as a sort of exception to the provisions contained in Order 18, Rule 4. The Commissions of Inquiry Act contains no provision similar to Order 18, Rule 4. Therefore, when Section 4(c) of the Act gives the Commission the power of receiving evidence on affidavits, it gives that as an independent power and not by way of an exception to the general rule of taking evidence viva voce in open Court. It would be natural in such circumstances to think that what the Act gives is only the power to take evidence by affidavit and does not intend to be subject to the proviso contained in Order 19, Rule 1. If it were not so, then the result really would be to require all evidence before the Commission

706. *Motahar Hossain* v. *Haratosh Chakrabarty*, 84 CWN 560.

to be given orally in open Court. If that was intended, it would have been expressly provided for in the Act. The number of witnesses swearing affidavits on the side of the Government may often be very large. The statute could not have intended that all of them had to be examined in open Court and subjected to cross-examination, for, then, the proceedings of the Commission would be interminable. The Act contemplates a quick disposal of the business before the Commission, for; otherwise the object behind it may have been defeated.[707]

In an enquiry before a Commission, the procedure is governed by Sections 8B and 8C of the Act and the Rules made by the State Government under Section 12 of the Act. Only when a witness is examined viva voce before the Commission the right to cross-examine that witness accrues under Section 8C to the person likely to be prejudicially affected. No such right arises when evidence is given on affidavits. The provisions of Sections 8B and 8C of the Act do not confer the right to summon parties who have given evidence on affidavit for cross-examination. The general right to cross-examination will accrue only when the evidence is recorded viva voce.[708]

Issuance of summons to a witness for his cross-examination is at the Commission's discretion. A person filing an affidavit before a Commission of Inquiry need not be summoned for cross-examination at the instance of other party. The person seeking issuance of such summons must make out a case for his claim. If the materials placed before the Commission are such which require an explanation by a person with reference to the terms of reference, then the Commission, in the interest of justice, may summon that person to the witness box to submit himself for cross-examination. Where no such explanation is warranted, that person cannot be compelled to the witness box for the purpose of cross-examination.[709]

---

707. *State of Jammu and Kashmir* v. *Bakshi Gulam Mohammad*, AIR 1967 SC 122, pp. 132-33.

708. *Mohd. Ibrahim Khan* v. *Sushil Kumar*, AIR 1983 Andhra Pradesh 69.

709. *Kailash Joshi* v. *State of Madhya Pradesh and Others*, AIR 1999 Madhya Pradesh 41.

Furthermore, every witness does not have a right to cross-examine every other witness examined before the Commission. Moreover, the proceedings of the Commission have to be controlled by the Commission and one witness cannot be permitted to cross-examine the other witnesses especially when he has no case that his rights will be prejudicially affected by the report of the Commission.[710]

A reading of Sections 8B and 8C would show that the Commission can permit any person to cross-examine the witnesses, if the reputation of such person is likely to be prejudicially affected by the inquiry. Of course, Section 8C provides that the Commission can also permit any other witnesses to cross-examine. But such permission can normally be given to only such person whose reputation is likely to be prejudicially affected by the inquiry.[711]

Applicability of Principles of Natural Justice to Inquiries Involving Civil Consequences

The question as to the applicability of the principles of natural justice to an inquiry to which the provisions of Sections 8B and 8C are not applicable, though such inquiry involves civil consequences, came up for consideration before the Orissa High Court in *Prafulla Chandra* v. *State of Orissa*.[712] Discussing the case law on the subject, the Court answered the question in the affirmative.

The aim of the rules of "natural justice", as has been explained in the decision reported in *A.K. Kraipak* v. *Union of India*[713] is to secure justice or to put it negatively, to prevent miscarriage of justice. Their lordships have further observed that these rules can operate only in the areas not covered by any law validly made and they do not supplant the law of the land but supplement it. Their lordships have noticed that the concept of "natural justice" has undergone a great deal of change in recent

---

710. *D. Guruswamy* v. *State of Tamil Nadu and Others*, AIR 2000 Madras 373.

711. *Ibid.*, p. 374.

712. AIR 1988 Orissa 18.

713. AIR 1970 SC 150 .

years. The following passage from the said decision would be profitable to quote in this connection.

> In the past it was thought that it included just two rules, namely, (1) no one shall be a judge in his own cause (*Nemo debet esse judex in propria causa*), and (2) no decision shall be given against a party without affording him a reasonable hearing (*audi alteram partem*). Very soon thereafter a third rule was envisaged and that is that quasi-judicial enquiries must be held in good faith, without bias and not arbitrarily unreasonably. But in the course of years many more subsidiary rules came to be added to the rules of natural justice. Till very recently, it was the opinion of the Courts that unless the authority concerned was required by the law under which it functioned to act judicially there was no room for the application of the rules of natural justice. The validity of that limitation is not questioned. If the purpose of the rules of natural justice is to prevent miscarriage of justice one fails to see why those rules should be made inapplicable to administrative enquiries. Often times it is not easy to draw the line that demarcates administrative enquiries from quasi-judicial enquiries. Enquiries which were considered administrative at one time are now being considered as quasi-judicial in character. Arriving at a just decision is the aim of both quasi-judicial enquiries as well as administrative enquiries. An unjust decision in an administrative enquiry may have more far-reaching effect than a decision in a quasi-judicial enquiry. As observed by this Court in *Suresh Koshy George* v. *University of Kerala,*[714] the rules of natural justice are not embodied rules. What particular rule of natural justice should apply to a given case must depend to a great extent on the facts and circumstances of that case, the framework of the law under which the enquiry is held and the constitution of the Tribunal or body of persons appointed for that purpose. Whenever a complaint is made before a Court that some principle of natural justice had been contravened the Court has to decide whether the

714. AIR 1969 SC 198.

observance of that rule was necessary for a just decision on the facts of that case.

In *City Corner* v. *Personal Assistant to Collector and Additional District Magistrate, Nellore,*[715] their lordships have held that the principle of natural justice should be followed as a requirement of law even where the statute in question itself does not so provide. In the enquiry in question in this case, even though it was administrative in character, the principle of natural justice as a requirement of law and as provided in the terms of reference itself, should be made applicable, as in such inquiry the report was capable of and in fact has prejudicially affected the petitioners.

The applicability of the principle of natural justice has been elaborately dealt with in the case of *Maneka Gandhi* v. *Union of India*[716] in which the passport of the petitioner of that case was impounded without giving opportunity to the petitioner to be heard. It was contended by the Attorney General in that case that giving such opportunity would have stultified and frustrated the provisions of the Passport Act. Their lordships held that the principle of *audi alteram partem* which mandates that no one shall be condemned unheard is a part of the rules of the natural justice. Quoting the law as stated by eminent jurists their lordships have gone to the extent of observing that natural justice is a principle which intends to invest law with fairness and to secure justice and over the years, it has grown into a widely pervasive rule affecting large areas of administrative action. In this case, their lorships have held[717] as follows:

> Now, if this be the test of applicability of the doctrine of natural justice, there can be no distinction between a quasi-judicial function and an administrative function for this purpose. The aim of both administrative inquiry as well as quasi-judicial inquiry is to arrive at a just decision and if a rule of natural justice is calculated to secure justice, or to put

715. AIR 1976 SC 143; (1976) 2 SCR 38.

716. (1978) 1 SCC 248; AIR 1978 SC 597.

717. (1978) 1 SCC 248; AIR 1978 SC, paragraph 10, p. 286 of (1978) 1 SCC 248.

it negatively, to prevent miscarriage of justice, it is difficult to see why it should be applicable to quasi-judicial inquiry and not to administrative inquiry. It must logically apply to both.

As observed by the Supreme Court in *Suman Gupta* v. *State of Jammu and Kashmir*[718] the exercise of administrative power vested in a public authority must be structured within a system of controls informed by both relevance and reason—relevance in relation to the subject which it seeks to serve and reason in regard to the manner in which it attempts to do so. Administrative power should be exercised within the defined limits in the reasonable discretion of the designated authority. The vesting of an absolute and uncontrolled power in such authority falls outside the Constitution.

Even administrative orders which involve civil consequences have to be passed consistently with the rules of natural justice, as held by the Supreme Court in the case of *State of Orissa* v. *Dr. (Miss) Binapani Dei*.[719] It may be useful to quote an extract from *S.G. Jaisinghani* v. *Union of India*[720] as under:

> In this context it is important to emphasize that the absence of arbitrary power is the first essential of the rule of law upon which our whole constitutional system is based. In a system governed by rule of law, discretion, when conferred upon executive authorities, must be confined within clearly defined limits. The rule of law from this point of view means that decisions should be made by the application of known principles and rules and, in general, such decisions should be predictable and the citizen should know where he is. If a decision is taken without any principle or without any rule, it is unpredictable and such a decision taken in accordance with the rule of law.[721] 'Law has reached its finest moments', stated Douglas, J, in *United States* v. *Wunderlich*[722] "when it has freed man from the unlimited

718. AIR 1983 SC 1235.

719. AIR 1967 SC 1269.

720. AIR 1967 SC 1427.

721. Dicey, *Law of the Constitution*, Tenth Edition, Introduction.

722. 1951 342 US 98.

discretion of some ruler.... Where discretion is absolute, man has always suffered." It is in this sense that the rule of law may be said to be the sworn enemy of caprice. Discretion, as Lord Mansfield stated it in classic terms in the case of *John Wilkes*[723] 'means sound discretion guided by law. It must be governed by rule, not by humour; it must not be arbitrary, vague, and fanciful'.

In *A.K. Kraipak* v. *Union of India,*[724] the Supreme Court has observed:

> The dividing line between an administrative power and a quasi-judicial power is quite thin and is being gradually obliterated. For determining whether a power is an administrative power or quasi-judicial power is quite thin and is being gradually obliterated. For determining whether a power is an administrative power or a quasi-judicial power one has to look to the nature of the power conferred, the person or persons on whom it is conferred, the consequences ensuing from the exercise of that power and the manner in which that power is expected to be exercised. In a welfare-State like ours it is inevitable that the organ of the State under our Constitution is regulated and controlled by the rule of law. In a welfare-State like ours it is inevitable that the jurisdiction of the administrative bodies is increasing at a rapid rate. The concept of rule of law would lose its validity if the instrumentalities of the State are not charged with the duty of discharging their functions in a fair and just manner. The requirement of acting judicially in essence is nothing but a requirement to justly and fairly and not arbitrarily or capriciously. The procedures which are considered inherent in the exercise of a judicial power are merely those which facilitate if not ensure a just and fair decision. In recent years are concept of quasi-judicial power....

---

723. 1770 4 Burr 2528, p. 2539.

724. AIR 1970 SC 150 (*supra*).

Administrative action must adhere to procedural safeguards fixed by it to avoid arbitrariness, failing which the action would be rendered invalid.[725]

In view of the aforesaid, the law must, therefore, now be taken to be well settled that even in an administrative proceeding that involves civil consequences, the doctrine of natural justice must be held to be applicable.

Protection of action taken in good faith.

9. No suit or other legal proceeding shall lie against the appropriate Government, the Commission or any member thereof, or any person acting under the direction either of the appropriate Government or of the Commission in respect of anything which is in good faith done or intended to be done in pursuance of this Act or of any rules or orders made thereunder or in respect of the publication, by or under the authority of the appropriate Government or the Commission, or any report, paper or proceedings.

Members, etc. to be public servants.

10. Every member of the Commission and every officer appointed or authorised by the Commission to exercise functions under this Act shall be deemed to be a public servant within the meaning of Section 21 of the Indian Penal Code.

Functions under this Act—Scope of

In *K. Krishna Warrier* v. *T.R. Velunny*,[726] the District Magistrate at Trichur, who was also the Commissioner of Inquiry under the Commissions of Inquiry Act preferred a complaint and sought dispensation of his examination by the Magistrate under the proviso (aa) to Section 200, CrPC. It was held that the complaint in the case fulfilled the definition of the term 'complaint' in Section 4(1)(h), CrPC and the Magistrate was competent under Section 190(1)(b), CrPC to take cognizance of the offence. Holding that the proviso (aa) to Section 200 CrPC

725. *B.S. Minhas* v. *Indian Statistical Institute*, (1983) 4 SCC 582; AIR 1984 SC 363.

726. AIR 1960 Kerela 350.

was not applicable in the case, it was observed that though as the Commissioner of Inquiry being a public servant, it was not a part of his duty to prefer complaint. It was further held that by the mere order of Government authorizing the complainant to prefer the complaint, he could not be deemed to be acting in the discharge of his official duty, because the Government Order did not confer any power on him to be exercised by him as an official, save that preferring the complaint. On the basis, that he had no official duty whatever to prefer a complaint, as the District Magistrate or as the Commissioner of Inquiry, it was difficult to hold that he purported to act in the discharge of official duty; he could not be deemed to have acted, in either of the two capacities.

Section 21 of the Indian Penal Code, 1860

Section 21 of the Indian Penal Code, 1860 defines the term "public servant". This term is to be distinguished from the expression 'servant of Government'. Section 14 of the Indian Penal Code, 1860 defines the expression 'servant of Government'. The term 'public servant' is of wider import than the expression 'servant of Government'. Every servant of Government is a public servant. But every public servant is not a servant of Government. Section 197 of the Code of Criminal Procedure, 1973 deals with prosecution of Judges and public servants. Sub-section (1) of this section provides "when any person who is or was a Judge or Magistrate or a public servant not removable from the office save by or with the sanction of the Government is accused of any offence alleged to have been committed by him while acting or purporting to act in the discharge of his official duty, no court shall take cognizance of such offence except with the previous sanction—(a) in the case of a person who is employed or, as the case may be, was at the time of commission of the alleged offence employed, in connection with the affairs of the Union, of the Central Government; (b) in the case of a person who is employed or, as the case may be, was at the time of the commission of the alleged offence employed, in connection with the affairs of a State, of the State Government: provided that where the alleged offence was committed by a person referred to in clause (b) during the period while a proclamation issued under clause (1) of Article 356 of the Constitution was in force in a State, clause (b) will apply as if for the expression 'State Government' occurring therein, the expression 'Central Government' wer substituted".

A member of the Commission of Inquiry and every officer of such a Commission are not included in the meaning of the term 'public servant' in Section 21 of the Indian Penal Code, 1860. Section 10 of the Commissions of Inquiry Act, 1952 creates a legal fiction in this regard and provides that every member of the Commission and every officer appointed or authorized by the Commission to exercise functions under this Act shall be deemed to be a public servant within the meaning of Section 21 of the Indian Penal Code. Thus, members and officers of the Commissions of Inquiry appointed under the Act become eligible to the protection of Section 197 of the Code of Criminal Procedure, 1973. Accordingly, no Court shall take cognizance of any offence alleged to have been committed by any member or officer of a Commission of Inquiry appointed under the Act while acting or purporting to act in the discharge of their duties except with the previous sanction of the appropriate Government. The underlying purpose is to save such members and officers from frivolous or vexatitious prosecution.

It will be expedient to reproduce the text of Section 21 of the Indian Penal Code, 1860 for ready reference as under:

> 21. Public servant—The words "public servant" denote a person falling under any of the descriptions hereinafter following namely:
>
> First— [727][****]
>
> Second—Every commissioned officer in the Military, Naval or Air Force of India;
>
> Third—Every Judge including any person empowered by law to discharge, whether by himself or as member of any body or persons, any adjudicatory functions;
>
> Fourth—Every officer of a court of justice (including a liquidator, receiver or commissioner) whose duty it is as

---

727. Omitted by the A.O. 1950.

such officer, to investigate or report on any matter of law or fact, or to make, authenticate, or keep any document, or to take charge or dispose of any property or to execute any judicial process, or to administer any oath, or to interpret, or to preserve order in the Court, and every person specially authorized by a court of justice to perform any of such duties;

Fifth—Every juryman, assessor, or member of a panchayat assisting a court of justice or public servant;

Sixth—Every arbitrator or other person to whom any cause or matter has been referred for decision or report by any court of justice, or by any other competent public authority;

Seventh—Every person who holds any office by virtue of which he is empowered to place or keep any person in confinement;

Eight—Every officer of the Government whose duty it is, as such officer, to prevent offences, to give information of offences, to bring offenders to justice, or to protect the public health, safety or convenience;

Ninth—Every officer whose duty it is, as such officer, to take, receive, keep or expend any property on behalf of the Government, or to make any survey, assessment or contract on behalf of the Government, or to execute any revenue process, or to investigate, or to report, on any matter affecting the pecuniary interests of the Government, or to make, authenticate or keep any document relating to the pecuniary interests of the Government, to make, authenticate or keep any document relating to the pecuniary interests of the Government, or to prevent the infraction of any law for the protection of the pecuniary interests of the Government;

Tenth—Every officer whose duty it is, as such officer, to take receive, keep or expend any property, to make any survey or assessment or to levy any rate or tax for any secular common purpose of any village, town or district, or to make, authenticate or keep any document for the ascertaining of the rights of the people of any village, town or district;

Eleventh—Every person who holds any office in virtue of which he is empowered to prepare, publish, maintain or revise an electoral roll or to conduct an election or part of an election;

Twelfth—Every person—

(a) in the service or pay of the Government or remunerated by fees or commission for the performance of any public duty by the Government;

(b) in the service or pay of a local authority, a corporation established by or under a Central, Provincial or State Act or a Government company as defined in Section 617 of the Companies Act, 1956 (1 of 1956).

ILLUSTRATION

A Municipal Commissioner is a Public Servant

Explanation 1.—Persons falling under any of the above descriptions are public servants, whether appointed by the Government or not.

Explanation 2.—Wherever the words "public servant" occur, they shall be understood of every person who is in actual possession of the situation of a public servant, whatever legal defect there may be in his right to hold that situation.

Explanation 3.—The word "election" denotes an election for the purpose of selecting members of any legislative, muncipal or other public authority, of whatever character, the method of selection to which is by or under, any law prescribed as by election.

Penalty for acts calculated to bring the Commission or any member thereof into disrepute.

[728][10A. (1) If any person, by words either spoken or intended to be read, makes or publishes any statement or does any other act, which is calculated to bring the Commission or any member thereof into disrepute, he shall be punishable with simple imprisonment for a term which may extend to six months, or with fine, or with both.

728. Ins. by Act 79 of 1971, Section 13.

[729](2) Notwithstanding anything contained in the Code of Criminal Procedure, 1973, when an offence under sub-section (1) is alleged to have been committed, the High Court may take cognizance of such offence, without the case being committed to it, upon a complaint in writing, made by a member of Commission or an officer of the Commission authorized by it in this behalf.

(3) Every complaint referred to in sub-section (2) shall set forth the facts which constitute the offence alleged, the nature of such offence and such other particulars as are reasonably sufficient to give notice to the accused of the offence alleged to have been committed by him.

(4) No High Court shall take cognizance of an offence under sub-section (1) unless the complaint is made within six months from the date on which the offence is alleged to have been committed.

(5) A High Court taking cognizance of an offence under sub-section (1) shall try the case in accordance with the procedure for the trial of warrant cases instituted otherwise than on a police report before a court of a Magistrate:

Provided that the personal attendance of a member of a Commission as a complainant or otherwise is not required in such trial.

(6) Notwithstanding anything contained in the Code of Criminal Procedure, 1973, an appeal shall lie as a matter of right from any judgment of the High Court to the Supreme Court, both on facts and on law.

---

729. Sub-section (2) was substituted by Act 63 of 1988, Section 3. The omitted sub-section reads as: (2) The provisions of section 198B of the Code of Criminal Procedure, 1898 shall apply in relation to an offence under sub-section (1) as they apply in relation to an offence referred to in sub-section (1) of the said Section 198B, subject to the modification that no complaint in respect of such offence shall be made by the Public Prosecutor except with the previous sanction,— (a) in the case of a Commission, or member or a Commission appointed by the Central Government, of the Central Government; or (b) in the case of a Commission appointed by the State Government, of the State Government.

(7) Every appeal to the Supreme Court under sub-section (6) shall be preferred within a period of thirty days from the date of the judgment appealed from:

Provided that the Supreme Court may entertain an appeal after the expiry of the said period of thirty days if it is satisfied that the appellant had sufficient cause for not preferring the appeal within the period of thirty days.]

Objects and Reasons

This clause seeks to insert a new Section 10A in the Act. The new section provides for penalty for acts calculated to bring the Commision or any member thereof into disrepute. The penalty proposed is simple imprisonment for a term which may extend to six months or a fine or both. Provisions of Section 198B of the Code of Criminal Procedure, 1898 have been made applicable to an offence under this new section. Subject to the modification that no complaint in respect of such offence shall be made by the Public Prosecutor except with the previous sanction of the appropriate Government (vide paragraph 30 of the Report).[730]

Section 10A of the Commissions of Inquiry Act, 1952 provides for penalty for acts calculated to bring a Commission of Inquiry or any member thereof into disrepute and provides for the procedure for taking cognizance of such offence. Under the procedure specified in the section, the provisions of the Code of Criminal Procedure will apply and no prosecution can be launched except with the previous sanction of the Central Government or the State Government, as the case may be. It is proposed to amend this section to change this procedure to provide that an offence under this section is triable by the High Court by ordinary procedure prescribed under the Code of Criminal Procedure on a report of the Commission of Inquiry concerned without committal proceedings and that the personal

730. Twenty-fourth Report of the Law Commission of India on the Commissions of Inquiry Act, 1952. Notes on Clauses, Clause 13, the Commissions of Inquiry (Amendment) Bill, 1971.

attendance of the members of the Commission of Inquiry as complainants would not be necessary.[731]

Nature and Scope of the Section

Chapter X of the Indian Penal Code, 1860, consisting of Sections 172 to 190, deals with the offences of contempt of the lawful authority of public servants. Sections 175, 178, 179 and 180 are relevant in the context of inquiry Commissions. These sections respectively deal with the offences relating to (i) omission to produce document to public servant by person legally bound to produce it (Section 175); (ii) refusing oath or affirmation when duly required by public servant to make it (Section 178); (iii) refusing to answer public servant authorized to question (Section 179); and (iv) refusing to sign statement (Section 180).

Chapter XI of the Indian Penal Code, 1860, consisting of Sections 191 to 229, deals with the offences of false evidence and offences against public servants. Section 228 of that Code is relevant in the context of inquiry Commissions. Section 228 deals with the offence of intentional insult or interruption to public servant sitting in judicial proceedings.

The above sections have been extended to Commissions of Inquiry in terms of Section 5 of the Commissions of Inquiry Act, 1952 and the Commissions are deemed to be Civil Court for this purpose.

Chapter XXI of the Indian Penal Code, 1860, consisting of Sections 499 to 502, deals with the offence of 'defamation'. Section 499 defines the term 'defamation'. The present section, i.e. Section 10A, is broadly on the lines of Section 499 of the Code. Of course, there are material differences. Yet the essence of the two offences remains the same. One may wonder as to what was the need for inserting Section 10A in the Act, especially when the provisions of the Code are otherwise available in the case of Commissions of Inquiry. One reason for this that can be gathered from the Statement of Objects and Reasons is the change of procedure that has been brought about by this Section.

---

731. Paragraph 1 of Statement of Objects and Reasons, the Commissions of Inquiry (Amendment) Bill, 1988.

Another reason could be to remove any ambiguity in the matter by making 'the act of bringing a Commission or its member into disrepute' a specific offence under the Act.

The essence of the offence of defamation in Section 499 of the Code is the harm to the reputation of a person. The essence of the offence under Section 10A is 'bringing the Commission or any of its members into disrepute'. The manner in which such harm to reputation of a person or, as the case may be, the Commission or any of its members is brought into disrepute is the same, that is to say, by words, either spoken or written/ published or 'any other act' which may include signs or visible representation or publication of any statement. This manner should be such as is calculated to bring the Commission or its member(s) into disrepute. The same result is brought about in Section 499 of the Code by using the expressions 'intending', 'knowing', or 'having reason to believe'.

It may be expedient to refer to the literal meanings of certains terms used in the two sections. For such meanings, reliance is made on the *New Collins Concise English Dictionary*. Accordingly, the word 'reputation' means "1. the estimation in which a person or thing is generally held; opinion. 2. a high opinion generally held about a person or thing; esteem. 3. notoriety or fame, esp. for some specified characterstic." The word 'repute' means "1.(tr. usually passive) to consider (a person or thing) to be as specified; he is reputed to be rich. –n. 2. public estimation; reputation; a writer of little repute."

The word 'defame' means "to attack the good name or reputation of; slander; libel." The word 'disrepute' means "a loss or lack of credit or repute".

The word 'calculated' means "1. undertaken after considering the likelihood of success or failure. 2. premeditated; a calculated insult".

Thus, the essential connotations of the offence under the Code and that under the present section of the Commissions of Inquiry Act are essentially the same. However, there is a marked difference between the two; namely, the offence of defamation under Section 499 of the Indian Penal Code is subject to ten exceptions. If a case falls under any of these exceptions, no offence of defamation will be made out. But the offence under Section 10A has not been statutorily subjected to any offence. The exceptions under the Code will not be applicable to offences under Section 10A of the present Act on their own. Nevertheless, it may be borne in mind that the exceptions are based on sound policy considerations, such as public good, good faith, fair comments and truth of the matter. These will certainly have material bearing on the interpretation of the term 'calculated to'. It may be useful to refer in this regard the provisions of Section 8 of the Contempt of Courts Act, 1971, which reads: "Nothing contained in this Act shall be construed as implying that any other defence which would have been a valid defence in any proceedings for contempt of court has ceased to be available merely by reason of the provisons of this Act." Section 8 indicates that the Act is not exhaustive on this aspect. It seems to have been inserted in the Act more by way of abundant caution. However, there is no corresponding provision in the Commissions of Inquiry Act. Nonetheless, one can gather from this section that there might be defences other than statutory ones that might be available in analogous proceedings under the general law of the land and the same are not intended to be taken away by the present Act. These would certainly enter into judicial consideration while adjudicating as to whether the impugned act is such as is calculated to bring the Commission and its members into disrepute. Thus, if something is said or done in good faith or for public good or bring about the truth to the fore or as a caution or fair comment, it may not be construed as calculated to, or intending to, bring the Commision and/or its members into disrepute as there would be no such motive, intention or mens rea to bring about that result. However, these aspects are yet to receive judicial consideration in the context of inquiry Commissions. With the development of case law on this aspect, the law will become more crystallise and certain in this matter. In any case, such exceptions will be viewed as mitigating factors, having bearing on the punishment to award in any case.

The offence under Section 10A is different from contempt of Court. Since a Commission of Inquiry is not a Court in its own right, there cannot be a contempt of Court in the case of such a Commission. The legal fiction in Section 5 of the Act whereby the Commission is deemed to be a Civil Court cannot be extended beyond its intended purpose and, as such, has to be strictly construed. The distinction between defamation and contempt of Court has been very aptly elaborated by the Apex Court[732] in the following words:

> A distinction must be made between a mere libel or defamation of a Judge and what amounts to a contempt of the court. The test in each case would be whether the impugned publication is a mere defamatory attack on the Judge or whether it is calculated to interfere with the due course of justice or the proper administration of law by his court. It is only in the latter case that it will be punishable as contempt.

Act to apply to other inquiring authorities in certain cases.

11. Where any authority (by whatever name called), other than a Commission appointed under Section 3, has been or is set up under any resolution or order of the appropriate Government for the purpose of making an inquiry into any definite matter of public importance and that Government is of opinion that all or any of the provisions of this Act should be made applicable to that authority, that Government may, subject to the prohibition contained in the proviso to sub-section (1) of Section 3, by notification in the Official Gazette, direct that the said provisions of this Act shall apply to that authority, and on the issue of such a notification that authority shall be deemed to be a Commission appointed under Section 3 for the purposes of this Act.

Applicability of the Section

This section applies to an authority, which is not set up as a Commission of Inquiry under Section 3 of the Act. A

732. *Perspective Publications (P.) Ltd. v. State of Maharashtra*, AIR 1971 SC 221, p. 230.

Commission of Inquiry can be constituted de hors the Act in which case it is an authority appointed in exercise of the executive powers of the Government and if such an authority has been or is set up under a resolution or order of the appropriate Government for the purpose of making inquiry into any definite matter of public importance, then upon the issue of a notification under Section 11 of the Act this authority is to be deemed to be a Commission appointed under Section 3 for the purposes of the Act. There is no question of such a resolution being bad for lack of authority, which is liable to be quashed. The resolution is the expression given to the exercise of executive power by the Government in setting up such an authority, which, by a fiction of law, is converted into a Commission appointed under Section 3 for the purposes of the Act. The issue of the notification under Section 11 of the Act would, therefore, result in the Commission appointed initially by the resolution becoming a Commission under the Act.[733] Any action that may have been taken by such a Commission under the Act prior to the issue of the notification under Section 11 of the Act will not be *per se* illegal and without jurisdiction. That will depend upon the powers conferred upon it under its terms of reference constituting it.[734]

In *Statesman* v. *Fact Finding Committee*,[735] the question of dismissal of the writ petition on ground of inordinate delay was determined with reference to the date on which the Committee was conferred the powers of the Commission of Inquiry as the starting point and not the date on which the Committee was originally appointed. The Committee in this case was constituted on 14-4-1972 and the writ petition was filed on July 1973, i.e. more than a year after the setting up of the Committee. It was accordingly argued that there had been an inordinate delay by the petitioners in presenting the writ petition to the Court and,

---

733. *P.R. Nayak* v. *Union of India*, ILR (1973) I Delhi 747.

734. This question was raised before Delhi High Court in *P.R. Nayak* v. *Union of India*, *supra*, but was not answered being unnecessary in the facts of that case as nothing was to follow therefrom to entitle the petitioner to any relief.

735. AIR 1975 Calcutta 14.

as such, on this ground alone, the petition should be dismissed. In answer to this contention of the respondents, Counsel for the petitioners submitted that so long the Committee was not conferred with the powers under the Act, or in other words, so long the Committee was not given the status of a Commission of Inquiry under Section 11 of the Act, the petitioners had no locus standi to move the Court. For the first time, on April 26, 1973, the Government by a notification under Section 11 of the Act directed that all the provisions of the Act excepting Section 5(1) thereof would apply to the Committee. It was submitted on behalf of the petitioners that since that date the petitioners felt aggrieved and on June 21, 1973, the second petitioner wrote letter to the respondent No. 2, the Chairman of the Committee. On July 7, 1973, there was an implied refusal by the respondent No. 2 to comply with the demand made by the petitioners and, as already stated, the writ petition was moved on July 19, 1973. It was, thus, contended that there had been no delay. This was upheld by the Court as the Court opined that the date on which the Committee was conferred with the powers of the Commission of Inquiry should be taken as the starting point and so considered, it appeared that there had been no delay on the part of the petitioners in moving the Court.

Power to make rules.

12. (1) The appropriate Government may, by notification in the Official Gazette, make rules to carry out the purposes of this Act.

(2) In particular, and without prejudice to the generality of the foregoing power, such rules may provide for all or any of the following matters, namely:

(a) the term of office and the conditions of service of the members of the Commission;

(b) the manner in which inquiries may be held under this Act and the procedure to be followed by the Commission in respect of the proceedings before it;

(c) the powers of civil court which may be vested in thc Commission;

[736]"[(cc) the traveling and other expenses payable to assessors appointed under Section 5B, and to persons summoned by the Commission to give evidence or to produce documents before it."]

(d) any other matter which has to be, or may be prescribed.

[737][(3) Every rule made by the Central Government under this section shall be laid, as soon as may be after it is made, before each house of Parliament while it is in session for a total period of thirty days which may be comprised in one session or [23]["in two or more successive sessions, and if, before the expiry of the session immediately following the session or the successive sessions aforesaid,"] both Houses agree in making any modification in the rule or both Houses agree that the rule should not be made, the rule shall thereafter have effect only in such modified form or be of no effect, as the case may be; so, however, that any such modification or annulment shall be without prejudice to the validity of anything previously done under that rule.

[738]["(4) Every rule made by the State Government under this section shall be laid, as soon as may be after it is made, before the State Legislature."]

Objects and Reasons

This clause seeks to insert a new sub-section to Section 12 of the Act making provisions for the laying of rules made under the Act before Parliament.[739]

Rules made by States under the Act

This section empowers appropriate Government to make rules to carry out the purposes of the Act. In exercise of its

---

736. Ins. by Act 63 of 1988, Section 4.

737. Ins. by Act 79 of 1971, Section 14.

738. Subs. and ins. by Act 4 of 1986, Section 2 and Schedule (w.e.f.) 15-5-1986.

739. Notes on Clauses, Clause 14, the Commissions of Inquiry (Amendment) Bill, 1971.

powers under this section, the Central Government has made the Commissions of Inquiry (Central) Rules, 1972. It is open to the State Governments to follow these rules instead of enacting their own rules. There are number of States and Union Territories that have not made any rules under this section. They are following the Central Rules. To mention, some of these States and Union Territories are: Assam, Arunachal Pradesh, Haryana, Lakshadweep, Andaman and Nicobar Administration, Mizoram, Nagaland, Punjab and Sikkim. Certain States have made their own rules but while doing so, they have merely adapted the Central Rules in whole with the condition that wherever the words "Central Government" have been referred to in the Commissions of Inquiry (Central) Rules, 1972, the same shall be construed as referring to the "State Government". An example of this is the Commissions of Inquiry (Manipur) Rules, 1993. There are, however, certain States that have made their own independent rules under this section. Some of these States are: Andhra Pradesh, Kerala, Madhya Pradesh, Maharashtra, Orissa, Rajasthan, Tamil Nadu, Uttar Pradesh. Chhattisgarh has been following the rules made by State of Madhya Pradesh. Jammu and Kashmir had its own Act and Rules on Commissions of Inquiry.

Commissioner not Subjected to Government's Control by Acting as per the Rules made by Government

The fact that a Judge of a High Court appointed on a Commission is liable to function in accordance with the rules of procedure that the State Government may make, does not render him subject to the State Government's control as a result of his accepting the appointment. Nor does this affect his status that is guaranteed to him under the Constitution. His appointment is not open to challenge on this count. "The rules may by virtue of powers conferred by an enactment, have the force of law, and to uphold the law or to work in accordance therewith cannot detract from the status of a Judge. In fact, it is his duty to interpret and apply the laws, even if enacted by

State Legislatures, and to uphold the limitations that they impose. Such regard for laws, irrespective of their source, cannot be derogatory to a Judge and cannot affect his status under the Constitution."[740]

740. *Samaruram Holiram* v. *B.K. Chaudhury*, AIR 1953 Nagpur 331, p. 333.